D1531417

The Life of
Robert Browning

BLACKWELL CRITICAL BIOGRAPHIES

General Editor: Claude Rawson

The Life of
ROBERT BROWNING

A Critical Biography

Clyde de L. Ryals

BLACKWELL
Oxford UK & Cambridge USA

PR
4231
.R9
1993

Copyright © Clyde de L. Ryals 1993

The right of Clyde de L. Ryals to be identified as author of this work has been asserted in accordance with the Copyright, Designs and Patents Act 1988.

First published 1993

Blackwell Publishers
238 Main Street, Suite 501
Cambridge, Massachusetts 02142
USA

108 Cowley Road
Oxford OX4 1JF
UK

All rights reserved. Except for the quotation of short passages for the purposes of criticism and review, no part of this publication may be reproduced, stored in a retrieval system, or transmitted, in any form or by any means, electronic, mechanical, photocopying, recording or otherwise, without the prior permission of the publisher.

Except in the United States of America, this book is sold subject to the condition that it shall not, by way of trade or otherwise, be lent, resold, hired out, or otherwise circulated without the publisher's prior consent in any form of binding or cover other than that in which it is published and without a similar condition including this condition being imposed on the subsequent purchaser.

Library of Congress Cataloging-in-Publication Data

Ryals, Clyde de L., 1928–
The life of Robert Browning : a critical biography / Clyde de L. Ryals.
p. cm. — (Blackwell critical biographies : 3)
Includes bibliographical references and index.
ISBN 1–55786–149–8 (alk. paper)
1. Browning, Robert, 1812–1889. 2. Poets, English—19th century-
–Biography. I. Title. II. Series.
PR4231.R9 1993
821'.8—dc20
[B]
92–30729
CIP

British Library Cataloguing in Publication Data

A CIP catalogue record for this book is available from the British Library.

Typeset in 10 on 11 pt Baskerville
by Graphicraft Typesetters Ltd., Hong Kong
Printed in Great Britain by T.J. Press Ltd, Padstow, Cornwall

This book is printed on acid-free paper

26401219

Contents

Illustrations

Preface

Structuralist and post-structuralist notions of the 'death of the author' have widely come to mean in theoretical circles that the author's life is of no signficance whatsoever in the study of his or her writings. Currently feminist critics almost alone are willing to consider the issues of biography and text. In general, the critic's task is regarded as (to borrow a term from Paul de Man) 'de-facement' of the text.

Such attitudes are, of course, not entirely new. The New Critical project demanded that a text be considered as autotelic, a verbal icon. T. S. Eliot stated in 'Tradition and the Individual Talent' that poetry is not an expression of personality but an escape from it. The 'I' who is the speaker in a poem is in no way to be related to the poet but to be viewed as a 'persona', distanced and distinct from the person who made the poem.

The Romantics, on the other hand, had quite a different view of poetry. For them it was primarily an autobiographical endeavour, and in many guises they indulged their passion for personal figuration. The Romantic critic, in consequence, was preoccupied with the figuration of the poet. 'A true allegory of the state of one's own mind in a representative history', said a late Romantic (David Masson) writing in the *North British Review* for August 1853, 'is perhaps the highest thing that one can attempt in the way of poetry'.

A typical (and influential) view of the mid-nineteenth-century critic's enterprise was expressed by the French critic Charles Augustin Sainte-Beuve in his *Causerie du Lundi* of 22 July 1862:

> Literature and literary production are not for me distinct or separable from the rest of the man and the organization; I can enjoy the work but for me it is difficult to judge it independently of knowledge of the man himself; and I will admit willingly: such and such a tree will bear such and such a fruit.

L'homme et l'oeuvre were necessarily joined, and Sainte-Beuve saw it as his business to portray 'a superior man distinguished by his work'.

In this study of probably the most paradoxical of poets writing in English I undertake a kind of paradoxical or antithetical criticism that is both Romantic and modernist (or post-modernist). That is, I show Browning's poetry as one of both biographical presence and biographical absence and this paradox as essential to his self-fashioning. Browning was born, but 'Browning' was scripted over a period of many years.

Relying chiefly on his own theatrical metaphors, I portray the poet as he depicted himself: as both the presenter and the presented. I assume that each of his works is what he himself called it – a performance – and that he produced and enacted it as part of a (biographical) script that was subject to constant modification. To a lesser degree I use the religious metaphors of immanence and transcendence and, in addition, suggest that the Christian Incarnation served as the paradigm for Browning's concept of the poet. In both metaphorical categories the word 'person' is of great importance; etymologically it is related to the Latin *persona*, theatrical mask. Recalling that 'person' is also cognate with the French *personne*, nobody, I want to show how Browning the person employs the *persona* to be (like the Shakespeare of Borges' story) 'Somebody and Nobody'.

I have previously written two books on Browning, which treat in detail the works of the poet's earlier and later career: *Becoming Browning: The Poems and Plays of Robert Browning, 1833–1846* and *Browning's Later Poetry, 1871–1889*. With the exception of one instance I have not referred to them in this book, and I suggest that readers desiring further information about individual poems might wish to consult them.

Part of chapter 15 was originally published in volume 18 of *Browning Institute Studies* (1990). I thank the editors for their permission to republish that material here.

Because I wish to trace Browning's poetical development, all quotations from his work, except as otherwise noted, are taken from the first London edition of individual volumes. Line numbers have been added to correspond with the Camberwell Edition, *Complete Works of Robert Browning*, ed. Charlotte Porter and Helen A. Clarke. I refer to this edition because none of the Ohio, Oxford and Longman editions, all currently under way, is yet complete. The Yale/Penguin edition does not include Browning's plays.

Browning makes frequent use of ellipsis points, especially in his early poetry. His ellipsis points are here typeset closed up, without space between, while my omissions are indicated by the customary spaced points.

C. de L. R.

Abbreviations

The following abbreviations are used in references in the text and notes to frequently cited works.

BIS	*Browning Institute Studies*
BSN	*Browning Society Notes*
Correspondence	*The Brownings' Correspondence.* Ed. Philip Kelley and Ronald Hudson. 10 vols to date. Winfield, Kan.: Wedgestone Press, 1984–.
Dearest Isa	*Dearest Isa: Robert Browning's Letters to Isabella Blagden.* Ed. Edward C. McAleer. Austin: University of Texas Press, 1951.
DeVane	*A Browning Handbook,* 2nd edn. By William Clyde DeVane. New York: Appleton-Century-Crofts, 1955.
Domett	*Robert Browning and Alfred Domett.* Ed. Frederick G. Kenyon. London: Smith, Elder, 1906.
Griffin and Minchin	*The Life of Robert Browning,* 3rd rev. edn. By W. Hall Griffin and Harry Christopher Minchin. London: Methuen, 1938.
Hood	*Letters of Robert Browning Collected by Thomas J. Wise.* Ed. Thurman L. Hood. London: John Murray, 1933.
Hudson	*Browning to his American Friends: Letters between the Brownings, the Storys, and James Russell Lowell.* Ed. Gertrude Reese Hudson. London: Bowes and Bowes, 1965.
Huxley	*Elizabeth Barrett Browning: Letters to Her Sister, 1846–1859.* Ed. Leonard Huxley. London: John Murray, 1929.

Irvine and Honan	*The Book, the Ring, and the Poet.* By William Irvine and Park Honan. New York: McGraw-Hill, 1974.
Kenyon	*The Letters of Elizabeth Barrett Browning,* 2 vols. Ed. Frederick G. Kenyon. New York: Macmillan, 1897.
Kintner	*The Letters of Robert Browning and Elizabeth Barrett Barrett, 1845–1846,* 2 vols. Ed. Elvan Kintner. Cambridge, Mass.: Harvard University Press, 1969.
Learned Lady	*Learned Lady: Letters from Robert Browning to Mrs. Thomas FitzGerald.* Ed. Edward C. McAleer. Cambridge, Mass.: Harvard University Press, 1966.
Letters to George	*Letters of the Brownings to George Barrett.* Ed. Paul Landis with Ronald E. Freeman. Urbana: University of Illinois Press, 1958.
Maynard	*Browning's Youth.* By John Maynard. Cambridge, Mass.: Harvard University Press, 1977.
NL	*New Letters of Robert Browning.* Ed. William Clyde DeVane and Kenneth Leslie Knickerbocker. London: John Murray, 1951.
Orr, *Handbook*	*A Handbook to the Works of Robert Browning.* By Mrs Sutherland Orr. 6th edn. London: G. Bell, 1927.
Orr, *Life*	*Life and Letters of Robert Browning.* By Mrs Sutherland Orr; new edn rev. Frederick G. Kenyon. London: Smith, Elder, 1908.
Peterson	*Browning's Trumpeter: The Correspondence of Robert Browning and Frederick J. Furnivall, 1872–1889.* Ed. William S. Peterson. Washington: Decatur, 1979.
PMLA	*Publications of the Modern Language Association of America*
SHBC	*Studies in Browning and His Circle*
TLS	*Times Literary Supplement* (London)
UTQ	*University of Toronto Quarterly*
VP	*Victorian Poetry*
VS	*Victorian Studies*
Wedgwood	*Robert Browning and Julia Wedgwood: A Broken Friendship as Revealed in Their Letters.* Ed. Richard Curle. London: John Murray and Jonathan Cape, 1937.

1

Growing Up in Camberwell

I

The Brownings were of Dorset yeoman stock. Robert Browning, the poet's grandfather, was born in Pentridge in 1749. He came to London at the age of twenty and began his career as a clerk in the Bank of England. By 1784 he had risen to the prestigious and lucrative office of principal clerk of the Bank Stock Office, earning him an annual salary of more than £500 and the right to sign his name Robert Browning, Esquire. At twenty-nine he married Margaret Tittle, whose family had wealth from their holdings on the island of St Kitts in the West Indies. The couple settled in suburban Battersea, where their son Robert, father of the poet, was born in 1782, and then moved to Camberwell, another suburb south of the Thames, in 1784. Five years later Margaret Tittle Browning died.

In 1794 the elder Browning, at forty-five, took a second wife, Jane Smith, aged twenty-three and of a prosperous family, by whom he had nine children. Conflict arose almost immediately in the household between the young Robert and his stepmother, and to rid himself of this cause of dissension Robert senior, who by all accounts was an arrogant and strong-willed man, sent his namesake off before the age of twenty to the West Indies to work on a sugar plantation, to which, through his deceased mother, he was a possible heir. The young Robert was revolted by the institution of slavery that he found there and, to his ambitious father's rage and disgust, soon returned to England.

Hoping to devote himself to painting, for which he had real talent, he was frustrated in this aim by his father, who refused to support him. In addition, at his jealous stepmother's insistence, his father declined to afford him a university education. It was plain that the elder Browning actively disliked his son and, in the view of his grandson, the poet, the old man 'continued to hate him till a few years before his death' (Kintner, 2:

1006). Forced to depend entirely upon himself, Robert junior found in 1803, with the help of a Bank director for whom he had worked in St Kitts after leaving the plantation, full-time employment as a clerk in the Bank of England, where he remained till 1852.

In contrast to his father, he was unambitious as far as his work was concerned; in fact, his need to earn a living at the bank caused him, according to his son, the poet, to 'consume his life after a fashion he always detested' (Kintner, 2: 1006). On the other hand, he was a man of cosmopolitan interests and scholarly bent. He read widely in a number of languages, including Hebrew, Greek and Latin as well as modern Continental languages, and collected an estimable library of some six thousand volumes, in which he made copious notes. In addition to drawing he also indulged in versifying.[1] On the whole, although he was something of a rebel, his pleasures were quiet ones.

In 1811 Robert Browning the second married, without his father's approval, Sarah Anna Wiedemann, a woman ten years his senior, of a cultivated, middle-class family from Dundee who had moved to Camberwell. Like her husband this Scottish lady delighted in the pleasures of home. She loved flowers and animals and, a talented pianist, was especially enthusiastic about music. Her most salient characteristic, however, seems to have been her strongly Protestant piety. Apparently her husband, who had been reared in the established Church, felt no compunction in joining her in Congregationalist worship at the York Street Chapel in Walworth, near to the cottage they took in Camberwell.

Soon the couple established themselves as, Thomas Carlyle remarked, 'people of respectable position among the Dissenters, but not wealthy neither'.[2] Until almost mid-century and the coming of the railroads Camberwell was still surrounded by fields and meadows that provided an almost uninterrupted view of the towers and spires of London to the north. Here in the eighteenth century several large houses had been built and they and their graceful gardens were still to be admired. Schools were plentiful, as were literary and philosophical societies. Just beyond Camberwell lay Dulwich, with its college and its handsome picture gallery, built in 1812 to the designs of Sir John Soane, containing magnificent paintings by Dutch masters, Velasquez, Titian, Poussin, Gainsborough and other Italian and English painters.

Into this Arcadia the poet Robert Browning was born on 7 May 1812, followed twenty months later, on 7 January 1814, by his sister Sarianna. By all testimony the boy was from infancy a conspicuous and precocious child who constantly insisted on showing off. He learned to read at an early age and from his mother and father gained a love of music and classical literature. When he was enrolled in a local dame school, probably at the age of five, he was so far in advance of the other children that he was sent home to avoid embarrassing the older boys. After a year or two of elementary studies at home, he went at the age of seven to the Misses Ready's weekly boarding school at nearby Peckham, from which he returned home at weekends. His first response to his new environment was one of lone-liness and boredom, and he never fully accommodated himself to the discipline of school life and the routine of a conventional education. In later years his chief recollection of life at the Misses Ready's school was of hair-brushing accompanied by singing of psalms and the hymns of Isaac Watts. At the time he mimicked the procedure and its attendant pieties so amusingly that even his devout mother was forced to laugh.

At about age ten the boy advanced to the tutelage of the Misses Ready's brother, the Reverend Thomas Martin Ready, master of the Peckham School, which focused on grammar and memorization of the rules of the Greek and Latin languages. Browning later said that it was with 'disgust' that he always thought of the school, being convinced that he was taught 'nothing there'.[3] Yet it was doubtless from the enforced discipline at the Peckham School that the young Browning gained a real foundation for his lifelong study and mastery of classical literature.

It was at home at weekends, however, that his real education took place. His father helped fix Latin declensions in his mind by turning them into rhymes and introduced the boy to Homer by making a game of the siege of Troy and then encouraging him on to the original Greek of the *Iliad* by means of Pope's verse translation. His mother instructed him in the names of flowers, taught him to play the piano and encouraged him in a love of music, while his father taught him to draw and took him to the Dulwich Picture Gallery, at the time the only public art gallery in the London area. In addition, the large library in the house offered him a world of imaginative and scientific literature and of engravings and other art works which he devoured. As an environment for learning and as a tutor, the Peckham School and the Reverend Thomas Ready paled in comparison.

The four Brownings were an extraordinarily closely knit family. When home from the bank, Robert senior was a potterer and hobbyist, spending no small part of his time in either drawing or reading and leaving the ordering of the household to his wife. To his children he was a loving companion, almost childlike himself, who would try to do almost anything they asked of him. The younger Robert was proud of him in every respect but especially because he 'conceived such a hatred to the slave system in the West Indies . . . that he relinquished every prospect', gaining thereby in his son's eyes 'infinite glory' (Kintner, 2: 1005–6). Later remarking upon her father's unworldliness, Sarianna observed that if she had gone up to him while he was engrossed in reading and said, 'There will be no dinner to-day', he would have replied, 'All right, my dear, it is of no consequence' (Orr, *Life*, p. 14).

Although their mother was the more responsible in daily affairs, she was not a domineering woman. On the contrary, she had the same sweet, gentle nature as her husband, which was readily communicated, to ani-mals as well as humans. Robert and Sarianna delighted in her piano–playing and gardening, in her love of nature and wild life. Like their father she had a 'childlike faith in goodness' and indulged her children in practically everything they wanted —'nor for liberty but it was conceded, nor confidence but it was bestowed' (Kintner, 2: 1070, 775). During the thirty-four years that Robert was to remain under their roof in the prolonged relation of childhood, 'it was his rule never to go to bed without giving [his mother] a good-night kiss. If he was out so late that he had to admit himself with a latch-key, he nevertheless went to her room' (Orr, *Life*, p. 43).

Little is known of the friends of his childhood other than his three cousins, the Silverthornes, sons of his mother's sister and the local brewer who lived close by. James, three years older than Robert, was his particular friend and frequent companion. Jim, as he was called, wanted to become an artist (although he ended up in the family brewery for a career), and with him Robert could share his ideas about art and poetry as they roamed the woods around Camberwell.

Robert left the Peckham School at the age of fourteen and for the next two years, from 1826 to 1828, was tutored at home with the aim of making him a gentleman, that highly desired but ill-defined ideal of nineteenth-century British culture. Middle-class though he was, he was nevertheless given the education that an aristocrat's son might be expected to receive. To be sure, his father never anticipated at this time that Robert would live a life of leisure, but he did intend that his son, whatever profession he might eventually choose, would be able to pass as a man of the world, at home in any sort of cultivated society. Where an earlier age had taken it for granted that a gentleman was born and not made, by the end of the eighteenth century it was conceivable that any male might, with the proper training and achievements, rise to that status. The industrial revolution was altering and by the mid-nineteenth century had practically obliterated the boundary lines between the upper and middle classes, as the newly powerful middle class aspired to the manners of the well-born and refused to be enslaved by their wealth. Yet the ultimate requirements for recognition as a gentleman remained a question of debate well into the century. The effort to clarify the social type can be seen, for example, in Newman's *Idea of a University*, which proposes the gentleman as the final product of intellectual cultivation at a university; in Thackeray's satires against snobbery; in Tennyson's long preoccupation with the character traits of Hallam in *In Memoriam* and of King Arthur in 'The Epic' and *Idylls of the King*; in Dickens's *Great Expectations*, which shows gentlemanliness dependent not upon money but upon moral worth; and in Ruskin's chapter 'On Vulgarity' in *Modern Painters*, where the gentleman's nature is contrasted with the vulgarian's selfishness and hardness of heart.

From his French tutor Robert learned the language and literature of France, in time speaking and reading it almost as easily as English. From his music teacher, John Relfe, the organist and composer, he acquired knowledge of music theory and composition, becoming so immersed in it that music more than any other of the arts was for several years his chief

interest. He was given lessons in dancing, fencing and boxing. He kept up
his Latin and Greek while he continued to explore his father's library for
books that interested him. During this two-year period there was very little
systematic education; rather, Browning's learning was by and large a matter
of eclectic reading which provided the wide-ranging erudition later to be
manifested in his poetry.

As for verse, he was making rhymes almost as soon as he could talk.
Although he appears to have known Shakespeare from earliest childhood,
his first enthusiasm was Macpherson's Ossian, in imitation of whom the
boy wrote down some of his earliest lines. From Ossian he moved on to
the English Romantics, probably initially to Wordsworth and Coleridge.
What Browning's earliest poems are like, we can have no idea, because he
destroyed them. A collection of them, modestly entitled 'Incondita', was
to his proud parents the work of genius. Hoping to find a publisher, his
mother stitched the poems together and showed them around to anyone
willing to have a look at them. But two poems dating from his fourteenth
year survive. One of them, 'The Dance of Death', is obviously modelled on
Coleridge's 'Fire, Famine, and Slaughter: A War Eclogue' (1798), which
deplored the war that Pitt's England was waging against France and which
appealed to the adolescent Browning's growing republican sympathies,
doubtless fostered by his father. The second poem evidences the influence
of Byron, the most famous English poet of the day.

When he first came to know the younger Romantic poet is uncertain,
but clearly by age fourteen he knew Byron well. 'The First-Born of Egypt'
shows the general Romantic predilection for apocalypse ('the dolorous
plaint, / The death cry of a nation') and specifically the Byronic hero's
claim to vast experience:

> I have seen many climes, but that dread hour
> Hath left its burning impress on my soul
> Never to be erased.

Byron had died at Missolonghi in 1824, and although Browning may have
heard of him earlier, the poet's death in a revolutionary cause made him
the boy's hero and chief poet. Browning loved everything about Byron
and, as he was later to say, took an enormous interest 'in the places he had
visited, in relics of him', would in fact 'have gone to Finchley to see a curl
of his hair or one his gloves' (Kintner, 2: 986). Byron's posturings and
attitudinizings – his 'curls' and 'gloves', his theatricality – appealed to one
who a few years later took to wearing yellow gloves as a means of asserting
himself in what he considered an alien society. The dandy that the young
Browning would be (and in later years was to become again) was enraptured
by the poet who sought not only ever wider experience but also integration
of his vision of self and the world.

After the imitative pieces of 'Incondita' Browning seems to have ceased
writing poetry for a period of five or six years. During this time music

became his chief means for finding expression, although, he said, he continued to hold 'a Poet's calling in pre-eminent reverence' (*Correspondence*, 3: 264). In addition, his enthusiasm for Byron began to wane as he increasingly perceived the poet's egotism and cynicism and as another Romantic poet, a contemporary of Byron's, came to exert his influence.

In late 1826 or in 1827 James Silverthorne gave Browning a copy of Shelley's *Miscellaneous Poems* (1826), an unauthorized collection of lyrics taken from the *Posthumous Poems* of the young poet who was drowned in the Gulf of Spezia in 1822. It was a cheap little book of duodecimo size. Why his cousin should have given him the book or where Jim had found it is a mystery, for Shelley was virtually unknown and his works almost unobtainable in the 1820s. In so far as he had any reputation at all it was as the author of *Queen Mab*, a poem inveighing against established institutions, including marriage and the Christian religion, written when Shelley was eighteen, published surreptitiously in 1813 and pirated frequently thereafter. When Shelley died, his patrician father, who had been scandalized by his son's atheism, republicanism and irregular love life, saw to it that nothing of his should be published or reprinted.

Although Browning had found in Byron the expression of many of the sentiments that he himself held, it was in Shelley that he discovered his own dreams and aspirations set forth with a startlingly fresh beauty. As he read poem after poem and marked them up with underlinings and marginal comments, a world undreamed of opened up to him. Here was much of what he had vaguely thought and hoped, forcefully expressed in the most exquisite musical verse. He must find out more about this poet. He wrote to the *Literary Gazette* to place a notice inquiring where Shelley's works could be obtained. What is probably the reply appeared in the *Gazette* for 24 November 1827 and directed him to a bookseller in Covent Garden. Browning asked his parents to give them to him, and his pious mother went with her son to the bookseller's, purchased most of the first editions of Shelley's works (only one having reached a second edition during the poet's lifetime) and, no doubt uncomprehendingly, presented him with the works of an evangelizing atheist. Browning had read Voltaire and been excited by his exhortations, but here in Shelley's poetry was a revolutionary and visionary zeal exceeding the French philosopher's. Here *écrasez l'infâme* was no longer a cry for the future; in Shelley's work all infamy had been destroyed and the future realized. The boy read Shelley and became an atheist and a vegetarian. For the next few years, said one of his boyhood friends, 'Shelley was his God' (*Domett*, p. 141).

Fired with Shelley's beliefs and Byron's dandyism, the young Browning 'gratuitously proclaimed himself', says Mrs Sutherland Orr, his first authoritative biographer, 'everything that he was, and some things that he was not'. In sum, 'he behaved as a youth . . . who knows himself to be clever, and believes that he is not appreciated, because the crude or paradoxical forms which his cleverness assumes do not recommend it to his elders' minds' (Orr, *Life*, p. 43). His mother was especially distressed as he seemed to reject her world of the York Street Congregational Chapel by displaying restlessness and boredom during the sermons of its minister, George Clayton. It was a period when, said his sister, 'he had outgrown his social surroundings', which were 'narrow', and 'he chafed under them' (Orr, *Life*, p. 45).

Seeking new company, he began to widen his acquaintance. He commenced calling regularly on the artistic, older Flower sisters, Sarah and Eliza, whom he had known since childhood and who had admired his 'Incondita'. Now living in north London with their father, they were extraordinarily intelligent young women whose mother had died while they were young chidren and whose father, Benjamin Flower, was a well-known printer and lay preacher of republican and unitarian views who had been fined and imprisoned by the House of Lords for libelling one of its members. Eliza, nine years older than Robert, was a talented musician, who became known as the composer of political songs and of music for hymns. In its obituary notice after her death in 1846 the *Westminster Review* referred to her as the greatest woman composer and the finest religious composer of her time (Maynard, p. 183). She may have have given Robert music lessons. Robert apparently idolized her for all her outstanding qualities and, as he said some years later, constantly wrote verses and letters to her instead of playing cricket and other sports as would the usual adolescent boy (Hood, p. 20).

Sarah, two years younger than Eliza and more emotional and sentimental, was interested in the drama and was admired by her friends for her readings from Shakespeare. For a short time, until her health gave way, she was an actress on the commercial stage. Sarah was also a poet and in 1841 published the long dramatic poem *Vivia Perpetua*; but her real fame resides in her authorship of the hymn 'Nearer, my God, to Thee'. Together the sisters exerted what the most authoritative biographer of the poet's youth suggests was probably 'the greatest influence on Browning in his early adolescence', he being drawn to them 'as models of artistic activity' (Maynard, p. 181). They provided him with a sentimental education.

Not unnaturally Browning spoke about his new beliefs to these young women brought up in a household of unorthodox views, and he evidently succeeded in unsettling at least one of them in her religious convictions. Sarah Flower wrote in November 1827 to her spiritual confessor:

> I would fain go to my Bible as I used to, but I cannot. The cloud has come over me gradually, and I did not discover the darkness in which my soul was shrouded until, in seeking to give light to others, my own gloomy state become too settled to admit of doubt. It was in answering Robert Browning that my mind refused to bring forward argument, turned recreant, and sided with the enemy.[4]

It is clear that in the 1820s the Flower sisters were of great importance to Browning, but later he and they alike found their interests too divergent to rekindle the old intimacy.

When fairly early in their friendship Browning's mother turned to Eliza Flower for help in finding a publisher for Robert's 'Incondita', Eliza showed the poems to the family friend William Johnson Fox, a unitarian minister and journalist. Fox's renown as a preacher and compelling personality was so great that his congregation had built a chapel specially for him in 1824, and soon South Place Chapel was the most fashionable dissenting pulpit in London. Fox was also a literary critic of some distinction as well as the co-editor and later proprietor of the *Monthly Repository*, to which such liberals as John Stuart Mill (as well as Browning himself) contributed. When the Flower sisters' father died in 1829, he became their guardian and took them into his home. When he became seriously ill, his wife apparently took no responsibility for nursing him or running the household; Eliza stepped in to fill the need and in effect replaced Mrs Fox, who nevertheless was jealous of Eliza and made life miserable for her. The news of Fox's domestic difficulties got out, and this, in addition to his increasingly liberal, free-thinking views, aroused the animosity of part of his congregation and his fellow unitarian ministers. Fox remained at South Place Chapel, but as an independent minister of a diminished congregation that nevertheless attracted a wide range of intellectuals, artists, and politicians.

Fox read the poems of 'Incondita' and thought they showed promise, although he recognized their derivative nature. He praised them to the young poet in person but advised against premature publication, probably pointing out their extensive debt to Byron. In the first issue of the *Westminster Review* in 1824 Fox had remarked on the popularity of Byron and the affectation and lack of seriousness that his example had fostered, and it may have been partly through Fox that Browning disavowed Byron's influence over himself. Robert took the criticism to heart, being neither offended nor dispirited, and retrieved and destroyed all copies of 'Incondita'. Fox's opinions were then and thereafter very important to the young poet, and Browning acknowledged Fox as his 'literary father' (Orr, *Life*, p. 43).[5]

After two years of tutoring at home, Browning began to look elsewhere for his education. His father, denied a university place himself, wished his son to have the benefit of such an education. Oxford and Cambridge could not be considered, both because of cost and because of the Brownings' dissenting persuasion. In 1825, when a group of men proposed founding a university in London that would be nonsectarian and inexpensive, the elder Browning subscribed £100, thereby becoming one of the original 'proprietors' and having the right to free tuition for his nominee. In April 1828, just three weeks after the first student had been admitted to The London University (as it was orginally called), Mr Browning applied for admission for his son, who, he said, was qualified by 'his unwearied application, for the last 6 years, to the Greek, Latin & French languages', and by 'Moral character' (Maynard, p. 268). Robert, eager to attend, was accepted, and his name was the sixteenth to be entered on the books.

Taking lodging in a rooming house in or near Bedford Square, the boy began his classes in German, Greek and Latin in late October. But his expectation was not matched by the reality of life at the new university. Student life was drab and the lectures were for the most part perfunctory. He soon withdrew from his student lodging and went back home to live. He tried to find profit in the education offered, but at the end of the academic year his father wrote to the warden on 4 May 1829 that his son was withdrawing from the university, '(an event as painful as it was unexpected)' (Maynard, p. 286). The truth was that Shelley was more exciting than his professors: what the poet advocated was more thrilling than anything they attempted to teach.

At seventeen Browning was forced to face the question of how he could make a living. He could take up his studies at home, but what would they lead to? Although his father had hoped that he might qualify himself for the bar by attendance at the university, that was no longer possible; besides, as he was later to say, he 'always had a supreme contempt for the profession' (Hood, p. 287) and would rather 'groom a horse . . . all day long than succeed . . . in the Solicitor-Generalship' (Kintner, 1: 193). His father then suggested a career in medicine. Browning visited Guy's Hospital, but his interest in medicine was that of a detached observer who would not submit to the discipline of the profession. Furthermore, he hated doctors and later would frequently ridicule them in his poetry. What else then was possible? He could find no answer, and so he simply studied with no goal in view, following an unsystematic but intense course of reading in his father's library. His parents doubtless had misgivings about their son's aimlessness, but apparently accepted it without dispute. As Browning was later to testify,

> by the indulgence of my father and mother, I was allowed to live my own life and choose my own course in it; which, having been the same from the beginning to the end, necessitated a permission to read nearly all sorts of books, in a well-stocked and very miscellaneous library. I had no other direction than my parents' taste for whatever was highest and best in literature; but I found out for myself many forgotten fields which proved the richest of pastures. (Orr, *Life*, pp. 378–9)

The next four years, from 1829 to 1833, form the least-known period in Browning's life. As he continued his self-education, the adolescent surveyed the whole of European culture. He read books on art, science, magic, history, politics, philosophy, theology: the subject matter that he sought to master was unending. The result was that Browning became, with the possible exception of Milton, the most learned of English poets. At this period, however, he still had not decided to become a poet, at least not primarily a poet. He thought first of a career as a musician, a composer of operas perhaps. Then he considered becoming a writer: a poet and, maybe, even a novelist. Perhaps, he thought, he might follow several

careers simultaneously. It was not till 1833, as we shall see, that he finally
chose the profession of poet.

During these years of self-cultivation Browning looked inward in an
effort to locate his true self, a central core of being that was the real
Robert Browning. What he discovered was that no stable centre of selfhood
is accessible to the thinking subject. The subject, he learned, is accessible
only obliquely, not in the continuity of its self-consciousness but in the
discontinuity of its shifting forms, in the different interrogations to which
it is submitted. As he followed the logic of this discovery, he perceived that
truth and meaning are not fixed but, instead, are always becoming. The
questions asked determine to no small degree the answers arrived at; the
angle of viewing limits vision of the whole. Not enough questions can ever
be asked, not enough points of view can ever be attained to yield a complete,
encompassing overview of any matter. At best one gains approximations of
the truth, which is always in advance of any formulation of it. Absolute
truth, therefore, is not resident in the phenomenal world, although in-
forming it. This means that the world known through the senses is to be
regarded in relation to the Absolute.

Such conclusions, which were to remain with him for life, forced
Browning to re-evaluate his beloved Shelley in a most radical way. Under
the influence of Rousseau and the *philosophes*, Shelley had argued that if
the 'infamy' of superstition and the institutions fostering it could be
abolished, mankind's natural goodness would stand revealed and perfec-
tion be attained. This was, no doubt, a noble dream; but, Browning con-
cluded, no more than a dream. In a world of becoming, humankind can
never reach perfection, although morally it must strive to do so. Moreover,
even were it attainable, perfection would have the most detrimental effect
morally: humankind would have nothing for which to strive; all would be
given, nothing need be worked for. Further, Shelley's argument for the
necessity of atheism proved groundless for the young man who had de-
duced the Absolute and its distance from the relative world of the senses.

It was to Shelley as poetic visionary that Browning at this time most
likely responded. Although an atheist, Shelley was a philosophical idealist
who believed in a realm beyond existential reality. He conceived of the
physical world as in essence like the spiritual world, phenomena being
veiled shows of the noumena behind. But, he confidently asserted, the
gifted person can discern appearances as signs or symbols of the spiritual
realm. The one who can read this language, intermediate between the
actual and the ideal, is a seer. The one who not only sees but also reveals
what he sees is a bard. Thus Shelley offers his work as the record, in the
complex language of analogies and symbols, of the authentic meeting of
his mind with the universal mind, what he calls the unseen Power. Brown-
ing himself apparently aspired to be such a bard, one of the small but
mighty band who are the unacknowledged legislators of mankind. From
his intermediate position between the concrete and the unseen he, like
Shelley, would in his verse provide connections of the one with the other.[6]

Soon, however, Browning recoiled from such a notion of the poet's work and from Shelley's whole mode of poetry. For Shelley the lyric was the chief means of expression, and what he sang of was himself, sometimes under other names but always recognizably as Shelley. What he aimed at was the elevation of himself into the mythic role of poet and redeemer of the world, and what he presented in his verse was an ideal of himself, which he considered to be representative of mankind, as, for example, when in the preface to *Alastor* he says that his poem 'may be considered allegorical of one of the most interesting situations of the human mind'. With himself as his hero and his own inner experience as his subject matter, his poems are works of mythopoeic creation. Such songs as Shelley sang were beautiful, but, Browning came to discern, they were untrue. They presented lovely visions, which were only visions, useless for mankind; in essence they were little more than dreams of wish-fulfilment. Shelley's poems can be prized as the sweetest songs ever sung, expressions of mankind's highest and noblest aspirations; but as mythic allegories their truth is no more than personal and private.

As Browning discovered, the self is culturally conditioned. Reflecting during this period of self-investigation on his own educational and cultural nurturing, he eagerly attempted to look behind and beyond the identity (such as he then possessed) derived from his culture and education. The more he read, the more he found that whatever he knew, whatever knowledge he possessed, was but a very small part of the vast symbolic realm of possibility. The more he studied, the more he was aware that if he were to know anything well, he would have to know everything, while in fact he, like the rest of mankind, remained ignorant of origins and purposes and the place of either. Having reached such conclusions, he necessarily disavowed Shelley's allegorical mode and Shelley's concept of the bard; he cast aside for ever all notions of the self as representative of mankind and of poetry as allegorical. With his acute consciousness of self and how it had been produced, Browning regarded himself as unique.

II

Breaking the spell of Shelley's influence did not, however, mean breaking with Shelley. He had, in fact, to fight off Shelley so as to be his own man. His first public act of exorcism was to occur in *Pauline; A Fragment of a Confession*, composed in late 1832. He kept the work secret from his parents, although his sister knew of it and perhaps told their aunt Christiana Silverthorne, who in any case volunteered to provide the £30 necessary for its publication by the firm of Saunders & Otley. The book appeared anonymously in an octavo volume of seventy-one pages in March 1833.

On Monday night, 22 October 1832, Browning saw Edmund Kean play Richard III in Richmond. Kean was well past his prime, in ill health because

of alcoholism and tuberculosis, but nevertheless gave a powerful im-
personation that held his audience in rapt attention. Browning marvelled
at Kean's power, his ability to command the complete concentration of his
audience. Seeing him act was as Coleridge had described it: 'like reading
Shakespeare by flashes of lightning'.[7] It was a thrilling, epiphanic experi-
ence and had an effect on the young man similar to that which a reading
of Chapman's Homer had on Keats: it opened up a new world.

As he walked the ten miles back to Camberwell after the play, perhaps
with his cousin Jim Silverthorne, with whom he often attended the theatre,
Browning reflected on what he had seen. Here on the Shakespearean
stage was history as spectacle, in which the major personages of the past
were actors. As Shakespeare had said in the famous passage from *As You
Like It*, 'All the world's a stage, / And all the men and women merely
players'. What if he, Robert Browning, were to regard life in the same
way? What if, like Shakespeare, he were to create a theatrical world and,
moreover, be, like Kean, its actor–manager? 'I will be gifted with a won-
drous mind', he wrote in *Pauline* in allusion to Kean (Griffin and Minchin,
p. 45),

> Yet sunk by error to men's sympathy,
> And in the wane of life; yet only so
> As to call up their fears, and there shall come
> A time requiring youth's best energies;
> And strait, I fling age, sorrow, sickness off,
> And rise triumphing over my decay.
>
> *   *   *   *
>
> And thus it is that I supply the chasm
> 'Twixt what I am and all that I would be.
>
> (670–7)

The excitement of the night of 22 October 1832 was owed to something
more than seeing Kean act. It was to the sight of his own future as an
artist: the acting of roles would bridge the chasm between what he was
and all he 'would be'. Henceforth his was to be a world of theatre.

As he considered his theatrical possibilities, the young man conceived
of a vast plan of artistic endeavour – a series of 'performances', he was
later to call it – in which he would write, under different names, various
works in different genres. The Browning theatre would include the whole
world of art. 'The following Poem', he was to say of the published *Pauline*,

> was written in pursuance of a foolish plan which occupied me mightily for
> a time, and which had for its object the enabling me to assume & realize I
> know not how many different characters;—meanwhile the world was never
> to guess that 'Brown, Smith, Jones & Robinson' (as the spelling books would
> have it) the respective authors of this poem, the other novel, such an opera,
> such a speech, etc. etc. were no other than one and the same individual.
> The present abortion was the first work of the *Poet* of the batch, who would

have been more legitimately *myself* than most of the others; but I surrounded him with all manner of (to my then notion) poetical accessories, and had planned quite a delightful life for him.

Only this crab remains of the shapely Tree of Life in this Fool's paradise of mine. (DeVane, p. 41)

Pauline is indeed more 'legitimately' Browning in that the poem shadows this 'first stage' of his life (885). The genre he chose was that of the lyrical narrative, doubtless suggested by Shelley's *Alastor* and perhaps in part *Epipsychidion*. He was at pains, however, to do what Shelley had not done: namely, to separate himself from his confessing speaker: 'I will tell / My state as though 'twere none of mine' (585–6). By this means he could trace his development and so review imaginatively and somewhat objectively his guilty past, which involved disloyalty to his family's religion, disappointment of their expectations for his education and subsequent career, and his betrayal of Shelley. As his friend Joseph Arnould was later to describe it to their mutual friend Alfred Domett, it is 'a strange, wild (in parts singularly magnificent) poet-biography: his own early life as it presented itself to his own soul viewed poetically: in fact, psychologically speaking, his "Sartor Resartus" ' (*Domett*, p. 141). In her note Pauline calls it an 'examen . . . de son âme, pour découvrir la suite des objets auxquels il lui serait possible d'atteindre' ('examination . . . of his own soul, carried out so as to discover the series of objectives that he could possibly attain').

The speaker of the poem is not only based on the poet himself but also derives from Byron's heroes, who are marked men with mysterious, guilty pasts, and from Shelley's idealistic heroes, who seek in reality the counterpart of their dreams. The auditor of his confession is Pauline, who may be the disguise of Eliza Flower. If, says Mrs Orr, in spite of Browning's denials, 'any woman inspired *Pauline*, it can be none other than she' (Orr, *Life*, p. 35), although more recently the poet's half-aunt Jemima (less than a year older than Robert), said to be the major love of Browning's early life, has been claimed as the model for Pauline.[8] At any rate, as an auditor she is no more than 'a mere phantom', as John Stuart Mill remarked;[9] she says nothing. The 'I' tells of, *inter alia*, his religious doubts, his renegade past, his lapsed worship of the Sun-treader, his faith in art and his need for Pauline. He is, as the epigraph in French from Clément Marot indicates, a man different from what he was and can never be again. This change in him is initially a cause for confusion and despair, but the more he talks, the more it becomes a source of self-confidence, seen as a necessary movement in the evolution of personal consciousness.

On the one hand, the speaker seeks permanence in the world of change. He wants to believe in God, to follow in the path of his idol the Sun-treader, to love Pauline and to cultivate domesticity. He wants, in brief, a world of being, represented by contraction and concentration. On the other hand, he is entranced by change and the dizzying elation that it entails. He desires not to be bound – by God, the Sun-treader, Pauline or the comforts of home; he wishes to assert his power, his unbridled self. Which is to say that instead of fixity and order he longs for a world of becoming, represented by expansion and decentring.

He begins his confession by acknowledging his acts of betrayal. First he had deserted Pauline and all the ease and solace of the familiar. Then he had forgone his inherited religious faith under the influence of the Suntreader, who taught him to put his trust in a new heaven and a new earth, in mankind and its perfectibility: 'Men were to be as gods, and earth as heaven. / And I – ah! what a life was mine to be, / My whole soul rose to meet it' (426–8). For a while he, like the young Wordsworth of *The Prelude*, was 'full of joy' (435), exhilarated by the notion of social transformation; but when he soon saw that earthly perfection was but a dream, he, again like Wordsworth, sought everywhere for a compensating belief and, finding none, yielded up moral questions in despair. Yet, curiously unlike Wordsworth and other nineteenth-century figures who faced similar crises such as Carlyle and John Stuart Mill, the speaker finds this no great loss, for 'new powers / Rose as old feelings left—wit, mockery, / And happiness' and so he 'cast / Hope joyously away' (462–4, 466–7). The strength he finds is totally within: it is a kind of ironic detachment that allows him to look on grief and time's changes as though they were no part of him. He becomes like a spectator at a play: 'spite of all life's vanity, no grief came nigh [him]'; though all around him, including body, were broken, still his would be 'a soul / Yet fluttering', hovering above it all (493–4, 497–8).

This sense of detachment and suspension is however hard to sustain. It is not, he found, easy to be a radical ironist. He would anchor his soul, 'turn with its energies to some one end, . . . one delight, . . . one rapture' (605–10). But as he surveys the world of possibilities he realizes that all he looks on holds some pleasure that his soul would grasp. Why then choose but one abode in which to dwell? Why settle on poetic fame or an earthly love or anything else?

> I cannot chain my soul, it will not rest
> In its clay prison; this most narrow sphere—
> It has strange powers, and feelings, and desires,
> Which I cannot account for, nor explain,
> But which I stifle not, being bound to trust
> All feelings equally—to hear all sides.
>
> (593–8)

Nevertheless, there remains a fear of total liberty; and a contrary impulse urges him 'to seize on life's dull joys from a strange fear, / Lest, losing them, all's lost and nought remains' (679–80).

For this reason he turns to Pauline and dreams of an English home and enclosure. Momentarily he is 'concentrated', but then follows the old restlessness: 'my soul saddens when it looks beyond; / I cannot be immortal, nor taste all' (808–10). His is but a history of 'struggling aims'. First the soul would rule, be monarch of all it surveys, only to find that 'commanding for commanding sickens it' and then, on second thought, it would 'rest beneath / Some better essence than itself—in weakness' (811–19). In sum, this is his 'confession', his record of a divided will that desires both continuity and change, primacy and secondariness, openness and enclosure, expansion and contraction.

Towards the end of the poem it appears that finally he is to submit to the world of limitations. In a culminating gesture he embraces God, the Sun-treader and Pauline, yet always with the knowledge 'that such pleasant life should be but dreamed' (985). Oddly, this confession that is throughout addressed to Pauline ends with an apostrophe to the Sun-treader, who is asked to be near him for ever as guide and to know that the speaker's last state is happy, free from doubt and fear. These final lines underscore what the reader has suspected all along: namely, that the poem is more about the speaker's anxiety *vis-à-vis* the Sun-treader than about his love for Pauline.

Although it is ostensibly a love poem, the real purpose of the monologue is self-analysis and on the poet's part self-definition. As we note the speaker's concerns, we see increasingly how Browning uses his speaker to objectify and evaluate his own situation: 'Sad confession first, / Remorse and pardon, and old claims renewed, / Ere I can be—as I shall be no more' (25–7). One of the subjects uppermost in his mind is remorse for desertion of his inherited religion. He can no longer embrace the forms of faith to which his parents subscribed. At one stage he 'could doubt / Even [God's] being' (304–5). Nevertheless, he has retained 'a need, a trust, a yearning after God' (295). And even though at the close he claims to believe in God, it is a highly qualified claim:

> I do not plead my rapture in thy works
> For love of thee—or that I feel as one
> Who cannot die—there is that in me
> Which turns to thee, which loves, or which should love.
>
> (827–30)

As far as God is conceived by religions such as his mother's, this expression of faith is weak. His strongest credence is lent to God as the Absolute, the Truth that mankind is always striving to reach: 'And what is that I hunger for but God?' (821).

The prime importance of the poet's relation to Shelley is indicated by the final verse paragraph addressed to the Sun-treader. His betrayal of Shelley is evidently a greater source of remorse than even his forswearing of his traditional religious faith. As all the images relating to him indicate, Shelley was the star, the sun, the guiding light in the young poet's life: he offered verses 'which seemed / A key to a new world; the muttering / Of angels, of some thing unguessed by man' (414–16). It was the apprentice poet's dream to follow in his footsteps, to be a new Shelley. But then the elder poet's vision proved unrealistic and unrealizable, and the younger man's adulation of him diminished. It is a cause of great sadness 'to see our idols perish; . . . / To see the painter's glory pass, and feel / Sweet music move us not as once' (546–52). It is a source of pain to acknowledge 'that I am not what I have been to thee' and 'never more shall I walk calm with thee' (192, 220). In effect, Browning bids farewell to Shelley so as to clear space for himself.

He does not, however, openly repudiate Shelley. Instead he releases himself from the older poet's pervasive influence by distancing and elevating Shelley into perfect light: the Romantic is hyperbolized as the Sun-treader and thereby transcendence erases immanence. Sealed into the artifice of eternity, Shelley is made a fixed star (171), on which the younger poet can hereafter 'lean' (1023) for the vision of perfection to which he aspires but which he can never attain.

Something of the same ambiguity that characterizes the speaker's relationship with God and the Sun-treader also marks his love for Pauline. He sees her as 'a last / Resource – an extreme want' (907–8). She will protect him, shelter him, 'bend o'er [him]', screen him from fear (2–5). But his dependency is brief, since soon she is 'standing beneath me— looking out to me, / As I might kill her and be loved for it' (901–2). The movement from contraction to expansion takes place constantly, and the speaker cannot yield to Pauline as a permanent source of value any more than he can fix on any certainty that would preclude other possibilities. The truth, he admits, is this: 'I can love nothing' other than provisionally (310). Even in the end, when he professes undying love for her and so can 'make an end in perfect joy' (1007), he concedes, in what is to become the hallmark of the Browning manner, that he might also 'be first to deny all' because he remains 'half afraid / To make his riches definite' (991, 998–9). He 'shall doubt not many another bliss awaits' (1009), as ultimately he turns to the Sun-treader and poetry, 'better love', for sustenance:

> I shall again go o'er the tracts of thought,
> As one who has a right; and I shall live
> With poets—calmer—purer still each time,
> And beauteous shapes will come to me again,
> And unknown secrets will be trusted me,
> Which were not mine when wavering—but now
> I shall be priest and lover, as of old.
> (1012–19)

In the end it is poetry, not love or religion, that is the speaker's chief concern. Indeed, the *raison d'être* of the monologue is poetry: as the speaker says at the beginning, till he confess 'it were vain / To hope to sing' (16–17). And what he confesses is how changes in his allegiances have affected his poetry. Tracing his artistic development, he tells how he began as a lyric poet. He had an impulse but no yearning – only sang. His verse an effusion indifferent to verbal meaning, he sang as he 'in dream [had] seen, / Music wait on a lyrist for some thought, / Yet singing to herself until it came' (376–9). Then he discovered the 'passion' of 'mighty bards', chief of whom was surely Byron, and found there

> the first joy at finding my own thoughts
> Recorded, and my powers exemplified,
> And feeling their aspirings were my own.
> And then I first explored passion and mind.
>
> (385–9)

What first attracted him to the Sun-treader was in fact the Romantic's exquisite, ardent lyricism, 'passion's melodies' (411), from which in time he sought 'to disentangle, gather sense from song' (413 in revised version). When he succeeds he discovers a beautiful political and philosophical idealism and learns that the lyric mode can be used to serve a prophetic purpose.

The speaker seeks to emulate the Sun-treader, to become a visionary bard who records the authentic meeting of his mind with the universal mind: 'ah, what a life was mine to prove! / My whole soul rose to meet it' (428–9). But having put his whole faith in the Sun-treader's beatific vision and discovered that reality is impregnable to its realization, he thereupon loses faith in 'freedom in itself / And virtue in itself—and then my motives' ends, / And powers and loves' (459–61). The Sun-treader's 'sweet imaginings are as an air, / A melody, some wond'rous singer sings' (221–2), perhaps the sweetest songs ever sung; but their truth is personal and private and has little or no relationship to life in the world. Hereafter the speaker gives up all notion of mythic allegories and bardic utterances. In effect he disavows the lyric for the dramatic mode. Turning away from the Sun-treader, the speaker forswears the subjectivity of lyric expression and adopts the objectification of self made possible by dramatic utterance: 'I will tell / My state as though 'twere none of mine' (585–6).

Writing to W. J. Fox in 1835, Browning called *Pauline* 'my first appearance on any stage (having previously only dabbled in private theatricals)' (*Correspondence* 3: 135); and in the preface to the 1888 edition of his works Browning spoke of it as the 'first of my performances'. Although to one familiar with his early life it is in parts autobiographical, the young poet went out of his way to make his first published poem as different from a lyrical narrative like Shelley's *Alastor* as possible, although basically the older poet's poem had served as a model. Not only did he insist on the dramatic nature of his speaker's utterance, he also supplied a kind of editorial apparatus to suggest that the confession was not his own. The note in French signed by Pauline at line 811, the Latin headnote from Agrippa, the motto from Marot in French, the affixed dates at the beginning and end – all these are signals that the work should be regarded as a fictional edition.[10]

In her role as editor Pauline has apparently performed several services. First, she has prepared the text for publication. She may even have arranged certain sections, as she speaks of considering how better to co-ordinate certain parts. Second, she has provided a critical note emphasizing the importance of genre in the evaluation of the poem and, further, pointing out its artistic defects. Third, she has prefixed two quotations, the one from Marot on the title page suggesting that change is the basic theme of the confession and the one from Agrippa on the reverse title page cautioning the reader that the poem is the work of a youth whose emotional extravagances should perhaps not be taken too seriously. Fourth, she has supplied the place and date of the poem's composition and of her final editorial work.

Editing is a way of distancing experience, of setting the fictional persona at a further remove from the author, of permitting him to 'tell / My state as though 'twere none of mine'. It separates story from narration and thus asserts the essential negativity of the fiction. More importantly, when regarded in the light of Browning's later career, the editorial apparatus was for the young poet a means by which to indicate the theatricality of the 'confession', to show how it had been managed and produced. The finished work was, then, purely dramatic, as the poet later said, although not dramatic in the sense in which it is generally understood, of being impersonal and objective. For the author himself *in propria persona* intrudes into the work in several ways. 'I wrote this work when I was less than a youth', the motto from Agrippa states; and following this there is the inscription 'V.A. XX', which Browning was later to explain as the Latin abbreviation of '*Vixi Annos*—"I was twenty years old"' (Hood, p. 256), exactly the poet's own age in January 1833, the date given following the motto. Finally, there is a place and date affixed at the end of the poem: '*Richmond: 22 October 1832*', where and when he saw Kean's Richard III.

Like his monologist Browning was possessed of 'a most clear idea of consciousness / Of self' that would be supreme: 'Most potent to create', it would 'call / Upon all things to minister to it' (269–76). Each act of creation – of the scripting of a performance – is thus a step forward in the growth of consciousness, as it 'give[s] back reflected the far-flashing sun' (364). Here as hereafter Browning paradoxically is at pains to distance his work from himself while simultaneously indicating, in various, sometimes clandestine ways, that he is its maker, a hovering, theatrical presence both in and out of his creation. Like the actors in *commedia dell'arte* he wears a half mask, which half conceals and half reveals.

Pauline displays an intellectual maturity and artistic daring beyond the poet's mere twenty years. Philosophically, Browning had even in this early poem pretty well worked out his notion of the doctrine of becoming, his conception of human history as the advance up a mountain of which the summit is unattainable. And lest his reader overlook the governing philosophical concept of the poem, he had his fictional Pauline comment in a note that in this 'examination of soul' the speaker was seeking to discover the sequence of objectives that he might attain and that, once attained, would form a plateau from which to discern other aims, which in their turn might be surmounted. Like the young Keats, whose *Endymion* (1818) and *Lamia* (1820) he had purchased at the same time that he acquired Shelley's works, Browning regards his future development as a leap into the unknown. The 'I' who speaks here is not only Browning but also the putative 'Browning', a presence somewhat indifferent to immediate personal concerns but sensitive to the formation of a poet who must create himself.[11]

Conceiving of personal and racial development as *Bildung* – growth, metamorphosis, moving on – he figured it as a perennial process whereby contradictions are resolved momentarily and the limitations of a current form of consciousness are temporarily overcome on the road to the unreachable Absolute. Formally, the enclosing of an open-ended 'fragment' within an editorial apparatus, a design reflecting the imagery of expansion and contraction in the 'confession', is indicative of the young Browning's sophistication and breadth of conception.

In writing *Pauline* – 'ce début sans prétention', the editor calls it – Browning was consciously attempting something new. As he says, by way of Pauline's note, this is a new genre, perhaps not well worked out and perhaps remaining no more than a sketch. But it remains an investigation of a 'soul', that is, a psychological examination of a person of a special cast of mind ('tournure d'esprit tout particulière'). It may be that the poet has not perfectly succeeded in executing what he was attempting, but as Pauline says, the conception is more important than the execution, a principle embraced by Shakespeare, Raphael and Beethoven. This philosophy of the imperfect or inadequate is an aesthetic theory to which Browning held all his life and, as thus articulated, is distinctively his.

The verse itself, however, is not distinctive, although the young poet Dante Gabriel Rossetti recognized Browning's hand when he came upon the anonymously published work in the British Museum almost fifteen years later. Take almost any passage and it can be recognized as a general Romantic style. For example:

> Night, and one single ridge of narrow path
> Between the sullen river and the woods
> Waving and muttering – for the moonless night
> Has shaped them into images of life,
> Like the upraising of the giant-ghosts,
> Looking on earth to know how their sons fare.
> Thou art so close by me, the roughest swell
> Of wind in the tree-tops hides not the panting
> Of thy soft breasts.
> (732–40)

In addition, the 'confession' appears to be in no way modified by the presence of an auditor, as Browning's later monologues were to be. As Mill observed, Pauline is 'a mere phantom', mainly spoken of as though she were not present. After its publication Browning did his best to forget his poem, not republishing it, even in his collected works, till thirty-five years later, when he was pressured to include it (he said in the preface) 'with extreme repugnance' in the collected edition of 1868.

2

Into the World

By 1833, when *Pauline* was published, Browning had not visited the Flower sisters and their friend W. J. Fox, with whom, since the death of their father, they now lived, for several years. But remembering Fox as one who had earlier spoken kindly of his boyhood verses, he wrote to Fox as soon as he had an available copy of *Pauline* to ask indirectly whether he might consider reviewing it for the *Westminster Review*. Fox evidently replied encouragingly, whereupon Browning sent him twelve copies of the poem for distribution to influential friends. Fox reviewed it in the April number of the *Monthly Repository*, praising it as a work of genius and quickly casting aside its defects as (borrowing from Pauline's note) 'a hasty and imperfect sketch': 'We felt certain of Tennyson, before we saw the book, by a few verses which had straggled into a newspaper; we are not less certain of the author of *Pauline*'.

Other reviews were mixed. *Fraser's Magazine* and *The Literary Gazette* were contemptuous of it as unintelligible. The *Atlas* and the *Athenaeum*, on the other hand, were enthusiastic, the latter's notice, Browning said later, having 'gratified me and my people far beyond what will ever be the fortune of criticism now' (Orr, *Life*, p. 14). The review most important to the poet was, however, one that was never published. Fox had given one of his twelve copies to John Stuart Mill, who in the 1830s was turning increasingly to literary pursuits from his work as a propagandist for utilitarianism. Mill read it, made a number of marginal comments, and wrote a thoughtful critique at the end of his copy. When he was unable to find a magazine or newspaper willing to publish his review, he returned his copy to Fox, who in October 1833 gave it in turn to Browning. Mill complained that 'the writer seems to me possessed with a more intense and morbid self-consciousness than I ever knew in any sane being'. Further, he found that Pauline was unreal and that the speaker '*pays her off* toward the end by a piece of flummery, amounting to the modest request that she will love him and live with him and give herself up to him *without* his *loving her*'. Yet 'the psychological history of himself is powerful and truthful—*truth-like* certainly, all but the last stage'. The young poet was doubtless stung to read what Mill had written, and in reply to some of Mill's marginal comments pencilled some defensive remarks in the same copy of *Pauline* that Mill had read. But Mill's observations had their effect. He had perceived that the poem passed too quickly from psychology to vision, that (in David Shaw's words) it presented 'no effective history compassing change and development'.[1] Browning took Mill's comments to heart, turning in his next long poem to history as the ground of meaning. The importance of Mill's review has, nevertheless, often been misunderstood and in a certain sense overplayed by Browning's biographers.[2] Its effect on the young poet was neither to silence him nor, apparently, to cause him seriously to question his manner of proceeding as a poet.

Several months after reading Mill's views of his poem, Browning took his first trip abroad. Two of his father's half-brothers – Reuben and William Shergold Browning – had taken a special interest in the young Robert. William, born in 1797, had first worked in the Bank of England and then, when his position was eliminated, had been placed by his father in the Paris office of Rothschild's. He was a cultivated man who wrote for the *Gentleman's Magazine* and other periodicals and was the author of novels and *The History of the Huguenots during the Sixteenth Century*, which went through several editions between 1829 and 1845. Reuben, only nine years older than his nephew, was the poet's favourite uncle. He too was a banker with the House of Rothschild but working in London rather than Paris; and he too was an author, of publications on income tax, bank notes and the currency, and other financial matters. Through one of these uncles Robert came to know Chevalier George de Benkhausen, consul general for Russia in England, who invited the young man to accompany him on a mission to St Petersburg to negotiate a Rothschild's loan.

The journey, in late February 1834, involved coach travel through the Netherlands, across Germany to Lithuania, and up the Baltic coast to the Russian capital. Browning seems to have been entranced by what he saw, and he was so taken with the court life he was permitted to observe that upon his return home in the spring he seems to have considered a diplomatic career for himself. At any rate the following year he applied, although unsuccessfully, to the government for appointment to a mission to Persia.

While in St Petersburg he was not so bedazzled by his heady experiences that he ceased to compose verse. Two monologues written in the foreign capital (according to Griffin and Minchin, p. 73) evidence Browning's growth as a poet over the past two years. Like *Pauline*, 'Porphyria's Lover' is a monologue addressed to a beloved, who here is even less of a presence than the 'phantom' Pauline. For Porphyria is dead, killed by her lover to preserve for ever the good moment when she was 'mine, mine, fair, / Perfectly pure and good'. The story told is full of stock material such as abounds in early nineteenth-century poems and novels: the lovers of different social class, the girl forced against her will to marry someone of higher financial and social status, her feelings of guilt, her slipping away from her engagement party to the boy's cottage during a storm, her giving herself to him sexually. It is much like the story told in Keats's *The Eve of St Agnes*, and it may be that the girl's name in Browning's poem was suggested by the lover's name, Porphyro, in Keats's.[3] 'Porphyria' seems to exemplify Keats's growing importance to the young poet several years after Shelley's influence had faded. As for the stock narrative details – Tennyson, for example, uses most of them in both 'Locksley Hall' and *Maud* – Browning manages to stamp them with his special mark. First, he gives his own twist to the story by having the lover kill the girl to prevent her marriage. Second, he makes the murderer the narrator. Though committed in a moment of passion, the killing was right, the speaker says: it was up to him to prevent the arranged marriage and keep the girl true to the one she really loved. 'I debated what to do', and then suddenly 'I found / A thing to do': it was to strangle her, almost ritualistically, with her long hair 'wound / Three times her little throat around'. It was so natural and painless ('I am sure she felt no pain'), and she seems in death as if she condoned the action. Neither she nor God utters a word of disapproval: 'all night long we have not stirred, / And yet God has not said a word!' Yes, surely, it was the 'thing to do'.

The other surviving poem from the Russian visit is 'Johannes Agricola in Meditation', identical in metre, rhyme scheme and length with 'Porphyria's Lover'. Here Browning turns for the first time to an historical personage as the subject for his poem. The protagonist is based on the German Protestant reformer, about whom Browning had read in his father's books, who broke with Martin Luther over antinomianism, according to which for the Christian the law is made void through faith. In the poem the speaker believes himself predestined for salvation and, thus unable to do wrong, exempt from the necessity of good works. Like the monologist in *Pauline*, he aims 'to get to God' and there rest in his 'own abode'. God has created him, 'guiltless for ever', as the vessel for His love; and so whatever he does, evil or otherwise, is turned to 'blossoming gladness' while the unelect, in spite of their good works, find 'all their striving turned to sin'.

These two intensely dramatic soliloquies were published in Fox's *Monthly Repository* in January 1836 under the general title 'Madhouse Cells'. Insane narratives of self-justification stated with matter-of-fact simplicity in a verse form – highly regular iambic tetrametre lines of male rhymes – suggestive of perfect rational control, both 'Porphyria' and 'Johannes Agricola', as they were originally entitled, exert intense ironic power. Already at so early a stage in his career, Browning was exploring the psychology of speech, showing its essential apologetic nature. When looked at from the

outside, both speakers in these poems appear to be little more than luna-
tics. But when looked at from the inside, so to speak, they evince how (in
Browning's opinion at least) every person has his own conception of good
that he uses to justify his deeds, no matter how wrong they appear in the
eyes of the world. In his *Notes on the Tragedies of Shakespeare* Coleridge had
spoken of the 'the motive-hunting of motiveless malignity' conducted by
Iago in soliloquy. With the notion of 'motive-hunting' as a stimulus for
speech Browning was in full agreement, but the idea of 'motiveless
malignity' he rejected, and set out to prove that there is no such thing. In
Browning's view human individuals are always defensive of personal actions
and give voice, to themselves and others, to justification of those actions.
The young poet had already arrived at the conclusion, which he never
tired of displaying, that all ratiocination is rationalization, and to dem-
onstrate this he was forced to resort to the dramatic mode.

In London in the summer of 1834 Browning met a young Frenchman,
four years his senior, with whom he was to develop an intimate friendship.
Count Amédée de Ripert-Monclar was an aristocrat who loved art and
literature and was in close touch with the cultural life of France. He was
a Bourbonist who held public office in Avignon for two years until the
1830 revolution, at which time he was briefly placed in jail. Browning met
him through his half-uncles William and Reuben. The young poet and the
French visitor quickly became close, and before the summer was out they
were seeing each other almost every day. Browning told Monclar, as he
told few others, about his authorship of *Pauline* and eventually gave him
a copy. When Monclar returned to Paris they corresponded often. Their
friendship was to remain affectionate until the 1840s, when they seem to
have drifted apart, although the poet continued to send Monclar copies
of his works through the decade. The Frenchman, a man of the world,
had apparently an important influence on Browning, especially enlarging
the poet's ever-expanding view of the world and increasing his already
deep interest in France, particularly in Paris, the cultural capital of Eu-
rope. Monclar seems even to have influenced Browning's poetic develop-
ment in that he was to suggest Paracelsus, the Renaissance physician and
alchemist, as the subject for a long poem (Orr, *Life*, p. 72).[4]

Browning was probably already acquainted with Paracelsus through his
father's three-volume edition of Paracelsus' works and his life as presented
in the *Biographie universelle* and other books on German medical men.
Browning began his poem in early October 1834, after Monclar's return
to France, and completed its 4,152 lines by mid-March 1835. The author
had some difficulty finding a publisher, but with the help of Fox he
persuaded Effingham Wilson, a small publisher who shared the radical
sympathies of Fox and Browning, to publish it when his father agreed to
bear the expense of publication. It was published on 15 August 1835 and
dedicated to Monclar 'by his affectionate friend, R.B.'.

The work is divided into five scenes and contains four characters, each
of whom speaks. But, the author insisted in the preface, it is 'a Poem, not

a Drama'; nor is it 'a Dramatic Poem'. The poet wanted this clearly under-
stood so that 'the Reader should not, at the very outset—mistaking my
performance for one of a class with which it has nothing in common—
judge it by principles on which it was never moulded, & subject it to a
standard to which it was never meant to conform'. Insisting that the work
is of a genre of a radically different nature from any previously undertaken
by any poet,[5] he says that he has attempted

> to reverse the method usually adopted by writers whose aim it is to set forth
> any phenomenon of the mind or the passions, by the operation of persons
> and events; and that, instead of having recourse to an external machinery
> of incidents to create and evolve the crisis I desire to produce, I have ven-
> tured to display somewhat minutely the mood itself in its rise and progress,
> and have suffered the agency by which it is influenced and determined, to
> be generally discernible in its effects alone and subordinate throughout, if
> not altogether excluded.

This means that each scene presents Paracelsus at a critical moment of
examination of his inner life in which he is brought by the articulation of
his 'mood' to new insights allowing him to act. In effect, the five scenes
are five monologues in which the auditors exist and sometimes speak in
order for the protagonist to iterate his 'moods'.[6] 'I go to prove my soul',
the hero says (1.559), as he, like the speaker in *Pauline*, engages in the
process of soul-making.

In *Pauline* Browning's speaker asks: 'O God, where does this tend—
these struggling aims?' Is there no goal, no *telos* towards which they point?
Further, he continues to inquire, 'What is this "sleep", which seems / To
bound all? can there be a "waking" point / Of crowning life?' (811–14).
To none of these questions does he find an answer. In *Paracelsus* Browning
turns again to the same questions but this time provides answers in a
conclusion whose 'drift & scope', said the poet, 'are awfully radical' (*Cor-
respondence*, 3: 134).

The protagonist of this work is not an imaginary character (or only
slightly veiled alter ego of the poet) but an historical personage, the
Renaissance mage and scientist Paracelsus, who was, as Browning explains
in a note, both a 'theosophist' and 'the father of modern chymistry'.
Living at a time of transition from the old medieval, religious conception
of the world as perfectly structured and enclosed to a modern, scientific
understanding of the universe as incomplete and evolving, Browning's
Paracelsus paradoxically embraces both world views. A seeker after know-
ledge, he aims to discover 'the secret of the world' (1.277) and, further,
'to comprehend the works of God, / And God himself, and God's in-
tercourse / With our own mind' (1.533–5).

In sum, Paracelsus seeks what Pauline's lover had repressed – 'a craving
after knowledge', which had been 'chained' but which was ready to rise up
if he should 'loose its slightest bond' (*Pauline*, 620–33). Unleashed, it

becomes for Paracelsus a monomania, 'one tyrant all- / Absorbing aim' that has 'made life consist of one idea' (2.152–3, 140). In quest of this abstraction he has rejected all earthly aids, including his predecessors and their works; asserting his own priority, he firmly believes in his self-origination and independence.

Paracelsus begins as a Shelleyan visionary. To him God is mind, 'the master-mind' to whom mind is 'precious' (2.229–30), and it is his role to encounter the divine and reveal the meeting of individual consciousness with universal consciousness to mankind. Every embodiment is 'a baffling and perverting' impediment that 'makes all error', and must be transcended (1.726–37). But Paracelsus – 'singled out' and called by God 'to be his organ' and 'commissary' (1.369, 295, 609) – releases the mind and truth imprisoned within himself to meet the One Mind that is Truth, and so gaze 'presumptuously on wisdom's countenance / No veil between' (1.517–18).

In Paracelsus' philosophy, which is similar to that expressed in Carlyle's *Sartor Resartus* (published in serial form in 1833–4), the phenomenal world is the vesture of the noumenal world. If the garments could be removed, then one could know the Thing-in-itself. 'I am priest', the philosopher says on the eve of his quest to locate the *Ding-an-sich* (1.801), and he will return as prophet when he uncovers 'the laws by which the flesh / Accloys the spirit' (1.775–6) and so discloses form without its clothing. With this as his aim 'Paracelsus Aspires', as the title of the first scene tells.

Nine years later, in scene two ('Paracelsus Attains'), the quester doubts his status as God's commissary but still believes that somehow he can gain direct access to the Absolute without mediation. If only he could strip nature of her vestures and escape from time, then he would see Truth. Insisting like the Romantic visionary that the individual mind can meet universal mind directly, Paracelsus rejects partial truths, 'single rewards', asking instead for truth 'in the lump' and insisting on 'all or nothing'. Though he has made a number of significant scientific discoveries, he regards them as of no value in that they fall 'short of such / Full consummation' (2.203–8). And so, despairing of science, he has turned to magic, the scene finding him in the house of a Greek conjuror. Browning wants to show how the Romantic quester's turn away from history is a sign of psychological regression.

Suddenly, as if indeed by magic, 'a voice from within' speaks. It is the voice of the poet Aprile. Paracelsus, the embodiment of power as it strives relentlessly after knowledge, meets his complement in Aprile, the personification of love as it seeks to appreciate all the beauties of the natural world. Where Paracelsus denies the value of the vestures of truth, Aprile worships its robe. Like Keats and the young Tennyson, whose two books of poems (of 1830 and 1832) had been praised by W. J. Fox and were almost certainly known to Browning, he loves beauty as an end in itself and never looks for signification beyond. It has been his aim to catalogue and capture life in all its loveliness. Yet, overwhelmed by the multitudinousness of the phenomenal world, he has been unable to focus on parts and replicate them in his art.

Like Paracelsus, Aprile has adopted an all-or-nothing attitude. He too would reach the Absolute directly, without mediation, which means that, asserting his priority, he rejects tradition. Yet now, near death, he perceives that no one can overleap time to eternity but each must work with present rude, limited tools in approaching the Absolute. What he learns, in other words, is what Browning, whose goal had been to be an entirely new kind of poet owing little or nothing to poetic tradition, was beginning to learn: his secondariness and dependency. In the first instance of a situation recurring in slightly different forms in Browning's poetry, a chorus of dead poets welcomes Aprile in an unearthly voice to their company and assures him that his endeavour has not failed utterly. They too have not attained all that they would, but each has made a step forward and thus advanced in some degree the poetic enterprise which is always a-building, 'still beginning, ending never' (2.324). Perfection is not of this world. 'Yes; I see now', Aprile says at death's door, only 'God is the PERFECT POET, / Who in his poem acts his own creations' (2.648–9). God alone is the great theatrical actor–manager who 'acts' and whose 'acts' are without flaw. To reformulate it in terms of the total 'love' that Aprile would express, only God is LOVE.

Paracelsus does not, however, comprehend what Aprile means. The scientist attributes the poet's failure to a lack of appreciation of knowledge and his own failure to a misvaluation of love. Envisioning Aprile and himself as 'halves of one dissever'd world', he vows that they must not part till the lover knows and the knower loves (2.634–7). He therefore abjures his aim to know infinitely so as to seek infinite love, which is to say that, heedless of the lesson Aprile learns, he retains his passion for ultimates. Thus does Paracelsus 'attain'.

Seeking love in its infinite varieties, he is made miserable when it does not come. He 'cannot feed on beauty for the sake / Of beauty only' (3.701–2); he cannot 'love' as Aprile did. Scene three finds him five years later suffering as a professor in Basel because he does not display the love which he believes Aprile had enjoined upon him; he will not accommodate himself to the chief requirement of teaching, namely, to the communication of knowledge. Characterizing his students as numbskulls, he makes no effort to lecture successfully but resorts to antics and grandiloquent speech, 'wild words' and 'foolish words' (3.308, 752), which, says Browning in a note added in a later edition, probably earned him the sobriquet 'Bombast'. It is, Paracelsus conceives, all a silly play, and he will rejoice when his 'part in the farce is shuffled through, / And the curtain falls' (3.591–2). He is no closer to God than he was earlier, 'knows as much of any will of His / As knows some dumb and tortur'd brute' (3.517–18). Yet he remains convinced that 'man must be fed with angel's food' (3.1015), that the eternal and the absolute can be realized in the present. But knowing now that he chose the wrong role when he attempted to play

Aprile's, he vows to return to his old quest for absolute knowledge even though aware of the futility of his search. He will play on a new stage.

The expected reaction against him in Basel having come, Paracelsus has fled to Colmar, the setting for scene four ('Paracelus Aspires'). The farce in which he fancied himself engaged in Basel here becomes absurd, and it matters not 'how the farce plays out, / So it be quickly play'd' (4.688–9). Recanting his former quest for knowledge, he will now seek knowledge in all aspects of experience, no matter how degraded they might be, and will accept 'all helps—no one shall exclude the rest' (4.239). For the first time he admits his dependency.

Throughout scene four Paracelsus is drunk. Much of what he says is, as he himself characterizes it, 'cant', 'petty subterfuges', a 'frothy shower of words' (4.627–8), as he comes increasingly to realize that truth cannot be encompassed in words. 'We live and breathe deceiving and deceived' (4.625), he says, not so much because general deception is the intention of mankind but because language is inadequate for truthful expression. Words are but vestures, not the thing itself; they 'wrap, as tetter, morphew, furfair / Wrap the flesh' (4.630–1). Indeed, some things, such as the notion of an afterlife, cannot be expressed at all because they cannot be clothed 'in an intelligible dress of words' (4.681). Nevertheless, words are to be valued as 'helps' in our approach to truth.

Paracelsus sums up his new understanding in the lyric 'Over the sea our galleys went', which he presents as a 'parable' (4.440–527). Mariners come to what they believe is an undiscovered island, where they begin to build shrines for their stone statues. They are no sooner finished than inhabitants from neighbouring isles arrive and invite them to bring their 'majestic forms' to other islands that offer more magnificent shrines already built. The mariners thus learn that there have been discoverers who came before them and who have erected other means for the presentation of truth. Departing, the mariners leave behind a pile of stones that future explorers may find and so learn from the 'tracings faint' that they are explorers in a tradition. Priority such as Paracelsus claimed is thus no more than a proud delusion. The way to truth is not 'trackless', as he initially thought (1.565), but is covered with 'tracings' of those who have gone before. With this in mind 'Paracelsus aspires'.

In the last scene ('Paracelsus Attains') the protagonist is on his deathbed, from which he is permitted a new perspective, a moment of insight into the nature of reality. Hearing the voices that Aprile also heard when dying, Paracelsus learns from them the futility of attempting to probe 'the inmost truth'. First, 'truth' is always in the making; it is never simply 'there' to be grasped. Second, even if it were graspable, it would not gladden or further the race; on the contrary, it would 'sink mankind / In uttermost despair' because there would be left no more to do, nothing to strive for (5: 143–6). There is always more to do and say; both scientists and poets are always beginning and never ending; but each one provides for successors a new rung on the endless ladder to the truth. The quest for the Absolute is doomed to fail, yet each person must search for truth in full knowledge that it will be success enough to fail as others previously have failed. Paracelsus asks of his 'sage peers' and 'rivals' from the past who 'join dead hands against [him]' to permit that 'the world enrol [his] name with theirs' (5.160–3).

Now clothed with the authority of deity as 'God speaks to men through [him]' (5.558), Paracelsus unfolds his philosophy of becoming as the divine plan. God, the source of all being, power and love, has set in motion the evolutionary process ending at present in man. This is not the culmination of the process, however, for mankind continues it by striving for perfection of himself; and were this goal to be attained, the evolution would not end even there, as man would aim Godward. 'Progress is / The law of life', Paracelsus reveals (5.741–2). Life spirals upwards, and history is the record of plateaux attained and ascents begun therefrom. Always beginning and never ending: this is 'the eternal circle life pursues' (5.776). There is no *telos* other than the striving itself.

At the close Paracelsus comprehends how his pursuit was misconceived. His Romantic quest for 'full consummation' (2.208) was an impossible one. He could not find 'the end' because in a world of becoming there is no such thing. First he sought for Godlike power, and then he sought to practise divine love. He did not understand the dialectic of power and love as a dynamic process: love preceding power, desiring power to set it free, and new power producing a growing access of love (5.856–9). In a world of plenitude the fertile abundance of life is always developing itself, by means of exhaustless energy, into new structures, or plateaux, of meaning. Thus one form yields to another, one past failure is the seed of a present success. Things in the present are, in this sense, shadows of their past embodiments. Hence what seems like evil is but the temporary eclipse of good; what appears to be hate is but a mask of love:

> To sympathize—be proud
> Of [mankind's] half reasons, faint aspirings, struggles
> Dimly for truth—their poorest fallacies,
> And prejudice, and fears, and cares, and doubts:
> All with a touch of nobleness, for all
> Their error, all ambitious, upward tending,
> Like plants in mines which never saw the sun,
> But dreamt of him, and guess where he may be,
> And do their best to climb and get to him.
>
> (5.875–83)

Embracing the doctrine of becoming, Paracelsus adopts a new theory of language. Like man's other attributes and experiences, language is generative. Words evoke responses, which in turn act as stimuli. This interanimation, which is evolutionary and developmental, leads to new stages of linguistic ability where new things can be expressed. Paracelsus learns not only that language is not static but also that words are not symbols mediating the noumenal and phenomenal: they do not permit 'vision' as the Romantics had taught; rather, they are signs that allow man to gain a larger grasp on himself and thus grow in understanding beyond present verbal constructs, 'narrow creeds of right and wrong, which fade / Before unmeasur'd thirst for good' (5.780–1). Hence Paracelsus' science has led to a new way of looking at the world, just as his contemporaries Martin Luther and Erasmus have pointed the way to new understandings of Christianity and humanistic learning. In that man not only deals with the world as language presents it to him but also realizes himself through words, it is mainly through language that 'in man's self arise / August anticipations ... / Of a dim splendour ever on before' (5.773–5). In this sense man writes himself and his beliefs.

It is, however, not only through language that humankind gains access to truth. Being phenomenal, language cannot speak of the noumenal. It is, rather, by means of nonverbal agency, a kind of intuition, that man penetrates to

> a vast perception unexpress'd,
> Uncomprehended by our narrow thought,
> But somehow felt and known in every shift
> And change in the spirit.
>
> (5.637–40)

Spiritual insight simply cannot be expressed in words, and hence Paracelsus cannot tell what he sees as he sets foot on the threshold of new and 'boundless life' (5.499–507). This is as it should be, for the knowledge attained by Paracelsus in his final hour would, if granted earlier, have rendered his life meaningless. There would have been no more for him to do.

Browning does not leave us, however, with Paracelsus. Rather, he leaves us with himself. Drawing on three works in his father's library, the poet appended a note to the poem stating: 'The liberties I have taken with my subject are very trifling; and the reader may slip the foregoing scenes between the leaves of any memoir he pleases, by way of commentary'. He then gives a translation of the account of Paracelsus taken from the *Biographie universelle*, together with his notes on that account. One point of his notes is to show that, in spite of all the liberties he *has* taken with the life of his hero, he has nevertheless made use of an historical personage for his work, thereby indicating that meaning is developed by reference to history as much as to consciousness. Another, and more important, purpose of the notes is to foreground the author himself. No matter how dramatic and thus impersonal the poem is said in the preface to be, there is nevertheless the author insisting on inserting himself into it. The preface had begun: 'I am anxious that the reader should not, at the outset— mistaking *my performance* ...'; and it ended by stating that this is 'an experiment *I* am in no case likely to repeat' (italics added). And the notes, here and there, state: 'I subjoin', 'I select', 'I shall disguise', 'I must give one specimen', 'I recollect a couple of allusions to it in our own literature'. These are no discreet signatures such as one might find in the corner of a painting. These are insistent demands for recognition of the producer of the 'performance'.

Paracelsus is indeed an experiment, as Browning had said. The ideas iterated are daring, if not from the perspective of the late twentieth century startlingly new. The notion of developmental formation or *Bildung* – a metaphor borrowed from biology – had been part of the cultural climate, at least at its upper levels, since being advanced in the late eighteenth century by Goethe; and recent scientific findings – such as Charles Lyell's work on fossils announced in his *Principles of Geology* (1830–3) – added impetus to the idea. The striking fact in Browning's case is that he had, at a young age, assimilated the idea to the extent that he could consider the possibility of human advancement in terms of biological evolution and spiritual or moral development, a postulate that Tennyson was to set forth in *In Memoriam* (1850). It is no wonder that Browning later in life could say of Darwin's theory of evolution, first elaborated in *On the Origin of Species* in 1859, that 'all that seems *proved* in Darwin's scheme was a conception familiar to me from the beginning: see in *Paracelsus* the progressive development from senseless matter to organized, until man's appearance' (Hood, p. 199).

The structures created in *Paracelsus* are likewise daring, as the work moves back and forth between enthusiastic creation of a construct or fiction and sceptical de-creation of it when as 'truth' or mimesis it is subjected to scrutiny. In its dialectical, discontinuous movement it reflects the fertile chaos of life-as-becoming. The poet was aware that such a work is not easily understood, and so in his prefatory remarks he insisted that it 'depends more immediately on the intelligence and sympathy of the reader for its success'. Indeed, he elaborates, 'were my scenes stars it must be his co-operating fancy which, supplying all chasms, shall connect the scattered lights into one constellation—a Lyre or a Crown'. That is, in this work of ironic discontinuity the reader must join in the process of creation. Thus does Browning announce his programme of reader response that is to become one of the hallmarks of his poetry.

Browning's concern with the co-operative reader reflects the crisis in poetry of the 1830s. Sir Walter Scott's easy-to-read verse narratives were exemplary of the kind of poetry that the public wanted; and even they were to some critics too demanding, the reviewer of Scott's *Rokeby*, for example, noting in the *British Review* for May 1813 that 'the mind ought not to be put upon any strong spontaneous effort'. By the 1820s verse requiring mental effort was almost impossible to sell. Thomas Love Peacock, a poet and novelist himself, wrote to Shelley, his intimate friend, that 'the poetical reading public, being composed of the mere dregs of the intellectual community, the most sufficing passport to their favour must rest on the mixture of a little easily-intelligible portion of mawkish sentiment, with an absolute negation of reason and knowledge'.[7] By the 1830s publishers were willing to print almost no poetry other than that appearing among the miscellanies of the gift books and picture annuals or by such sentimental versifiers as Letitia Elizabeth Landon ('L.E.L.') and Felicia Dorothea Hemans.

Browning recognized that the readers of poetry of any intellectual pretension were few and that his audience was limited to those who would make a determined effort to understand it. As Arthur Henry Hallam said, in his promotion of his friend Alfred Tennyson's poems in *The Englishman's Magazine* for August 1831, real poetry is not meant for 'the stupid readers, or the voracious readers, or the malignant readers, or the readers after dinner'. Browning demanded that readers of his verse be willing to engage with the poet, through the exercise of their 'co-operating fancy', in the creation of the poem, linking the 'scattered lights' into 'a Lyre or a Crown'.

The early reviews of *Paracelsus* were largely favourable, and John Forster's review in the *Examiner* for 6 September 1835 was encomiastic. Forster, soon to become a great friend of Browning's, guessed that the author of *Paracelsus* was a young man and predicted for him 'a brilliant career'. Fox, who had heard Browning read the poem in manuscript, applauded the work in the *Monthly Repository* for November as a poem of ideas, finding the protagonist 'not a personification indeed, but an individualisation of humanity, in whom he exhibits its alternation of aspiration and attainment'. Other favourable notices followed, and in a second article on *Paracelsus* Forster, writing in the *New Monthly Magazine and Literary Journal* in March 1836, named 'Mr Robert Browning at once with Shelley, Coleridge, and Wordsworth'. Browning, he said, 'has in himself all the elements of a great poet, philosophical as well as Dramatic'. In short, if the poem did not gain its author a great deal of money, it was nevertheless a *succès d'estime*, and for a number of years thereafter the title pages of Browning's new works bore the legend 'By the Author of *Paracelsus*'.

II

It is always difficult to get at the precise nature of Browning's political views. In so far as his letters address political issues, they are foreign ones – Italian liberty or the Franco-Prussian War – not English concerns. We may suppose, however, that he originally shared his father's Whig and later liberal opinions and that under Shelley's influence, which he had partially cast off but never entirely repudiated, these were to some degree radicalized. It is a fact that he found his warmest reception among the circle of political radicals and moderates that gathered around W. J. Fox, who after his disaffiliation from the unitarians in 1834 turned with increasing fervour to the urgent social and political concerns created by the industrialization and subsequent urbanization of the nation. But whatever his political persuasion, Browning never presented himself as a man of the people. He was very much a man of the middle class and never pretended otherwise, although he adopted the dress and perhaps early on the attitudes of the dandy. To Fox's young daughter Tottie he cut a dashing figure: 'He was then slim and dark, and very handsome; and . . . just a trifle of a dandy, addicted to lemon-coloured kid gloves and such things: quite "the glass of fashion and the mould of form" '.[8] To others he seems to have affected Italian ways. In Russia (as in Paris in 1837) he was taken for an Italian (Maynard, p. 129). There seemed to many people whom he encountered a cosmopolitan air about him, as though he were not English and not overly interested in English affairs.

Yet the persons most taken with him were men of intense political and social concerns. Through Fox he met Mill, Thomas Carlyle, Leigh Hunt and Harriet and James Martineau. Carlyle was originally 'anything but favourably impressed' by the young man who wore such clothes as a 'smart green coat' of cut-away shape (*NL*, p. 263). Probably others were of like opinion; but in time they discerned beneath the dandified surface a serious although ironic personality. Fox knew literary men who also shared his opinions, men such as Charles Dickens, Thomas Noon Talfourd, Edward Bulwer, R. H. Horne and John Forster, and soon Browning came to know them too.

In late November 1835 Browning made the acquaintance of the actor–manager William Charles Macready, who, famous in both Britain and America, had replaced Edmund Kean as the dominant theatrical personality of the English stage. They took to each other immediately. Macready, almost twenty years Browning's senior, subsequently invited the young poet and John Forster to his home for New Year's Eve. Forster, the same age as Browning, had also entered the University of London in 1828 and had studied law at the Inner Temple. By the mid-1830s he was well known as a man of letters, having served as dramatic and literary critic for several journals, and was now the chief critic of the *Examiner*, of which in time he was to become editor. As a result of this pleasant meeting at Macready's home the three men quickly became good friends, the theatre being their chief topic of conversation when they met thereafter.

On 26 May 1836 Macready presented Talfourd's play *Ion* to a stellar audience at Covent Garden and was received with wild enthusiasm. After the performance sixty persons, including Browning and Forster, repaired happily from the theatre to Talfourd's home in Russell Square for supper. Among a number of toasts, Talfourd proposed Browning, 'the youngest poet of England' (Orr, *Life*, p. 82). Walter Savage Landor, poet and author of *Imaginary Conversations*, raised his glass; and Wordsworth is said to have leaned across the table and whispered: 'I am proud to drink to your health, Mr. Browning' (Griffin and Minchin, p. 77). Most important of all, Macready asked the young poet to write a play for him, hoping to awaken in Browning 'a spirit of poetry whose influence would elevate, ennoble, and adorn our degraded drama'.[9]

Browning did not accept the invitation immediately, for, he wrote Macready, he was already engaged in the writing of a long poem, but if he was unable to complete it within a month he would attempt a tragedy. The month passed with the poem unfinished, and it is not unlikely that the earl of Strafford came to mind as a subject for his drama because he had recently completed a biography of Charles I's minister that Forster, who had been commissioned to write the lives of prominent Commonwealth statesmen, had begun but, owing to unforeseen circumstances, had been unable to finish. In any case, Browning was and remained intensely interested in the period of the Civil War and Commonwealth, and he turned, as he said in the preface, to writing a play about Strafford so as 'to freshen a jaded mind by diverting it to the healthy natures of a grand epoch'.

Almost certainly the neophyte dramatist first conceived of his play as a psychological study of an historical personage whose monarchist views were so different from his own. In the person of Strafford he thought he saw a man whose basic instincts were on the side of representative government.[10] What, he must have asked himself, could make such a promising statesman go wrong, turn his back on the persons and party whose aims he had espoused? The key to such a personality, the young playwright conceived, could be shown to reside not in self-interest and betrayal but, paradoxically, in self-abnegation and loyalty to one unworthy of it. Here was a man undone by virtue, virtue that proved ill. It was on this basic irony that the poet began to build his play.

During the autumn of 1836 and winter of 1837 he worked on it, revising it to meet Macready's many objections. Forster acted as something of a go-between, constantly expostulating that Macready was being too fussy and taking too long to produce the play. Browning went through the text line by line with Macready and made whatever changes the latter suggested, only to have them afterwards rejected by the very person who had insisted on them. By March 1837 the author 'looked very unwell, jaded and thought-sick'.[11] Macready then went through the text with Forster, hoping that this practical man could rescue for the stage what seemed to the actor a piece of confusion and lifelessness. Forster tinkered with it and began to act as if the play were in fact his. 'There were', said Macready, 'mutual complaints—much temper—sullenness . . . on the part of Forster, who was very much out of humour with Browning, who said and did all that man could do to expiate any offense he might have given'. Forster was, however, unbending, and what followed 'was *a scene*'. Afterwards Browning told Macready that Forster frequently was unable to control his temper and that this was the cause of 'Forster's *unpopularity*', tales of which Macready had heard from others. At the end of this meeting, on 12 April, 'Browning assented to all the proposed alterations, and expressed his wish, that *coûte que coûte*, the hazard should be made, and the play proceeded with'. The actor–manager, however, continued to worry over it, becoming 'convinced that the play must be utterly condemned' and asking for still further deletions, additions and clarifications of the text; and the author became so disheartened that he almost withdrew it.[12] *Strafford* was nevertheless produced on 1 May 1837 and printed the same day so as to preclude Macready's making further changes in the script. It was the only one of Browning's volumes prior to his marriage in 1846 to appear at the expense of the publisher.

Although the play was poorly staged, owing to the near bankruptcy of the management of Covent Garden, and for the most part indifferently acted, it received vehement applause from the crowded house on opening night, and qualified approval from the press next day. The audience on the second night was less enthusiastic, and unexpectedly Forster's review in the *Examiner* of 7 May deemed the play more poetic than dramatic. The fourth night was more encouraging, and a fifth performance was promised for 11 May. But when one of the actors dropped out, Macready did not see fit to replace him and the play reappeared on stage for a fifth and final time on 30 May. Throughout, Macready recorded, Browning 'evinced an irritable impatience about the reproduction of *Strafford*',[13] and relations between the two men remained cool for the next two years.

Macready was bothered by 'the meanness of plot' and the lack of 'dramatic power; character . . . having the [supposed] interest of action'.[14] The audience was likewise perturbed by the lack of action. The response of the young William Bell Scott, who was later to become a well-known Pre-Raphaelite painter, was probably typical. Scott had been a great admirer of *Paracelsus* and was determined to go and applaud *Strafford* 'without rhyme or reason'. But soon it became plain 'that applause was not in order'. For nothing seemed to be happening on the stage other than talk: 'The speakers had every one of them orations to deliver, and no action of any kind to perform'.[15] Browning, however, was not interested in displaying the conventional kind of dramatic action that his producer and audience expected. In acted drama as in dramatic poetry he was concerned with *Bildung*, the development of soul – which is to say, with character, not with character as an agent of plot. In *Paracelsus* his focus, he explained in the foreword to that poem, was on 'the mood itself in its rise and progress', which required subordination of 'the agency by which it is influenced and determined'. In *Strafford* his aim again, as his preface relates, was on 'Action in Character rather than Character in Action'. In short, Browning was attempting a dramatic form that would retain the detachment and objectivity of drama but would also allow for the subjective action of the lyric. As Terry Otten says, the budding dramatist was seeking 'to break down the barriers between lyric and dramatic form and discover a means of giving subjective matter objective expression'.[16] Or to put it another way, Browning wished to write ironic drama, drama that originates in the incongruity of the reflexive activity of the self observed and observing.

With the completion of *Paracelsus* and its enunciation of the doctrine of becoming in the final scene, Browning had achieved a philosophical basis for his irony that allowed him to enlarge his conception of it. In his poems of 1833 and 1835 the poet had investigated the local ironies of soul-making. But once he arrived at the idea that being is also becoming – that *a* is both *a* and not-*a* – then the way was opened to the kind of irony that is not so much a form of irony as a way of presenting it. In writing *Strafford*, Browning proposed to show two equal and opposite points of view, each having plausible claims and specious reasons to allege. His characters, their motives and principles, would be brought into hostile collision, of which there could be no possible reconciliation and in which good and ill are so blended that each demands equal sympathy from the audience. Hence *Strafford* is probably the first play in English consciously designed as a dramatization of irony.

The chief characters are far from being 'the healthy natures' of whom Browning spoke in the preface. At best Strafford and Pym are monomaniacs, each devoted beyond all reason to the furtherance of an idea – the monarchist principle in the case of Strafford, the parliamentary in the case of Pym. The two antagonists had been friends in earlier days, and even as they are presented in the first act Strafford is susceptible to Pym's plea to return to his old friends in parliament. Yet the king manages to captivate him, to seduce him away from his former friends. For in spite of the fact that Strafford is fully aware of the king's waywardness and personal disloyalty, he vows, 'I am yours— / Yours ever . . . / To the death, yours' (2.2.36–8). Hereafter, with the brief exception in 3.3, in spite of Charles's every act of perfidy and faithlessness, Strafford, like a romantic lover, besottedly remains devoted to 'the man with the mild voice and mournful eyes' (2.2.292–3).

Pym displays a contrary movement. Where Strafford casts off notions of office in manifesting his love for the person, Pym puts aside the notion of love and friendship to serve the office. Although he woos Strafford and pleads with him almost successfully to return to their old friendly ways, Strafford removes his hand from Pym's when the king appears in 1.2. As time passes and Pym sees how Strafford increasingly devotes himself exclusively to Charles, he, like a scorned lover, conceives of himself as 'the chosen man that should destroy / This Strafford' (4.2.159–60) and as the embodiment of the will of England that seeks 'England's great revenge' (3.1.29). Only at their last meeting, where their paths irrevocably diverge, does Pym again speak of his love for the doomed man: 'I never loved but this man—David not / More Jonathan! Even thus, I love him now . . .' (5.2.287–8).

Both Pym and Strafford are too blinded by passion and prejudice to do justice to the views of the other; and wedded to their causes, they condone methods and actions of which they would otherwise disapprove. Strafford is loyal to a person whom he knows to be worthless and pursues a course of action that he knows to be futile. Pym places his faith in Strafford despite his former friend's known opposition to the parliamentary cause, and when it becomes plain that Strafford will support the king under all circumstances, he resorts to acts in total violation of parliamentary principles, including connivance with the king and collusion with the king's party. This means that the audience is faced with the paradox that the better man represents the worse cause, since the play leaves us in no doubt of the moral superiority of the parliamentary faction even though it has a demagogue for its leader.

The dialectical movement of the antagonists provides an ironic structure for the play much like that of *Paracelsus*, in which true aspiration leading to false attainment is followed by the reverse pattern. From the second act on, it is inevitable that the diverging paths of Pym and Strafford must cross again. 'Keep tryst! the old appointment's made anew,' says Pym. 'Forget not we shall meet again!' And Strafford replies, 'Pym, we shall meet again!' (2.2.154–5, 166). In act three Strafford submits to his antagonist as the embodiment of the will of England (3.3.96–7). But this proves not to be the true meeting, for Strafford discovers that he was 'fool enough / To see the will of England in Pym's will' (4.2.74–5). He impeaches Pym, and far from there being a meeting of the two, the occasion is one in which Pym shrinks from, and quails before, Strafford (4.2.50, 59). To the parliamentarians, who demand that Pym bear parliament's pardon to Strafford, Pym says, 'Meet him? Strafford? / Have we to meet once more, then?' (4.2.186–7). And Strafford says in similar vein: 'I would not look upon Pym's face again' (4.2.106).

Up to this point there has been an ironic reversal. Pym, the just man with a just cause, has grown in attitude and behaviour to resemble the royalists, whose cause he detests and whose conduct he abominates – all because of his hate for Strafford. Even the king recognizes Pym's motives (4.3.38–40). Strafford, on the other hand, grows in strength and dignity. Whereas in act one he was willing to perform any kind of deed for the sake of the king, even though it offended conscience and common sense, in act four he marshals his energies for more apparently reasonable ends, though still on the king's behalf: 'From this day begins / A new life, founded on a new belief / In Charles' (4.2.101–3). This new life leads however only to the Tower and the inevitable final encounter with Pym.

The conflict between Pym and Strafford was almost certainly the germ of the play, which is to say that it was conceived as an ironic drama of character. Yet here as in *Paracelsus*, where the notes tell of the protagonist's real achievements in science and medicine, Browning was not content to allow an undefined irony of movement and countermovement. This is suggested by Strafford's final utterance – 'O God, I shall die first' – which is full of ambiguities: after him will follow not only the king and Pym but also thousands of Englishmen killed in the Civil War. History not only forestalls closure in this 'historical tragedy' (as the playwright subtitled his drama) but also grounds meaning.

Browning further sought to define his irony by introducing the character of Lady Carlisle into the midst of the dialectical movement. Pym and Strafford were the historical *données*, and, according to the preface, the portraits of them were 'faithful'. But 'Carlisle, however, is purely imaginary'. Browning invented her to provide not only a conventional romantic interest but also a moral centre. If everyone in the play was to be fickle, self-serving or blindly deceived, at least in Lady Carlisle there would be one character who was faithful, selfless and aware of the deceptions practised by herself and others.

Carlisle is sensible of playing a role, regarding herself and others as actors in a play; and the other characters too are conscious of being *dramatis personae*, which means they become ironic observers and victims of irony to the extent that they doubt the meaningfulness of their actions in the drama. At the beginning the puritans fancy that Strafford has turned Ireland 'to a private stage' (1.1.41), has superseded other royalists 'whose part is played' (1.1.151) and has tried to persuade Pym that 'a patriot could not play a purer part / Than follow in his track' (1.1.115–16, as the passage reads in the 1863 revision). But Strafford's role, which he self-consciously plays, is not the one the puritans envision. He perceives that the king wears a mask (2.2.123) and that in order to save the monarchy he must do the same. Thus when parliamentarians arrive just at the moment that Strafford discovers the king's double dealings, Strafford immediately drops to his knee before Charles in a gesture of hurried but loyal farewell. As Lady Carlisle says, 'there's a masque on foot' (2.2.260).

In this play within a play, conspirators teach their henchmen to recite to others 'all we set down' with 'not a word missed' and 'just as we drilled' (3.1.8, 21). Strafford is to be kept 'in play' (3.2.126). As in a theatre the king witnesses the impeachment proceedings against Strafford from a screened box, which 'admits of such a partial glimpse' and whose 'close curtain / Must hide so much' (4.1.17–26). The royal party judge that the trial 'was amusing in its way / Only too much of it..the Earl withdrew / In time!' (5.1.17–19). At the end Strafford wonders whether history will declare the chief part in this masque to have been played by an actor named 'the Patriot Pym, or the Apostate Strafford' (5.2.57).

Sensible of their status as actors in a play, the characters feel, like those in *commedia dell'arte*, their lack of independence, of willed action, as though they were puppets pulled by a master puppeteer. Pym and his group feel that their actions are predestined. More than once Pym speaks of his fated course and of himself as 'the chosen man' (4.2.159). This is not merely the Calvinist doctrine of election, for the royalists too believe their actions controlled. 'There's fate in it—I give all here quite up' (2.2.195), says Strafford; and the king feels, 'I am in a net.. / I cannot move!' (4.3.82–3). In effect, the actors suggest that behind the scene there is the figure of the playwright constantly manipulating them.

The actors in the masque are also aware of the superfluity of words enveloping the action; they are almost conscious of their literary status. The opening scene is devoted to those who 'will speak out' (36) and those who say that there has been 'talk enough' (263), the need being that 'word grow deed' (243). The second scene shows how the monarchical party have 'decried' Strafford's service, made no 'precise charge' (39) and 'eschew plain-speaking' (53, 39, 141). Charges and countercharges make up much of the play, as the characters not only see themselves as actors in a play whose words alone convey the action but also regard themselves and their circumstances as part of a text to be interpreted. The parliamentary party are obsessed with the reading of reports. Pym charges the king with attempting 'to turn the record's last and bloody leaf' so as to record a new 'entry' on a 'new page' (1.1.153–9). Strafford thinks of himself as a figure in a romance in which he 'shall die gloriously— as the book says' (2.2.169–81). Both puritans and royalists carefully scrutinize the text of every proposal. A set of notes seals Strafford's fate (4.1.65). Only 'the busy scribe' of time and fame will provide the 'curious glosses, subtle notices, / Ingenious clearings-up one fain would see' (5.2.52–5). The characters give the impression that they know they are part of the script of *Strafford: An Historical Tragedy By Robert Browning, Author of 'Paracelsus'* (as the title page read).

Browning also calls attention to his dialogue as words because, as he was never tired of saying, words are signs of things, not the things themselves, and require interpretation. As he depicts 'Action in Character', he shows how humans use words to justify their actions and how understanding of them necessitates going beyond their words to get at their motives. That is why interpretation of the dialogue assigned to his actors requires semiotic and psychological agility on the part of the reader or auditor.

In Browning's world language is a deceptive veil through which it is impossible fully to penetrate. At best, comprehension of meaning is approximate. Nevertheless, language is the means by which characters realize themselves – that is, advance themselves in soul-making. In *Strafford*, more clearly than in his two previously published poems, Browning represents speech as the active, formative force of the mind in the process of self-articulation. Full of asides, interjections, partially completed statements, interruptions, the dialogue is characterized by numerous semantic breaks that offer possibilities for extension of meaning. We see this in the colloquy between Carlisle and Strafford near the end of the second act, when Strafford has just discovered the full egoism of the king and Carlisle comprehends the extent of his foolish love for Charles:

> CARLISLE: The King!—
> What way to save him from the King?
>   My soul..
> That lent from his own store the charmed disguise
> That clothes the King..he shall behold my soul!
> Strafford...(I shall speak best if you'll not gaze
> Upon me.)...You would perish, too! So sure!...
> Could you but know what 'tis to bear, my Strafford,
> One Image stamped within you, turning blank
> The else imperial brilliance of your mind,—
> A weakness, but most precious,—like a flaw
> I' the diamond which should shape forth some sweet face
> Yet to create, and meanwhile treasured there

Lest Nature lose her gracious thought for ever!...
STRAFFORD: When could it be?...no!...yet...was it the day
We waited in the anteroom till Holland
Should leave the presence-chamber?
CARLISLE: What?
STRAFFORD: —That I
Described to you my love for Charles?
CARLISLE: (*Aside.*)   Ah, no—
One must not lure him from a love like that?
Oh, let him love the King and die! 'Tis past...
I shall not serve him worse for that one brief
And passionate hope..silent for ever now!
                                        (2.2.225–46)

This staccato dialogue reveals how Strafford and Carlisle repress their true emotions and thus suppress true communication. He seems to know what she is getting at, but then with that resolute 'no!' returns to the king, while she with her 'What?' delays understanding him until she utters as an aside what she was about to declare openly. In this instance, as in many others, Browning clearly represents language as an instrument of deception, not only of others but of oneself as well. As Paracelsus said, 'We live and breathe deceiving and deceived' (4.625).

It is to be wondered at that *Strafford* was received enthusiastically at its first performance. Its dialogue was totally unlike that for which the audience was prepared; its action lay largely in its language; it lacked a conventionally sympathetic hero or heroine. Again Browning was conscious of attempting something radically new, as his preface makes clear. To focus on his protagonist's psychological development – to achieve 'the represented play, which is one of Action in Character rather than Character in Action' – would mean that 'considerable curtailment will be necessary'. The outward, historical facts would be cut to a minimum and would have to be supplied by the audience. As in the preface to *Paracelsus*, the poet was again insisting that in a work of ironic discontinuity the reader must join in the process of creation – employ 'his co-operating fancy' – in order to perceive the facts within. While his play's success would be gratifying, failure would not wholly discourage him: 'experience is to come, and earnest endeavour may yet remove many disadvantages'. He was sure he was on the right track and working in the right mode. Like *Pauline* and *Paracelsus*, *Strafford* was a 'sketch' of what he ultimately wanted to do. To later audiences – readers properly, for it has rarely been revived for theatrical presentation – the play has been chiefly of interest in the charting of Browning's development.

3

Taking Stock: *Sordello*

Following the exertions and disappointments of dealing with *Strafford*, Browning turned from English history and the English stage to foreign concerns. Ripert-Monclar visited London in June–August 1837, and Browning saw him nearly every day. Further, during that year Robert visited Paris with William Browning and met a number of his uncle's literary friends. More important, however, was his three-month tour of Europe in the spring of 1838 – important because the journey had a profound effect upon the long poem that he had been writing, or attempting to write, for the past four or five years.

During the summer of 1834 Browning had been at work on a poem devoted to the thirteenth-century Italian troubadour Sordello, about whom he had learned from Dante's *Purgatorio* and the *Biographie universelle*. He had intended to publish this poem and *Paracelsus* together, but in December 1834 he changed his conception of *Sordello* and had to start again.[1] When he did publish *Paracelsus*, he referred in the preface, dated 15 March 1835, to 'other productions which may follow in a more popular, and perhaps less difficult form'; and in a letter to Fox of 16 April he wrote of 'another affair on hand, rather of a more popular nature' (*Correspondence*, 3: 134). A year later he believed that he was almost finished; he wrote Macready on 28 May that he would have his poem completed within the month (*Correspondence*, 3: 173). But then *Strafford* intervened, as the preface to the play tells: 'I had for some time been engaged in a Poem of a very different nature, when induced to make the present attempt'. The advertisement at the end of *Strafford* announced, however: 'Nearly ready. Sordello, in Six Books'. Then in July 1837 appeared a long poem by Mrs W. Busk in six cantos on the same subject, entitled *Sordello* and somewhat in the manner in which Browning had conceived his work. The reviewer in the *Athenaeum* for 15 July 1837 asked concerning Mrs Busk's poem: 'Is this founded upon the same subject as that chosen by the author of "Paracelsus" for his announced poem?' This gave the young poet pause

Plate 1 'Robert Browning, 1837'. Drawing by Count Ripert-Monclar. Courtesy of the Armstrong Browning Library.

and caused him to reconsider his plan for his own work so that it could in no way be taken to resemble Mrs Busk's.

Nevertheless, he wrote Monclar on 9 August that *Sordello* was 'undergoing a final revision' and was to be published 'in a few months' (*Correspondence*, 3: 265). Less than two weeks later he was less sure. 'I am working well enough at Sordello, never fear', he wrote another correspondent on 20 August; 'I shall soon get the better of the monster, and..

but to anticipate is unluck[y]' (*Correspondence*, 3: 280). In late December he called on the writer Harriet Martineau, whom he knew through the Flower sisters, and told her that his poem was still unfinished. In her diary Martineau noted: 'Denies himself preface and notes. He must choose between being historian or poet. Cannot split the interest. I advised him to let the poem tell its own tale'.[2] Clearly at an impasse, Browning decided to visit Italy, intending, he wrote to a friend, 'to finish my poem among the scenes it describes' (*Correspondence*, 4: 24).

A Rothschild shipment to Trieste offered him the means of getting there, and on 13 April 1838 he left London on a seven- week voyage, the first part of it, as the ship crossed the stormy Bay of Biscay, causing the most desperate seasickness in the young traveller. After Gibraltar the sea was calmer, but adventure awaited off the coast of Algiers, where a wrecked smuggler full of dead bodies was encountered. Stripped by the English crew of everything valuable, the battered hulk then, Browning reported, 'reeled off, like a mutilated creature from some scoundrel french surgeon's lecture-table, into the most gorgeous and lavish sunset in the world' (*Correspondence*, 4: 68).

The ship landed in Trieste on 30 May, and from there Browning took a steamer for Venice, where he spent two weeks enraptured by San Marco and the palaces along the canals, the gondoliers, the markets, the *contadine* bearing their fruits and vegetables, and all the other sights and sounds of the Veneto. From there he went to the mountains, to 'delicious Asolo' (*Correspondence*, 4: 68), the fortified town with its view northward across the Brenta plain to the Alps. Asolo was an enchanting city of almost terrifying beauty. As he was to say of it in the prologue to *Asolando*, his last volume of verse,

> I found you, loved yet feared you so—
> For natural objects seemed to stand
> Palpably fire-clothed! No—
>
> No mastery of mine o'er these!
> Terror with beauty, like the Bush
> Burning but unconsumed.

After visiting Vicenza and Padua, he went back to Venice and thence to Verona, where he gathered yet more local colour for *Sordello*. He crossed the Tyrol into Germany and Würzburg, the scene of the first part of *Paracelsus*, and then down the Rhine to a Channel steamer, arriving home in July.

He did not, however, manage to finish the poem among the scenes described in it; in fact, he wrote only four lines during the three months he was away (*Correspondence*, 4: 67). Nevertheless, he returned to England refreshed and apparently spent the next year and a half working on it. *Sordello* was published in March 1840 by Edward Moxon, W. J. Fox's friend and Tennyson's publisher, at the expense of the poet's father.

It is evident that Browning's conception of the poem changed several times over the years during which he was at work on it.[3] Mrs Orr says that he studied all the chronicles of that period of Italian history that were in the British Museum (Orr, *Handbook*, p. 32), yet the published poem is profoundly unhistorical.[4] Browning himself said in his dedication to the reworked *Sordello* of 1863: 'The historical decoration was purposely of no more importance than a background requires; and my stress lay on the incidents in the development of a soul: little else is worth study'. The poem treats Sordello's development as a poet, his love for Palma, his military exploits – material largely invented but placed in a highly detailed historical background. It is told by a narrator who has no stable identity, being sometimes a nameless third person, sometimes the poet himself and sometimes the consciousness of Sordello. On the surface it would seem that the poet, facing several different versions of his poem, could not fuse his intractable materials into an harmonious union. To Browning, however, this was no drawback, for conventional formal unity was in no sense what he desired, formal perfection and logical coherence being in his view the attributes of the poetry of the past. What he wanted was something new, something distinctive, something radically different from the work of his predecessors. His aim was to be one of the 'setters-forth of unexampled themes, / Makers of quite new men' (1.26–7). This is why his speaker in the beginning bids Shelley depart: 'Thou, spirit, come not near' (1.60). And it is only with 'Shelley departing', as the elucidatory page heading reads in the 1863 version of the poem, that this work of approximately 5,800 lines of iambic pentameters in rhymed couplets gets down to business.

Because this was to be a narrative of a new kind, it would have to be told in a new way. With his experience in the dramatic mode, the poet would have preferred to render his narrative as a monologue, thereby 'making speak, myself kept out of view / The very man as he was wont to do, / And leaving you to say the rest for him' (1.15–17); but this would not do, because makers of the new

> Had best chalk broadly on each vesture's hem
> The wearer's quality, or take his stand
> Motley on back and pointing-pole in hand,
> Beside them; so for once I face ye, friends.
>
> (1.28–31)

The poet has to appear in the poem as the presenter so as to indicate that the work is in essence a point of view, *his* novel manufacture that makes no pretence of being 'bardic' or representative.

> Who will, may hear Sordello's story told:
> *His* story? Who believes *me* shall behold
> The man, pursue his fortunes to the end
> Like *me*; . . .
> Only believe *me*.
>
> (1.1–4, 10; italics added)

The novelty of the narrative presentation also necessitated an experiment in genre. This could not be a conventional kind of verse narrative – as the verse romance of Scott, for example – nor could the fictional narrative be entirely modelled on the prose novel, already in the 1830s the most popular form of literature.[5] As we have seen, Browning was interested in self-inscription not only as a display of the showman but also as a means of indicating the particularity of context; and neither genre would permit the open presence of the writer and his response to the work. Clearly what was required was a blend of genres, something approximating *Don Quixote*, in which the author destroys the pretence of historical objectivity by interrupting the narrative with reflections upon himself, his work, his readers and the society of his day. It would be 'a Quixotic attempt' (as the 1863 page heading indicates):

> as the friendless people's friend [Don Quixote]
> Spied from his hill-top once, despite the din
> And dust of multitudes, Pentapolin
> Named o' the Naked Arm, I single out
> Sordello.
>
> (1.4–8)

The chief characteristic of such generic experimentation would, then, be parabasis, which in Greek drama is the stepping forward of a chorus or an actor to break the dramatic illusion and speak directly to the audience. Hence the composition would confound and deconstruct the narrative order and determinable meaning that it pretended to offer. No better possibility could there be for one who plainly wished to present himself as the manager of the performance.

Conceived as example of a genre inclusive of many genres, *Sordello* is part novel, part puppet show, part carnival and many other things as well.[6] As an illusionist, the master of the performance repeats the command 'appear / Verona'. As a painter (or perhaps a tailor) he 'chalk[s] broadly on each vesture's hem' (1.28). As a clown or stage-manager in *commedia dell'arte* he 'take[s] his stand / Motley on back and pointing-pole in hand / Beside them' (1.29–31). As a storyteller to an imaginary audience, he 'face[s] ye, friends, / Summoned together . . . / To hear the story I propose to tell' (1.31–4). The poet–showman's stances are numerous.

The presenter is not, however, merely a fictional presence distinct from the poet: he is that, but he is the poet also.[7] As the poem proceeds, Browning constantly exploits the perpetual discrepancy in narrative between author and narrator and, further, between narrator and character. The poet actually appears recognizably as Robert Browning in three different places: where he refers to his own birthday (2.296–7), where he alludes to himself musing on the palace steps in Venice (3.676–7) and where he apostrophizes his friend the poet Euphrasia Fanny Haworth and the revered writer Walter Savage Landor (3.950–74).

Yet the poet in no way authorizes the presenter to speak on his behalf; he is always careful to keep the exact degree of identity ambiguous, as the showman haltingly tells the story and comments on the means by which it is told. In other words, the presenter is also the metapoet whose commentary on the poem's own means and ends is inextricable from the actual presentation. He is, on the one hand, the 'archimage' whose poetry, like a 'transcendental platan' of pyrotechnical brilliance, is addressed to an audience from whom he is totally 'apart'. Yet, on the other hand and more precisely, he is like a god who comes and goes in his creation: he can 'entrance' his audience and depart, 'as a god may glide / Out of the world he fills', later 'returning into it without a break / I' the consciousness' (3.595–614).

Browning had promised an evocation of an historical figure: to show 'the very man as he was wont to do' (1.16). But in his several reworkings of his material he found that 'the very man' was irrecoverable. He could try to present the historical Sordello within the medieval poet's own cultural system, but there were obviously severe limitations on his achieving this. How could a man of the late 1830s recreate life of the late eleventh and early twelfth centuries? He realized that he was bound by time and place, and hence must forgo the impossible task of reconstruction in favour of an historical perspective. Thus, viewing the past from a certain station, he would honestly admit his partiality by foregrounding the differences between his circumstances and his language and those of Sordello's. In short, Browning became a New Historicist *avant la lettre.*

In the first half of the poem the presenter appears to be more concerned with his own situation than with Sordello's. His announced subject is Sordello, yet Sordello does not appear till line 328 of book one, at which point the audience is given a flashback to Sordello's youth in Goito lasting some two thousand lines. To put Sordello in his proper setting, the showman attempts to create Verona. And having announced his choice of subject, he says, like a necromancer, 'Appears / Verona'. But Verona does not appear; in its place are reasons for the way the story will be told. Then a second time Verona is unsuccessfully summoned to appear. Finally, on the third call, Verona appears, only to disappear and be replaced by Goito (1.10–11, 59–60, 77–8). Not until book three does Verona again briefly appear (3.261), this time followed by a digression lasting for the rest of the book, at which point the audience is promised that 'you shall hear Sordello's story told'.

The poem, then, is half over before we get to what was initially promised. And realizing this, the poet asks why he should continue when his narrative will not shape itself, will not yield what he wants. Having in desperation fled to Venice (in 1838, as we have seen), Browning ponders how to continue his poem. He needs a muse, a 'queen' for inspiration (3.679–81). Suddenly his heart leaps up when he sees a group of market girls – young, strong and healthy – and he is moved to ask for the oppressed people of the world what these girls now possess, the opportunity for happiness.

Where formerly, in his Shelleyan phase, he had thought it possible for the human race to achieve perfection, he now realistically lowers his expectation, asking youth, strength and health for each of the poor and dispirited, nothing more.

Taking now for his muse the 'sad dishevelled ghost' who plucks at his sleeve and whom he sees as a type of poor and disempowered humankind (3.696–745), the poet reconsiders his art. He cannot achieve artistic perfection, because his means are not adequate to his vision; but he does have the opportunity to work towards it. His aim will be to impart the gift of seeing to his audience, to permit them to see what he sees; he will be the 'Maker-see' (3.928); and with new purpose he lets his narrative unfold in the last three books less haltingly. As Browning wrote to Fanny Haworth in an excellent example of his frequently tortured prose, he had left off his verse writing 'with a notion of not taking to it again in a hurry', when there appeared the dishevelled form that he typified and figured as 'Mankind, the whole poor-devildom one sees cuffed and huffed from morn to mid-night, that, so typified, she may come at times and keep my pact in mind, prick up my republicanism and remind me of certain engagements I have entered into with myself about that same, renewed me, gave me fresh spirit, made me after finishing Book 3^{d} commence Book 4th' (*Correspondence*, 4: 269).

Having from the start accepted parabasis as a necessary condition of his narrative, Browning was constrained to work out a dialogic relationship between the poet–narrator and the protagonist. In book one the world is experienced from Sordello's point of view, as the narrator invites us to pass into the castle at Goito and into the mind of Sordello (1.389–92). The boy does not speak, but the narrator relates his experiences, at times adding comments about the boy's development. These comments are addressed not only to the audience but to Sordello as well, as though the narrator were tugging the boy into consciousness.[8] As an adolescent wrapped up in himself, Sordello lives in a dream world, in which he aspires to be both chief ruler and chief poet, emperor and Apollo; and he is allowed to express his fantastic hopes.

In book two Sordello is grown to manhood, and the narrator converses with him more directly, although also projecting his thoughts by means of indirect discourse, as Sordello takes on a separate life of his own. While Sordello is increasingly merged into the narrator in the first three books, in the last two there is a growing separation, so that in the end the narrator loses almost all sympathy for him and sums up Sordello's life as 'a sorry farce' (6.849–50). Plainly Browning uses Sordello as the persona by which to trace his own development until, having gained a certain self-knowledge and hence a certain superiority over his material, he separates himself from his hero.

In *Sordello* as in *Pauline* Browning deals with a protagonist who would be a Shelleyan legislator of mankind. In the later poem, however, the poet locates his aspiring young bard, for reasons that we shall see, in the historical past, at a moment of transition from one cultural climate to another, 'beside the flow / And efflorescence out of barbarism' (1.570–1), from the Middle Ages to the Renaissance. Growing up alone in Goito, Sordello calls upon all nature to minister to his sense of self as he in turn endows nature with his own values; in isolation he exerts the powers of imagination exclusively for his private pleasure. Soon, like the young Browning who believed himself capable of mastery of all arts, he fancied that he could grow to any height, be 'equal to being all' and so could 'display completely here / The mastery another life should learn, / Thrusting in time eternity's concern' (1.548, 564–6). Impersonating first the poet Eglamor and then the emperor Frederick, he ultimately selects the god Apollo, as concentrating all excellence, for his model. And then one day he wanders away from Goito and comes upon a court of love near Mantua presided over by the princess Palma.

Sordello wins out over Eglamor, the consummate formalist, in the song contest, reworking the older poet's materials into 'the true lay with the true end' (2.82). He becomes chief minstrel in Mantua and must 'think now', where 'hitherto / He had perceived' (2.123–4). Pure lyric ceases to be adequate. But what body, instrument or vehicle for expression will serve? He experiments but finds none satisfactory. For to his dismay he discovers that for what he thinks he wants to say, traditional poetic language 'scarce allowed a tithe / To reach the light'. His only recourse is then to transform his province's form of the Latin language, and so he 'slow re-wrought / That Language, welding words into the crude / Mass from the new speech round him, till a rude / Armour was hammered out' (2.570–7).

Yet the armour is inadequate. For although he can embody thought, he cannot make language exhibit perception: 'Because perceptions whole, like that he sought / To clothe, reject so pure a work of thought / As language'. To be sure, 'Thought may take Perception's place', but it cannot re-present the perception that thought has usurped. Language is linear and thus can only render 'the Whole / By Parts, the simultaneous and the Sole / By the Successive and the Many' (2.588–95). Sordello learns that there is no 'wondrous vehicle' that would allow him 'to become Apollo' (2.601–3). Hereafter his must be the language of silence as he turns to the world of action for the 'body' that his soul requires.

Summoned to Verona by Palma, he becomes there an instrument of her ambition. Up to this point Sordello had barely heard of the Guelfs and Ghibellins, the parties espousing the cause of the Pope and the Lombard barons on the one hand and the cause of the emperor on the other. But never seriously questioning his ability as a politician or warrior, he resolves to be

> Gatevein of this heart's blood of Lombardy,
> Soul to their body—have their aggregate
> Of soul and bodies, and so conquer fate.
> (3.555–61)

At last, he deceives himself, he has found the body for his soul, the means for self-display that poetry had not vouchsafed. But Sordello's difficulties as a man of action are roughly the same as those he had as a poet: where he tried to manifest himself fully in words, he now wishes to do the same with deeds, 'to display here / The mastery another life should learn, / Thrusting in time eternity's concern' (1.564–6). He wishes to ally himself with the good and serve mankind. But how is the good – his goal of uplifting the masses – to be achieved? The chief political parties are no guide. What he requires is 'a Cause' that 'fate ordained' and can provide him with the means to pursue (4.950–2). And so the old quandary remains. Where he could imagine verbalization of whole perception but discovered his medium of language incapable of rendering it, he now imagines a perfect society – a new Rome, a universal and continuing city sheltering all mankind – but finds no means of achieving it. There is no more possibility of building it 'all at once' than of saying it 'all at once'.

His vision of a new Rome, he soon realizes, is another in 'the dull / List of devices—things proved beautiful / Could they be done, Sordello cannot do' (5.71–3). But then suddenly he has a new vision – not unlike that of Paracelsus on his deathbed – in which a voice says:

> God has conceded two sights to a man—
> One, of men's whole work, time's completed plan,
> The other, of the minute's work, man's first
> Step to the plan's completeness.
>
> (5.85–8)

Where Sordello had failed, the voice says, was in attempting to take the last step first, to overleap time, which meant that he was engaged in a deluded Promethean adventure: 'You were God: be man now!' (5.97).[9]

Living men build on dead men's accomplishments: this is as true in practical affairs as in poetry. And in doing so, they are acquiescing in the evolutionary scheme – the fundamental plan of becoming – that God has devised. If, as Aprile in *Paracelsus* discovered, only God is the perfect poet, then no mortal, even though he mimic God's creative act and God's ability to be both immanent and transcendent, can be 'a whole and perfect Poet' (5.116, in the revised *Sordello*). As the ghostly voices of his fellow poets tell Sordello, the collective poet surpasses what the individual poet can do. The song begun by a predecessor is carried on by a present singer, whose works in turn will be furthered and modified by a future poet till 'time's mid-night / Concluding' (5.117–18). It is the irony of incomplete completion – the work offered as a finished product that is but a stage in a continuous process – that ultimately dictated Browning's decision to cast *Sordello* as an offering to, and a dialogue with, his poetic predecessors.

Speaking of his disappointment concerning the reception of his work, the poet tells his audience, dead spirits summoned from heaven and hell, that he regards them as his 'lovers', a brotherhood who have returned 'to see how their successors fare'. But he dismisses one, who in the 1863 headnotes is identified as Shelley, because his presence would make the narrator self-conscious and induce in him a feeling of presumption. The narrator feels, in other words, that he must define his own difference as a poet.[10] Just as Sordello must free himself of the influence of Eglamor, so must Browning show himself a different kind of poet from Shelley.

In this process of self-definition the narrator traces the evolution of poetry throughout the ages – from the epoist to the dramatist–analyst to the synthetist (as the headings in the 1863 version call them).[11] The fraternity of poets is ever engaged in the corporate, fraternal enterprise of making and dismantling the 'complex gin' of poetry, whose ultimate goal is said to be the unveiling of man's inner life. In the past the poet and his predecessors – or the poet and his audience – were hardly 'brothers'. In the beginning deeds gave birth to song, which in turn inspired both deeds and thoughts. Then came the art of the epoist, which was allegorical in that it exaggerated the good and bad qualities of human beings. When this was perfected, 'Next age—what's to do?' The dramatist, or analyst, came along to portray men and women realistically. What then was required? The art of the synthetist, whose chief interest is psychological, arose to show man's inmost life. In this history or 'masque' of the progress of poetry, each stage involves an increasing role for the audience/reader to play, so that the last – synthetist poetry, which works on the principle of complementarity – demands dialogue. Casting 'external things away', the synthetist asks his audience to employ the 'co-operating fancy' spoken of in the preface to *Paracelsus* and 'yourselves effect what I was fain before / Effect, what I supplied yourselves suggest, / What I leave bare yourselves can now invest'. Conversing 'as brothers talk', the poet and his audience will engage in 'brother's speech, . . . where an accent's change gives each / The other's soul' (5.584–637).

This does not mean, however, that the synthetist entirely discards the works of the past. On the contrary, he is constantly aware and appreciative of a rich and copious poetic tradition. The poetry of previous ages, symmetrical and rounded in its formal architecture, served its purpose for its time. What is needed now is not an elaboration of those older forms but instead a reduction and transformation of them:

> a single touch more may enhance,
> A touch less turn to insignificance
> Those structures' symmetry the Past has strewed
> Your world with, once so bare: . . .
> . . . need was then expand,
> Expatiate . . .
>
> (5.631–4, 638–9)

Hence the present poet joins the brotherhood of poets, not shoving them aside or being immobilized by competition with them but making use of them by building on them: 'my art intends / New structure from the ancient' (5.642–3).

The aesthetic theory expounded by Sordello is reflective of the narrator's expressed in book three, which forswears poetic closure and all sorts of objectivist art in which the poet and the poem are one. Real life – which, the poet–narrator insists, is what modern art aims to reflect – cannot be fully transcribed or transcripted: there is always something left over, a surplus, a singular world in which the poet becomes aware, creates, lives and dies. Synthetists, unlike Eglamor, feel no 'need to blend with each external charm, / Bury themselves, the whole heart wide and warm, / In something not themselves' (1.507–9). Nor are they 'bards', who from their poetic heights prophesy and promise more than they can deliver. In their view poets are of three different kinds: the worst say they have seen; the better tell what they saw; and the best impart the gift of seeing. The synthetists advance on this last type and ask their audiences who, 'having seen too what I saw, be bold / Enough encounter what I do behold / (That's sure) but you must take on trust' (3.912–15). This poetics of dialogue is what Browning aimed for in the composition of *Sordello.* Hoping that 'Man's inmost life shall have yet freer play', he casts away all externals, 'And natures varied now, so decompose that... Why, he writes *Sordello!*' (5.616–19).[12]

Sordello, however, even with his new understanding of the evolutionary process resulting in an art of full-fledged audience participation, does in fact accomplish nothing. The heart of his problem is one that Browning had previously considered, especially in *Paracelsus* – namely, the conflict of power and love. The career of power exemplified in the general Salinguerra cannot be reconciled with the younger man's love for the people and his desire to relieve their suffering. Perhaps, Sordello figures, he could use his poetic gift to persuade Salinguerra, who prosecutes the Ghibellin cause, to champion instead the Guelf cause, which serves Rome's. And as he addresses the general with this aim in view, Salinguerra all of a sudden confers the emperor's badge upon him and Palma reveals that he is Salinguerra's son. The result is total perplexity. For given the power to take on Salinguerra's strength, Sordello cannot come to a decision as to what to do.

All along the narrator has hinted that what Sordello lacks is some belief – some world view or governing myth – to guide him. Others with not half his accomplishments had succeeded in various pursuits because they had some inner 'core' or submitted to 'some moon' drawing them on. In short, they had a 'function' (5.57–60) because they had a controlling purpose supplied by something outside themselves, 'a transcendent all-embracing sense, / Demanding only outward influence, / A soul . . . above [them]' (6.39–41). Sordello, however, was devoid of these. Neither Palma, the representative of love, nor Salinguerra, the figure of power, would, the narrator says, have proved equal to swaying *all* Sordello, but the love and strength they respectively offered would have provided at

least a partial sense of purpose. Yet Sordello could embrace neither be-
cause neither was sufficient 'moon' to 'match his sea' (6.89–93). His is the
predicament of Pauline's lover and other earlier Browning protagonists:

> Since
> One object viewed diversely may evince
> Beauty and ugliness—this way attract,
> That way repel, why gloze upon the fact?
> Why must a single of the sides be right?
> Who bids choose this and leave its opposite?
> (5.441–6)

Where, in other words, is the 'abstract Right' (5.447), the power and love
that will sanction life in the finite world?

Retiring to an upper room, Sordello ponders what he should do. The
world as he sees it is all possibility – 'The real way seemed made up of all
the ways' – and taking one course of action is equivalent to denying the
validity of all others. Why 'brutalize' soul by enclosing it within a restraining
body? Why yield eternity for the 'single sphere—Time' (6.575, 555)? Finding
no answer to these questions, Sordello has it supplied by the narrator. 'Ah
my Sordello', he says,

> I this once befriend
> And speak for you. A Power above him still
> Which, utterly incomprehensible,
> Is out of rivalry, which thus he can
> Love, tho' unloving all conceived by Man—
> What need! And of—none the minutest duct
> To that out–Nature, nought that would instruct
> And so let rivalry begin to live—
> But of a Power its representative
> Who, being for authority the same,
> Communication different, should claim
> A course the first chose and this last revealed—
> This Human clear, as that Divine concealed—
> The utter need!
> (6.590–603)[13]

Although he does not place his formulation within a specifically Christian
context, it is clearly the Incarnation of Christ that the narrator 'induces'
from his (and his protagonist's) 'utter need'. For the Incarnation, as con-
ceptualized here, stands as the pattern for one seeking to comprehend
how power and love find satisfactory manifestation in the phenomenal
world, or, to use Sordello's terms, how soul is embodied with meaning and
purpose. God condescends to time and matter as spirit becomes flesh, and
in so doing provides a model for human self-realization. If He finds the
joy that comes 'when so much Soul is wreaked in Time on Matter', surely
it is hubris for anyone, artist or politician, to 'let Soul attempt / Matter

beyond its scheme'. The Sordellos of this world must take God's act as exemplary and hence 'fit to the finite [their] infinity' (6.493–9). In so doing they will accomplish what the young Sordello desired but never achieved – 'true works' reflecting passion, power and knowledge 'far / Transcending these, majestic as they are' and forcing the audience to 'recognise / The Hid by the Revealed' (3.622–8, 570–1).

It is to the myth of the Incarnation that Browning's three previously published works have been leading. This is not to say that the poet embraced the orthodox Christian doctrine of the Incarnation; rather, it is to say that he embraced it as a mythic pattern, a model of organization for his life as artist. The obsessive subject matter of his prior work – the sense of the infinite power of the imagination and the concern to channel it – is surely reflective of the poet's own struggle to fit imagination, felt to be boundless, to the quotidian world. He had many gifts but he lacked 'some point / Whereto those wandering rays should all converge' (*Paracelsus*, 5.690–1). The Incarnation provided this point, especially in offering a paradigm for poetic practice. The poet as God living among his creatures, giving and drawing sustenance from them – the notion was compelling to one who wished to be a 'Maker-see' (3.928), both subjective and objective, immanent and transcendent, not sequentially but simultaneously. In the mystery of the Incarnation lay the perfect symbolization of the irony that Browning had felt drawn by and had displayed.

The irony that Browning embraced does not permit conclusion, in that it forms a cycle of contradictory senses perpetually defying the principle of non-contradiction. Where this irony is concerned, a thing is simultaneously that which it is and that which it is not: *a* is not only *a* but also *a becoming b*. In so far as the work of art is concerned, it affirms both the nullity of the work that it supports and inspires and the transcendent value of that work.

We see the truth of this when we examine the structure of *Sordello*. The poem seems to be lacking in structural unity, appearing to be two main parts separated by the personal digression in book three. The first part, the first 'round' of Sordello's life (3.563) covering thirty years and emphasizing narrative and concrete details, is circular, as it begins in the present, retreats to the past and finally returns to the present. The second part, focusing on abstract discussion and psychological exploration of motive and covering three days, is horizontally linear, bringing the tale to an end with Sordello's death.

But there are other ways to view its structure. If we regard *Sordello* as cast in the epic mould, as the narrator suggests (1.360–73), then we see that it opens *in medias res* with present action followed by a long flashback to explain how the present moment of crisis is reached, the personal digression in book three being a variation on the traditional epic invocation to the muse. If we view the poem as an account of the development of the protagonist's moral consciousness, then its shape, which leads from the despair of solipsism to the bliss of self-negation and 'triumph' over 'extreme despair', can be figured as a rising diagonal, a kind of Dantean comedy. Or if we view it as a narrative of Sordello's accomplishments, it must be figured as a circle, as the narrator castigates his protagonist vigorously for all the things he did not do (6.756–69, 829–51) and reports the return of his body to his mother's tomb at Goito. Underscoring the circularity is the frequent recurrence of the figure of the circle and the idea of return in the last 260 lines; in addition, the very last line, except for the verb tense, repeats the opening line of the poem.

There are, then, carefully worked out structures. But Browning no sooner sets up possible structures than he calls them into question. For as the poem closes, he has his narrator suggest that the real subject of the work is not the story of Sordello but, rather, the poet himself and his efforts to write the poem. The narrator relates how, a week earlier, an old priest had told him that the Ghibellin Alberic's skeleton had been recently brought to light after six centuries and also, apparently quite superfluously, that June is the month for carding off the first cocoons that silkworms make. This is, the narrator says, 'a double news, / Nor he nor I could tell the worthier. Choose!' (6.795–6). Which is the more important – the present or the past, an unearthed piece of history or the act of fabrication, the seer or the fashioner? We as readers must choose, and if we let ourselves, with our 'co-operating fancy' be guided by the end of the poem, we must choose both.

For the conclusion of the poem returns us to the playful irony that disappeared in books five and six and in effect cancels, in a fashion that was to become typically Browningesque, what had appeared likely to become the centre of the poem, a philosophical–moral centre. Sordello's apparent 'triumph' in discovering the power and love of which the narrator spoke as needful promised the victory of meaning over irony. But this is true only if we read the narrator's befriending speech (6.590–603) as the last word, as so many commentators do. 'Is there no more to say?' the narrator asks (6.819). Of course there is, as is always the case with Browning. History does not provide the last word; its word is at best equivocal and paradoxical. Sordello was a failure but also a small success. He did not achieve what he should have achieved, but nevertheless lives on, through a small snatch of his verse, among the glorious company of poets. No, the last word belongs to the showman Robert Browning, who, as master of the performance, turns to his audience to say, in effect, that the imaginative *donnée* of his poem is irony, which forgoes meaning for metaphysical and aesthetic play.

This playfulness is especially evident in the verse style of *Sordello*. Like its theme and structure, which are perfectly fused, the one giving rise to the other that in turn informs the first so that this one may illuminate the other, the verse style evidences the constant process of interaction and reflection. Let us take, for example, this passage following Palma's kissing the dead (or dying) Sordello:

By this the hermit-bee has stopped
His day's toil at Goito – the new-cropped
Dead vine-leaf answers, now 'tis even, he bit,
Twirled so, and filed all day – the mansion's fit
God counseled for; as easy guess the word
That passed betwixt them and become the third
To the soft small unfrighted bee, as tax
Him with one fault – so no remembrance racks
Of the stone maidens and the font of stone
He, creeping thro' the crevice, leaves alone.
                                        (6.621–30)

The bee and Sordello and Palma are all fused, not only in ambiguous pronouns but also in suggestive actions. In addition, the rhyme – and thus the pause at the end of the line – causes a line to be read first one way and then, when the reader goes on to the next line, in another.[14] Added to this process of fusion are constant punnings in the fashion of the Metaphysical poets and lengthy compounds that anticipate the manner of Gerard Manley Hopkins – all of which make the reading of *Sordello* a taxing but invigorating experience. Although in his later works Browning was to modify to some degree the verse style here displayed, *Sordello* is the first that is characteristically Browningesque.

   Sordello is a wonderful, zany poem. Carefully ordered but appearing unstructured, announcedly historical but deeply personal, constantly reflecting both itself and its author, generically indeterminate, stylistically complex, it is without counterpart in literary history. As Ezra Pound, who once looked to it for a model, was to say, 'Hang it all, there can be but one *Sordello*!'[15]

4

Bells and Pomegranates

The poem that Browning had believed would make him popular had entirely the opposite effect.[1] For the next two decades it blighted his reputation, which since *Paracelsus* had been regarded as promising. Few copies of *Sordello* were sold, and its critical reception was almost universally condemnatory. The *Atlas* for 28 March 1840 found it full of 'pitching, hysterical, and broken sobs of sentences'. The *Athenaeum* of 30 May called it replete with 'puerilities and affectations'. The May issue of the *Dublin Review* thought it might better be entitled 'Sordello a conundrum'. No one seemed able to understand it. Jane Welsh Carlyle, whose literary acuity was equal to her husband's, claimed, no doubt partly facetiously, that she could not discover whether Sordello was a man, a city or a book. Douglas Jerrold, a playwright and journalist, said that he tried to read it upon recovering from a serious illness and, finding it incomprehensible, believed he had gone mad. Alfred Tennyson declared that he had understood only the first and last lines – which stated that Sordello's story would be and then had been told – and both were lies.[2] Macready recorded in his diary for 17 June 1840: 'After dinner tried—another attempt—utterly desperate—on *Sordello*; it is *not* readable'.[3] Browning wrote ruefully to Fanny Haworth, who had been memorialized in the poem as 'Eyebright': 'You say roses and lilies and lilac-bunches and lemon-flowers about it while every body else pelts cabbage stump after potato-paring . . .' She and Carlyle were among the very few who had a kind word to say (*Correspondence*, 4: 269). Within three months of its publication the poet had become notorious for obscurity and his poem a target for jokes and derision of all kinds.

Browning did not allow the obloquy directed at him to daunt his spirits. During the years 1840–4 he became a great diner-out who took advantage of every invitation. Social life was, however, not merely an end in itself but also a means of establishing himself among intellectuals and literary figures of the time. Even if his books of poetry were unsold, he would at least be known as the *author* of these unappreciated works.

According to his friend Joseph Arnould, about whom and whose circle at Camberwell we shall presently have more to note, he was adept at conversation, and this came 'from the habit of good and extensive society'. Where earlier the poet seemed hardly to do 'justice to himself in society', he now was 'quite the reverse—no one could converse with him without being struck by his great conversational power' (*Domett*, p. 86).

The persons whom Browning knew socially he met by and large through the Flower sisters and W. J. Fox. Leigh Hunt was one of these. The poet and essayist, who had been the friend of Byron, Shelley and Keats, had outlived his friends and remained to play the part of the ineffectual romantic rebel in the Victorian age. Imprisoned for libelling the Prince Regent in 1813, Hunt had become something of a legend in his own time. He had a large family that he was unable to support, and he was notorious both for his debts and for his borrowings from his friends. Dickens caricatured him in *Bleak House* as Skimpole, who disguised his selfishness under the assumption of utter irresponsibility. Browning liked him, however, for his childlike nature and because he had known and loved Shelley. When Shelley's drowned body had been relegated to the funeral pyre on the beach at Viareggio, the poet's heart had been saved from burning, and it now belonged to Hunt, who was a great collector of literary relics. In time he was to give Browning a lock of Milton's hair.

Another person whom the poet met through Fox and whom he came to see increasingly often during the early 1840s was Richard Henry (later Hengist) Horne, ten years his senior. Horne had been expelled from Sandhurst and crossed the Atlantic as part of a naval expedition to Mexico, where he contracted yellow fever. After recovering he had made a vagabond journey through the United States and Canada, encountering all sorts of terrifying adventures. Returned to England, he briefly edited the *Monthly Repository*, wrote plays that were never acted and gained fame with the epic *Orion*, which was published in 1843 to sell for a farthing and soon went through five editions. In 1844 he published, with the assistance of Elizabeth Barrett, a general estimate of contemporary literature, *A New Spirit of the Age*, in which Browning was declared a great but little-known poet. Browning was indebted to him even before then for some generous critical attention and was grateful to him for it.

It was probably by means other than Fox's that Browning met Richard Monckton Milnes, later the first Baron Houghton. Poet, politician, traveller and *bon vivant*, Milnes had been at Cambridge with Tennyson and Thackeray and remained close to them. He was a short, jolly man who seemed to know everyone of any importance in the literary, social and political circles of London as well as those on the Continent. He had a large library of pornography, including the works of the Marquis de Sade, from which Swinburne was to draw nourishment and excitement. He was also the author of the *Life, Letters, and Literary Remains of John Keats* (1848), which revived the reputation of the near-forgotten Romantic. After the poet–banker Samuel Rogers, and like him the subject of both admiration and ridicule, Milnes was the most famous giver of breakfasts in London, and at these Browning met persons knowledgeable about the world and capable of advancing his career. Milnes was among those to whom the young poet sent copies of *Sordello*, and he was among the first to write to congratulate Browning upon his marriage.

As part of his campaign to redeem his reputation, Browning wished to publish three plays that he had been working on and had then set aside to finish *Sordello*. At the suggestion of Edward Moxon, the publisher of *Sordello* and another friend met through Fox, he determined to have his works printed in a series of inexpensive paperbound pamphlets, the cost of publication again to be borne by his father. As a general title he chose *Bells and Pomegranates*, a name that mystified most readers until in the last number he explained that it was meant 'to indicate an endeavour towards something like an alternation, or mixture, of music with discoursing, sound with sense, poetry with thought; which looks too ambitious, thus expressed, so the symbol was preferred'. In all there were eight pamplets, containing seven plays (two in the final number) and two collections of poems, published over a five-year period from April 1841 to April 1846.

I

The initial number was *Pippa Passes*, which was probably composed in spring 1839 after the completion of *Sordello*. Its setting is north-eastern Italy in contemporary times and reflects the poet's visit there in 1838. The idea for the work seems to have occurred to Browning one day as he was walking alone in a wood, 'when the image flashed upon him of some one walking thus alone through life; one apparently too obscure to leave a trace of his or her passage, yet exercising a lasting though unconscious influence at every step of it; and the image shaped itself in the little silk-winder of Asolo, Felippa, or Pippa' (Orr, *Handbook*, p. 55). Clearly, smarting from the dismal reception of *Sordello*, Browning was thinking of himself as a poet unappreciated and unknown but having a lasting influence upon those who read or heard his verse.

Pippa is a friendless young girl who longs for community and affection but who nevertheless uncomplainingly accepts her lonely state. What sustains her is her keen perception of nature and her ability to render it in lyric song. Like Sordello's at Goito, hers is a Keatsian world of brilliant, sensuous images, of nature observed in its minutest and most detailed aspects; and in this world the only human figure is herself, the 'queen' of nature (introduction, 90–100), whose song if heard at all is overheard only from afar and in no direct relation to mankind.

Behind the conception of *Pippa Passes* lay Romantic notions of poetry as essentially lyric effusion. Wordsworth's emphasis on poetry as the spontaneous overflow of powerful feeling, Coleridge's insistence on the intutitive nature of the creative act, Shelley's belief in the evanescence of artistic inspiration, Keats's assertion that intensity is the hallmark of artistic excellence – all these views informed the demand made throughout a good part of the nineteenth century for a literature of lyrical intensity. John Stuart Mill provided a critical summing up in two essays published in Fox's *Monthly Repository* in 1833, entitled 'What is Poetry?' and 'The Two Kinds of Poetry', in which he expressed as dogma the view that lyric is more eminently and peculiarly poetry than any other type because it is the poetry most natural to the truly poetic temperament. For Mill this meant that the greatest poetry is by nature soliloquy, not heard but overheard, the poet being totally unconscious of a listener.

To Browning, who had been at some pains to expound a poetics of dialogue, this was nonsense. And in writing *Pippa* he undertook to criticize such a view.[4] What if his heroine, whose only mode of utterance is lyric poetry, were to sing and be overheard by others? In working out the answer to this question Browning would show that the poet has, willy-nilly, a dialogic relationship with the audience and a responsibility from which he or she cannot escape. Poetry, like all the other arts, is not autotelic. It is theatre, performance before an interactive audience.

On her annual holiday from the silk mill, for which she prepares by singing a song full of Keatsian images of nature, Pippa is eager to live her one free day fully and fancifully by pretending to participate in the lives of others. Singing as she passes among a crowd of pimps, prostitutes, hired assassins, paid informers, murderers, debauched students, adulterous lovers and cynical clergymen – many of whom she presumes to be the town's happiest inhabitants – she is untouched by them, entering their world only unknowingly or fancifully; and she comes away from it confirmed in her delusion that those who have heard her song are Asolo's happiest ones.

Yet at the end of her day Pippa, who regards herself as one of God's puppets, is forced, almost against her will, to admit that fancy is not adequate to sustain life: she is 'tired of fooling' (4.293). What she wants and needs is what Sordello (and Browning also) realized was needed: namely, the world of men and women, the world of action. She longs for dialogue and relationship, wishes, in other words, to transform her lyric song into drama. She wants to 'approach all these I only fancied being . . . , so as to touch them, . . . move them . . . some slight way' (4.340–2). As the young Keats came to realize, the lyricist must forgo make-believe – pretences about men and nature – for the agony and strife of human hearts.

One of the chief evident ironies of the poem is that Pippa 'touches' her audience in ways she never dreams of. In the first episode, 'Morning', Ottima and Sebald have cast themselves in the roles of romantic lovers willing to sacrifice all for love. Having read Shelley and Keats and perhaps Byron, they embrace the Romantic notion of salvation through passionate love. To escape the quotidian and live fully in love has necessitated Sebald's killing of Ottima's old husband. As initially conceived, the deed was to be one of reckless passion committed for love's sake; but in the aftermath guilt and shame arise. Sebald would 'throw off / This mask' of romantic lover (1.40–2), but Ottima wishes the little drama to continue and with passionate words convinces him to remain in his role: 'Crown me your queen, your spirit's arbitress, / Magnificent in sin. Say that!' (1.217–18). Sebald begins to repeat her words and just then Pippa appears outside singing about the world's divinely mandated order: 'God's in his heaven— / All's right with the world' (1.227–8). Hereupon Sebald denounces Ottima as a wicked enchantress and casts off his role as romantic lover. He is now free – but free to do what is left, as so often in Browning, indeterminate. This episode is, as Irvine and Honan claim, perhaps 'the most impressive single scene of poetic drama written in the nineteenth century' (p. 97).

Sebald has conceived of love as a religion and his beloved as his 'spirit's arbitress' (1.217). When that role fails him – or he fails it – he is totally undone: his sense of self decomposes, as is indicated by the images of disintegrating consciousness in his final speech. What he senses, dimly and never fully comprehendingly, is that the self in modern times is unstable. Without God in the world – without, that is, the order of the Great Chain of Being to which Pippa alludes – personal identity, the self, becomes problematical. Inner vacuity, the absence of Presence, makes role-playing inescapable. That is why Sebald, when forced to give up one role, must adopt another. The idea of punishing himself suggests the new role – the penitent and punisher of vice. Pippa's song does not stimulate him to love of God but only to a role that has no moral or religious content. Sebald is among the many of Browning's characters who sustain themselves by assuming roles.

In the second episode, 'Noon', Jules seeks salvation not in romantic love but in art. A sculptor who has doubtless gained much of his aestheticism from Keats and Tennyson and who is a kind of ur-Pre-Raphaelite, he aims to manifest ideal beauty in his art by capturing 'the human Archetype' (2.86). The artist, as represented in his sculpture, is a visionary who sublimates desire for vision:

> Quite round, a cluster of mere hands and arms,
> Thrust in all senses, all ways, from all sides,
> Only consenting at the branches' end
> They strain towards, serves for frame to a sole face,
> ... The Praiser's, who with eyes
> Sightless, so bend they back to light inside
> His brain where visionary forms throng up, ...
> Sings, minding nor the palpitating arch
> Of hands and arms, nor the quick drip of wine
> From the drenched leaves o'erhead, nor who cast
> Their violet crowns for him to trample on –
> Sings, pausing as the patron-ghosts approve,
> Devoutly their unconquerable hymn!
>   (2. 65–77)

Thus far unsuccessful in his delineation of the visionary and his visions, Jules discovers Phene, whom he immediately perceives from afar as the living embodiment of his ideal. But his perception is based on illusion; for Phene is not what she seems. She is in fact an ignorant girl, whose beautiful letters during their epistolary courtship have been written by Jules's fellow art students. The scene opens after the wedding ceremony, Jules declaring his eternal devotion to her as living art, a kind of *tableau vivant*. But eventually she is forced to speak – to become real, in other words – and repeats the scurrilous doggerel of the perpetrators of the malicious hoax.

Jules's first inclination is to disavow Phene and seek revenge from the students. But then Pippa passes by singing of a page's love for a queen who lived in Asolo long ago; and her song evokes in Jules new emotions and new insight. Curiously he identifies himself with the queen – 'I find myself queen here it seems!' (2.287) – and electing to play her part, not the page's, he will shape Phene as he has shaped marble, 'evoke a soul' from the raw materials she presents. As 'queen' he will take her to an island in far-off seas and there possess her utterly as he moulds her anew. But this is hardly an endeavour to be applauded, as so many critics have supposed.[5] For Jules does not rise to true love, a relationship between subjects; Phene remains for him an object, one to be possessed and used to confirm him in his self-constructed role of Pygmalion.

In the third episode, 'Evening', which first evidences Browning's concern for Italian independence, the adolescent Luigi elects to play the role of political martyr, though like Sordello he has not the foggiest idea about politics.[6] As his mother reasons with him and tries to dissuade him from his foolish intention to assassinate the Austrian emperor, he hears not her but echoes of his own voice (3.1–15). For, unable to find meaning in modern life, Luigi has chosen a role in a little drama that will give import to his situation. Envisioning himself in 'handsome dress' for the occasion – 'White satin here to set off my black hair' – he will march straight in past the emperor's guards: 'I have rehearsed it all' (3.104–11). Watched from their spiritual heights by the glorious company of martyrs for the cause of Italian freedom, he will kill the tyrant as he cries out, 'Italy, Italy, my Italy! / You're free, you're free' (3.120–1). And then he will be captured and put to death, with no effort on his part to escape – 'to wish that even would spoil all!' because 'the dying is the best part of it' (3.64–5).

As his mother continues trying to dissuade him, pointing out that this kind of grand gesture is 'the easiest virtue for a selfish man / To acquire' (3.125–6), Pippa passes by singing of a good king of ages long ago who was preserved from an attack by a python. Luigi applies the song to himself and, strangely enough, instead of deciding against the assassination, as the sense of Pippa's song would seem to suggest, rushes out to do the deed; whether he accomplishes it or not is left undisclosed. Plainly, Luigi has chosen a role and regards everything, no matter of what nature, as confirming him in it.

In the last episode, 'Night', the Monsignor plays to perfection the role of ecclesiastical grandee and is known only by his title. In dialogue with the intendant he discovers that the latter did not, as he has long believed, murder his niece, Felippa (Pippa), to keep her from inheriting the family estate. Fearing the special knowledge that the intendant has, the Monsignor ceases to be the bishop and becomes the pawn. Passively he listens to the intendant's plan for doing away with Pippa, uttering no demur and seemingly offering assent (4.205–9). Then Pippa passes by singing a song of an early appreciation of the music of nature and an imminent understanding of the harmony of the spheres when 'suddenly God took me' (4.233).

But instead of God taking him or his submitting to God, the bishop thereupon has the intendant gagged and removed, and in the process becomes inarticulate. He has almost ceased to be 'the Monsignor', and now to recapture his role he must resort to the proper language for that role: '*Misere mei, Domine!* quick, I say!' The episode ends, like the one preceding, with Pippa's song serving to recall the hearer to a sense of personal identity with his chosen role. The outcome however is left unclear, the bishop giving no clue as to whether Pippa's rightful inheritance will be restored to her.

Each of the four episodes concludes with the protagonist left alone with his self-conceived role and employing language to minister to the psychological need that the role satisfies. Although Browning had explored this irony earlier, in *Pippa Passes* he shows for the first time how human beings filter language to meet their requirements, hearing only what they wish to hear: the actors in each of the little dramas either misinterpret or contort Pippa's songs to make them mean what they, the actors, want them to mean.

It is Browning's belief that every human is indeed an individual; that is, everyone sees the world from his or her own special angle of vision. We live, the poet suggests, in a conditional world, and so, as Paracelsus observed, 'We live and breathe deceiving and deceived' (*Paracelsus*, 4.625). As *Pippa Passes* demonstrates, things are never what they seem: the characters in the four episodes are not happy and enviable people, all is not right with the world, Pippa in fact touches many lives, she is not a mere working girl but the heiress to a fortune. Appearances seem to have no reality at all, not because humankind are wilfully purblind but because their faulty perceptions are owing to the boundedness of their locations: various points of view necessarily yield varying reports of things observed.

Pippa Passes is Browning's first work of perspectivist art, and it dramatizes the poet's belief, held increasingly strongly through the rest of his life, that point of view cannot be transcended. Does this then mean that human beings are in large part determined, enslaved by their psychological needs and the locus of their perception? The answer that the poem gives is far from clear-cut. To Pippa we are all 'God's puppets' (introduction, 194). She herself, a figure of such great importance in the lives of the people who hear her song, is portrayed as resembling one of the Fates, engaged in 'silk-winding, coil on coil' (introduction, 71). Sebald feels himself caught in a web of Ottima's hair (1.247). Jules believes that 'all's chance here' (2.250). Luigi, confident that he is possessed of 'God's gift', holds that 'heaven / Accords with me' (3.150, 73). The Monsignor – 'I, the bishop' – also holds that 'my glory springs from another source' (4.109–11). In addition, within the poem everyone is subject to the domination of someone else: Pippa's life is controlled by Luca, her employer, who is killed by Sebald, who in turn is enslaved by his 'queen', Ottima. Phene is exploited by the students to get at Jules, who then will 'mould' her. Luigi is manipulated by political schemers. The intendant is at the mercy of the Monsignor, who almost becomes the intendant's accomplice and thus subject to blackmail. In short, everyone is the puppet of someone else, and all, according to Pippa, are the puppets of God.

Is it then the final meaning of the poem that humans are but the playthings of a God who presumably uses them for his own amusement?[7] Browning's irony does not permit such a limited interpretation of the poem. We of course can never know what God knows, he alone knowing whether men and women are puppets or not. As readers we have an overview of the events of New Year's Day in Asolo – we have, as it were, the world in microcosm – and yet we finally know little more than the characters in the poem about God's ways. All we can know for sure from the evidence of the poem is that God's ways are inscrutable and can be neither justified nor explained. It is the ironic import of the poem that there is nothing more to be known. As the title is perhaps intended to suggest, Pippa – and in so far as we identify with her, we too – we and Pippa pass through most of life uncomprehendingly.

Pippa Passes is a highly experimental work, combining the lyric, dramatic and narrative modes in verse and prose. Like *Paracelsus* it presents a series of lyric moments treated dramatically, but here those moments are more fully concentrated and dramatized. Like *Strafford* it is a dramatization of irony, but here the characters' decisions to act are more clearly focused. *Pippa*, which Browning originally called a poem and only later a drama, is a fully lyrical drama: it is song which brings the drama into being, song that evokes the crucial decision in each scene (the resulting action from which is not dramatized) and song that moves the narrative from morning to night. In this respect *Pippa* looks forward to the dramatic lyrics that the poet was to publish only a year later.

The title of the work is ultimately suggestive of the author's own relationship to his creation. If we stress the first word in the title, we gain one understanding of the poem – of its personal, lyric nature – and if we stress the second, we gain another – of its dramatic nature as something seemingly distinct and apart. Browning never wants us to forget that this is art, not life, we are witnessing, that (to use Pippa's analogy) his characters are puppets and he the puppeteer.[8] In many ways he designed his lyric drama to call attention to itself as an artifice. What could be more obviously artificial or contrived than the fact that Pippa just happens by at the crucial moment in the lives of eight people and that her singing, which they just happen to overhear, provokes four of them to actions overweeningly important in their own lives and the lives of others? What could be more artificially circumstantial than that the intended victim of the fourth episode is the one whose song stimulates one co-conspirator, who is also her uncle, seemingly to reverse his momentary inclination to permit her to be done away with? Such contrivances abound in *Pippa Passes* because its author wished to make himself known as the creator of them and thus show forth as master of the performance. Thus does Browning allow how 'the magnitude of all achieved / Otherwise, may be perceived' (epilogue, 80–1).

II

Pippa was, Browning said in the advertisement prefacing the work, 'the first of a series of Dramatical Pieces' intended by 'the cheap mode in which they appear' to help him 'to a sort of Pit-audience' such as had applauded *Strafford*. But in the event he was disappointed. *Pippa* was not widely reviewed and, except for his friend John Forster's glowing evaluation of it in the *Examiner*, was coolly received where it was noticed. Furthermore, sales were poor. A letter from Carlyle, however, helped mitigate the poet's disappointment.

By 1841 Thomas Carlyle was widely recognized as one of the most profound thinkers of his age. He had first come to prominence with his essays and biographical works of the 1820s in which he introduced recent German philosophy and literature to the English-speaking world, which was generally ignorant of German language and culture. Then with the publication in the mid-1830s of *Sartor Resartus*, which set forth the philosophical doctrine of becoming in terms that made it applicable to all of nineteenth-century life, Carlyle reached an audience of young persons who longed for spiritual values no longer to be discovered in the dead letter of traditional Christianity. With its insistence on a dynamic life of action and exercise of will, *Sartor* became the bible of those who wished to throw off the despair of Byronism and embrace a metaphysics offering an organic universe of purpose and change in which entities are formed so as to be transformed. In the three volumes of *The French Revolution* in 1837 Carlyle solidified his reputation as a thinker by demonstrating how the doctrine of becoming operated in a recent piece of history, and with his lectures on *Heroes and Hero-Worship* in 1840, which showed how the Absolute had manifested itself in great men throughout history, was acknowledged as a true Victorian sage.

Browning first met Carlyle in April 1836 at the home of Leigh Hunt. Even though the young man seemed something of a dandy, Carlyle nevertheless liked him, and thereafter they met from time to time. When Browning attended Carlyle's lectures on *Heroes* in May 1840, the older man invited the poet to visit him at his home in Chelsea. Browning called at Cheyne Row and met Mrs Carlyle, who found the young man affected and did not much care for him, then or later. As already noted, Carlyle had some good things to say about *Sordello*, a copy of which Browning sent to him; and these encouraging words prompted the poet to send him a copy of *Pippa Passes* in May 1841. Carlyle wrote to the poet, apparently for the first time, on 21 June 1841, thanking him for the two books:

> Unless I very greatly mistake, judging from these two works, you seem to possess a rare spiritual gift, practical, pictorial, intellectual, by whatever name we may prefer calling it; to unfold which into articulate clearness is naturally the problem of all problems for you. This noble endowment . . . you are *not* at present on the best way for unfolding;—and if the world had loudly called itself content with these two Poems, my surmise is, the world could have rendered you no fataller disservice than that same! Believe me I speak with sincerity; and if I had not loved you well, I would not have spoken at all.
> A long battle, I could guess, lies before you, full of toil and pain, and all sorts of real *fighting*: a man attains to nothing here below without that. Is it not verily the highest prize you fight for? Fight on; that is to say, follow truly, with steadfast singleness of purpose, with valiant humbleness and openness of heart, what best light *you* can attain to; following truly so, better and ever better light will rise on you. The light we ourselves gain, by our very errors if not otherwise, is the only precious light. Victory, what I call victory, if well fought for, is sure to you.

Carlyle then advised, as he seems to have advised every poet but Tennyson, to write in prose.

> Not that I deny you poetic faculty; far, very far from that. But unless poetic faculty mean a higher-power of common understanding, I know not what it means. One must first make a *true* intellectual representation of a thing, before any poetic interest that is true will supervene. All *cartoons* are geometrical withal; and cannot be made till we have fully learnt to make mere *diagrams* well. It is this that I mean by prose. . . .
> But enough of this: why have I written all this? Because I esteem yours no common case; and think such a man is not to be treated in the common way.[9]

In this letter we can discover certain aspects of Carlyle's thinking that had a strong impact upon the poet: the importance of work; the doctrine of courage, perseverance and endurance; the aim of striving for the highest and best; the salutary effect of failure. If we add to these qualities the stylistic qualities of *Sartor Resartus* – its grotesque imagery, its spasmodic but dynamic cadences, its jagged and often contorted syntax – we can discern some of the influence that Carlyle had upon the young poet.

Browning was encouraged by Carlyle's letter and thanked him for it. In spite of dashed hopes for a welcome reception of *Pippa*, he persevered and the following March published the second number of *Bells and Pomegranates*. This was *King Victor and King Charles*, the first in the series of six plays designed for stage production.

The plays are probably rightly regarded as unsuccessful diversions from what the poet properly should have been doing. Browning was deluded that he would achieve popularity as a playwright, as time after time he tried to find a producer for his dramas, and it took several years and harsh words for him to realize that this quest for fame in the theatre was chimerical. Presented with *King Victor*, Macready termed it 'a *great mistake*' and 'called Browning into [his] room and most explicitly told him so'.[10]

Foiled here, the playwright then turned to a play having as its subject 'the most wild and passionate love, to contrast with [*King Victor*]' (*Correspondence*, 3: 257). This was *The Return of the Druses*, published as the fourth of the *Bells and Pomegranates* pamphlets in January 1843. Macready read it and wrote: 'with deepest concern, I yield to the belief that he will *never write again*—to any purpose. I fear his intellect is not quite clear'. Nevertheless, he suggested revisions, which Browning willingly made, but none of them caused the actor–manager to alter his opinion that the play, 'mystical, strange and heavy', was unfit for the stage.[11]

With Forster's help the young dramatist did, however, prevail upon Macready, after weeks of bitterness and recriminations between the two, to produce *A Blot in the 'Scutcheon* in February 1843. The chief complaint about his earlier plays was that they were almost devoid of action, but here, so Browning assured the actor–manager, was a new one with '*action* in it, drabbing [whoring], stabbing, et autres gentillesses,—who knows but the Gods may mean me good even yet?' (*Correspondence*, 4: 293). Against his better judgement, Macready, who was convinced that the playwright 'is for ever gone',[12] grudgingly agreed to put it on. Argument after argument ensued between the playwright and the producer. It was withdrawn after three performances, at which point Browning's break with Macready was complete, as were, effectively, the playwright's hopes for the stage. *A Blot* was published as the fifth pamphlet on the same day as its first performance so as to forestall Macready, who was constantly making changes in it, from further alteration of the text.

When he had a new play ready, Browning turned to another theatrical manager, Charles Kean, who suprisingly liked it and offered a goodly sum for it, although he could not promise to produce it before a year later. Browning felt he could not afford to wait: 'something I *must* print, or risk the hold; such as it is, I have at present on my public; . . . and two or three hundred pounds will pay me but indifferently for hazarding the good fortune which appears slowly but not mistakeably setting in upon me, just now' (*Correspondence*, 8: 252). And so *Colombe's Birthday*, though not produced on the stage, appeared as the sixth pamphlet in April 1844.

Browning was by now fed up with the commercial theatre and also beginning to tire of the drama as a literary form, for which, however, he never conceded that he had little talent. By spring 1845 he was thinking about two new plays – one, *A Soul's Tragedy*, finished but in need of revision; the other, *Luria*, conceived but yet not set down on paper (Kintner, 1: 26, 18). He seems to have had little pleasure in dealing with these two pieces, but felt that they had to be 'got rid of': some things he would 'like to preserve and print now, leaving the future to spring as it likes, in any direction,—and these half-dead, half-alive works fetter it, if left behind' (Kintner, 1: 26, 493). Further, he told his old friend Alfred Domett, 'I felt so instinctively . . . that unless I tumbled out the . . . conceptions, I should bear them about forever, and year by year get straiter and stiffer . . . , and at last parturition would be the curse indeed' (*Domett*, p. 127).

By 1845 Browning had written five plays for the theatre, only two of which had been produced on the stage, and they with indifferent success. He had had a tempestuous relationship with Macready and become convinced of the mindlessness of theatrical people in general. '[I]t never entered into my mind', he wrote to a friend about Charles Kean's dealing with *Colombe's Birthday*, 'that anybody, even an actor, could need a couple of months to study a part, only, in a piece, which I could match with such an other in less time by a good deal' (*Correspondence*, 8: 252). In addition, his growing aversion to the theatre was encouraged by his new epistolary friend, Elizabeth Barrett, who frankly told him: 'I have wondered at you sometimes, not for daring, but for bearing to trust your noble works into the great mill of the "rank, popular" playhouse, to be ground to pieces between the teeth of vulgar actors and actresses'. 'And what is *Luria*?' she asked hopefully about the new work he told her he was writing, 'A poem and not a drama?' (Kintner, 1: 22).

Apparently Browning had pretty well decided to quit writing for the theatre by the time he began correspondence with Elizabeth Barrett in early 1845. Answering her question about genre, he replied: 'That "Luria" you enquire about, shall be my last play..for it is but a play, woe's me!' (Kintner, 1: 26). In the event, he did complete it and published *Luria* and *A Soul's Tragedy* together in April 1846 as the eighth and last number of *Bells and Pomegranates*, with a dedication to Walter Savage Landor stating that these were his 'last attempts for the present at dramatic writing'.

Few persons have ever regretted that Browning gave up writing plays. Yet there is much to be said for them. Unfortunately they (like many of the poet's works – *Sordello*, for example) appeared before an audience was sufficiently educated and sensitized to understand them. In the conventional sense they offer little plot and almost no action. In the preface to *Strafford*, Browning explained that he was intent on portraying action in character rather than character in action, and of *Luria* he said, in private, almost the same thing: 'It is all in long speeches—the *action, proper*, is in them—they are no descriptions, or amplifications – but here..in a drama of this kind, all the *events*, (and interest), take place in the *minds* of the actors' (Kintner, 1: 381). For the typical audience of the 1830s and 1840s, however, this psychological delving was simply not enough. Macready had complained of *Strafford's* 'meanness of plot' and its lack of 'dramatic power; character . . . having the [supposed] interest of action'; and he correctly predicted 'that the play must be utterly condemned'.[13] William Bell Scott's response to *Strafford*, noted earlier, was typical of the general response to that play and the later ones as well. In short, audiences found Browning's plays both boring and puzzling.

It was not only the static quality that alienated them. It was also that they could find few characters to focus on or to sympathize with, because in many instances the author had designed his plays to make several different and sometimes conflicting points of view equally sympathetic. Speaking of the protagonist of *Luria* and its other characters, Browning admitted that 'for me, the misfortune is, I sympathise just as much with these as with him' (Kintner, 1: 26). And as its title indicated, *Luria* was a tragedy, a form which traditionally calls for a hero superior in nearly every way to those around him.[14] Clearly it was ironic drama that Browning aimed to present, and his audiences were not sufficiently elastic to stretch their sympathies to characters representing views antithetical to each other.

The root conception of the plays seems to have been the conflict between love and duty or love and power, which is for the most part worked out within a political situation.[15] Contemporary audiences understandably believed that the political motives, as in Shakespeare's history plays, would be the primary focus in them. In fact, the interest resides very little if at all in statecraft. It lies rather in a kind of moral or psychological conflict within the characters themselves, and politics is nothing more than a form of theatre.[16] In *King Victor and King Charles* the son must find a way to accommodate his love for his father with the father's ruthless exercise of power, a resolution made possible only by a kind of melodramatic miracle when Charles gives the crown to his father, who promptly dies, leaving Charles king. In *The Return of the Druses* Djabal falsely represents himself initially as Hakeem the god of power, only in the end to realize by means of the selfless love of Anael that through love alone can power grow to godhead. *A Blot in the 'Scutcheon* shows young love and life cruelly cut off by one whose interest lies solely in the power derived from the ways of the world, the lovers themselves finding fulfilment only in death. In *Colombe's Birthday* the heroine does not win the handsome lover who also turns out to be a powerful prince but instead chooses a poor, plain suitor who is no other than he appears and can offer her only his love; love and power go their separate ways, each diminished without the other. *Luria* demonstrates the superiority of love to power as the protagonist kills himself so as not to destroy his dream of Florence, the city in which, he deludedly believes, love has a claim equal to power. *A Soul's Tragedy* presents a happy ending in which love wins through as Luitolfo and Eulalia are left to live happily ever after and power is left in the hands of the wise and benign priest Ogniben.

In all the plays the actors are conscious of their status as *dramatis personae*, and references to their participation in theatrical productions of all types abound. They feel that they have little or no freedom of will, that their lives are ruled by scripts and that the arena of their actions is limited. Thus in *King Victor* the old king sees the events about to unfold as in a play: 'the masque unmasque / Of the King, crownless, grey hairs and hot blood,— / The young King crowned, but calm before his time' (2.1.181–3). Thus does Djabal, like the others in *Druses* who are constantly putting on and taking off costumes, 'dare / Assume my Nation's Robe' when he understands 'what I am to personate' (4.149–50). Thus does Tresham in the end of *A Blot* proclaim that

> There are blind ways provided, the foredone
> Heart-weary player in this pageant-world
> Drops out by, letting the main Masque defile
> By the conspicuous Portal.
>
> (3.2.137–40)

Thus in *Colombe*, so numerous are the documents passed around, studied and quoted that they are elevated from the position of subtext to become part of the actual text from which the characters read and speak, in effect playing parts in a drama whose text has become a 'rescript' (2.182). Luria also conceives of himself as ruled by texts written by others and sees that 'an alien force like mine / Is only called to play its part outside / [The Florentines'] different nature' (2.85–7). He is and must remain 'the Moor' (3.398). Like others he is ruled by 'words' that become 'life's rules and ordinance of God' (4.66–7). In *A Soul's Tragedy* the populace are so accustomed to the theatricalities of politics that they ask their recently appeared 'saviour' to 'come and harangue us in the market-place!' (1.390).

In sum, Browning's plays constantly call attention to themselves as artifice and hence remind us that behind the work there stands the playwright manipulating his creatures in an imagined world. It is perhaps this aspect of his plays that Browning's audiences found more unsettling than the lack of action or plot. The *commedia dell'arte* quality of them could not be tolerated till twentieth-century playwrights such as Pirandello and Beckett taught audiences that the theatre is a place of illusion that makes its own reality.

Browning was attempting a new type of drama that he was never able to work out. Most of his plays he tried to force into a tragic mould – and they simply would not fit. Tragedy demands that there be *a* way of viewing a hero and his actions, and its meaning is largely unproblematical on the level of story and plot. Browning's 'tragedies', on the other hand, are ironic in that they suggest there are at least two – and sometimes contradictory – ways of looking at a question. This is particularly true when the question is one of free will or determinism. By the time he was writing his last 'tragedy' Browning appears to have been consciously rebelling against tragedy as the type of drama that he himself should write.

A *Soul's Tragedy* is designed to show that 'who thinketh he standeth [should] take heed lest he fall' (2.653–4). This could have been the stuff of tragedy, but in the poet's hands it is worked out so that in the end his surrogate pronounces the benediction: 'And now give thanks to God, the keys . . . to me, and yourselves to profitable meditation at home'. The puppeteer puts his puppets back in the box and in effect bids farewell to the formal drama.

III

Surveying the signs of the times under the influence of Thomas Carlyle, Browning was acutely aware of the enthronement of reason that had been forced on the Western world by the despotic Enlightenment. Like the later philosophers of the Frankfurt School, he was convinced that reason can be emancipative only if it frees itself of the received norms of rationality that pass for truth. He believed that truth does not lie in an ahistorical or acontextual reason. As he shows in nearly all his work, we can undertand 'truth' – the operation of reason – only when we perceive how it is historicized and psychologized, that is, placed within a context. Anticipating the work of Michel Foucault, Browning's poetry offers a plurality of counterpositions, of lifestyles, of points of view that constitute not 'truth' but 'truths'.

With this conviction, already explored in *Sordello*, Browning turned to a different form of ironic art, which, as Vladimir Jankélévitch says, is '*l'art d'effleurer*'.[17] The art of glancing at or touching lightly adopts, one after another, an infinity of points of view in such a way that they tend to correct each other, thereby allowing the author to bypass the drive towards totalizing – being – that is ever seeking to subvert the doctrine of becoming. This different form of perspectivist art was the dramatic monologue – a term Browning himself never used, referring to these works, variously, as dramatic lyrics or dramatic romances.

The dramatic monologue internalizes plot so that instead of an open conflict of forces as on the theatrical stage there is an interior conflict of which the speaker is frequently not consciously aware and, as often as not, a conflict in the reader/listener's understanding of that speaker. As Browning defined it in the prefatory statement to *Dramatic Lyrics*, the third of the *Bells and Pomegranates* series, the poems in this form are 'for the most part Lyric in expression, always Dramatic in principle, and so many utterances of so many imaginary persons, not mine'. This means that the utterance by the fictitious speaker is lyric to the degree that it is expressive of self and dramatic to the degree that it is suggestive of conflicting motives and tendencies. As reader/listeners, we come upon the speaker in the act of talking to another person (or him- or herself), and as we listen we follow the speaker until we gain insight into his or her personality and hence his or her real as opposed to ostensible purpose for speaking. As a literary form, the dramatic monologue is fragmentary and open-ended.[18]

'My Last Duchess', the most famous of the 1842 poems, may be taken as the paradigm of how in Browning's hands what he called the dramatic lyric and what is now called the dramatic monologue operates.[19] The lyric part of the duke of Ferrara's monologue is that in which this cultivated aristocrat gets carried away – into song – when talking about his artefacts, of which his last duchess, 'painted on the wall', is now one. His utterance is an example of how Browning shows language to be generative, one utterance begetting another which in turn modifies the former. Like so many of the poet's monologists, perhaps most of them, the duke speaks not in accordance with what the dramatic context requires – that is, what a future bridegroom should be saying to the agent of the father of a future bride; on the contrary, he speaks in violation of the demands of the dramatic context, speaks simply because he has spoken, because one utterance engenders another, because one musical phrase begs to be made into song.

The dramatic aspect of the duke's monologue is that in which his motives for speaking are manifested as conflicting. Browning's monologues dramatize how speech is the means humans employ to justify themselves and their actions, how ultimately almost all speech is little more than rationalization. In 'My Last Duchess', although having a design upon the envoy (to get the marriage contract concluded to his satisfaction), the duke also attempts to justify – if not to the envoy, then to himself – why he should have done away with his wife. Even the sixteenth-century duke of Ferrara is not so depraved that he commits murder on a whim, for the fun of it. As the poet–narrator in *Sordello* asked concerning those the world calls 'evil men past hope':

> don't each contrive
> Despite the evil you abuse to live?
> Keeping, each losel, thro' a maze of lies,
> His own conceit of truth? to which he hies
> By obscure tortuous windings, if you will,
> But to himself not inaccessible;
> He sees it . . . ;
>   some fancied right allowed
> His vilest wrong.
>
> (3.787–95)

There is, in other words, no such thing as motiveless malignity. Yes, the duke tells himself (and the envoy), there was a good reason why he had to get rid of his wife. He did the deed, justifiably, and enough said. Having told the tale stimulated by the portrait, he turns to another art object, makes a comment on it, and, casting aside all differences in rank, goes down the stairs side by side with the envoy.

Browning's point is that any view, coming from the mouth of an accomplished speaker, can be made compelling. During the moment of speaking we the reader/listeners are swept away by the duke's song; we are fascinated by him, as is apparently the envoy, who offers no demur. Yet in the end, as the instant of lyric and dramatic intensity passes, the spell is broken and we see this proud and haughty man for what he is. But even then, even after we reflect on what he has said, our judgement of the duke does little to diminish our image of the man as larger-than-life-size. It is the special irony of Browning's monologues that we are given – and caused to hold – two conflicting views of the same speaker.

But the poet is not content to let his monologues, for all their psychological insight and verisimilitude, pass merely as realistic conversation. Here, as in his plays and longer poems, the element of self-display is an essential part of the work: the performance has a manager. For Browning arranges in various ways to remind us that 'My Last Duchess' is not life but art. First, he casts the poem in rhymed couplets, which he playfully conceals by enjambment until almost the very close, when he end-stops the last lines and thereby calls attention to them as rhyming couplets. Second, he has the speaker call attention to the poem as a poem when the duke refers to Neptune, 'taming a sea-horse, thought a rarity, / Which Claus of Innsbruck cast in bronze for me'. In this passage, whatever the speaker may or may not have intended by it, we are invited by the poet to see the statue as a summarizing symbol of the duke, the man always in control. In short, Browning signals us that the duke's monologue stands apart from the real world and that its relationship to that world is fixed by the indwelling poet, who reminds us that the speaker's words are, after all, but words put into the speaker's mouth by the poet himself.

'My Last Duchess' has justly become one of the best-known poems in English. Thought to be amenable to New Critical techniques of analysis, it has been adopted into the canon of English literature and is perhaps the one poem by Browning that nearly every educated person knows fairly well. When it first appeared, it was entitled 'Italy' and was paired with 'Count Gismond' (then called 'France') under the joint title 'Italy and France'. The companion poem, however, is not nearly so well known, mainly because of its more apparent ambiguities and inconsistencies. The speaker is a woman, in the traditional reading of the poem understood to be wrongly defamed and then restored to virtue by a knight who suddenly appears to defend and afterwards marry her. As more recent readers have noted, there are many objections to such an interpretation.[20] Why, for instance, does she lie to her husband at the end of her monologue? Why, further, does she offer such apparently extraneous details as her champion's bloody sword touching her side? We can never be certain what really happened. But then, on the other hand, we can never be sure of many of the details in 'My Last Duchess'. We can only guess at the envoy's future action. And on certain points the poet himself was not of much help. When asked what happened to the duchess, Browning said that 'the commands were that she should be put to death, . . . or he might have had her shut up in a convent' (DeVane, p. 109). Much – in fact, most – of Browning's poetry is ambiguous, and to seek for determinate meaning in the narrative is often to misread his monologues.[21] For as the poet said in the dedication to the revised *Sordello* in 1863, his interest lay not in conventional story or plot but in the development of a soul (his own as well as his characters') as attained through language.

Nearly every one of Browning's monologists has a near obsession with words. The duke of Ferrara constantly refers to speech: what people do not ask ('seemed as they would ask me, if they durst'), what Fra Pandolf said, how the duchess talked or would have talked, what he himself said, could not say and is now saying. The speaker of 'Count Gismond' is similarly concerned with speech – who said what, and when, and how what she says now will influence the future – as she repeatedly uses the word 'lie', in the end changing the subject and prevaricating about what she has been saying when her husband returns: 'have you brought my tercel back? / I was just telling Adela / How many birds it struck since May'. The predatory falcon is very much like Neptune taming a seahorse in 'My Last Duchess', functioning as a concluding symbol of character and as a means by which the poet makes known his presence, as the writer of these words. It is as though the monologists, who are never at a loss for words, see themselves as mouthers of scripts in theatrical situations.[22]

Consciousness of fate or of being manipulated is especially strong in the poems of 1842 that deal with love. 'In a Gondola', often and mistakenly said to reflect Browning's belief that love is triumphant over all,[23] is a study in the psychology of romantic love, recalling the Ottima and Sebald episode in *Pippa Passes*. Conceived as an illustration of a picture by Daniel Maclise, it aimed, said the poet, 'to cataloguize . . . in rhyme and unreason' all the romantic 'properties' of storybook love (*Correspondence*, 5: 189). The lovers, an apparently married woman and her paramour, meet only in the dark to engage in little dramas to sustain their passion. 'Say after me, and try to say', she directs her lover, 'My words as if each word / Came from you' (8–10). But theatre is not enough: 'Since words are only words' (19), physical dissolution alone will permit their spirits to blend in full, permanent union. And so, they believe, it was ordained that they should die, which is what happens: he at the hands of 'the Three' and she presumably later by her husband, although they themselves had actively courted death.

Where love is concerned in these poems, the notion of being caught in a kind of web where they are 'fixed' is paramount in the minds of the lovers. In 'Cristina', also traditionally said to be expressive of Browning's most cherished beliefs about love,[24] the speaker claims that when he met the queen she fixed him with her eyes and their souls rushed together. She was aware of the affinity ('she knew it / When she fixed me') but out of worldly concerns withdrew, while he has remained faithful and thus grown greater than she: 'She has lost me—I have gained her'. One can wonder, however, about the sanity of the speaker, who repeatedly claims to have been 'fixed' and thus to have had time stopped at the moment of ecstasy.[25]

The belief in 'fixation', of having captured the good moment and living exclusively in it, is closely allied to the theological doctrine of election. Thus in the companion poems 'Madhouse Cells', discussed earlier in another context, Johannes Agricola acts and speaks as he does because God has ordained it and Porphyria's lover believes himself justified in the murder of his beloved because 'God has not said a word' of condemnation. These insane narratives of self-justification scripted in highly regular tetrameter lines that, mostly end-stopped, call attention to the strongly patterned male rhyme – these are the words of speakers aware that they are creatures of a creator who governs their every move. It is Browning's genius that permits us as reader/listeners to believe in them as characters having a life of their own and at the same time to recognize them as pure artifice, over or behind whom hovers the figure of the poet.

The two poems of 'Madhouse Cells' are soliloquies, and in a certain sense many of Browning's dramatic monologues, even those where there is an audience present, are soliloquies. For the speakers are so absorbed in their own orbits of value that they cannot go beyond the encircling, isolating walls of ego to engage in dialogue. Often they are captives of systems, institutions and other kinds of embodiments from which (to use Browning's own terminology) the soul has fled. This is particularly true of those holding dogmatic religious views or functioning within a religious institution.

The 'Soliloquy of the Spanish Cloister' (originally entitled 'Cloister [Spanish]') is a beautiful example of this. The speaker knows everything there is to be known about religious ritual and formal ecclesiastical practices but nothing of the informing principle from which they were derived. Believing himself a model Christian monk, he unwittingly damns himself as a kind of Satan and shows up the hated Brother Lawrence as a living saint. Like most of Browning's characters the speaker is not what he seems, either to himself or to others. The would-be manipulator is himself in fact controlled by his creator.

Probably the most formally complex of the *Dramatic Lyrics* is the one that was of most personal interest to the poet. In his early adult years Browning was a member of a club called the Colloquials, whose members were all from Camberwell. Among them were Alfred Domett and Joseph Arnould, both of whom, university men and members of the Church of England, were to become lawyers and distinguished public figures, the former as prime minister of New Zealand and the latter as a supreme court judge in India. Arnould had married in 1841 and Domett had suddenly emigrated to New Zealand in May 1842, leaving the poet 'in real sorrow of heart' (*Correspondence*, 5: 328), deprived of the fairly constant companionship of two of his close friends. In 'Waring' he expresses his deep sense of loss at Domett's departure, said to have been caused by the latter's lack of recognition in England. In the first part of the poem, a monologue, the speaker expresses his guilt for not making more of his friend. On the night on which he departed, the speaker left Waring to be with the new prose-poet, a 'distinguished name' such as the 'I' is always apparently courting. But as he speaks, the monologuist recognizes Waring for his true worth and asks him to come back to England, where the 'distinguished names' seem 'as if they played at being names / Still more distingushed' (202–4). In the second part, a dialogue, another speaker reports having seen Waring in foreign parts, to which the first responds, concerning his earlier prophecy of Waring's unrealized potentialities: 'In Vishnu-land what Avatar?' (261–2).

As the poem proceeds, it becomes apparent why Waring left London: namely, to escape the kind of empty life that the speaker, who is evidently a clubman, leads, a life among prose poets and other minor celebrities who are to be valued as 'distinguished names'. The speaker obviously loves Waring but claims him more as a potential 'name' than as a friend. 'You saw Waring?' (211) he asks incredulously when his fellow clubman reports sighting him. 'You?' he says, as though no one but him had a right to Waring in any way.

'Waring' is mainly interesting just to the extent that it shows how Browning could take a matter close to him, objectify it, and treat it ironically. It is a very good example of how he could transform the lyric, the song of self, dramatically into what his prefatory disclaimer had called one of the 'many utterances of so many imaginary persons, not mine'.[26]

Dramatic Lyrics is a landmark in literary history, marking, along with 'Ulysses' in Tennyson's *Poems* published in the same year, the first appearance of the dramatic monologue in English. This was to become the chief genre which Browning was to employ – to experiment with and elaborate – for much of the remainder of his career. In large part because of Browning's use of it, the dramatic monologue was to be the dominant poetic genre of the next hundred years. Rossetti's 'Jenny'; Eliot's 'Prufrock', 'Portrait of a Lady', even *The Waste Land*; Pound's many monologues, especially those of the early drafts of his first *Cantos* and those of the *Personae* volume – all owe a tremendous debt to Browning's dramatic monologues.

IV

Not long after its publication in April 1844, Browning sent a copy of *Colombe's Birthday* to his friend Alfred Domett and said: '. . . I feel myself so much stronger, if flattery not deceive, that I shall stop some things that were meant to follow, and begin again'. Things to follow were presumably more plays, and beginning again apparently referred to shorter pieces of the kind that appeared in *Dramatic Lyrics*. 'I really seem to have something fresh to say,' he believed (*Correspondence*, 9: 69), but felt himself in need of a change, a trip to southern Italy that would complement his 1838 visit to northern Italy, where he had found artistic renewal. This second Italian journey, between August and December 1844, proved remarkably fruitful: he not only wrote verse on the way there and back but also was inspired by Italy for poems written upon his return.

He landed in Naples in September, visited Sorrento and Amalfi, and then headed north for Rome, where he saw the graves of Shelley and Keats. From there he went to Florence and Leghorn, where he called on Edward John Trelawny, the friend of Byron and Shelley, and gained first-hand information about the Romantic poets whose works had been so influential on his adolescent years. By the end of the year he was back in England.

On his first Italian visit the young poet had apparently been most taken by the tourist's Italy – the scenery and the historical monuments. In Venice he had noted the prevailing poverty and had incorporated his feelings about the downtrodden in the third book of *Sordello* when he made the poor waif of trembling thin lips and tear-shot eyes his muse; and in the third episode of *Pippa Passes* Luigi was determined to play the patriot and assassinate the Austrian emperor. But in general Browning's poetry prior to 1844 had taken little direct notice of contemporary politics. In the summer of 1844, however, the Austrian occupation of Italy had become a matter of topical concern when it was discovered that the English government was opening the mail of the Italian revolutionary Giuseppe Mazzini, who was living in exile in England, and reportedly providing the Austrian government with information as to its content. Like his friend Thomas Carlyle, who spoke out in *The Times* on behalf of Mazzini in condemnation of the government's action, Browning was evidently much exercised over the affair; and when he sailed for Italy he was more than ever mindful of the injustices that the Italians suffered at the hands of the Austrians, who had effectively dominated the Italian states since 1815. What he felt and saw on this second visit to Italy provided a good part of the material for the seventh number of *Bells and Pomegranates*, published as *Dramatic Romances & Lyrics* in November 1845.

Nearly all the poems in the pamphlet touch on the question of loyalty and to whom it may properly be owed. 'The Lost Leader' deals with what Browning considered the apostasy of Wordsworth, once the fiery radical in both poetry and politics, in becoming a Tory and then in 1843 accepting the laureateship. Even more than a lost leader, he is a 'lost soul' whose defection is an 'insult to God'. Yet, with a typical Browning twist, reminiscent of Pym's forgiveness of Strafford in the 1837 play, the speaker allows that, in spite of his disloyalty, the lost leader's work remains and this entitles him to be 'pardoned in Heaven, the first by the throne'. This opinion is consonant with Browning's appreciation expressed to the president of the Wordsworth Society in 1880: 'I keep fresh as ever the admiration for Wordsworth which filled me on becoming acquainted with his poetry in my boyhood' (Maynard, p. 169).

'The Italian in England' (originally called 'Italy in England') is the monologue of a revolutionary exile very much like Mazzini who recounts how a *contadina* helped him escape from the Austrian police. Looking back over an episode that happened long ago, he reveals how the intervening years have taken their toll of his youthful fervour and openness to spontaneous emotion. For in the constant process of finding support for his nationalistic cause he has become in effect a professional patriot, dead to all save The Cause. Yet in recalling the old days in Italy, he experiences something of his old emotion. Thinking what he might possibly wish for, if he were to spend three wishes on himself, he still turns to The Cause for the first two: the bloody murder of Prince Metternich, the Austrian minister, and the slow death of his traitor friend who deserted The Cause. For his third wish he would see the girl who rescued him now grown into a happily married woman with children. Realizing he can never know the joys of domestic affection because he has wedded The Cause, which has sapped his soul's energy, he nevertheless wishes for an instant that his life had been different. Such thought is, however, but 'idle wishing—how / It steals the time! To business now!'

Browning enters the poem by means of the imagery of rebirth. The story takes place during Holy Week, while the man, who has been betrayed by a friend, is hidden in a 'crypt'. A young girl, figured as a type of the Virgin Mary, comes to him and is asked to serve as mediatrix between himself and those in the Duomo. As a result of her ministrations help comes within seven days – on Easter – and he rises from his hiding place and leaves Italy by sea.[27] The narrator's heart goes out to her, and years later he thinks of her in the same innocent way in which he had regarded her earlier. By his imagery Browning would have us see that, were the revolutionary to moderate the obsessiveness that is his 'business', there remains for him the possibility of rebirth. The poem touchingly reveals the loneliness of one fixed by a cause that has become a monomania.

In the companion monologue, 'The Englishman in Italy' (originally titled 'England in Italy. [Piano di Sorrento.]') the speaker comforts a small peasant girl, frightened by the scirocco, by describing his impressions of the preceding day of drought and the first stirring-up of the wind. The storm has passed and soon a festive celebration will begin. ' "Such trifles" you say?' he asks the child. Well, yes, for in England on this very day parliament is debating whether abolishing the Corn Laws, which increased the price of bread for the poor by taxing imports of grain, be 'righteous and wise'. Why, they might just as well debate whether the scirocco should vanish in black from the skies. This Englishman has, however, done little to further the cause of abolition of the Corn Laws, which were a matter of grave political and social concern during the 1830s and 1840s; for he is a tourist amusing himself with observation of the 'sensual and timorous beauty' of southern Italy. Where the Italian in England has his country's freedom as his 'business', the Englishman in Italy gives but passing mention – and this to a child – to one of the most serious causes of starvation in his homeland.[28]

Browning again enters clandestinely into the poem by the imagery of rebirth, introducing echoes of Shelley's 'Ode to the West Wind' for ironic effect; for the scirocco, which is a hot and dry south wind, heralds no new birth.[29] Shelley's poem also plays a part in 'Pictor Ignotus', the monologue of an unknown Florentine painter of the early sixteenth century whose purpose is to justify his failure to gain fame. He has been tempted to paint in the new style of Raphael and the others of the High Renaissance; but the expenditure of psychic energy thus required would be too great, for it would mean nothing less than a spiritual rebirth. He has, consequently, elected to work in an older mode already perfected by medieval painters. If this means that he must remain unknown, at least, he claims, he has not pandered to the crass materialism of collectors of Renaissance art like the duke of Ferrara in 'My Last Duchess' or debased his art by abandoning his formal perfection. 'Blown harshly, keeps the trump its golden cry? / Tastes sweet the water with such specks of earth?' he asks at the end. These questions – of conception and its realization, of the relation between artist and audience – that were of such great importance to Browning's Romantic predecessors, are here given ironic significance in images of prophetic creativity. Gabriel's trumpet awakens the dead to new life; Shelley's west wind is a trumpet of prophecy; Moses strikes the rock to bring forth water from the earth for the thirsty Israelites. By such means Browning intrudes into the poem so as to make himself known.

'Pictor Ignotus' perfectly reflects Browning's understanding of theatricality as a certain ontological and social condition. Viewing theatricality historically, the poet dramatizes the movement from the medieval notion of acting as an allegorical personification of vices and virtues to the Renaissance notion of acting as impersonation of various types of individualized human beings. As he paints, Pictor Ignotus acts on the very cusp of historical change. He sees the possibilities offered by the coming age. He dreams of acting on a bigger stage, of commanding a vast audience, of 'making new hearts beat and bosoms swell' to the four corners of the earth, of being loved and praised, and then at the end not going to heaven but lingering on earth among those who admired him. But 'glimpses of such' have given him stage-fright. For the Renaissance stage is too crowded, too colourful, too boisterous – in short, too secular. And so he retreats from dialogue to monologue, from the secular to the sacred, to the smaller medieval stage where he can enact with competence and precision the allegorical roles of Hope, Rapture and Confidence spoken of in the poem.

For Browning the Middle Ages were to be identified with dogmatic faith, which, in his opinion, smothers life. The early Renaissance, on the other hand, was a period of transition, which unsettled dogma and thereby stimulated vitality; and the poet seemed to find an analogy between the early Renaissance and his own day. The medieval revival in the nineteenth century was to him a revival of medieval superstition; and so, as Dwight Culler has suggested, Browning's project was to create a 'Victorian

Renaissance' in opposition to it.[30] It was not the Renaissance of the later sixteenth century but the Renaissance of the fourteenth and fifteenth centuries, the transitional period, that struck him as the most interesting stage of history and that he chose to take for his own. By the time the sixteenth century was well advanced the actors had by and large settled into fixed roles, and when Browning sets his stage during this period, his actors exemplify the rigidities of role-playing.

This is particularly evident in 'The Bishop Orders His Tomb at St Praxed's Church' (initially titled 'Tomb at St Praxed's'), inspired by the poet's first visit to Rome. A Renaissance clergyman, the bishop is oblivious to all but the outward forms of his religion. Like the soliloquizer of the Spanish cloister, he knows everything about Christianity but its meaning. And like so many of the speakers in the monologues of 1842 and 1845, he is fixated on one subject: in his case, a magnificent tomb whereby he can triumph in death, as he apparently did not in life, over his arch-rival in love and ecclesiastical preferment. Lying on his deathbed, he begs, pleads and bargains with his sons (who may or may not be all his and whom he, a supposedly celibate clergyman, euphemistically calls 'nephews') for the kind of tomb he believes he deserves. Yet it is clear that the more he talks to these sons, who seem to have heard it all before, the less likely he is to get what he wants. He recognizes this too; but like the duke of Ferrara he is so caught up in his role and the language that ministers to it that he cannot cease, although his utterance is at odds with his strategic intent. In the end he takes refuge in the drama of liturgy that permits him to imagine his displacement from his deathbed to his tomb in St Praxed's Church.

Browning called the poem 'a pet of mine' and believed it 'just the thing for the time – what with the Oxford business, and Camden Society and other embroilments' (*NL*, pp. 35–6). In 1833 the so-called Tractarian Movement was initiated at Oxford and was continued under the leadership of John Henry Newman in *Tracts of the Times*. Its purpose was to revive Church doctrines, such as the Apostolic succession, the importance of the sacraments, and in general the Catholic foundation of the Church of England, that had become almost obsolete among most of its members. Earlier in the decade Newman had turned increasingly away from the Anglican Church towards Rome, and there was widespread concern over his almost-certain conversion to the Roman Catholic Church, which was to take place in 1845. The Camden Society, founded in 1838, was devoted to historical studies and publication of early English documents, and its researches were much used in the Tractarian controversy. As one always suspicious of doctrine, dogma and formalism, Browning had little patience with Tractarianism, and his feelings about the matter are clearly reflected in 'The Bishop Orders His Tomb'.

It is surely one of the poet's most brilliant monologues. Browning designed it as an exemplum, a sermon by example, on the text *Vanitas vanitatem*, the first line (in translation) of the monologue. It is a sermon preached unknowingly by the speaker, who time and again lapses into the homiletic mode that over the years he has practised. The preacher here proves his text by the revelation of his own character, and his plea for sympathy and understanding becomes a literary form – that is, a sermon – that stands in judgement of him. The monologue thus announces itself as an artifice, a work of words.

Several of the lyrics as well as the 'romances' are concerned with language. 'The Flower's Name' deals with the preservative power of language, while its companion, 'Sibrandus Schafnaburgensis', deals with the uncreating word. In 'The Laboratory' the female speaker attempts by language to make of murder a fine art as, wearing a mask of glass as well as a mask of words, she speaks of chemical poisons as though they were flowers. The poem's companion, 'The Confessional', focuses on the word 'lie' in both its physical and its linguistic meanings and concludes with the imprisoned young woman's perception that for her the truth is the physical 'lying' of passionate lovers, not the 'lying' of the Church. 'The Glove', whose dominant motif is rhetoric, lights up the difficulty of ever penetrating the webs and veils of language to arrive at the truth of a situation; for in the end the reader is left to ponder the impossibility of reconciling two contending strains of narrative.

In general the *Dramatic Romances & Lyrics* are more allusive and more densely packed than the earlier *Dramatic Lyrics.* Dealing with contemporary matters of widespread concern in the mid-1840s, they show how the poet was increasingly turning towards a sociocultural scene to make meaning.[31] But as 'The Bishop Orders His Tomb' exemplifies, Browning was also providing an ironic reading of society and history embodied in a form only superficially a little less extravagant than that of *Sordello* or *Pippa Passes.*

Writing on Browning in *A New Spirit of the Age,* published in 1844, R. H. Horne noted that the poet's prime excellence was 'dramatic portraiture'. Yet, as we have noted, for some years the poet had been forcing his native talent into a literary form alien to it – namely, the dramatic tragedy. Only with the greatest wrenching of the plot could he force it to yield the ironic possibilities of character portrayal that he found most congenial. Approaching the end of his *Bells and Pomegranates* series, he realized that he would have to give up writing plays and focus on the form suited to an author who hangs between immanence and transcendence, involvement and detachment, the lyric and the dramatic. In *Dramatic Romances & Lyrics* he perfected this form – the dramatic monologue. Though hereafter he was to write other exquisite monologues, they were formally to be but variations on those in this collection.

With the *Dramatic Romances & Lyrics* the poet could lay claim to attention as a major poet. Although the volume was not widely reviewed, its critical reception in the press was mildly favourable. The greatest praise of it was, however, to come from other quarters. The poet Walter Savage Landor, whom Browning had long revered, wrote and published in the

Morning Chronicle of 22 November 1845 a poem attesting to his majority. In one of the most generous compliments ever paid by one poet to another, Landor recognized that his younger friend had become 'Browning', a name to be listed, along with Chaucer and Shakespeare, among the greatest English writers. And another poet, whom Browning had recently come to know, was equally enthusiastic. Elizabeth Barrett wrote, prior to the publication of *Dramatic Romances & Lyrics* but after having seen some of the poems in the collection: 'To judge at all of a work of yours, I must *look up to it – & far up* – because whatever faculty *I* have is included in your faculty, & with a great rim all round it besides!' (Kintner, 1: 125).

5

Courtship and the Early Years of Marriage

I

Under Shelley's influence the young Browning had wished to be an heroic redeemer of mankind. In time he recognized that such an aim was unrealizable and so disavowed it. But the notion of rescue remained constantly with him and was to figure thematically in much of his poetry. During his boyhood and young manhood one of his favorite works of art was the *Andromeda* of Polidoro da Caravaggio, representing Perseus' rescue of the maiden from a dragon. He kept a print of it over his desk at both Camberwell and New Cross, another London suburb south of the Thames to which the Brownings moved in 1840, and he alluded to it in both *Pauline* (655–6) and *Sordello* (2.211). Later the Perseus–Andromeda myth modulated in Browning's work into the myth of St George and his rescue of the princess Sabra.[1]

Browning saw himself, however, as something of an ambiguous saviour. His heroes – Pauline's lover, Paracelsus, Sordello, Luria – express the desire for full independence and command, while at the same time they acknowledge their need for dependency and servitude. Pauline's lover, for instance, confesses his need for both Pauline and the Sun-treader, but he also admits his desire to be free of them both. As Constance Hassett observes, 'the roles of Perseus and Andromeda are by no means mutually exclusive. A defenseless innocent may create her own savior, and the strong savior may be the morally needier of the two'.[2] Thus in Browning's life and works alike there is a certain interdependence and interchangeability of victim and rescuer.

Another notion that the young poet constantly harboured was the lack of appreciation that genius is forced to endure. Although most of his work had not been widely reviewed – with the exception of *Sordello*, which was harshly condemned and dismissed as a perversion – the critical reception

Plate 2 Gavin Hamilton, engraving after Polidoro da Caravaggio, 'Perseus and Andromeda', Schola Italica picturae, etc . . . , 1773. A print of this painting hung over Browning's desk at Camberwell and in his room at New Cross. (British Library shelfmark 1899.d.18.) Reproduced by courtesy of The British Library, London.

of his work had not been severe. In fact, it was for the most part mildly enthusiastic. Browning, however, had expected something more. 'They take to criticizing me a little more, in the Reviews', he wrote to Alfred Domett in 1843, 'and God send I be not too proud of their abuse! For there is no hiding the fact that it is of the proper old drivelling virulence with which God's Elect have in all ages been regaled' (*Correspondence*, 7: 125). Overly sensitive to criticism, he was always eager to hear of – and to meet – people who liked his work.

The two notions of rescue and appreciation coalesced when Browning met Elizabeth Barrett, the most famous woman poet of her day. Browning had known of Miss Barrett personally through their mutual friend John Kenyon, a wealthy bachelor and amateur of the arts who had been a schoolmate of Robert Browning senior. He now lived near the Barretts, who were his distant cousins, and from him the poet learned that the erudite and poetic Miss Barrett was an invalid who lived almost hermetically sealed within her room and that the household of unmarried children in Wimpole Street was strictly presided over by a father who demanded that his orders be obeyed.

The Barrett family had until earlier in the century long lived in the West Indies and had amassed considerable wealth. Elizabeth, born in 1806, the eldest of eleven children, was the first Barrett in several generations who had not been born there. Her father, Edward Moulton Barrett, had resettled in England and built a manor house, Hope End, near Malvern in Herefordshire, and there Elizabeth and her eight brothers and two sisters led the active life of children in the country. Like Browning she was a precocious child who loved literature and wrote verses, and like Browning she read avidly, with certain restrictions, the books in her father's library. When her eldest brother, Edward, began to study Greek she shared his lessons. At eleven or twelve she had completed an epic in four books, *The Battle of Marathon*, that her father had printed in fifty copies in 1820. Her parents were as proud of her as the Brownings were of their son.

In 1828 her mother died; her father locked up his wife's rooms and forbade her name ever to be mentioned again in his presence. Not long thereafter the children learned that the family fortunes had been declining. Hope End was sold and the family moved to Sidmouth, in Devon, where they lived for three years. In 1835 the Barretts moved to London, first to Gloucester Place and then to 50 Wimpole Street. Elizabeth, who had loved the countryside close to the Malvern Hills and the sea-coast of Devon, disliked London and its yellow fog, and she hardly ever left the house to go out in it. In 1838 she had a severe cough that resulted in a burst blood vessel in her chest. Years earlier she had suffered a severe illness and it is evident now, as it was not then, that she had been stricken with tuberculosis and that it had remained more or less dormant over the past seventeen years. Her doctor insisted that she escape the London weather by going to southern Europe. Her father, however, never wishing his children to be long away from him, refused to let her go, and only after a great deal of persuasion on the part of her brothers and sisters, who suggested Torquay as a compromise, did he relent. Elizabeth remained at Torquay for three years, during which, at Mr Barrett's command, various of his sons and daughters were sent bustling back and forth between London and Devonshire.

The eldest Barrett son, Edward, was thinking of marriage, in spite of his father's reluctance to see any of his children in any way independent of him. Elizabeth, who was certain she was dying, tried to make over her small fortune to her brother, but her father intervened to prevent her. During this time of family upset in 1840 two deaths occurred: Samuel, six years younger than Elizabeth, died of yellow fever in Jamaica, where he had been sent on business by his father; and Edward was drowned in a boating accident in Torquay. Both deaths, especially the latter's, were severe blows to Elizabeth, who was overcome with grief. 'For more than three months I c$^{\underline{d}}$ not read – c$^{\underline{d}}$ understand little that was said to me. The mind seemed to myself broken up into fragments' (*Correspondence*, 5: 82–3). Only when she turned to the work of literary composition did she find any effective relief.

Plate 3 'Elizabeth Barrett Barrett with her dog Flush', May 1843. Pencil drawing by Alfred Moulton Barrett. From *The Browings' Correspondence*, ed. P. Kelley and R. Hudson, frontispiece to vol. 7, 1991. Reproduced by kind permission of Wedgestone Press, Kansas.

Elizabeth had published, at her father's expense, books of verse and translations from Aeschylus in 1826 and 1833, and with *The Seraphim and Other Poems* in 1838 she became a recognized poet. Returning in 1841 to the sooty air of London, a less salubrious place than which can hardly be imagined for someone in her condition, she was confined to one room and to one sofa in it and constantly relied on morphine to alleviate the pain caused by her illness. Nevertheless, she continued to work away and to keep up, by means of periodicals, books, visitors and correspondence, with the literary life of England. When her *Poems* in two volumes were published in 1844, she was acclaimed, both in England and America, a leading poet.

Robert Browning liked Elizabeth Barrett's poetry, and he had been delighted with her praise of him in an article in the *Athenaeum* in 1842 and with a highly complimentary allusion to him in her poem 'Lady Geraldine's Courtship', published in 1844, in which the heroine has read to her lover 'from Browning some "Pomegranate", which, if cut deep down the middle, / Shows a heart within blood-tinctured, of a veined humanity'.

Browning was full of gratitude, and assured by Kenyon that Miss Barrett would be pleased to hear from him, he posted a letter to her on 10 January 1845, out of '*purely personal obligation*' as he later told her (Kintner, 1: 271). 'I love your verse with all my heart, dear Miss Barrett,' the letter began, and then after praise of her works it continued, 'and I love you too' (Kintner, 1: 3). One wonders how the recipient reacted to such words, but apparently she was less startled by them than might have been expected, for she replied the next day expressing thanks 'for this cordial letter & for all the pleasure which came with it' and proclaiming herself 'a devout admirer & student' of his works (Kintner, 1: 5). Hereafter they began to exchange letters every few days.

From the beginning both were aware that they were not merely exchanging pleasantries, were on the contrary deeply earnest. She is curious about the real Robert Browning, to which he replies that his poems are but 'mere and very escapes' of his inner powers and give little indication of the man himself, but that one day he will write '"R.B. a poem"'(Kintner, 1: 17–18). She, on the other hand, fending him off when he asks to meet her in person, says that she has put her best self into her work: 'I have lived most & been most happy in it, & so it has all my colours; the rest of me is nothing but a root, fit for the ground & the dark' (Kintner, 1: 65).[3]

Finally the day comes when they meet. And despite all the fears that her 'New Cross Knight' (Kintner, 2: 1019) would enter her darkened castle and discover not sleeping beauty but an ageing invalid (known to her family by the childhood nickname 'Ba') some six years his senior lying on a sofa and wrapped in shawls and rugs, Browning entered 50 Wimpole Street on 20 May 1845 to fall in love with her almost at first sight, as he was soon to tell her in letters. On her side she was reticent, unable to believe that someone could love a seemingly incurable invalid and terrified that her tyrannical father, who had forbidden his children to marry, would learn about her ardent admirer. 'Imagine, you who know him', Joseph Arnould was later to write to Alfred Domett, 'the effect which his graceful bearing, high demeanour, and noble speech must have had on such a mind when she first saw the man of her visions in the twilight of her darkened room. She was at once in love as a poet-soul only can be' (*Domett*, pp. 134–5). But she wrote to him guardedly and forbade him to speak of love. In the meantime they wrote and talked of their shared interests in literature and in Nonconformist Christianity, to which they both adhered.

Browning had published the first nine sections of 'The Flight of the Duchess' in *Hood's Magazine* in April, and although he had already composed other parts, under Elizabeth's influence the poem began to take a new direction. The poem came in fact to resemble his own and Elizabeth's situation, in that it recounts the story of a vibrant lady rescued from a stultifying marriage to a tyrannical husband to pursue a freer life of emotional fulfilment. Other poems also to be published in November in *Dramatic Romances & Lyrics* likewise reflect Browning's constant thoughts of Miss Barrett and in addition incorporate many of the changes that she suggested.[4] 'The Glove' tells of a virtuous youth, who wins a lady spurned by a knight, made to prove his love with deeds instead of words. 'Time's Revenges' shows a lover demanding obstacles to be erected so that he can prove himself 'that sea / Of passion' he 'needs must be'. 'The Lost Mistress' portrays a rejected suitor whose beloved has relegated him to the status of friend but who none the less remains faithful: 'Mere friends are we,—well, friends the merest / Keep much that I'll resign'.

By the time that the seventh number of *Bells and Pomegranates* was published in November 1845, Elizabeth was ready to declare her love in forthright terms, although she told none of her friends or family. Her two sisters guessed her secret, which she confirmed to them, but said nothing to her brothers, who nevertheless were suspicious. Arabella (called Arabel) and Henrietta helped spirit her gentleman caller, who was now calling her 'Ba', in and out of the house as surreptitiously as possible. Meeting without calling notice to Robert's visits necessitated all sorts of deviousness. 'By the time all this is over', Elizabeth said, a month before their wedding, 'we shall be fit to take a degree in some Jesuits college—we shall have mastered all the points of casuistry' (Kintner, 2: 951).

Elizabeth had been told by medical authorities that unless she went south, her health would never improve. She (and Robert) thought of her going to Pisa, and when her father, who had become suspicious of Robert's visits, positively forbade her to leave the house, she came to recognize him for the despotic egoist that he in fact was.

> I told him that my prospects of health seemed to me to depend on taking this step, but that through my affection for him, I was ready to sacrifice those to his pleasure if he exacted it—only it was necessary to my self-satisfaction in future years, to understand definitely that the sacrifice *was* exacted by him & *was* made to him,..& not thrown away blindly & by a misapprehension. And he would not answer *that*. . . . I had better do what I liked:—for his part, he washed his hands of me altogether—(Kintner, 1: 211)

Now she was ready to discuss the possibility of marriage, and as the pair considered it, they also continued to speak of Robert's works.

Elizabeth saw *Luria* in January 1846, when it was almost finished. She had expressed surprise early in their correspondence that Browning should write for the stage and had almost suggested that he give it up. Having apparently already made up his mind to quit writing for the theatre, he assured her: 'That "Luria" you enquire about, shall be my last play..for it is but a play, woe's me!' (Kintner, 1: 26). But later, in extenuation, he said that it was to be 'for a purely imaginary Stage' (Kintner, 1: 251). In any event, Browning had a hard time writing it, especially delineating his heroine, whom he meant 'should propose to go to Pisa with [Luria], and begin a new life' (Kintner, 1: 451) but whom he could not realize. In other words, he wished in the end to make his heroine a type of Elizabeth. But he understood that it was all wrong, his play merely 'a pure exercise of *cleverness*': 'I say . . . in excuse to myself,—*unlike* the woman at her spinning-wheel, "He thought of his *flax* on the whole far more than of his singing"—more of his life's sustainment, of dear, dear Ba . . . , than of these wooden figures—no wonder all is as it is!' (Kintner, 1: 551).

A *Soul's Tragedy*, the other play published in the last number of *Bells and Pomegranates*, was composed prior to the poet's acquaintance with Elizabeth, and so, he told her, it had 'no trace of you . . .—you have not put out the black face of *it*—it is all sneering and *disillusion*' (Kintner, 1: 451). She liked it however, finding it 'full of hope for both of us, to look forward & consider what you may achieve with that combination of authority over the reasons & the passions' (Kintner, 2: 569). Clearly, as the correspondence shows, Robert was willing to reorient his art along the more 'didactic' lines that Elizabeth seemed to prefer (Kintner, 1: 406). And in bidding farewell to the formal drama he was inclined towards poems that unfold in less ironic fashion. 'If I had not known you *so far* THESE works might have been the *better*', he said. 'If you take a man from prison and set him free..do you not probably cause a signal interruption to his previously all-ingrossing occupation, and sole labour of love, of carving bone-boxes, making chains of cherry-stones, and other such time beguiling operations—does he ever take up that business with the old alacrity?' His plays, he implies, had been but time-serving. Now he is ready for more serious enterprises: 'ploughing, building (castles . . . , no bone-boxes now)' (Kintner, 2: 580).

One obstacle to their marriage was money. Robert had himself never earned a shilling and was entirely dependent upon his parents for financial support – 'my simple expenses', as he called them (Kintner, 2: 1005), which they had gladly provided. Elizabeth, on the other hand, had inherited from relatives a fortune that yielded her about £350 annually, which was more than enough to live on should they settle in Italy. Robert however would not hear of taking any money from her and proposed quixotically several careers that he might take up. At last the money question was settled when he agreed that they would live on her income but that she must write a will bequeathing her property after her death to her brothers and sisters. Further, the pair agreed that Elizabeth's maid, Wilson, and her spaniel, Flush, would accompany them to foreign parts.

On 9 September 1846 Mr Barrett decreed that his family should vacate the Wimpole Street house and remove to the country while the house was being redecorated. Robert saw this as his opportunity for spiriting Elizabeth away: 'We must be *married directly* and go to Italy – I will go for a licence today and we can be married on Saturday [the twelfth]' (Kintner, 2: 1059). He told his parents of his plan, which they approved, as they did of everything else that Robert wanted. 'They have never been used to interfere with, or act for me—and they trust me', he told Elizabeth. 'If you care for any love, *purely* love—you will have theirs—they give it you, whether you take it or no' (Kintner, 2: 1006). On the eleventh he paid his last visit to the Barretts' home and made arrangements for the wedding. On Saturday morning Elizabeth, accompanied by Wilson, left the house on the pretence of taking a drive in the park; went to a cab stand; called at a chemist's shop for some sal volatile to steady her nerves; and drove to St Marylebone Church, where Robert was waiting for her. At approximately eleven o'clock they were married in the presence of two witnesses, Wilson and Robert's cousin James Silverthorne. Elizabeth returned home alone, they having agreed that scruple would not permit Robert's visiting the house again. On the nineteenth the couple, joined by Wilson and Flush, fled by train, boat and coach to Paris, where they rested for several days; thence by rail, coach and river steamer to Avignon and Marseilles; thence by ship to Leghorn; and finally by train to Pisa, where they arrived on 14 October. For most of the journey Robert had to lift and carry Elizabeth, who was so weak and thin that the jolting of the carriages bruised her badly and who was forced to take increasingly heavy doses of morphine.

In Pisa they found an apartment near the Campo Santo and settled in for the winter of 1846–7. In Italy Elizabeth's health immediately improved. She was, she wrote three weeks after their arrival, not merely '*improved*, but *transformed* rather' (Kenyon, 1: 306). Reporting what Robert had written him, Joseph Arnould told Domett 'that the *soi-disante* invalid of seven years, once emancipated from the paternal despotism, has had a wondrous revival, or rather, a complete metamorphosis; walks, rides, eats and drinks like a young and healthy woman'; in brief, the couple 'are in Love, who lends his own youth to everything' (*Domett*, p. 136).

For the first times in their lives Elizabeth and Robert were living independently of their parents, in a home of their own. Elizabeth was none the less anxious about her family. Upon learning of her elopement her father charged her with deceit, disinherited her, and thereafter spoke of her as if she were dead. Her brothers were almost as indignant as their father, although they relented after some months, almost forgiving Elizabeth but accusing Robert of having married their sister for money. Robert missed his parents and his sister. He was especially concerned about his mother, Elizabeth wrote to Sarianna, and was always 'so anxious' about her: 'How deeply and tenderly he loves her and all of you' (Kenyon, 1: 321–2). In spite of their acute feelings of separation from their families, both Elizabeth and Robert nevertheless happily went about setting up a household and learning Italian ways of managing it. The prolonged child-hoods of each of them – Robert was now thirty-four and Elizabeth forty – were at last over.

In March 1847 Elizabeth had a miscarriage, but Robert seems to have suffered from it more than she. In mid-April they set out for a tour of northern Italy with every intention of returning to Pisa; but at their first stop, Florence, they almost immediately fell in love with the city and soon decided to make their home there. They set about looking for permanent lodgings and, after trying furnished rooms at four different addresses, finally rented an apartment of seven unfurnished rooms in Casa Guidi, almost opposite the Pitti Palace and just a short walk from the Arno and the Ponte Vecchio. It was to be their home for the next thirteen years.

With the exception of Paris, Florence, under the easy, indolent rule of the Grand Duke Leopold II, was the most cosmopolitan city on the Continent, the home of Englishmen and Americans who for various reasons, not least the cheap cost of living and moderate taxation, had decided to settle there. There was gaiety and liveliness everywhere. There were book-stores that catered to a French- and English-speaking clientele. There were the opera and picture stalls. There were masked balls and musical soirées at the grand ducal palace. There were numerous other palaces, splendid gardens, walks along the river and over the famous bridges. In short, Florence was enchanting.

The Brownings soon set upon an active life in the city. They loved walking among the narrow streets and strolling along the Arno. Robert, who liked things – furniture, pictures, *objets* – quite as much as Henry James, scoured the city for paintings, tables, chairs and sofas; Elizabeth marvelled at what he discovered. They soon came to know most of the large English colony, and they met large numbers of the English and American visitors passing through. Already their marriage and retreat to Italy had become the stuff of storybook romance, and they – along with Giotto's tower and Ghiberti's bronze doors – themselves became one of the sights of Florence. Like most of the English and Americans living in Italy, they seem to have had almost no Italian friends. The Florentines they knew were almost entirely of a lower class, servants and tradesmen.

They were as happy as they ever dreamed they could be. But, as Eliza-beth wrote in December 1847, 'being too happy doesn't agree with literary activity as well as I should have thought' (Kenyon, 1: 353). While she had written several poems, Robert, who before marriage had been so prolific, managed to compose only one during the two-year period following their arrival in Italy. This was 'The Guardian Angel', which relates Browning's viewing of a picture by Guercino in a church at Fano on the Adriatic coast, which he and Elizabeth had visited in July 1848. In theme and style the poem is more nearly like *Pauline* than anything he had written since 1833. Invoking the angel in the picture to 'bend' over him, he wishes to rest his head 'beneath thine' while the angel's healing hands cover his eyes,

Plate 4 'The Salon at Casa Guidi', 1861. Oil painting by George Mignaty. Courtesy of the Armstrong Browning Library, Waco, Texas.

'Pressing the brain, which too much thought expands, / Back to its proper size again' and 'smoothing / Distortion down till every nerve had soothing'. If only this could happen, 'all worldly wrong would be repaired' and he would see 'with such different eyes'.

The poem is largely a 'song', as it is called in the last stanza, different in mode from the dramatic lyrics that he had been writing only a few years earlier. It is clearly regressive, almost in the Freudian sense, as the speaker, who is undifferentiated from the poet, voices his need for dependency. Here at Fano – 'My angel with me too' – he recalls seeing other works by Guercino elsewhere, almost certainly at the Dulwich Gallery with his friend Alfred Domett, who is addressed by name. Those days however are past: 'My love is here'. But, 'Where are you, dear old friend? / How rolls the Wairoa at your world's far end?' The poem seems to suggest some degree of dis-ease on the part of the poet, although it may have been nothing more than homesickness and a longing to see his family and friends after such a long separation that led him to give voice to the same desire for

protection and support that he expressed years earlier in *Pauline*.[5] Eliza-
beth, on the other hand, seemed positively to relish her independence in
Italy and continued to grow in physical strength, in spite of a second
miscarriage in March 1848. 'Children may be kept for those who have not
such a husband as I, perhaps!' she wrote to a friend in April 1848 (Irvine
and Honan, p. 245).

The main interest of 1848 was the revolutionary fervour being mani-
fested all over the Continent. The election as Pope in 1846 of Pius IX, who
in marked contrast with his predecessor was democratic in attitude, had
led to an outburst of liberal enthusiasm as he proclaimed amnesty for
political prisoners, relaxed the censorship laws and established a munici-
pal council in Rome. His popularity grew throughout Italy and encouraged
liberal sentiment in the peninsula. In October 1847 the king of the Pied-
mont yielded to liberal agitation in consenting to amendment of restric-
tive laws. In January 1848 a revolutionary movement broke out against
Bourbon rule in Sicily that resulted in its king's granting a liberal consti-
tution in February. Grand Duke Leopold of Tuscany was likewise obliged
to grant a constitution, as was the king of Piedmont in early March, soon
followed by the Pope's introducing a constitution in Rome. The revolu-
tionary fervour of the *Risorgimento* began to spill over into France, Ger-
many and Austria: kings were deposed or had their powers limited and
new republics were established.

In Italy Milan rose up against Austrian rule, a Venetian republic was
proclaimed, Piedmont declared war on Austria and the papal forces,
enlarged by contingents from Naples and other parts of Italy, joined the
Piedmontese. During April there was wild enthusiasm almost everywhere.
But a papal encyclical at the end of April disclaimed any intention of
making war on Catholic Austrians, thereby paralysing all action by papal
troops. The revolution in Naples collapsed in mid-May, and Neapolitan
troops withdrew from the north. The Piedmontese were defeated by the
Austrians in late May and withdrew from Lombardy.

During the summer and autumn of 1848 rebellion in all the Italian
states seemed to have been put down for good. In mid-November there
was however an insurrection in Rome and the Pope, who had retreated
from his earlier liberal stance, was forced to appoint a democratic ministry.
Alarmed by radical agitation, Pius retreated from Rome to the protection
of Naples, where he tried unsuccessfully to maintain his power in Rome
through a regency. In February 1849 a Roman republic was proclaimed,
with Mazzini as chief of the governing triumvirate, and the grand duke of
Tuscany deposed. In the following month Piedmont, owing to radical
pressure, denounced its armistice with Austria, which led only weeks after-
wards to the decisive defeat of the Piedmontese. In May Grand Duke
Leopold returned to Florence under protection of Austrian troops. In
July, in large part because of French intervention, the Roman republic was
dissolved after fierce fighting and the Pope returned to his dominions,
never again to display the democratic tendencies of his early reign. By

August Venice, besieged by the Austrians and ravaged by cholera and starvation, had fallen and the revolutionary movement everywhere in Italy had been suppressed.

Both Brownings had espoused the Italian nationalist cause while in England, and now in Italy, with the establishment of republics in Venice, Tuscany and Rome and the various uprisings against the Austrians in the Piedmont, they became enthusiastic partisans of Italian liberty. Before the collapse of the revolutionary states Elizabeth wrote the first part of *Casa Guidi Windows*, extolling Florence and liberty while damning Austria and tyranny. Things were happening so quickly that her hopes rose only to be soon dashed, and her letters, which recount her and Robert's responses to events, are full of accounts of the chief actors in the swiftly unfolding drama. In February 1849 she thought that 'though Mazzini is virtuous and heroic, he is indiscreet and mistakes the stuff of which the people is made, if he thinks to find a great nation in the heart of it. The soldiers refuse to fraternize with the republicans, and Robert saw a body of them arrested the other day' (Huxley, p. 101). Her fears proved well founded when at the end of April fighting between soldiers and republicans broke out in Florence and 'Robert barely managed to get home across the bridges' (Kenyon, 1: 401). When the Austrians entered Florence, she was 'sick at heart, and so is Robert, at the prospect of the country'. As for the poor, simple grand duke, she 'shed some tears when he went away, and could cry again for rage at his coming back'. Much disheartened, she wrote her sister, 'Robert and I agree that it is melancholy work to live on here' (Huxley, p. 105).

II

In the midst of this excitement Elizabeth was pregnant for the third time. This pregnancy however was to end more happily than the previous two. On 9 March 1849 at Casa Guidi she gave birth to a son, Robert Wiedeman Barrett Browning. He was called Wiedeman (soon to be corrupted, by his mispronunciation, to 'Penini', 'Peni', and eventually 'Pen') in honour of Robert's mother, whose maiden name was Wiedeman(n), and 'her own father and mother, whom she loved so much' (Hood, p. 24). Robert was delighted that, with no complications, Elizabeth had produced this healthy and beautiful son. Although a nurse was hired immediately to look after the child, Robert insisted on holding him frequently and helping with the baby's bath.

But his joy was diminished only a few days later by three letters from his sister stating first that their mother was seriously ill and then that she had died. Actually she was dead before any of the three was written, but knowing the effect that the news would have upon her brother, Sarianna wrote the first two to prepare him. Robert was none the less distraught, and Elizabeth was anxious for him, knowing how he had 'loved his mother as such passionate natures only can love' (Kenyon, 1: 399). She explained: 'While he was full of joy for the child, his mother was dying at a distance, and the very thought of accepting that new affection for the old became a thing to recoil from . . . So far from suffering less through this particular combination of circumstances, as some people seemed to fancy he would, he suffered much more, I am certain, and very naturally' (Kenyon, 1: 404). Nothing seemed to cheer him up. More than a month later he was, wrote Elizabeth, 'in the deepest anguish . . . I never saw a man so bowed down in an extremity of sorrow . . . and sometimes when I leave him alone a little and return to the room, I find him in tears. I do earnestly wish to change the scene and air' (Kenyon, 1: 399).

Adding to the general depression in the Browning household was, of course, the defeat of Italian liberty everywhere. In late June, soon after Pen's baptism in the French Evangelical Protestant Church, the Brownings went to Bagni di Lucca, a wooded spa in the Tuscan hills north-west of Florence, for a change of scene and to escape the heat of the city. Initially Robert's genial spirits seemed to revive as, Elizabeth wrote, 'Robert and I go out and lose ourselves in the woods and mountains, and sit by the waterfalls on the starry and moonlit nights' (Kenyon, 1: 415). Elizabeth showed him for the first time the forty-four sonnets, to be published as *Sonnets from the Portuguese* in 1850, that she had written to him during their courtship, the last being dated two days before their wedding. For all his genuine appreciation of them and his humble pleasure at being the subject of such noble poems, he could not however shake off his sadness, which was aggravated by his being at a loose end for something to do. Elizabeth's letters recount her many efforts to help him find occupation. 'What am I to say about Robert's idleness . . . ?' she wondered at the beginning of October. 'I scold him about it in a most anti-conjugal manner' (Kenyon, 1: 422).

In February 1846 Robert had told Elizabeth: 'I mean to take your advice and be quiet awhile and let my mind get used to its new medium of sight—, seeing all things . . . thro' you: and then, let all I have done be the prelude and the real work begin' (Kinter, 1: 455). In 1849 he published – with Chapman & Hall, Moxon being judged too slow – the 'prelude', the first collection of his works, which included in two volumes everything but *Pauline, Strafford* and *Sordello*. And he had been silent, having apparently over the past three years written only one poem. Evidently seeing everything through Elizabeth's eyes entailed a difficult refocusing of vision. But he persisted, beginning a new poem in late 1849, and completed *Christmas-Eve and Easter-Day*, which was published the following spring.

It was perhaps inevitable that, having suffered the shock of his mother's death so soon after the experience of extreme joy at the birth of his son, when Browning roused himself from his idleness and took up a new poem he should turn to religion for its subject. Indeed the passages on death and hope for an afterlife are probably the core of 'Christmas- Eve', around which were clustered the elements of an elaborate dream vision dealing with different modes of worship. His previous poetry had by and large never dealt directly with organized religion; it was, so to speak, metaphysical without being religious, *Sordello* being a perfect example. In his discussions and correspondence with Elizabeth in 1845–6 the subject of religion arose from time to time, he agreeing with her that Christianity is a 'worthy *myth*, & poetically acceptable' (Kintner, 1: 43); and they spoke of the forms of worship Christianity may take. She confessed, fairly early in their acquaintance, that she was from a dissenting background although not really interested in sectarianism as such, 'hating . . . all that rending of the garment of Christ, . . . & caring very little for most dogmas & doxies in themselves . . . & believing that there is only one church in heaven & earth, with the one divine High Priest to it'. In reply Browning acknowledged that he too was from a dissenting family but did not elaborate other than to say that this was not a 'point of disunion' between them (Kintner, 1: 141, 143).

A year later the pair again turned to the subject of sectarianism, and in explanation of her position Elizabeth spoke of her unwillingness 'to put on any of the liveries of the sects': 'I could pray anywhere & with all sorts of worshippers, from the Sistine Chapel to Mr [W. J.] Fox's, those kneeling & those standing. Wherever you go, in all religious societies, there is a little to revolt, & a good deal to bear with'. As for her own personal preference she opted for 'the simplicity of the dissenters' (Kintner, 2: 962). Browning agreed: 'If in a meeting house, with the blank white walls, and a simple doctrinal exposition,—all the senses should turn (from where they lie neglected) to all that sunshine in the Sistine with its music and painting, which would lift them at once to Heaven,—why should you not go forth?' (Kintner, 2: 969).

Throughout their correspondence Elizabeth had hinted that her suitor might consider a new course as a poet. She was full of praise for his dramatic poems, in which he had his 'creatures speak in clear human voices', but now she also wanted him, the man himself, to speak: 'I do not think that . . . only your own personality should be dumb' (Kintner, 2: 731–2). Perhaps, she implied, it would be salutary if he were to address himself directly to some of the great issues facing humankind.

Browning no doubt wished to heed his wife's advice and speak in his own voice when in the summer of 1849 she set him the task of composition to relieve his sorrow and idleness. Yet when he thought of elaborating the core passages of his poem into considerations of modes of worship more or less along the lines of their earlier correspondence, he found that he could not speak *in propria persona* any more easily than he could in January 1845, when he allowed to his future wife that he could 'only make men & women speak—give you truth broken into prismatic hues, and fear the pure white light', although he was 'going to try' to do what she did and 'speak out' (Kintner, 1: 7). Possibly he conceived of the device of the dream vision as a means of distancing himself from his material; but upon reflection even this would in the end mean pinning himself down to a certain stance. It was simply not in him to be anything other than a showman, an ironist, who could reveal himself only as the master of the performance.

The sole solution that he saw was the one he had adopted earlier in *Sordello* and in his reply to Elizabeth's remarks on sectarianism. Having agreed with her and outlined his ideas about forms of worship, he then, after an elaborate, highly fanciful metaphor, said: 'See the levity! No—this sort of levity only exists because of the strong conviction, I do believe! There seems no longer need of earnestness in assertion, or proof..so it runs lightly over, like foam on the top of a wave' (Kintner, 2: 969).

'Christmas-Eve' is a dramatic narrative of events that befell a certain unnamed speaker in London on Christmas Eve 1849. To escape the rain he enters a dissenting chapel, in which an ugly and mean congregation are preached to by an ignorant man. He withdraws to the open air and congratulates himself upon his own mode of worship, which entails direct communication with the divine without any kind of earthly mediation. Suddenly a rainbow appears and from it issues forth what seems to be the figure of Christ (although he is never named), who gathers the speaker up in his robe and transports him on a magical mystery tour to Rome, where he witnesses the midnight mass at St Peter's, and to Göttingen, where he hears a lecturer, espousing the Higher Criticism of the Bible made famous by German scholars in the 1830s, demythologize the Christian story. Noting that Christ had apparently been present in the chapel and had entered into the observances at both Rome and Göttingen while he, the speaker, had been left outside with only the hem of Christ's vesture to hold, the speaker realizes that there is a residuum of faith in all these various celebrations of Christ's birth. After a storm arises and Christ disappears, the speaker reflects that his own absolutism is wrong, that the truth he had been regarding as absolute is truth only to him. Admitting that there are many perceptions of truth and that each man's realization of it is true for him if for no one else, the speaker is vouchsafed a return of the wondrous robe, which carries him back to the chapel and ordinary consciousness. Henceforth he will not deny to other modes of worship their own validity. As a personal matter he prefers that way which employs fewest earthly aids, and so instead of 'attacking the choice of my neighbours round, / With none of my own made—I choose here!' (1340–1).

Commentators on 'Christmas-Eve' have long taken the poem as Browning's evaluation of the relative merits of the three modes of worship and as 'his decision in favor of the Dissenting Chapel, for the Chapel seems in the poet's opinion to have received most fittingly the gift of God's Son to the world' (DeVane, p. 202). Such judgement does not, however, take into account the ironic 'levity' undercutting whatever direct statement of belief may or may not be iterated. For Browning makes sure to leave us at the end with no notion that this is his final word on the subject; in fact, he causes us to question whether this dream vision has even been a serious consideration of the subject.[6]

First, although the poem is carefully organized, its structure being circular, with an introduction and a coda, the effect is not of careful organization but of cramming and stuffing, of fantasy and unreality; in this respect it is like *Sordello*. Many passages have little to do with modes of worship but concern, for example, the Incarnation (in the scene at Rome) and the need for accepting the divinity of Christ (in the scene at Göttingen). The impression of the poem as something of a grab bag is heightened by the hudibrastic verse form, which lends a tone of grotesquerie and facetiousness to content often of intense seriousness.

Second, the speaker questions the reality of the experience: if he has been transported to various parts of the world, how is it that he has heard the sermon in the chapel and been able to note in detail its deficiencies? Third, he admits to what some people might call 'undue levity' in dealing with 'the holy and the awful' (1346–7), this being in no small part owing to the language itself, which does not permit adequate discussion of the infinite because of its finite nature. Fourth, the poem ends with a complete violation of the pretence that this has been a dramatic poem, as in the last few lines the speaker says: 'I put up pencil' (1355). This has been no fictional character but the poet himself speaking: 'The giving out of the hymn reclaims me' (1342). It recalls him from fantasy to himself – the master of the performance – who comes forth to say that this is not the representation of an experience but a poem, not life but art. He reminds us that 'Christmas-Eve' offers not creeds but fictions of faith, not a generalized statement but a point of view.[7]

Where 'Christmas-Eve' is a monologue addressed to an unnamed auditor, its companion poem is the first of Browning's 'parleyings', a dialogue in which the poet divides himself up into two voices. 'Easter-Day' deals not with the 'vestures' of belief, as Carlyle had called them in *Sartor Resartus*, but with faith itself. 'How very hard it is to be / A Christian', the first speaker says (1–2): not just to live up to the ideal of Christian practice in the world but to lend credence to Christianity itself. In response the second speaker suggests possible ways in which the finite life might be related to the supremacy of the infinite life. But to each of these the first speaker offers objections and insists that modern men and women demand there be no self-delusion in the matter but rather a firm trust and that this be reconciled with the Christian God's clear requirement that the world's gain is to be accounted loss.

He then offers a personal experience which happened three years ago when he was crossing the common near the chapel that 'our friend spoke of, the other day' (375), in 'Christmas-Eve'. As he was musing on his personal belief and wondering whether, were he to die at that very moment, he would lie faithful or faithless, all at once there came a vision, in which he found himself at Judgement Day. Standing before the throne of judgement, he chooses, like Aprile of *Paracelsus*, the world and the beauty of nature. Christ allows his choice. In a transport of joy as he relishes the sense of full possession of earthly beauty that is to be his, he soon realizes that what he has chosen is mere 'partial beauty', which is but 'a pledge / Of beauty in its plenitude' (769–70). Recognizing the insufficiency of nature, he then opts for art in its place. And in this choice he again comes to understand that were he to achieve that perfection of form to which artists, such as Eglamor in *Sordello*, constantly aspire, that completion when repeated would be dreary: 'The good, tried once, were bad, retried' (834). Thirdly the speaker, like Paracelsus, chooses mind, the intellectual life, which also is proven deficient in and of itself in that it lacks inspiration to lure mankind onward. Finally and belatedly the speaker chooses love, which he now sees was all about him and which is the true channel to the infinite; love alone gives the light of life to all the earthly things which he desired – the beauty of nature and art and the joy of mental activity.

Now convinced that mankind's belief in the supremacy of the infinite lies in the perception of the infinite through the finite, the speaker awakes and rejoices that it is hard to be a Christian and that he is not condemned to earth and ease for ever. Unlike the dreamer in 'Christmas-Eve' who awoke to affirm for the moment that his vision was true – 'True as that heaven and earth exist' (1245) – the dreamer of 'Easter-Day' immediately wonders, 'Was this a vision? False or true?' (1010). Further, at the onset of the visionary experience he believed that it could be no more than 'a dream—a waking dream at most!' (609). The echoes of Keats's 'Ode to a Nightingale' are unmistakable. Moreover, the speaker's descriptions of nature and his election of art as his chief good also suggest Keats.

Browning had been familiar with Keats's verse almost as long as with Shelley's, and in time Keats seems to have exerted an important influence over him. Yet he also seems to have recognized the limitations of the aestheticism and sensualism that Keats embraced. *Pippa Passes* had offered a critique of the Keatsian world of nature in Pippa's introduction and epilogue and had questioned whether the artistic imagination is sufficient to counterbalance the human's need for relationship and community. In the mid-1840s Robert and Elizabeth had discussed Keats on several occasions, he even once quoting the final line from the 'Nightingale Ode' alluded to in 'Easter-Day' (Kintner, 1: 189). He showed Elizabeth a lengthy criticism of Keats that Jane Welsh Carlyle had sent him; and while admitting that Keats was indeed a poet of the senses but the senses idealized, Elizabeth detected 'the want of thought as thought' in his poetry (Kintner, 1: 187). Later Robert criticized Keats to her very much along the lines set forth in 'Easter-Day', saying that the beauty that Keats praised so will die but that love opens out to the eternal (Kintner, 1: 378–9). In addition, the publication of his friend Richard Monckton Milnes's edition of Keats's poems and letters in 1848 had served further to bring the Romantic poet to the forefront of his consciousness.

Yet for all the distrust of the Keatsian enterprise implicit in the poem, 'Easter-Day' is by no means a disavowal of Keats. Indeed, the echo of Keats in the final lines underscores the artistic nature of the poem and reminds us by its ironic undercutting of meaning that the thoughts expressed in the 'vision' are but the expression of one point of view – namely, that of the artist, Robert Browning.

There is little levity in 'Easter-Day'. In fact, Elizabeth 'complained of the *asceticism*' in it, and Robert explained that 'it was "one side of the question"' (Kenyon, 1: 449). Probably most readers agree with her. In any case, the poem has never been popular. Yet along with *Paracelsus* it provides some of the best examples of Browning's thoughts on change and development, especially of his notion of Godhead as an evolutionary process, of God pursuing 'His progress through eternity' (851). 'Easter-Day' insists that the God of becoming, who does 'expand, expand' (1004), is also the God of love who provides for human evolvement and does not condemn mankind to stasis. So convinced, the speaker declares himself a fighter ready to 'go through the world, try, prove, reject, / Prefer, still struggling to effect / [His] warfare' (1019–21) against all obstacles in the way of advancement to ever higher spheres of being.[8]

Christmas-Eve and Easter-Day was published on 1 April 1850 by Browning's new publishers, Chapman & Hall. It was respectfully but not widely reviewed. Within a fortnight 200 copies were sold, and thereafter almost none. When Wordsworth died on 23 April, Elizabeth was proposed by the *Athenaeum* and other journals as his successor as Poet Laureate. The new edition of her *Poems* in two volumes was published in the autumn and received, as usual, far more reviews than Robert's poem. For the most part, Robert had to enjoy critical esteem vicariously.

6

At Home And Abroad, 1850–1854

In late July 1850 Elizabeth suffered a miscarriage from which, Robert reported, 'she had lost over a hundred ounces of blood within the twentyfour hours' (Hood, p. 28) and which for six weeks left her enfeebled. At her doctor's suggestion the Brownings rented a villa above Siena for several months to enjoy the cooler country air, returning to Florence in November. Elizabeth recovered beautifully and was, Robert later said, 'at the very height of her health' (*Dearest Isa*, p. 232).

Young Wiedeman, soon to learn to talk (mainly in Italian) and call himself 'Penini', was growing and being pampered by Wilson and his adoring parents, who were ever anxious, often needlessly, about him. While at Sienna Pen –'our poor little darling', as Elizabeth wrote – suffered for a day from 'a species of sunstroke': 'Terrible, the silence that suddenly fell upon the house, without the small pattering feet and the singing voice. But God spared us: he grew quite well directly and sang louder than ever' (Kenyon, 1: 459). Screaming however was more often to be heard than song from the child who, like Flush, was more than a little spoiled. 'If Flush is scolded, Baby cries as a matter of course' (Kenyon, 1: 469).

By 1850 the Brownings had established an interesting circle of friends in Florence, including a large number of Americans. The sculptor Hiram Powers had set up a studio there in 1837, having gained fame in the United States for his portrait busts of noted statesmen, including Andrew Jackson, Daniel Webster and John Marshall. Elizabeth was particularly impressed by him, finding him, 'like most men of genius', almost childlike, 'quiet and gentle, calling himself "a beginner in art" which is the best way of making a great end' (Huxley, p. 29). She greatly admired his statue of the chained and naked girl, *The Greek Slave*, and wrote a sonnet about it expressing her horror of slavery.

Another American sculptor whom they came to know more intimately was William Wetmore Story, seven years younger than Robert. The Brownings had met him and his wife, Emelyn, and their two children, Joe and Edie (or Edy), in 1848. Story's father was a famous lawyer – founder and first professor of the Harvard University Law School and an associate justice of the US Supreme Court – and the son had likewise become a lawyer, successful in private practice and highly regarded as the author of several legal treatises. On the side he wrote verse and studied painting, sculpture and music. By the time the Brownings met him he had pretty much settled on being a sculptor, and he and his family had been living in Italy off and on since 1846, by and large alternating between Rome and Florence. The Storys were highly cultivated and interesting people and were among the closest friends that the Brownings made in Italy.

About the same time they came to know the Storys the Brownings met Margaret Fuller. The daughter of an American congressman who had personally educated her in a way almost as demanding as that supervised by John Stuart Mill's father, she was a feminist who had conducted 'conversations' with a group of ladies in Boston as a means of general cultural education. For a while she was associated with the utopian Brook Farm community in Massachusetts; and, a friend of Ralph Waldo Emerson's, she served as editor of the *Dial*, the organ of American transcendentalism. As literary editor of the New York *Tribune* she had established a reputation as one of America's finest critics. She had come to Europe in 1846, stopping first to meet Carlyle and other luminaries in London, and then proceeding to the Continent, where, as foreign correspondent, she wrote articles for the *Tribune*. In 1847 she met and married in Rome the Marchese Angelo Ossoli, with whom she took part in the 1848 revolution and by whom she had a child.

Fleeing from Rome with the collapse of the republic, the Ossolis arrived in Florence in late 1849 on their way to the United States. The Brownings found the Marchese amiable but not overly clever; Margaret, however, was brilliant, and both Elizabeth and Robert were strongly drawn to her, admiring not only her intelligence but also her honesty and courage. On the night before she left Florence, she gave a Bible from her son to Pen. Not long afterwards, on 19 July 1850, she and her husband and child were drowned when their ship was wrecked off the coast of New York.

The news of the tragedy arrived soon after Elizabeth's miscarriage, and Robert tried to keep it from her. Elizabeth heard of it nevertheless and grieved not only for the loss of the Ossolis but also once again for her brother Edward who was also drowned at sea. Robert wrote to John Kenyon of 'this dreadful loss of dear, brave, noble Margaret Fuller': 'We loved her, and she loved Ba, coming here oftener as the time for departure approached.' Her last letter to them, from Gibraltar, began 'Dear precious friends' (Hood, p. 31).

Among English friends and acquaintances was the dilettante painter Seymour Kirkup, who had studied at the Royal Academy and known William Blake and Benjamin Robert Haydon. Because of pulmonary weakness he had come to Italy before 1820 and had been present at the funerals of both Keats and Shelley. Settling in Florence, he became a devoted Dante scholar and in 1840 had discovered a portrait of Dante that, according to tradition, had been painted by Giotto. The Brownings liked him and valued his artistic opinions. Robert, who loved hunting for old pictures, would often consult Kirkup. 'The other day', Elizabeth wrote in May 1850 about one of her husband's finds, 'he covered himself with glory by discovering and seizing on (in a corn shop a mile from Florence) five pictures among heaps of trash; and one of the best judges in Florence (Mr Kirkup) throws out such names for them as Cimabue, Ghirlandaio, Giottino, a crucifixion painted on a banner, Giottesque, if not Giotto' (Kenyon, 1: 448). Neither Robert nor Kirkup was, however, a perfect judge, and many of Robert's attributions later proved incorrect.

By 1850 the Brownings had come to know Isabella Blagden, the 'Dearest Isa' of Robert's later years. She was a spinster, six years Robert's junior and of mysterious origins: it was rumoured that she was the daughter of an unwed English father and Indian mother, although at her death her nationality was given as Swiss. As much as Margaret Fuller she was given to passionate friendships with women, but she evidently was to have a romantic affair with the diplomat and author Robert Lytton. Herself an undistinguished poet and novelist, of slight frame and dark complexion, she welcomed to her home in Florence famous English and American residents and visitors. In the later 1850s, as Elizabeth grew more frail and more dependent on narcotics and at her request, Robert took to going into society alone and was to be found at Isa's villa four nights a week. She was, for both Brownings, 'our best & dearest friend' (Dearest Isa, p. 71); and it was to her that Robert was to turn at the time of his greatest bereavement.

Yet for all the liveliness and sociability of Florence there remained the attraction of England and the family and friends whom they had not seen in almost five years. In May 1851, having let their apartment in Casa Guidi, Robert, Elizabeth, Pen, Wilson and Flush set out for Venice on a voyage that was eventually to land them in England. Elizabeth was beguiled by her first sight of the city that John Ruskin had praised in the first volume of his Stones of Venice, published the previous March. After the delights of Venice – trips by gondolas, tea in the Piazza San Marco, visits to spots associated with Byron – they proceeded via Padua (with an excursion to Arqua because of Petrarch), Milan, Lake Maggiore and the St Gotthard to Paris, where they met the Alfred Tennysons, who were on their way to Italy and Florence.

Elizabeth had been an emotive admirer of Tennyson's for many years and in 1842, acclaiming him 'divine', had had no hesitation in ranking him higher than Browning (Correspondence, 6: 54, 220). She had had a slight correspondence with the poet whose 'shoetyes' she was 'ready to kiss ... any day' and who for his part, John Kenyon reported, had said, 'There is only one female poet whom I wish to see..& that is Miss Barrett' (Correspondence, 7: 36, 4). In his letters Robert had been less adulatory, no doubt acutely aware of his own lack of recognition as compared with Tennyson's, but admitting 'how good when good he is' (*Correspondence*, 6: 32). Robert had met him in person on two or three occasions but did not know him well. Tennyson, whom the queen had appointed Laureate in 1850 following the astounding success of *In Memoriam*, had married Emily Sellwood in June 1850 after a long engagement, he then aged forty-one and she thirty-seven. Both Brownings were charmed by the Tennysons, who invited them (although they declined) to make use of their house in Twickenham while in England. Thereafter the relationship of the Brownings and the Tennysons was cordial if not, owing to the geographical distance between them, intimate; but after Elizabeth's death Robert's relations with the Tennysons and their children grew increasingly close.

In Paris they had slight misgivings about returning to London: Elizabeth was apprehensive about her reception by her family, and Robert was saddened to consider visiting beloved spots without his mother's presence. Nevertheless they determined to go and finally arrived in London on 22 July, taking a house in Devonshire Street, near the southern edge of Regent's Park and within walking distance of the Barretts' home. Elizabeth visited her two sisters (one of whom, Henrietta, had, like her, been disowned by their father for marrying, and had come from her home in Somerset) and her five brothers, only one of whom, George, became fully reconciled to her and Robert. She and the baby called at Wimpole Street while her father was out, though once while in Arabella's room she heard her father's voice on the stairs. Both Elizabeth and Robert wrote to Mr Barrett, who returned their letters, along with a packet of Elizabeth's to him for the past five years, unopened. 'He said he regretted to have been forced to keep them by him until now, through his ignorance of where he should send them', Elizabeth wrote to a confidante (Kenyon, 2: 20). There was to be no reconciliation.

Robert spent long hours with his father and sister at New Cross, and they were enchanted by Elizabeth and Pen, both of whom they were seeing for the first time. John Kenyon, who had supplemented Elizabeth's income by the gift of £100 annually after Pen was born, called on them frequently. They met each other's old friends like John Forster and Joseph Arnould, who wrote to Alfred Domett in New Zealand: 'I caught a glimpse of them while in town. He is *absolutely* the same man: her I like of all things—full of quiet genius' (*Domett*, p. 142). The Carlyles Elizabeth saw in person for the first time. A warm admirer of Carlyle's, she was, she told Robert early in their correspondence, 'a devout sitter at his feet—and it is an effort to me to think him wrong in anything' even though 'he told me to write prose and not verse' (Kintner, 1: 24). Meeting him, she said, 'I liked him infinitely more in his personality than I expected to like him', finding that 'his bitterness is only melancholy, and his scorn sensibility. Highly picturesque too he is in conversation' (Kenyon, 2: 27). Everything about London during that summer of the Great Exhibition in the Crystal Palace seemed lively, and they hated to leave, despite Elizabeth's depression resulting from her father's behaviour, Robert's vivid awareness of his mother's absence, and his concern about the effects of the filthy air on Elizabeth's health. For Robert, Elizabeth said, 'it had been pure joy . . . , and I do believe he would have been capable of never leaving England again'. As for herself, she left with 'mixed feelings': 'Oh England! I love and hate it at once'; and on balance 'there was relief in the state of mind with which I threw myself on the sofa at Dieppe' (Kenyon, 2: 23).

In late September they travelled to Paris accompanied by Carlyle, who was his way to meet his friends Lord and Lady Ashburton. While in England, Elizabeth had coughed 'perpetually', and 'no sooner [did she] get to Paris than the cough vanishes' (Kenyon, 2: 23). Finding lodgings on the Champs-Elysées, they almost immediately immersed themselves in the capital's social and cultural life. They met the poet Alphonse de Lamartine, who had served in the provisional revolutionary government in 1848 as minister of foreign affairs. Through Carlyle they had obtained a letter of introduction from Mazzini to the novelist George Sand, whom Elizabeth adored and called 'the greatest female poet the world ever saw' (*Correspondence*, 8: 240). On the several occasions when they did meet George Sand, a married woman whose liaisons with the poet Alfred de Musset and the pianist–composer Frédéric Chopin had contributed almost as much to her fame as her novels had, she and Robert did not find each other sympathetic. Now forty-eight, she was still something of a *femme fatale*, and when the Brownings called was receiving the admiration of her male admirers with calm disdain. Robert was more than a little shocked by these 'crowds of ill-bred men who adore her *à genoux bas*, betwixt a puff of smoke and an ejection of saliva. Society of the ragged Red diluted with the lower theatrical' (Kenyon, 2: 63).

Most importantly, they met and often saw Joseph Milsand, who was the antithesis of all that George Sand represented and who was to become Robert's closest male friend. A *bon bourgeois* native of Dijon, a Protestant who had converted from Roman Catholicism, an amateur painter who had once thought of taking up art as his profession, a family man, and a lover of Italian and English literature, Milsand had recently published in the *Revue des Deux Mondes* a perceptive and laudatory article on Robert's poetry, and was at work on an essay on Elizabeth's poetry. Robert was greatly impressed by Milsand, on whose judgement and knowledge of English poetry he soon came to rely, even to the extent of sending Milsand his proofsheets for final revision before publication and in turn commenting on Milsand's work before it was sent to the printer. Elizabeth loved him also, not least because, in addition to understanding her own verse, he, almost alone among critics, did justice to Robert's work.

Not long after the Brownings established themselves in Paris, Robert was commissioned by his old publisher Edward Moxon to write a preface to twenty-five letters by Shelley that Moxon had purchased and proposed to publish. The *Essay on Shelley*, as it has come to be called, is Browning's major critical document. Nine years previously he had written another prose piece, ostensibly a review, on the boy-poet Thomas Chatterton, who had forged a number of poems in the late medieval manner, met with some success, and then in despair committed suicide. Appearing anonymously in the *Foreign Quarterly Review* in the first number of which John Forster was the editor, July 1842, the piece had argued in typical Browningesque manner that the case was not what it seemed and Chatterton's death not an act of desperation but the moral victory of one disavowing deceit. In effect, the *Essay on Chatterton* (as it is now known) is a kind of dramatic monologue expounded in the third person. The *Essay on Shelley* is an altogether more ambitious and important text.

Using the nineteenth-century commonplace critical terms 'objective' and 'subjective', Browning contrasts two different kinds of poets. The objective poet is mimetic, aiming to represent men and women and their actions. He is a maker, and the world he fashions in the narrative and dramatic modes is distinct from himself. The subjective poet, on the other hand, is an illuminator who looks beyond things external and tries to see what God sees. Making no effort like the objective poet to be impersonal, he creates in the lyric mode a world that is projected from, but not separate from, himself. For the objective poet there is no need for a biography to enlighten his work. But for the subjective poet like Shelley every piece of biographical information, like the letters at hand, is useful. Shelley was a great and good poet, Browning goes on to say, and though he was a youthful atheist, his vision was essentially religious and his poetry was 'a sublime fragmentary essay' towards presenting 'the correspondency of the universe with Deity'. Had he lived, he would in time 'certainly have ranged himself with the Christians'.

Having defined the two types of poets, Browning then proceeds to show, as in *Sordello*, that literary history has proceeded dialectically, in cyclically alternating periods when one or the other type was dominant. But, Browning suggests, there is no reason why those two modes of poetic faculty might not be combined in 'the whole poet' who fully displays the objective and subjective modes. Beholding the universe, nature and man 'in their actual state of perfection in imperfection', the whole poet looks to 'the forthcoming stage of man's being' and presents 'the ideal of a future man'. Rejecting 'ultimates' and aspiring always toward a 'higher state of development', he strives 'to elevate and extend' both himself and the race as a whole. He will never attain 'an absolute vision' but his goal will be 'a continual approximation to it'. In short, the whole poet is the poet of becoming, the kind of poet that Browning conceived himself to be. And in apparently writing about Shelley, he was in fact writing about himself, who was, as Elizabeth had called him, a poet who has 'in [his] vision two worlds' and is 'both subjective & objective' (Kintner, 1: 9).

Browning sent off his introductory essay to Moxon in December, and it was published in the *Letters of Percy Bysshe Shelley* early in 1852. The letters, however, were soon discovered to be spurious and the book was suppressed. Browning himself cared little for the essay but Carlyle liked it, not least because it was written in prose. 'Give us some more of *your* writing, my friend', he responded upon receipt of the volume. 'Nor do I restrict you to Prose, in spite of all I have said and still say: Prose or Poetry, either of them you can master; and we will wait for you with welcome in whatever form your *Daimon* bids'.[1]

For the moment, however, political events in France impressed themselves upon the Brownings. Early in December President Louis Napoleon staged his *coup d'état* that dissolved the National Assembly and led, a year later, to his assumption of the title of emperor. As the military machinations were reported in the press, the Brownings' friends and relatives became fearful for their safety. The worry was needless, for never were they in any danger, although Wilson was told to keep Pen inside and not go walking on the boulevards. There was, however, dissension in the household about the president's unconstitutional seizure of power. Elizabeth forcefully insisted that, given the unsettled state of affairs in Paris and the country as a whole, Louis Napoleon had acted in the only way possible. Robert, on the other hand, regarded the president's actions as nothing more than a cynical grab for personal power and foresaw where it would lead. There were real differences between the pair. 'Robert & I', Elizabeth wrote to her brother George in February 1852, 'have fought considerably upon all these points'. 'Is it not strange', Robert asked George Barrett also on the same day, 'that Ba cannot take your view, not to say mine & most people's, of the President's proceedings? I cannot understand it—we differ in our appreciation of facts, too—things that admit of proof' (*Letters to George*, pp. 165, 169). Their differences about Louis Napoleon were to continue for the rest of their married life, and the subject became a barely buried bone of contention between them.

James Silverthorne died in May 1852, and Sarianna wrote to say that Robert should surely come over from Paris to attend the funeral of his favourite cousin. Elizabeth, however, was terrified of being left alone, and Robert felt that he could not leave her. He commemorated his cousin in 'May and Death', to be published five years later, recalling their earlier days when they walked 'arm in arm' in the 'long evening-ends' as they returned from the theatre and other nocturnal pleasures.

The summer of 1852 the Brownings spent in London, in part because of a judgement of £800 in damages that the Court of the Queen's Bench, in early July, found against Robert Browning senior. The elder Browning had proposed marriage to a widow, whom he subsequently and erroneously believed to have been illegally married to her second husband. He wrote to her breaking off the engagement and charging her with misconduct. She sued him for breach of promise and defamation of character and won. Robert *fils* – who was mortified by his father's foolishness and, probably more particularly, what he considered disloyalty to his mother's memory, only three years after her death – arrived in England several days after the trial to find his father and sister in deep depression and determined to move to foreign parts to escape paying the damages. He accompanied Robert senior and Sarianna to Paris in mid-July and saw them settled in an apartment.

Later in the month Robert returned to London, where he and Elizabeth remained to enjoy their numerous friends and relatives. They frequently saw their benefactor John Kenyon, who had W. S. Landor as a guest. Elizabeth was surprised and delighted to hear Landor, 'full of life and passionate energy', say that Louis Napoleon was a man of genius (Kenyon, 2: 78). They met the Christian Socialist author and clergyman Charles Kingsley and the American poet James Russell Lowell. Jane Carlyle brought Mazzini to meet them, and they made a fuss over him and were reluctant to let him leave. 'I was thinking, while he sate there', Elizabeth said, 'on what Italian turf he would lie at last with a bullet in his heart, or perhaps with a knife in his back, for to one of those ends it will surely come' (Kenyon, 2: 78). She liked Mrs Carlyle, who found her '*true* and *good*, and the most *womanly* creature' but who, 'in spite of Mr C.'s favour for him', thought Robert to be '"nothing", or very little more, "but a fluff of feathers!"'[2]

The Brownings dined with W. J. Fox, with whom Elizabeth waxed eloquent about George Sand and Louis Napoleon; lunched with the Ruskins, not long before Mrs Ruskin, whom Elizabeth found lovely and elegant but not overly intelligent, was to leave her husband for the painter John Everett Millais; went for drives with R. M. Milnes and his wife of a year and attended the christening lunch held for their infant daughter. They cemented their friendship with the Tennysons and were invited to the christening of Hallam, the Tennysons' first child, which Robert attended alone because of Elizabeth's frail health. Altogether their pleasure in London was mitigated by the deleterious effect that the weather had on Elizabeth.

They departed in October for Paris, where Robert as always was invigorated by that city's life. Pen looked at a parade in which Louis Napoleon rode on horseback ten paces ahead of his escort and 'was in a state of ecstasy' when he cried 'Vive Napoléon' and the president 'took off his hat to him directly' (Kenyon, 2: 90). By mid-November they were home in Florence, from which they had been absent for a year and a half. Elizabeth was pleased to be back, but, she told Sarianna Browning, 'Robert has been perfectly demoralised by Paris, and thinks it all as dull as possible after the boulevards: "no life, no variety"' (Kenyon, 2: 93).

Nevertheless, the winter of 1852–3 passed pleasantly, especially because Elizabeth was in good health. They were delighted to see their old friends, 'Kirkup wonderfully well, and Powers moving into a larger house' (Hood, p. 38). They also met two new friends. Frederick Tennyson, Alfred's elder brother, was a poet and accomplished musician who had distinguished himself at Trinity College, Cambridge. Coming into an inheritance he had moved to Italy, married the handsome daughter of Sienna's chief magistrate, and settled in Florence with four children while remaining, as Elizabeth observed, 'intensely English nevertheless, as expatriated Englishmen

generally are' (Kenyon, 2: 113). Like most of the Tennysons he possessed
a number of eccentricities and passed among the Florentines as a type of
the mad Englishman. His main preoccupation was religion, particularly
the Second Coming which he expected imminently.

Their second new friend was Robert Lytton, the son of Sir Edward
Bulwer-Lytton, the novelist, poet and playwright whom Robert had first
met through John Forster and whom he had come to know well. Lytton,
who in his early twenties had fairly recently arrived in Florence as secretary
of the British legation, was himself later to be, under the pseudonym
Owen Meredith, a fairly successful poet and, as a professional diplomat
who was created first earl of Lytton, ambassador to France and viceroy of
India.

Both Frederick Tennyson and Lytton, whom Elizabeth found 'intelligent
and interesting persons' (Kenyon, 2: 99), were strongly enthusiastic about
spiritualism, and in a short time the vogue for spiritualism, given impetus
by recent 'manifestations' in America, took Florence's English-speaking
community by storm. Elizabeth turned to it wholeheartedly: 'We read of
a prophecy concerning "angels ascending and descending upon the son
of man". What if this spiritual influx and afflux is beginning? It seems to
me probable' (Huxley, p. 190). Robert, who at first tried for his wife's sake
to be sympathetic, grew increasingly hostile and finally exasperated and
disgusted. Spiritualism was to prove a serious difference between them,
one that was never reconciled.

Another difference between them concerned the dress of young Pen,
whom Elizabeth decked out in lace and frills. Dressed in 'a white felt hat,
white satin ribbons and feathers . . . with a trimming of blue satin ribbon
inside at each cheek', Pen was, Elizabeth declared, 'lovely'. 'People stare
at him, Wilson says, and turn round to stare again' (Huxley, p. 146).
Strangers in fact asked Wilson whether he was a girl or a boy. Robert of
course wanted his son to appear more like a little boy than a little girl. But
whatever contentions may have arisen, Robert, mindful of Elizabeth's weak
health, seems generally to have deferred to her. No wonder that Elizabeth
referred to him as 'the prince of husbands, . . . lenient to my desires'
(Kenyon, 2: 63).

Summer 1853 was spent again in Bagni di Lucca, where the Storys
were also staying. It was for the Brownings an unexpected pleasure to find
them here. They went back and forth between each other's houses, took
long walks and enjoyed picnics in the woods. In October both families
returned to Florence and the next month went on to Rome, a journey of
eight days that included stops at Perugia, Assisi and the falls at Terni.
Installed in Rome in lodgings the Storys had arranged for them, the
Brownings were introduced into 'the best society' (Kenyon, 2: 159), which
meant the foreign colony, for here as in Florence they made no effort to
meet Italians. They were introduced to Thackeray and his daughters and
were happy to find the author of *Vanity Fair*, which Elizabeth thought 'very
clever, very effective, but cruel to human nature' (Kenyon, 1: 401), genial

and amusing. They met Hans Christian Andersen, the Danish author of fairy tales, who at one of Story's parties read to the children 'The Ugly Duckling' followed by Robert's reading of 'The Pied Piper of Hamelin'. They made the acquaintance of the American sculptor Harriet Hosmer and the English painter Frederic Leighton. They were visited by Fanny Kemble the actress and her sister Adelaide Sartoris, now retired from the operatic stage. They frequently called on the painter William Page, known as the American Titian, who lived in the same building. They went on picnics into the Campagna, sometimes with three carriages full of people. Rome was more exciting than Florence.

But their stay in Rome was marred by several occurrences. Little Joe Story was taken ill and died soon after they arrived. His sister, Edie, was also stricken, and her nurse developed the same symptoms. Elizabeth was alarmed: 'I fell into a selfish panic about my child', she wrote (Kenyon, 2: 153). Happily both Edie and her nurse recovered. The burial of Joe in the Protestant cemetery, near Shelley's grave, was very sad, and even visits to the famous sights of Rome did not relieve their gloom. Then there was Elizabeth's renewed interest in spiritualism, which she practised more fervently and with which Robert was even more impatient than he had been in Florence. In addition, the city was expensive, Pen was struck by Roman fever and Robert was unable to accomplish any work. By late spring they were ready to give up on Rome for ever.

7

Men and Women

By early June 1854 the Brownings were home. 'I am delighted to say that
we have arrived', Elizabeth wrote to Sarianna, 'and see our dear Florence,
the queen of Italy, after all' (Kenyon, 2: 167). Settled into a more orderly
routine than they had followed in Rome, they diligently set to work. Robert
had a certain stock of poems on hand that were, he told John Forster, 'of
all sorts and sizes and styles and subjects . . . the fruits of the years since I
last turned the winch of the wine press. The manner will be newer than
the matter. I hope to be listened to, this time, and I am glad I have been
made to wait this not very long while' (*NL*, p. 77). He continued to fill the
wine vat, writing during the morning and showing Elizabeth his manu-
scripts in the evening. She read them and pronounced them 'magnifi-
cent', confidently predicting that they 'will raise him higher than he stands'.
'We are up early working, working', she wrote her sister in April 1855.
'Penini's lessons I never neglect—then I write.— Then dinner—then I
criticise Robert's MSS. Altogether I have scarcely breath for reading'
(Huxley, p. 216). Despite Elizabeth's several chest attacks and Robert's
almost constant attention to her, he managed to compose 8,000 lines of
verse by June 1855.

For some time they had been planning a visit to London, and when in
June they heard rumours that cholera had broken out in a street near
Casa Guidi, they hurriedly packed their belongings, bought new clothes
for Pen and headed to Leghorn for a ship that would take them to
Marseilles. There they discovered Elizabeth's brother Alfred Barrett, who
was about to marry without his father's approval and who, like Elizabeth
and Henrietta, would be disinherited as a consequence.

Arriving in Paris on 24 June they took an apartment in the same build-
ing near the Invalides where Robert's father and Sarianna lived. Their stay
was prolonged by the necessity of getting Wilson, who was pregnant, married
to the father of the child, their manservant Ferdinando Romagnoli. Wilson

was Protestant and Ferdinando was Catholic and resolving the difference proved tedious, Wilson in the end however relenting and allowing herself to be married by a priest on 10 July. The Brownings nevertheless took time to see Milsand and Thackeray and his daughters, to visit the painter Rosa Bonheur and to meet prominent Frenchmen such as the writer Prosper Merimée.

On 12 July they were once more in London, where they settled into an apartment in Dorset Street, not far from Wimpole Street; sent Wilson north to her family for her confinement; and gave Ferdinando responsibility for household chores. Elizabeth had been shocked by Wilson's premarital pregnancy but was more distressed by the fact that Wilson would no longer sleep beside Pen and watch over him at night. Ferdinando was appalled by the English weather and impressed upon Pen the advantages that Florence had over London. Arabella regularly took Pen to the Barrett home, where on one occasion he was seen by his grandfather Barrett, who upon asking and then learning who the child was and why he was there, changed the subject and turned away.

Over the next three months the Brownings saw many of their friends and relatives. Dante Gabriel Rossetti, an old admirer, drew Robert's portrait. Tennyson called and read his *Maud* while Rossetti, noticed only by Sarianna, surreptitiously made a sketch of the Laureate. At the same soirée, at which Arabel Barrett, Rossetti's brother, William Michael, and other prominent Pre-Raphaelite artists – William Holman Hunt, Ford Madox Brown and Thomas Woolner – were also present, Robert read 'Fra Lippo Lippi'. The two readings were markedly different, Tennyson's being lyrical and Browning's dramatic. Elizabeth found the Laureate 'captivating with his frankness, confidingness and unexampled *naïveté*! Think of his stopping in "Maud" every now and then – "There's a wonderful touch! That's very tender. How beautiful that is!" Yes, and it *was* wonderful, tender, beautiful, and he read exquisitely in a voice like an organ, rather music than speech' (Kenyon, 2: 213). Rossetti noted that on this 'night of the gods' Robert read 'with as much sprightly variation as there was in Tennyson of sustained continuity'.[1]

Others whom the Brownings saw on this visit to London included Carlyle, Fox, Mrs Sartoris and Fanny Kemble. They lunched with John Ruskin on Denmark Hill near Camberwell and saw his collection of paintings by Turner. They met, apparently for the first time, Philip J. Bailey, the author of *Festus*, the dramatic poem that had enjoyed enormous popularity since it was first published in 1839 and continued to be lengthened. At a breakfast party given by John Kenyon they encountered 'half America and a quarter of London' (Huxley, p. 218). Elizabeth insisted on meeting the famous American spiritualist Daniel Dunglas Home, of whom she had heard in Florence, from Hiram Powers among others, and who was now taking London by storm. At the séance that she and Robert attended, Home summoned spirits that played an accordion, lifted a table, and crowned Elizabeth with a wreath of clematis. She was thrilled; Robert, predictably, was disgusted and not reluctant to show his feelings about the matter.

Browning took his manuscript to his publishers Chapman & Hall almost as soon he arrived in London. It was decided that the material should appear in two volumes, printing of which began almost immediately. A final poem was added in September and Browning was reading proofs before the end of the month. In October he and Elizabeth retired to Paris to await publication on 10 November. The two volumes, together containing fifty-one poems, were entitled *Men and Women*. The title recalls the poet's second letter to Elizabeth Barrett, in which, contrasting himself with her, who speaks out, he allowed that he himself could 'only make men & women speak' (Kintner, 1: 7); it may also refer to the opening lines of the twenty-sixth of the *Sonnets from the Portuguese*: 'I lived with visions for my company / Instead of men and women, years ago'. In subject matter the poems deal mainly with love, art and religion.

The love poems predominate and, unsuprisingly, touch on matters of deep personal concern to the poet and his wife. 'A Lovers' Quarrel' alludes to differences between them concerning, first, Louis Napoleon, who had proclaimed himself Emperor Napoleon III in December 1852, and who had 'taken a bride / To his gruesome side' in January 1853; and secondly, the spiritualism that had been so fashionable in Florence in 1852–3. The speaker regrets his 'sudden word' on these subjects and awaits his beloved's forgiveness 'as before'. Although not properly a love poem, 'Mesmerism', written in the same anapestic metre as 'A Lovers' Quarrel', treats the psychic practice to which Elizabeth had been attracted before her introduction to spiritualism. The mesmerist relates how he draws to him the body and soul of the woman he desires, only in the end to pray that he be restrained from control of another's individuality. As the narrator of 'A Light Woman' says, "Tis an awkward thing to play with souls'.[2] 'A Woman's Last Word', on the other hand, expresses the lady's weariness with contention and promises, should her lover require it, to lay flesh and spirit in his hands, 'tomorrow / Not tonight'. The gentle irony of the ending of these poems mitigates any suggestion of rancour on the part of the speakers.

Several poems dealing with inconstancy in love were perhaps suggested by Robert Browning senior's proposal of marriage that led to the breach-of-promise court case. The speaker of 'Any Wife to Any Husband' lays guilt on her husband by prophesying that after her death he will be attracted by women incapable of the spiritual and physical union characterizing their marriage. In 'A Pretty Woman' the speaker reflects on a woman whose beauty is her most salient and almost her only quality. Why, he asks, should men endow her with qualities that she does not possess? Instead, he advises, treat her like a rose, whose beauty alone is sufficient excuse for her being: 'Smell, kiss, wear it—at last, throw away!' The soliloquizer of 'In a Year' laments her lover's fickleness and his belief that 'Love's so different with us men', while the woman of 'Another Way of Love' considers a course to take with her lover who is bored by her perfect constancy. In 'Misconceptions' the lover who thought to have found perfect joy is undeceived when he learns that his mistress has casually used him in order to move on to other happiness.

Many of the love lyrics represent what Browning told Milsand he was aiming at: 'a first step towards popularity . . .—lyrics with more music and painting than before' (DeVane, p. 207). And although many are brief and seem to exist simply for the sake of blending sight and sound in song, they nevertheless are expressive of the poet's profoundest ideas. In 'Love in a Life' the speaker presents love as an ideal that is never captured: 'door succeeds door' and 'she goes out as I enter'. In the companion lyric 'Life in a Love' the speaker spends his life in love's attainment. In neither poem, however, does the speaker despair; for the quest itself is sufficient for satisfaction. 'Who cares?' he asks in the first, and in the second declares that striving is all:

> No sooner the old hope goes to ground
>   Than a new one, straight to the self-same mark,
> I shape me—
> Ever
> Removed!

Even in those poems where the speakers have gained the loved ones they sought and where constancy is not to be questioned, there is never any expression of desire on their part to submerge their wills in another's or to rest in the perfection of love that they have thus far attained. In the charming monologue 'By the Fire-Side' the speaker anticipates a reminiscence in old age of the scene and time of a crowning moment of love, a 'moment, one and infinite' (181), when love and marriage supervened friendship. Probably reflecting the Alpine landscape near Bagni di Lucca known to the Brownings from their visits there in 1849 and 1853, it is full of personal details such as references to Elizabeth's 'great brow' and 'spirit-small hand' in the penultimate stanza. As for the events, Robert was later to say, 'all but the personality is fictitious—that is, the portraiture only is intended to be like—the circumstances are a mere imaginary framework'.[3] The poem has a double focus, on the present and the past, as the monologist treads back down a path that led 'to an age so blest that, by its side, / Youth seems the waste instead' (124–5). But even thus blissful, the husband sees the time as but a provisional resting place on the journey to a new world beyond death where his wife will be 'just before' and 'see and make me see, for your part, / New depths of the divine' (138–40). Rehearsing the perfect joys of their past and present together, the speaker avoids closure not only by projecting their present into the future but also by forecasting, in the final stanza, that he will think over 'the whole' when autumn comes, 'which I mean to do / One day, as I said before'.[4]

As in all Browning's work, the present is never allowed to be more than a temporary stop, nowness ever and always flowing to the future. The 'infinite moment' is, in fact, no more than a moment in time, and to locate one's whole self in that instant, as did the speaker of 'Cristina', is to submit to stasis and living death. As the speaker of 'Two in the Campagna' says, 'the good minute goes'. Evidently having read Shelley, the lover in that poem would, like him in 'Epipsychidion', submerge his identity in his beloved. 'I would that you were all to me', he says to her; 'I would I could adopt your will, / . . . —your part my part / In life'. But she remains 'just so much, no more'. In spite of himself he can be 'fixed by no friendly star', even though it be, as in 'My Star', one of great beauty and illumination. For, like Pauline's lover, he finds that finitude, phenomenal reality, cannot encompass his infinite desire. And so in the end he is left with the recognition of 'infinite passion, and the pain / Of finite hearts that yearn'.

Such a recognition is denied to the monologist of 'Love Among the Ruins', which, like 'Two in the Campagna', also takes place in a pastoral landscape once filled with the noble edifices of a past civilization. The former, however, is framed in light ('This morn of Rome and May'), while the latter repeats the crepuscular setting of Gray's 'Elegy in a Country Churchyard', as the sheep 'tinkle homeward through the twilight' and leave the world to darkness and to the soliloquizer. Contrasting the past with the present, the speaker in 'Love Among the Runs' reflects on the culture that once flourished here. In this flattened country which 'does not even boast a tree', there was once a 'domed and daring palace' that shot its spires up over the giant wall encircling it. And in the city 'a multitude of men breathed joy and woe', as the desire for glory lured them on and the dread of shame kept them conscientious. But as Gray noted, the paths of glory lead but to the grave. All that remains is a 'single little turret' which marks 'the basement whence a tower in ancient time / Sprang sublime'. Yet in that turret there waits for him a girl with eager eyes and yellow hair, 'breathless, dumb / Till I come', at which point she will not speak but 'give her eyes the first embrace / Of my face'.

Moralizing on the situation, the speaker asserts that the past, for all its architectural splendour and courageous activity, was motivated by imperial conquest and the lust for gold. The city sent forth a million warriors, it built its gods a sky-high pillar, it lived in luxury. And yet in the end what did it all mean? Folly, noise, and sin! They, 'with their triumphs and their glories and the rest'—'Shut them in', the speaker says. For 'Love is best'.

Nearly all readers of the poem have accepted the truth of the moral. After all, it is a constant theme in Browning's work that life and love are better than history and art. Yet, the curious reader is left to wonder, is the love that the soliloquizer envisions indeed best?[5] To him it signifies peace, quietness and utter immobility. Not once does the 'good moment' that he foresees lead to anything other than a release of *his* passion; it is a moment of power and control, qualities that he ironically attributes to the civilization he condemns. The object of it is a young woman – not unlike

Tennyson's solitary Lady of Shalott – who lives in a turret awaiting her lover. Described as almost lifeless ('breathless, dumb'), she and her environment exist in marked contrast to the city and its inhabitants of yore. In the tower 'whence the charioteers caught soul / For the goal, / When the king looked', she motionless is said to look now for her lover, who will hardly give her 'soul'. The love that he praises is, like the present landscape, flat, almost totally lacking in character. It is the love of being, not of becoming, not of the *ewig weibliche* that, in 'By the Fire-Side', leads the lover on to ever greater heights.

The notion of love as striving is perhaps best displayed in 'The Last Ride Together'. Like most of Browning's love poems it is strongly erotically charged,[6] but unlike most erotic literature the emphasis is not on fruition but on postponement. The emphasis is on 'ride' and not on 'last' as the speaker considers the perils of an ending and disclosure. 'Who knows but the world may end tonight?' he asks, and then immediately answers, 'Hush!'

This 'good moment' may in fact not be the last. Although he has failed to secure his mistress's total commitment, at least for the time 'here we are riding, she and I'. And if he has failed to possess her fully, so have others likewise not succeeded in gaining the ambitious ends for which they aimed.

> What hand and brain went ever paired?
> What heart alike conceived and dared?
> What act proved all its thought had been?
> What will but felt the fleshly screen?

The statesman, the warrior, the poet, the sculptor, the musician have all tried to tell what is fit and proper for their hearers and viewers to be and do. Yet none has been able to encompass life itself, as many times they have pretended or deludedly believed. And, for the speaker at least, this is the way things should be; apocalypse is ever to be postponed. If, Faustlike, he had signed a bond granting him all the bliss his heart desired, would he have been content? Most assuredly not. For nothing fixed will ever satisfy for long. And so gladly accepting that 'heaven and she are beyond this ride', he finally considers the possibility that even heaven itself might be a place for riding, where, 'the instant made eternity', he and she might 'for ever ride'.

In Browning's world love is never a matter for the faint-hearted. Indeed, those lovers who are not courageously defiant of the world and its ways are to be condemned. The lovers in 'Respectability' declare that had they followed the conventions of society, which are in fact hypocritical, instead of daring to love as they do, they would have lost time. The lovers in Browning's last and briefest play, the one-act 'In a Balcony', pay the penalty for failure to act on their love. In the first line of the play Norbert says, 'Now!'; and Constance, wishing to maintain their standing with the queen, replies, 'Not now!' Only when it is too late do they cease dissembling and openly avow their love, which, had they done so earlier, might have led to life and happiness.

The debt to be paid for lovers' conformity to social conventions is the subject of 'The Statue and the Bust', and it was a matter of such concern to the poet that he added a coda to point up the moral. Taking Shelley's familiar theme of the rescue of the maiden in the tower (which in a slightly different form Browning had long since adopted as his own) but reworking it, the poem tells of a bride who on her wedding day looks out from her window to see the great duke of Florence riding by. At first sight they fall in love but out of worldly considerations fail to act on their feelings. Temporizing day by day and then year by year, they look upon each other from afar as the duke rides by ('For I ride—what should I do but ride?'). There is however never a 'ride' together, and eventually they find youth and love gone. In the end art is brought in to memorialize the pair, but the bronze statue in the square and the terracotta sculpture are as fixed in their apartness as the lovers were in life and instead of commemorating their love ironically mock them and their cowardliness.

The story is told by a Florentine who after the first stanza never employs the first person. In the coda, on the other hand, which is separated by a line from the main narrative, an unidentified voice speaks as 'I' to point up the implications of such faint-heartedness. It is as though the poet were so eager to make sure that his readers understood what he was getting at that he felt compelled to enter and speak in his own voice. If the lovers had eloped (as, by implication, he and Elizabeth had), they would have got to bliss on earth and thereafter seen God in heaven, where dwell the courageous 'soldier-saints'. As the narrator tells us, for the lady 'the past was a sleep, and her life began' (30) when she fell in love with the duke. Yet unlike Robert, the duke did not spirit her away. And this inaction was nothing less than a crime, although elopement would in the world's eyes have been criminal.

Life's a game, says the 'I', and one should do one's best if one chooses to play. Punning on the world 'Guelph' in the line about the button offering 'the stamp of the very Guelph', referring to both the Florentine and the British ruling dynasty, the poet shows himself in a moment of parabasis attempting to make sure that the moral to be derived from the game is understood to be applicable to his 'virtuous' British readers. Shockingly, the sin he charges to 'each frustrate ghost' is 'the unlit lamp and the ungirt loin', even though the end in sight was a vice. And then, like a Greek chorus, turning directly and challengingly to his audience, the 'I' joins issue and asks the virtuous: 'how strive you?' '*De te, fabula* [This story is about you]', he charges. The unarticulated answer to his question may be, as the pun on 'Guelph' suggests, that in England one strives for money.

In 'The Statue and the Bust' as in his other poems, meaningful action is dependent upon daring. 'Let a man contend to the uttermost / For his life's prize, be it what it will' (242–3), the 'I' of the coda says. The end is little or nothing; what matters are the vision and energy driving the quester on. Nowhere else is this idea more prominent than in the poems dealing with artists. It is presented insistently in 'Fra Lippo Lippi', which delineates not only Browning's own aesthetic ideals but also his poetic way of proceeding.

The poem is based on the early *quattrocento* painter whose works the poet had seen in Florence and whose life he had read about in Vasari's *Lives of the Artists*. What chiefly interested Browning was that Lippo was said to have been the first naturalist and realist in painting and thus the originator of a new kind of art. In the poem Lippo is conscious of being a groundbreaker, of inaugurating something new. 'I've broken bounds', he proudly says (223), and 'paint now as I please' (226), although, breaking with the traditions of ecclesiastical painting, he has often been excoriated. Why, asks the prior of his monastery, does he not continue to paint as Giotto more than a century earlier had painted? Others say that his work betokens 'art's decline' (233) from that of his predecessors, that he is 'not of the true painters, great and old' (234). Lippo is, however, aware of working within a tradition, of being part of the 'complex gin' spoken of in *Sordello* that artists are always making and dismantling. As his work superseded that of Lorenzo Monaco and Fra Angelico, so will his own be radically altered by successors such as 'Hulking Tom', the youngster now painting in his convent.

Significantly, Lippo has been apprehended by the watch as a potential law-breaker, and in explaining why he is in such a situation, a 'monk out of bounds' (341), he simultaneously explains why he paints as he does. Lippo is, in other words, the kind of painter he is because of the kind of man he is. He has broken all the rules that he as a monk should be observing, and in defence of his behaviour he suggests that his art, now approved by so exalted a patron as Cosimo de Medici, reflects the life that he lives. As Browning noted in the *Essay on Shelley*, 'greatness in a work suggests an adequate instrumentality', and there is therefore a correspondence between the man and the work he produces. Lippo was a street urchin who was literally given to the Church. Having faced deprivation, he became sensitized to the world; experience increased his power of observation: 'soul and sense of him grow sharp alike, / He learns the look of things' (124–5). And when he took up painting, he painted what he saw. This, of course, was not what his immediate artistic predecessors had done. Like the unknown painter of 'Pictor Ignotus' they had, in their attempt to exalt the spirit and denigrate the body, painted men and women not as they are but as ethereal beings of hieratic attitudes who look as though they took a mess of shadows for their meat. His fellow monks, who were simple men, loved Lippo's work because it resembled what they actually saw, and delighted in pointing out the familiar figures that they discerned therein represented. The prior, on the other hand, would have none of it, insisting that the painter's business is to make his viewers forget the flesh and to paint soul: 'Give us no more of body than shows soul'

(188). To Lippo this makes no sense, and he then proceeds with his
defence of realistic painting.

> God created the world, he says, and so it must be good.
> —The beauty and the wonder and the power,
> The shapes of things, their colours, lights and shades,
> Changes, surprises,—and God made it all! . . .
>   This world's no blot for us
> Nor blank; it means intensely, and means good.
>   (283–5, 313–14)

Why not, then, paint these things 'just as they are, careless what comes of
it?' (294). But, as Lippo proceeds dialectically, it can be objected, what
is the good of such an enterprise? God's works already exist and can be
seen by everyone. Unless you improve on nature (as eighteenth-century
aestheticians were to insist), what is the point? Lippo's answer is that the
artist is (what is called in *Sordello*) a maker-see. It is the purpose of his art
to defamiliarize that which has become dulled for us by habituation;

> we're made so that we love
> First when we see them painted, things we have passed
> Perhaps a hundred times nor cared to see;
> And so they are better, painted—better to us,
> Which is the same thing. Art was given for that;
> God uses us to help each other so,
> Lending our minds out.
>   (300–6)

And in so doing, painting higher things – Creation, the saints – with the
same realistic truth that shows 'the value and significance of flesh' (268),
the early Renaissance painter assumes in an increasingly secular age the
hermeneutic function historically reserved to the clergy: 'Interpret God to
all of you!' (311). It is no wonder that his prior is so uneasy with Lippo's
work.

Lippo is quick to admit, parenthetically (298), that art cannot reproduce
nature. As his creator had frequently pointed out, the artist can but re-
present.[7] This does not mean, however, that if words or paint cannot
capture an existing reality there is no such thing. Although he is ever
aware of, and occasionally seems to lament, the inability of art to capture
nature or truth, Browning did not believe, like some late twentieth-century
deconstructionists, that it was a mere logocentric prejudice that an in-
dependent, metaphysical reality exists beyond texts. What he through Lippo
wishes to make clear, however, is that it is *his* perception of reality that
informs his art, and for it to do so he must represent himself in his work.
In the intended picture, *Coronation of the Virgin*, that Lippo will paint for
the Sant' Ambrogio convent, he will depict himself and on a scroll in the
painting will write '*Iste perfecit opus* [This man did the work]'. Like the
poet, Lippo is sure to make his presence known.

It is part of Lippo's (and Browning's) aesthetic credo that all art is praise, even though it is inadequately rendered. At the end of his monologue Lippo tells the watch a little parable. In the picture he is to paint of God, the Madonna and babe, surrounded by saints, he is, as he said, himself to be depicted, appearing from an unexpected corner. But he is no sooner entered into this holy scene than he is amazed and paralysed to find himself in such presence. Looking for a way to escape, he all of a sudden is stopped by an angel, who says that his art, for all its earthly realism, is celestially approved. So he scuttles off to some safe bench, still holding the angel's hand: 'And so all's saved for me, and for the church / A pretty picture gained' (388–9). The point of the story is to indicate that Lippo is not entrapped by the fiction that is his art. His painting is not heavenly purity; it is Lippo's rendition of it that he has violated by his presence in it; it is not *the* truth but *his* fiction of representation.

Such a disclaimer and such modesty could never issue from Browning's Andrea del Sarto. A companion monologue to 'Fra Lippo Lippi', 'Andrea del Sarto' is also a pendant to 'Pictor Ignotus'. It is however a more complicated poem than 'Pictor', as indeed nearly all the monologues of *Men and Women* are more complex than those printed in the 1840s. As Herbert Tucker notes, these later speakers are more aware of what they are doing when they speak; they know that their monologues are fabrications put forth tendentiously.[8] Like 'Pictor', 'Andrea' is a confession, a confession of failure. The speaker alone knows what he might have been, and although he tries to place the blame for his lack of achievement on his wife, he knows, no matter how hard he tries to hide the truth from himself, that such attribution is a fiction. This is why Andrea speaks as a kind of manic-depressive, alternating between states of elation and constriction.

The poem is parenthetically entitled '(Called "The Faultless Painter")', and it is the chief irony of the poem that Andrea's unforgivable fault is to be faultless. In technique and skill he has achieved perfection, but beneath the flawless surface of his paintings there is only spiritual vacuity, the lack of what Browning characteristically calls soul. For Andrea has mastered his art and ceased to strive for more ambitious goals. Enunciating the famous Browningesque philosophy of the imperfect, Andrea confesses that he has rested content in the present and forgone anticipation of the future, has painted himself in, as it were; and thus encircled he, like the formal perfectionist Eglamor in *Sordello*, has had nothing left over for other work to come. Other painters have not achieved his matchless technical perfection, and yet 'there burns a truer light of God in them' than in 'this low-pulsed forthright craftsman's hand' (79, 82). Whatever fire of spirit might once have burnt within him is now almost extinguished, leaving only a grey ember reflected in his 'silver-grey / Placid and perfect . . . art' (98–9).

Andrea's aesthetic inadequacy stems from a failure of energy, an unwillingness to strive. And this hoarding of his talents has led to moral failure as well. During the year spent at Fontainebleau, in the employ of

King Francis, he managed to overleap the confining walls of ego and paint in a wholly different fashion. Touched by alterity, he saw with others' eyes and burnt with others' fire. But in time 'too live the life grew, golden and not grey' for 'the weak-eyed bat' that had been tempted 'out of the grange whose four walls make his world' (168–70). Though exhilarated, he could not maintain the energy required in the open world. And so he, like Pictor Ignotus, retreated to the sterile safety of enclosure.

Cowardly as he is, Andrea places the blame for his artistic failure on Lucrezia, his wife, who like Fra Lippo wants to escape confinement, from the four walls of 'the melancholy little house' (212) to the open air and vitality offered by the so-called 'cousin' down below. 'And had you not grown restless', Andrea charges her, he would have continued at Fontainebleau, where he was doing his best work. And at the end he also shifts blame to her for his crimes as well as for his artistic failure. But not once does he make his denunciations so squarely and forthrightly as to cause her to defend herself; for no sooner does he charge her with something than he quickly withdraws the accusation.

All along Andrea is aware of being judged, judged in comparison with Leonardo, Michelangelo and Raphael. Had Lucrezia, with all her physical virtues, which he has displayed in the paintings in which she has served as model, also given him 'soul', 'we might have risen to Rafael, I and you', might have lived 'side by side with Agnolo' (119, 130). These others have prevailed, however, because they had no wives. And, victim that Andrea is, his present situation 'must suffice [him] here' (259). But what if, in heaven, he were given one more chance, 'four great walls in the New Jerusalem' (261) for him and the three other great painters to cover? 'At the end', Andrea had said earlier, 'God, I conclude, compensates, punishes,' and so it is better 'that I am something underrated here' (141–3). In so far as he thinks of the future at all it is in imagining how he must be the eternal victim. For still the award escapes him in heaven as on earth, and the three great painters overcome because, he says, 'there's still Lucrezia, —as I choose' (266). Whatever the cost, the status quo is preferable to change and the demands that it entails, and so he elects to fail in both art and love. 'Go, my Love', he says, permitting his wife to betray him and portraying himself as more pitiable than ever in the role of victim of infinite resignation.[9] Andrea's failure of both artistic vision and moral courage is suggested by the fact that the heaven he conceives and would feel most at home in is an enclosed room of four great walls.

In both 'Fra Lippo Lippi' and 'Andrea del Sarto' artistic creativity is linked to sexual vitality. Lippo sports abroad with prostitutes (and other ladies as well), while Andrea at home is unable to satisfy his wife and keep her from her lover. It is tempting to read these poems in biographical terms and to see in them Browning's delight in marriage as a stimulus to his renewed poetic activity in the 1850s.[10] Yet when we recall 'Pictor Ignotus' (or even *Pauline*), we note that from earlier years – and indeed, as we shall see, almost throughout Browning's poetry – artistic creation is an aspect of sexual potency. This is in striking contrast to Tennyson's verse, where sexual frustration finds release in artistic creation. It is telling that the best-known formulation of Browning's philosophy of the imperfect – 'a man's reach should exceed his grasp' ('Andrea', 97) – should be expressed in sexually suggestive terms.

Browning's two chief poems dealing with music are spoken not by the composers themselves but by performers who seek in the music they play a kind of sexual energy that they do not find. Although monologues, they are different from the dramatic monologues dealing with painters in that the performers converse with the composers about the meaning of their music. Formally these poems are more like the parleyings of the 1880s than the dramatic monologues of the 1840s and 1850s. Ironically, in both 'A Toccata of Galuppi's' and 'Master Hugues of Saxe-Gotha' the speakers ask of music, the most fluid of the arts, a fixed meaning; and in them Browning treats a matter that was later to become of such importance to him, namely, why art loses its emotional charge for later ages.

In 'A Toccata of Galuppi's' the performer, an Englishman who has never left home, has an idea of eighteenth-century Venice that is totally at variance with what he hears in the music that so delighted the people of that time. For the speaker, Venice of the preceding century represents love and life in colourful, romantic gaiety. The inhabitants were truly alive, always on the move, living both in the pleasurable moment and in anticipation of future enjoyments. They 'made up fresh adventures for the morrow' (12), never considered endings, of either kisses or life itself. And amidst all this vitality Galuppi played his music, which they found utterly gratifying. How could this be? For when the speaker, a scientist who is ever searching for the answer to earth's puzzles, tries to reason out the meaning of Galuppi's toccata, he discerns only 'cold music' that betokens a moral judgement passed on the frivolous Venetians who never realized that 'the kissing had to stop' (42). 'Dust and ashes, dead and done with' (35) – mortality, finality, closure: that is the fixed meaning of the music for him. Galuppi tells that 'Venice spent what Venice earned' (35), the performer sadly says, using one of Browning's favourite economic metaphors. But the 'dear dead women, with such hair, too—what's become of the gold / Used to hang and brush their bosoms' (44–5)?

The monologue is in effect a dramatization of a man's failure of imagination.[11] A repressed Englishman, the speaker obviously longs for the erotic freedom that for him Venice signifies. The chief irony of his monologue resides in the fact that while on the conscious, rational level Galuppi bespeaks a moral meaning that the speaker takes 'with such a heavy mind' (3), on the unconscious, emotional level desire rises to a mighty pitch as the pianist performs. 'I can hardly misconceive you; it would prove me deaf and blind', the speaker says in the beginning. But as it turns out, for all his alleged rationality, he is proven uncomprehending of both Galuppi's music and his own sexual desire. Because of a kind of scientific prejudice the speaker is blocked from accepting the emotional release of his vicarious 'performance'. In the end, desire not spent but saved, he leaves off playing and admits, 'I feel chilly and grown old'.

In 'Master Hugues of Saxe-Gotha' the performer on a church organ asks in a 'colloquy' (9) with the composer what meaning resides in his giant, difficult fugues. 'Dead though, and done with' (8), Hugues nevertheless enjoys the performer's conviction that behind the intricate interplay of voices there is something in his music that was significant and made it prized in its composer's time. Yet with its 'affirming, denying, / Holding, riposting, subjoining' its 'import' cannot be grasped (89, 91–2). And unable to make it speak its meaning, the speaker makes of the music a 'moral of Life' (106), which with its interweaving of human thought and actions obscures truth and nature. In the end, however, the speaker is unsure of his moral and suggests that the fugue he plays may provide nothing more than an opportunity to play joyfully, 'unstop the full-organ, / Blare out the *mode Palestrina*' (139–40). And that's enough, for the performer at least. Not everyone can be a hermeneuticist: 'Do I carry the moon in my pocket?'

'Transcendentalism: A Poem in Twelve Books' takes up the question of meaning more forthrightly. Doubtless addressed to Carlyle, who had advised Robert, Elizabeth and every other poet who would listen to cease writing verse, which was meant for earlier, simpler ages, and take up prose, the proper medium for modern thought, the parleying is a defence of lyric expression, a poetry of spareness and suggestive imagery that recalls us to an earlier life of feeling that has been overlaid by adult rationality. A philosophical poem, unadorned with sights and sounds, provides only the 'subtler meanings of what roses say' (36), while song can yield 'the sudden rose herself' (39), thereby 'pouring heaven into this shut house of life' (45). In the end the speaker urges his brother poet to turn to the harp again.

The brotherhood of artists working in all media is the basic concern of the parleying by someone very like Browning with Giotto and other antique painters in 'Old Pictures in Florence'.[12] Dead long since, they now live with God and 'have all attained to be poets' (55); they are far from being done with, as the witless believe. Taking up a familiar theme from *Sordello*, the speaker insists, 'Old and New are fellows: / A younger succeeds to an elder brother' (62–3). Yet the world soon forgets its artists or, not forgetting, separates them from their successors by naming them Old Masters. Embracing Browning's philosophy of becoming, the speaker vehemently asserts that all life is one. There is a common soul in 'the race of Man / That receives life in parts to live in a whole, / And grow here according to God's clear plan' (110–12).

Yet such a plan is often not discerned. For many the great artists of the past are stumbling blocks; they and their attainments are so great and we of the present are so small. We can, however, learn from them, and once having gained what they can teach, we can, in a manner of speaking, shove them aside: 'What's come to perfection perishes' (130). It is the speaker's 'fancy' that when this life is ended there is new work for the soul in another state, that life continues in unlimited stages though on different scales. 'Yet I hardly know', the speaker is quick to say, insisting that such utterance is but a 'fancy' of the moment. Very much aware that human thought is conditioned by time and place, he is quick to admit that 'what and where depend on life's minute' (138).

Browning's interest in the possibility of an afterlife is reflected especially in the two companion epistolary monologues 'An Epistle Containing the Strange Medical Experience of Karshish, the Arab Physician' and 'Cleon', both set in the first century AD. Karshish is a medical man travelling in Judea. He has met someone named Lazarus who claims to have died and then been restored to life. Reporting the encounter to his medical teacher, he intermixes the story of Lazarus with accounts of herbs and other medical curiosities. Attempting to explain how Lazarus' version of the miracle is attributable to mania induced by trance, he characterizes Jesus as a master physician who wrought the cure. He tries to strengthen his naturalistic explanation further by describing Lazarus as a fifty-year-old man of child-like disposition, one unable to make distinctions and appreciate the relative value of things. Karshish cannot, however, put out of his mind that the miracle might really have been as Lazarus reported. If so, it is plain that one who has encountered the infinite is totally unfitted for life in the world, thus 'professedly the faultier that he knows / God's secret, while he holds the thread of life' (200–1). Further, he is set apart from his fellows by his special knowledge and his inability to speak of it. In sum, Lazarus is rendered inert by his encounter with the Absolute and can do no more than love all humanity while awaiting another death.

Near the close of his letter Karshish writes, with embarrassment, that Lazarus regards his curer as the living God, 'creator and sustainer of the world, / That came and dwelt in flesh on it awhile' (269–70). What sane man can believe such a possibility? Yet in a postscript Karshish reveals the impact that the story has had upon him. Would it not be wonderful, he says, if the God of power were also the God of love? If God were to say: 'Thou hast no power nor mayst conceive of mine, / But love I gave thee, with myself to love' (310–11)?[13] But ironically undercutting the expression of all his heart longs for and using the same words as he previously employed to characterize other medical curiosities, Karshish ends, 'The madman saith He said so: it is strange'.

In 'Cleon' the writer is a Greek who regards himself as the summation of Greek culture. Poet, painter, sculptor, musician – 'In brief, all arts are mine' (61) – he possesses everything that material culture can provide. Yet replying in the manner of Greek dialectic to the ruler Protus who has written to ask what comfort is to be found in facing death, Cleon admits that in spite of all his accomplishments he finds no solace when thinking of his mortality. He offers only the consolation that one must be 'glad for what was' (237).

It is apparent from the beginning that Cleon does not accept Browning's philosophy of becoming, does not understand the Browning notion that 'imperfection means perfection hid' (185). He wishes Protus the reward of 'eventual rest' 'within the eventual element of calm' (33, 42). As an artist he is appreciative of tradition, as the speaker of 'Old Pictures in Florence' was, but unlike the monologist in that other poem he sees the artistic enterprise not in terms of setting up and then dismantling but of working towards some 'composite' (65), 'a synthesis [where] the labour ends' (94). Though he has not equalled Homer, Terpander or Phidias and his friend in their separate spheres of excellence, he has nevertheless triumphed by 'running these into one soul' or consciousness (144), the fully cultivated man able to perfect what others inaugurated.

Yet for Cleon this is not ultimately a cause for happiness: for the gift of culture is self-consciousness. All too aware of our limited capability to perform what we can envision, we are inevitably led to the sad conclusion that 'life's inadequate to joy, / As the soul sees joy, tempting life to take' (249–50). What is required is more time, more opportunity for further life. Protus had said that Cleon did in fact possess immortality through his art, but this is a notion that Cleon is quick to refute; art is not life, is indeed less than life:

> Say rather that my fate is deadlier still,
> In this, that every day my sense of joy
> Grows more acute, my soul (intensified
> By power and insight) more enlarged, more keen;
> While every day my hairs fall more and more,
> My hand shakes, and the heavy years increase—
> The horror quickening still from year to year,
> The consummation coming past escape
> When I shall know most, and yet least enjoy.
>   (309–17)

Inducing from his own need the necessity for an afterlife, Cleon envisions a future 'unlimited in capability / For joy, as this is in desire for joy' (326–7). But alas, though he has allowed the human race to evolve to its present state of physical and artistic perfection, Zeus has not granted the gift of immortality – 'and alas, / He must have done so, were it possible!' (334–5).

Obsessed by apocalyptic closure,[14] Cleon shuts out possibility, one example of which the letter-writer alludes to in his postscript. Protus has asked about a visitor to the Greek isles named Paulus who preaches the gospel of Christ and to whom he also has written, presumably to enquire about his sect's views on death. How, Cleon asks, could the king possibly believe that this barbarian Jew has access to knowledge denied to Greeks? What Paul preaches is a doctrine that no sane man could hold. Like Karshish, and even echoing his words, Cleon is prevented by a cultural prejudice from embracing the answer that lies so closely at hand.

Browning probably cast both 'Karshish' and 'Cleon' in the form of letters to suggest an ironic or parodic relationship to the Pauline epistles of the New Testament. Where Paul's letters, addressed to the Christian faithful, are written by one ready and willing to give his life for Christ, Karshish's and Cleon's, addressed to recipients almost totally ignorant of the Christian story, are written by persons who approach Christianity with minds as blank slates and induce Christian belief as a result of their own spiritual needs.[15]

'Saul' likewise deals with the 'induction' of Christianity and formally with biblical parallels. The first nine sections of the poem were published in the *Dramatic Romances & Lyrics* of 1845. Elizabeth thought that they were sufficient to make a complete poem (Kintner, 1: 173), but Robert was not satisfied that they had reached a proper conclusion and so printed them with a promissory note ('End of Part the First') that more was to come. This first part, sung to the spritually benumbed King Saul by the shepherd boy David, recalls earth's beauties and bounties, great moments in Jewish history, his people's hymns of aspiration, the greatness of Saul's accomplishments – all the things that Saul has to be thankful for. Yet the king, who has every reason to praise and thank God, is unable to utter a word or lift his eyes to heaven. Generically this fragment is unlike anything else in the 1845 volume. What it most resembles is a Davidic psalm; that is, David sings in the manner of the reputed author of Psalms.[16] Browning recognized that a song of a different nature was necessary to bring Saul out of his lethargy and so complete the poem. The solution he eventually hit upon was to go beyond Psalms, as in the first nine sections he went beyond the Historical Books, to the Prophets.

David realizes that Saul cannot be comforted by an account of the past but must be persuaded of a future:

> thou doest well in rejecting mere comforts
> that spring
> From the mere mortal life held in common by man and
> by brute:
> In our flesh grows the branch of this life, in our soul
> it bears fruit.
>
> (148–50)

David, in other words, expounds in song the philosophy of becoming and in doing so offers a prophecy. Through his own love for Saul, his willingness to sacrifice himself for his beloved king, he infers and then prophesies the Incarnation. If he possess this sacrificial love, can God do less? God is revealed in nature as power and law, and in his, David's, own love God is revealed to him as love. God can accomplish what he, David, only desires to accomplish; God can give him continuing life, offering 'the next world's reward and repose, by the struggles in this' (286). This is the God infinite in the power to love but weak in the power to be beloved; and it is this 'weakness in strength' (308) that David seeks in Godhead. And finding it, he predicts that

                                                    it shall be
A Face like my face that receives thee; a Man like to me,
Thou shalt love and be loved by, for ever: a Hand like
                              this hand
Shall throw open the gates of new life to thee! See the
                          Christ stand!
                                                      (309–12)

It might be expected that the poem would end here at its climax. Yet it continues for another twenty-three lines with David's departure from the tent in which Saul has been revived from his benumbed state of death-in-life. The last section in fact has nothing to do with Saul at all but records the experience of David as he goes home. Around him there were 'witnesses', 'cohorts', 'angels', and 'powers' that were, curiously, 'unuttered, unseen' and that he 'repressed'. In a situation similar to that in 'Christmas-Eve', amidst celestial fireworks, with earth awakened and the crew of hell set loose, he was impelled forward by 'the Hand' that 'supported, suppressed' the tumult until finally earth came to rest. Nevertheless, on the following morning the birds and the flowers reacted with awe when he approached and the brooks murmured with 'hushed voices – "E'en so, it is so!"'

This ending with its sense of awe is reminiscent of Tennyson's symbolic closes and on the face of it seems highly uncharacteristic of Browning. Yet when we investigate the passage more carefully we see that almost every assertion is undercut or negated. Nothing is actually seen or heard, at least by the physical senses, and this leads us to question, as in 'Christmas-Eve' and 'Easter-Day', whether anything happened at all. In this respect, the final section of 'Saul' is very Browningesque to the extent that dogmatic assertion is not allowed to stand unqualified.

The longest poem in Men and Women treats directly the whole question of dogma. It is also the cleverest poem in the two volumes but because of its length almost too clever by half. 'Bishop Blougram's Apology' is the defence made by a Roman Catholic bishop of himself and his faith to a journalist, Gigadibs, who believes him hypocritical. The question that Gigadibs implicitly asks is: How can any intelligent person believe in Christianity? In answering this Blougram says that one cannot live by ideals that cannot be realized but must deal with what is. Thus when faced with religious belief or unbelief, neither of which can be proven, he has chosen belief because it is the best principle by which he and others can live and be happy. And having elected belief, he has embraced it in its more dogmatic, authoritarian form because this not only yields better results but also suits his dominating nature. He admits that enthusiasm for belief or even unbelief were perhaps preferable to his own qualified credence, but he goes on to say that doubt proves faith, in that faith is dynamic and is a matter of constant discovery: 'If you desire faith—then you've faith enough' (634). The facts don't matter:

It is the idea, the feeling and the love,
God means mankind should strive for and show forth
Whatever be the process to that end,—
And not historic knowledge, logic sound,
And metaphysical acumen.

(621–5)

He closes by also noting that belief pays off in a worldly sense: he finds
material rewards in belief while Gigadibs has nothing to show for his
unbelief. Having been absolutely frank with the journalist, Blougram now
challenges him to print the substance of the interview, which no one will
believe.

Bishop Blougram was modelled on Nicholas Wiseman, who had been
named cardinal and archbishop of Westminster when the Roman Catholic
hierarchy was introduced into England in 1850. Much of the discursive
monologue appears jesuitical, and much of it is expressive of some of
Browning's most cherished beliefs. In a coda the reader is told that
Blougram believed 'half he spoke' and 'said true things, but called them
by wrong names' (980, 996). Gigadibs is said, in a final passage that was
designedly made ambiguous, to have departed for Australia to settle there.
'I hope', says the narrator, 'By this time he has tested his first plough, /
And studied his last chapter of Saint John'. Did Gigadibs leave England
because he was revolted by people like Blougram? Has he taken up intensive
study of the Bible? Has he given up study of the Gospels? Did he read the
final chapter of St John's Gospel in which Jesus thrice tests Peter, each
time commanding, 'Feed my sheep', this being a comment on the inad-
equacy of Blougram's pastoral responsibility? The answer to these questions
is that we shall never know. What we are left with in the end is the poet
offering us himself and undecidability.[17]

The ambiguity of the final line of 'Childe Roland to the Dark Tower
Came' in like manner leaves us with questions. In this poem Browning
takes up the familiar motif of quest and struggle and locates it in a waste
land. 'My first thought was, he lied in every word', the monologist begins,
distrusting any guide that might lead him to the tower that he has been
seeking for years and iterating his belief that he is left with himself alone
in pursuit of his goal. Yet even though he suspects a trick, he nevertheless
follows in the direction pointed by the 'hoary cripple, with malicious eye'
(2). As he wanders through uncharted territory, Roland can see no progress.
To fail as others, 'The Band', have failed to reach the tower would be
success enough. Still he continues through a hateful terrain of horror and
death, and with each step he feels that he is just as far from the end as
he was at the beginning. Suddenly, through a kind of transformation of
consciousness, he sees what he has been looking for: 'Burningly it came
on me all at once, / This was the place!' (175–6). And what he sees is a
loathsome landscape in the midst of which lies the Dark Tower, which is
as abhorrent as the natural scenery surrounding it: a 'round squat turret,

blind as the fool's heart, / Built of brown stone, without a counterpart / In the whole world' (182–4).

When most isolated, Roland paradoxically had been most united with his predecessors who had made the quest. For he had been constantly mindful

> Of all the lost adventurers my peers,—
> How such a one was strong, and such was bold,
> And such was fortunate, yet each of old
>   Lost, lost!
>
> (195–8)

Yet when he gains the tower, which comes to him and not he to it, he sees his forerunners, standing on the hillside in a sheet of flame, there to watch the last of him; he recognizes them all, forming 'a living frame / For one more picture!' (200–1). And yet he dauntless gives a blast on his horn: '"*Childe Roland to the Dark Tower came*"'.

What does the horn blast signify? Is it a gesture of praise or dispraise? It is probably of neither one nor the other but of both – of praise of himself for enduring and of dispraise of what he has had to endure. The quest has been hateful and the goal unworthy, yet he has been relentless and finished with panache. At the very least, even though it cannot be known whether the quest has succeeded or failed, it has proven a triumph of personality,[18] and in blowing the horn Roland makes his personality known, in effect signing his monologue in somewhat the same way as Browning signs his poems. 'Look', says Roland as he sounds his horn, 'Look, it's me, Childe Roland, who has said and done all this'.

The poem has been often read as an allegory. Questioned about it, Browning claimed that it came upon him 'as a kind of dream' and was no more than 'a fantasy' with no allegorical intention. Yet when asked if it meant 'he that endureth to the end shall be saved', Browning answered, 'Yes, just about that' (DeVane, pp. 229, 231). It is, however, most tempting to read the poem as an allegory of the poet's own aesthetic adventure, of his sense of traveling along difficult, uncharted paths to a goal which Shelley and other prior poets had in fact reached in their own ways and under whose inspiration he proceeded.[19] Sordello's view of the gin of poetry is surely coincident with Roland's discovery that he has in fact been following in the same direction as his lost peers.

The issue of the quest is also prominent in 'A Grammarian's Funeral'. The unnamed Renaissance scholar was single-minded in pursuit of mastery of the Greek language and succeeded in clearing up many of the fine points of its grammar. But in doing so he gave up ordinary life – 'decided not to Live but Know' (139) – and aged quickly. Fittingly he is to be buried on the heights, removed from the world of men and women: 'Lofty designs must close in like effects' (145). But what is the significance of this lonely tomb on high?

The question that the monologue implicitly asks is this: Is the grammar-ian to be applauded or condemned?[20] Again, as is usual in Browning's work, the answer is neither one nor the other but both. From the vitalist point of view that the poet constantly expounds, the grammarian is to be found guilty of pursuing an unworthy goal. At the expense of living he worked on what Browning in 1863 told Tennyson was intended to be 'the biggest of the littlenesses':[21]

> He settled *Hoti's* business—let it be!—
> Properly based *Oun*—
> Gave us the doctrine of the enclitic *De*.

And in so doing he became – what to Browning with his praise of Eros was among the gravest defects – 'dead from the waist down' (129–32). This was a life thrown away for almost nothing. Yet whatever the goal, the grammarian endured in his quest of it. It was his whole life and he will-ingly sacrificed everything for it, moving like Roland in his own kind of waste land. 'Cramped and diminished', he

> stepped on with pride
> Over men's pity;
> Left play for work, and grappled with the world.
> (38, 43–5)

Rightly, then, he is to be praised for having gained his resting place on high 'where meteors shoot, clouds form, / Lightnings are loosened, / Stars come and go' (141–3).

In Browning's monologues there is always an anterior life. 'Let us begin and carry up this corpse', the grammarian's disciple commences. Corre-spondingly in the poet's work there is always more to be said, as in the final line of 'The Grammarian's Funeral' where the world goes about its business 'living and dying'. Appropriately the first poem of *Men and Women*, 'Love Among the Ruins', takes the past as its present point of departure, while the last monologue in the two volumes begins by alluding to the prior 'fifty men and women' and ends with the offering of a picture imagined but unpainted and a song conceived but unsung.

Dedicated to Elizabeth and entitled 'One Word More', the final poem was written in September 1855 after the rest of the poems had gone to press. On the manuscript Browning gave it the title 'A Last Word, to E.B.B.' and then changed it in proof. In choosing the new title Robert was perhaps thinking of Elizabeth's letter to him of 31 August 1845 when, rejecting any thought of their life together, she said: 'Therefore we must leave this subject—& I must trust you to leave it without one word more' (Kintner, 1: 179). More importantly he doubtless gave it its present name in a move consciously designed to forestall closure.

In 'One Word More' the poet frankly identifies himself as the speaker, pretending to 'speak this once in my true person' (137). This is of course an ironic statement, since we have noted how time and again the poet injects himself into the previous poems. In the coda to 'The Statue and the Bust', in 'By the Fire-Side' or 'Old Pictures in Florence' the speaker's voice and situation are hardly to be differentiated from the poet's. Further, there are little personal footprints all along the way, as when in 'A Light Woman' the speaker offers the subject of the poem to 'Robert Browning, you writer of plays' (55). Everywhere there are, as in Fra Lippo Lippi's paintings, signs that '*Iste perfecit opus* [This man did the work]' ('Fra Lippo', 377). In 'One Word More' Robert admits that he has gathered men and women so as to 'enter each and all, and use their service, / Speak from every mouth' (131–2). But for this once he will speak 'not as Lippo, Roland or Andrea' (138).

As K. W. Grandsen remarks, in this poem 'the ironic mode is itself the persona: the poet wears the mask of art'.[22] For the voice is not new: it is presented in another way, just as the speaker says that he employs unrhymed trochaic pentameter lines for the first and last time in his poetic career so as to make 'a strange art of an art familiar' (124). Browning's aim in 'One Word More' is essentially the same as in the previous fifty poems: to de-customize the familiar by lifting it out of the field of ordinary perception and placing it within a new artistic network of relationships.

In this case, the speaker says, it is the attempt to express his love spontaneously and artlessly that prompts him to employ a different mode. Raphael wrote sonnets to his beloved, and Dante wished to paint a picture of Beatrice. Attempting to express feelings in ways impossible in their usual modes, they hoped to 'leave the artist, / Gain the man's joy, miss the artist's sorrow' (71–2). Obviously reflecting on the failure of his work to gain wide approval and implicitly linking his exile in Italy with Dante's in Ravenna and Israel's in Egypt, Browning moves from Dante to Moses to point out that the work of the innovating artist is always subject to denigration. It is the artist's sorrow that in condescending to a material medium, he desecrates the ideal: 'Heaven's gift takes earth's abatement' (73). Further, he cannot help remembering, like Moses who smote the rock to provide the Israelites with water, that the crowd always expects him to be the artist, the miracle worker, and has no sympathy for him as a man. So, then, to gain the man's joy, he who cannot fittingly paint, carve statues or make music must resort to verse alone – 'I stand of my attainment' (112) – although in a new way, 'a semblance of resource' (117).

The pretence of self-revelation for the nonce leads the speaker to the myth of the moon goddess showing a different side to a mortal lover, one that is for ever unseen by the ordinary world, as the divine vision of Moses and Aaron must remain a mystery to others. Every person has 'two soul-sides, one to face the world with, / One to show a woman when he loves her!' (185–6). What he shows here is for Elizabeth alone, although 'One Word More' is a poem to be published and thus to be shown and, perhaps, unappreciated, by the world at large. Significantly, the last of *Men and Women* ends with the poet's refusal to articulate meaning, as looking

on his own, the hidden side of his 'moon of poets', he sees 'the novel /
Silent silver lights and darks undreamed of, / Where I hush and bless
myself with silence' (188, 195–7). In silence he preserves the possibility of
the one word more that Robert Browning, the showman of *Men and
Women*, might say.

8

The Last Years Together

The popularity that Browning had hoped for did not come. As they read the reviews of *Men and Women* in their Paris apartment, both Robert and Elizabeth were dismayed and disheartened. To many of the reviewers the matter was arcane, the style was bizarre and inappropriate, the poems seemed to lack unity and order; in short, still charging obscurity as Browning's great fault, they almost uniformly failed to understand that the poet was not working in conventional modes but exploring new territory.

Defending himself to John Ruskin, who had written in puzzlement about the poems and offering advice, Browning provided as clear a statement of his poetic procedure as he was ever to enunciate. In his view, he said, poetry was a putting of the 'infinite within the finite'. 'I *know* that I don't make out my conception by my language', he acknowledged. 'You would have me paint it all plain out, which can't be'. Yet, he went on, 'by various artifices I try to make shift with touches and bits of outlines which *succeed* if they bear the conception from me to you'. In other words, not by language alone but also by discontinuities and manipulation of perspective he hopes to communicate 'the whole [that] is all but a simultaneous feeling with me'. Do not ask for logical copulas that will get the reader from one place to another. 'In *prose* you may criticise so—because that is the absolute representation of portions of truth, what chronicling is to history'. Therefore, he tells Ruskin, 'in asking for more *ultimates* you must accept less *mediates*, nor expect that a Druid stone-circle will be traced for you with as few breaks to the eye as the North Crescent and South Crescent that go together so cleverly in many a suburb'.[1] In sum, Browning was characterizing his as protosymbolist art, symbolism being the art of juxtaposing without links.

After most of the reviews of *Men and Women* had appeared, Browning wrote to his publisher, Edward Chapman, from Paris in April 1856, excoriating critics and public alike:

the public . . . cry out for new things and when you furnish them with what they cried for, 'it's *so* new', they grunt. The half-dozen people who know and could impose their opinions on the whole sty of grunters say nothing to *them* . . . and speak so low in my own ear that it's lost to all intents and purposes. (*NL*, pp. 92–3)

Yet various appraisals of the 1855 poems were not so universally damning as Browning pretended. Carlyle privately acknowledged Browning's 'keenest just insight into men and things . . . Rhythm there is too, endless poetic fancy, symbolical *help* to express; and if not melody always or often . . . , there is what the Germans call *Takt*, – fine *dancing*, if to the music only of *drums*'.[2] George Eliot, at this time unknown to the poet but later to become a friend, wrote perceptively in the *Westminster Review* for January 1856. 'To read poems is often a substitute for thought', she said. But let the reader

> expect no such drowsy passivity in reading Browning. Here he will find no conventionality, no melodious commonplace, but freshness, originality, sometimes eccentricity of expression; no didactic laying-out of a subject, but dramatic indication, which requires the reader to trace by his own mental activity the underground stream of thought that jets out in elliptical and pithy verse. To read Browning he must exert himself . . . Indeed, in Browning's best poems he makes us feel that what we took for obscurity in him was superficiality in ourselves. . . . Turning from the ordinary literature of the day to such a writer as Browning, is like turning from Flotow's music . . . to the distinct individuality of Chopin's Studies or Schubert's Songs.

Milsand understood precisely what Browning was up to and spoke out publicly in praise of him, in a review in the *Revue Contemporaine* (15 September 1856) that included a good number of translations of the 1855 poems.

In general, however, the reception of *Men and Women* was a bitter disappointment, not least because Browning seems truly to have thought that the poems would make him popular. No matter how hard he tried to escape the charge of 'obscurity' that had hung over his work since *Sordello*, he seemed to be for ever condemned as an egotist who simply wished to parade his novel talents and would in no way condescend to make his poetry accessible to the reading public. He was what the title of an unsigned article in *Chambers's Journal* (7 February 1863) was later to proclaim him to be: 'A Poet Without a Public'. This was a matter of great sadness and frustration for a writer who conceived of his poetry as a matter of dialogue with his reader. The situation continued to depress him for the rest of his life in Italy. Five years later, in March 1861, Elizabeth wrote to his sister that 'his treatment in England affects him' for 'nobody there, except a small knot of pre-Raffaellite men, pretend to do him justice. Mr. Forster has done the best,—in the press. . . . —and for the rest, you should see Chapman's returns [from sales]!' (Orr, *Life*, pp. 233–4).

To keep up their spirits Robert and Elizabeth led an active social life in Paris in addition to seeing to Robert senior and Sarianna. 'Little Penini', Elizabeth wrote, 'has been blossoming like a rose all the time. Such a darling, idle, distracted child he is, not keeping his attention for three minutes together for the hour and a half I teach him, and when I upbraid him for it, throwing himself upon me like a dog, kissing my cheeks and head and hands. . . . Oh, such a darling that child is!' (Kenyon, 2: 227–8). For occupation Robert took to drawing and produced some quite respectable heads. But by spring 1856 they had had enough of the French capital.

They went to London in late June to occupy the home of John Kenyon, who was recovering from a serious illness on the Isle of Wight. Elizabeth, who had been working on her verse novel *Aurora Leigh* for the past three years, completed the book-length poem in London and submitted the manuscript to the publisher in early August, while Robert gave up writing almost entirely and devoted himself to helping with his wife's work.[3] September was spent on the Isle of Wight, where they followed the younger Barretts, who were commanded to leave London when the elder Mr Barrett discovered that the Brownings were living close by in London, and where they visited Kenyon. For three weeks in London in October Elizabeth and Robert read proofs and then left the particularly foul weather for Florence, where they arrived in early November.

Aurora Leigh was published in mid-November and immediately became a critical and popular success as edition after edition was called for. Ruskin, whose praise of *Men and Women* had been stinting, wrote to Robert extolling *Aurora Leigh* as the greatest poem in English and the finest poem that the nineteenth century had produced in any language.[4] Robert himself seemed to bask in the praise. 'That gold-hearted Robert', Elizabeth wrote to his sister, 'is in ecstasies about it—far more than if it all related to a book of his own' (Kenyon, 2: 242). To Edward Chapman, however, Robert admitted that, happy as he was with the reviewers' generally lavish praise of his wife, he could not forget how they treated him. They were

> like those night-men who are always emptying their cart at my door, and welcome when I remember that after all they don't touch our bread with their beastly hands, as they used to do. Don't you mind them, and leave me to rub their noses in their own filth some fine day. (*NL*, p. 97)

As the Brownings were considering how the royalties from the sales of *Aurora Leigh* would lighten their financial situation, they received news of the death of John Kenyon and his bequest to them of £11,000. Deeply saddened by the loss of their old friend, they were nevertheless aware that hereafter they need have no worry about money.

The winter of 1856–7 passed uneventfully, marked mainly by Robert's depression over the reception of *Men and Women*. He could not bring himself to turn again to writing poetry. When Elizabeth's father died in mid-April, he was however forced to rouse himself from his lethargy to support Elizabeth in her grief. 'Ba was sadly affected at first; miserable to see and hear', Robert wrote. 'After a few days tears came to her relief. She is now very weak and prostrated' (Kenyon, 2: 263). At the end of July they went for the summer to Bagni di Lucca but found little respite from troubles. Robert Lytton, accompanied by Isa Blagden and one of her friends, arrived soon after the Brownings and almost immediately came down with gastric fever. Isa undertook to nurse him and Robert was more or less forced to help. 'Through sentimentality and economy combined', Robert wrote his sister, 'Isa would have no nurse (an imbecile arrangement), and all has been done by her, with me to help: I have sate up four nights out of the last five, and sometimes been there nearly all day beside' (Kenyon, 2: 268). Soon after Lytton recovered, Pen fell ill of the same disease, and Elizabeth, mindful of little Joe Story, was terrified. Pen however recovered nicely as the summer drew to a close. When the family returned to Florence it was in continuing gloom, Robert restless and Elizabeth drained of energy; and it was thus, enlivened mainly by American visitors such as Nathaniel Hawthorne and Pen's piano-playing and educational accomplishments, which included learning to read German and French as well as Italian, 'for which', Elizabeth wrote, 'Robert deserves the chief credit' (Kenyon, 2: 277), that they continued pretty much through the winter of 1857–8.

In early summer 1858 they set out for France, stopping in Dijon to visit Milsand and then going on to Paris. Robert was pleased to find his father and sister in good health and was invigorated by Parisian life, although Elizabeth continued in a weakened state. After two weeks they set off with Mr Browning and Sarianna for Normandy, eventually settling in Le Havre. Renting a large house, they were visited by Elizabeth's siblings and Milsand, and after two months, during which Elizabeth grew stronger, they returned to Florence for six weeks.

In November they went to Rome in search of warmer weather. Elizabeth remained at home with Pen while Robert walked in the mornings and went to parties and stayed up late. 'Dissipations decidedly agree with Robert', Elizabeth told Sarianna (Kenyon, 2: 311). One especially notable incident of Robert's social life was a dinner with the seventeen-year-old Prince of Wales, whose governor had called and explained that '*it would be gratifying to the Queen that the Prince should make Mr. Browning's acquaintance*' (Huxley, p. 310). Robert found the young man sprightly and intelligent and talked to him about the political situation in Italy.

With the defeat of Mazzini and his followers in 1849 leadership of the *Risorgimento*, whose aim was a united Italy, fell to the Piedmont, specifically to King Victor Emmanuel II and his chief minister, Count Camillo Benso Cavour. Cavour saw that it was possible to defeat the Austrians if he could enlist the military aid of one of the great powers; and he succeeded in capturing the support of Napoleon III. Piedmont began to arm, after its king's declaration in January 1859 that he was acutely aware of the widespread cry for political freedom throughout the peninsula. Austria demanded on 23 April that Piedmont disarm. Piedmont refused, Austria declared war, and then France declared war on Austria.

Excited by this turn of events, the Brownings returned to Casa Guidi in May 1859 to discover French troops encamped in and about Florence. Pen was delighted with the colourful French soldiers, Robert contributed money to the cause and Elizabeth threw her heart and soul into the war, almost delirious over the exploits of the French emperor and the Piedmontese king. 'Tell M. Milsand, with my love', she wrote to Sarianna, 'that if I belonged to his country, I should feel very proud at this time. As to the Emperor, he is sublime' (Kenyon, 2: 314). When, in spite of great victories over the Austrians at Magenta and Solferino in June, Napoleon III, having gained the military glory he always craved, made peace with Austria in July, Elizabeth suffered a physical collapse, all her hopes for a united Italy completely erased. For three weeks she was prostrate, during which time, she wrote Sarianna, 'Robert has been perfect to me. For more than a fortnight he gave up all his night's rest to me', while during the day he gave Pen his lessons (Kenyon, 2: 320). To provide a change of scene, Robert arranged for a stay in Sienna, where they were joined by the Storys and the octogenarian Walter Savage Landor.

Landor's had been a life of intemperate behaviour. Expelled from Rugby, sent down from Oxford, driven into exile by his libellous attacks on various authorities, he had married and gone to Italy in 1815, moving from city to city as he was ordered to leave each by local officials because of his insults. Settling in Florence and then in nearby Fiesole, he wrote most of his *Imaginary Conversations.* In 1835 he quarrelled with his wife and left his family for England, where he lived primarily at Bath and was dutifully looked after, from the distance of London, by John Forster. In 1858 he was forced by yet another libel suit and a judgement against him to flee England and rejoin his family at Fiesole. His wife could not tolerate his irascible behaviour and soon turned him out, whence he started, with only a few coins in his pocket, for Casa Guidi. After an interview with Mrs Landor and with the financial support of the old man's brothers, Robert assumed through Forster (whom Landor had also turned against) a guardianship. Robert was grateful for Landor's generous praise of his early work and, further, had been greatly influenced by Landor's *Conversations,* which are, like Browning's dramatic monologues, abbreviated dramas in which the speakers urge and defend their own points of view. 'Robert always said that he owed more as a writer to Landor than to any contemporary,' Elizabeth told Sarianna, adding, after personal experience of the old man's temper tantrums, that 'my Robert has generously paid the debt' (Kenyon, 2: 354).

The Brownings remained in Sienna till October, when they returned briefly to Florence and settled Landor into a house not far from Casa Guidi. This was the home of Wilson, now Romagnoli, who after the arrival of a second child had left the Brownings' service. Here Landor was to stay

Plate 6 'Elizabeth Barrett Browning, Rome', 1859. Crayon drawing by Field Talfourd. Courtesy of The National Portrait Gallery, London.

Plate 5 'Robert Browning, Rome', 1859. Crayon drawing by Field Talfourd. Reproduced by Courtesy of The National Portrait Gallery, London.

Plate 7 'Elizabeth and Pen Browning, Rome', 1860. Reproduced by kind permission of the Master and Fellows of Balliol College, Oxford (Photograph: Thomas Photos.)

till his death in 1864. The winter of 1859–60 the Brownings spent in Rome, again so as to take advantage of a warmer climate for Elizabeth, whose health continued to be bad and who was increasingly dependent upon the morphine which she had now been taking, often to Robert's alarm, for many years. The Storys, who found lodgings for them, feared that she would not make it through the winter. 'Suffocations, singular heart-action, cough tearing one to atoms'—these were her afflictions (Kenyon, 2: 355). In March 1860 she published her *Poems before Congress* expressing her initial exaltation and subsequent revulsion concerning the political situation over the past year but nevertheless continuing to praise Napoleon III. In their responses to the new volume the reviewers were almost as caustic in their denigration as they had been enthusiastic in their praise of *Aurora Leigh*.

In June 1860 the Brownings were back for a short while in Florence, where they learned that Kirkup had tried to convert Landor to spiritualism and Landor had responded with a fit of laughter. They passed the summer in Sienna, where the Storys had again taken a villa close by and Isa Blagden a cabin not far away. In Rome again for the next winter they learned that Elizabeth's sister Henrietta, whose illness they first heard of in Sienna, had died. From this shock Elizabeth never fully recovered, although she tried, as Robert told Isa, to 'eat a little, listen to talking, attend to Pen, & so on' (*Dearest Isa*, p. 68). Robert himself wrote no poetry but spent his time nursing her and tending to Pen's education. They had intended to pass the summer of 1861 in France, Robert not having seen his father and sister for three years; but when they returned to Florence in late spring Elizabeth was obviously in no shape for further travel. In June she caught a cold, which brought on inflammation of the lungs. It was obvious that her situation was grave. 'I had to fetch a Doctor in the middle of the night who stayed with us till morning', Robert wrote to the Storys on 23 June; 'it really seemed as if she would be strangled on the spot,—and that for six hours together!' (Hudson, p. 72). Elizabeth however was less alarmed than either Robert or the doctor, whose diagnosis was 'that one lung was condensed (the right) and that he suspected an abscess in it'. 'It is the old story', she maintained. 'This is only one of my old attacks' (Hood, p. 60).

Nevertheless, over the next few days she grew worse and worse. Robert sat by her day and night, trying to make her comfortable. On 28 June Isa came to try to divert her with political news, but Robert, recognizing his wife's precarious hold on life and fearing she would become excited, sent Isa away. Wilson came to help with Elizabeth's toilette and thought her much better. Pen, upon coming to say goodnight, asked his mother whether she was really better, to which she replied affirmatively; the boy was nevertheless afraid. As Robert watched over her that night and noted her 'heavy, troubled breathing, and waking with oppression', she assured him that she was better; and when he sent the porter for the doctor, she said, '"Well, you *do* make an exaggerated case of it"' (*NL*, p. 138). Soon thereafter, in the early morning of Saturday, 29 June, she died in Robert's arms, having told him only a few minutes earlier, 'Our lives are held by God!' (Hood, p. 62).

Isa came later that morning and took Pen home with her. Robert sat beside Elizabeth's body. 'How she looks now', he wrote Sarianna, 'how perfectly beautiful!' (Hood, p. 63). The Storys came from Leghorn as soon as possible and found Robert in better control of himself than they had anticipated. 'The cycle is complete', he told them. 'Looking back at these past years I see that we have been all the time walking over a torrent on a straw'.[5] For some time he had been unsettled, unable to write or to do anything other than, first, drawing, and, recently, studying sculpture with Story and modelling. 'The consequence of which is', Elizabeth had written Sarianna only three months earlier, 'that he wants occupation, and that an active occupation is salvation to him with his irritable nerves' (Orr, *Life*, p. 232). But now – well, things would be different. The day after Elizabeth died he wrote to his sister: 'My life is fixed and sure now. I shall live out the remainder in her direct influence, endeavouring to complete mine, miserably imperfect now, but so as to take the good she was meant to give me'. He would make a complete break, rid himself of both his dependency on and responsibility for Elizabeth. 'I go away from Italy at once, having no longer any business there' (Hood, p. 62). Ever a faithful adherent to the philosophy of becoming, he almost instinctively refused to be inactivated by the past; instead, he looked to the future.

In the meanwhile there were the funeral and burial to be tended to. The funeral that took place on 1 July was a Church of England service that was attended by fewer people than Story had expected,[6] but the shops in the neighbourhood were shut and the procession to the grave in the Protestant cemetery in Florence was followed by a considerable crowd as 'the coffin was carried with two great crowns, of laurel and white flowers, thro' the streets'. There were, said Robert, 'extraordinary demonstrations of sorrow: everybody understood' (*NL*, p. 132).

After the burial Robert wasted no time in reordering his life. Almost immediately he had Pen's hair cut and the boy dressed in long trousers. 'The golden curls and fantastic dress', he told his sister, were 'gone just as Ba is gone' (*NL*, p. 133). When a representative of one of the most illustrious Florentine families and himself a leader of the Italian revolutionary movement called on Browning on 12 July to ask that he remain in Florence and rear Pen as a Tuscan, Robert declined politely but was evidently revolted by the very idea. 'Of course', he told Forster, 'Pen is and will be English as I am English and his Mother was pure English to the hatred of all un- English cowardice, vituperation, and lies . . .' (*NL*, p. 140). As Jacob Korg observes, the Florentine's request must have caused Browning to realize that he did not share the relationship to Italy that Elizabeth, the Italian patriot, and Pen, who had been born in Italy, enjoyed: 'He had never identified himself with Italy, or idealized it, but had observed it, from an affectionate distance, as an arena of moral and spiritual drama'.[7]

Plate 8 'Robert Browning senior'. The poet's father, Paris, c. 1860. Crayon drawing by Sarianna Browning. Courtesy of the Harry Ransom Humanities Research Center, The University of Texas at Austin.

For too long he had lived the life of an exile; he was tired of it, and he was relieved to give vent to his momentary xenophobia. 'Oh, to be in England', he thought, like his speaker in the 1845 'Home-Thoughts, from Abroad'.

'I shall go away from Italy for many a year', he wrote to Frederic Leighton on 19 July. 'Don't fancy I am "prostrated"' (Orr, *Life*, p. 239). 'I want my new life to resemble the last fifteen years as little as possible', he told the Storys. In future, 'I shall have no ties, no housekeeping, nothing to prevent me from wandering about, if circumstances permit' (Hudson, pp.

76–7). 'I shall grow, still, I hope', he told Fanny Haworth, 'but my root is taken and remains' (Orr, *Life*, p. 241). Unlike his Cleon, who could only be 'glad for what was' (337), Browning, the poet of becoming, could look back with affection over the past fifteen years of love that even he, the most imaginative of men, could not have imagined, but he refused to be stultified by what was now over. Elizabeth, he wrote to Sarianna, 'is with God, who takes from me the life of my life in one sense,—not so, in the truest' (Hood, p. 62). He packed furniture and other belongings at Casa Guidi during the day, and he and Pen spent their nights at Isa's home. Robert and Pen and Pen's pony (Flush had died in 1854) departed Florence on 1 August for Paris 'accompanied by Miss Blagden, who has devoted herself to me & Peni, disregarding health, convenience & all other considerations' (Hudson, p. 75). Isa left Paris after a few days while Robert and Pen stayed on with Mr Browning and Sarianna in Paris and Brittany till October, and then with the pony went to England. Robert was never to set foot in Florence again.

9

In London Again

In London Robert and Pen took temporary lodgings at 1 Chichester Road, Upper Westbourne Terrace, before locating (with John Forster's help) and settling (in June 1862) in the rented house at 19 Warwick Crescent. For the next twenty-five years this was to be home. It was not far from Elizabeth's sole surviving sister, Arabel, whom Robert and Pen saw almost every day and in whose company the widower found much comfort. Except for the summers, which he now began to enjoy on the Breton coast, and occasional visits to Paris to see his father, Sarianna and Milsand, the former traveller, who had spent the past decade moving from one place to another, was settled in London for good and glad to be there. He was however lonely. Besides seeing to the education of Pen, for whom, again with the aid of Forster, he soon found a satisfactory tutor, he mainly occupied himself in solitary walks.

He missed Florence and some 'authentic news' from there (*Dearest Isa*, p. 97). One heartening piece of information that came was that the municipality was to place a commemorative tablet on Casa Guidi, where, so the inscription (in translation from the Italian) read, 'wrote and died Elizabeth Barrett Browning who in the heart of a woman united the wisdom of a sage and the spirit of a poet and made her verse a golden link between Italy and England. Grateful Florence places this memorial'. To make sure that he would keep up with the goings-on of his old friends in Italy, he arranged with Isa Blagden that they would write to each other every month, she on the twelfth and he on the nineteenth.

Browning was too sociable a being to remain long solitary. At first he met with old friends like Forster and Carlyle, and by the spring of 1862 he had begun what for the rest of his life would, besides his writing, which always took place every morning, be his chief occupation: namely, dining out. He was elected in February to the Athenaeum, a distinguished club in Pall Mall, and afterwards was often to be seen there, especially in its splendid library. He was also in demand to lend his presence to various gatherings. 'I go out every night to dine in a cold-blooded way', he told the Storys, meeting 'all these people . . . whose very names I forget next day'. But, he added, 'I cannot say I am dull here—I work, or, at least, am employed all day long' (Hudson, pp. 106, 114).

One cheering event was the offer in March 1862 of the editorship of *The Cornhill Magazine* upon the retirement of Thackeray. 'I really take it as a compliment', he wrote to the Storys, but declined the position by answering that 'my life was done for & settled, that I could not change it & would not'. Furthermore, 'they count on my attracting writers,—I who could never muster *English* readers enough to pay for salt & bread'. The offer was a sign, whether he wished to believe it or not, that 'people are getting goodnatured to my poems' (Hudson, pp. 100–1).

Before turning to his own work, he guided Elizabeth's *Last Poems* (1862) through the press (dedicating it, in allusion to the tablet at Casa Guidi, to 'grateful Florence') and prepared a group of her essays for publication under the title *The Greek Christian Poets and the English Poets* (1863). He then began revisions for the second collected edition of his works, the first having appeared in 1849. This three-volume edition, which contained everything published up to this point save *Pauline*, was printed in 1863 and dedicated to Forster, his 'old friend' who was the 'promptest and staunchest helper' of the works therein. The poems of 1842, 1845 and 1855 were broken up and regrouped, and *Sordello* was radically revised in syntax and punctuation and enlarged by 181 lines. 'Let the next poem be introduced by your name', Browning said in his dedication of the new *Sordello* to 'J. Milsand, of Dijon', and 'therefore remembered along with one of my deepest affections, and so repay all trouble it ever cost me'. A volume of *Selections* (1863) was put together by John Forster and the lawyer–poet B. W. Procter ('Barry Cornwall'), an old friend known through Fox and the dedicatee of *Colombe's Birthday*, who in their preface claimed Browning as 'among the few great poets of this century'. 'There's printing a book of "Selections from RB"', Browning wrote to Story,

> which is to popularize my old things: & so & so means to review it, and somebody or [other] always was looking out for such an occasion, and what's his name always said he admired me, only he didn't say it, though he said something else every week of his life in some Journal. The breath of man! (Hudson, p. 101)

Both the collected works and the selections sold so well and were received by the reviewers so respectfully that the poet was persuaded by his publisher to postpone publication of a new volume of poems till the next year. Browning, *mirabile dictu*, was at last *popular* – and was to become more so when *Dramatis Personae* appeared on 28 May 1864.

The monologues of *Men and Women* had touched on a great number of topical concerns, far more than had the monologues of the 1840s; and the eighteen poems of *Dramatis Personae*, are again more anchored in contemporary matters of importance than those of 1855. Biological evolution, spiritualism, current social conditions, Higher Criticism of the Bible, modern love – these are but some of the topics of the poems included in what the poet called 'a new book of "Men & Women"' (*Dearest Isa*, p. 128).

Yet the poems of 1864 are by and large quite different from those of 1855. As Lawrence Poston remarks, they give hints of the disputatiousness characteristic of much of Browning's later poetry.[1] Moreover, the monologists are conceived less as independent characters (through whom the poet of course speaks) than as persons in a play, *dramatis personae* in Robert Browning's theatre. In this respect they somewhat resemble the characters of Browning's monologues and plays of the 1840s who are ever aware of their fictive status but who nevertheless seem to have more of a life of their own.

Since all the poems touch on love and religion, it is tempting to read them in the light of Elizabeth's death three years earlier. Yet several of them seem to have been conceived or composed before she died. In May 1860 Elizabeth wrote from Rome that Robert had been 'working at a long poem which I have not seen a line of, and producing short lyrics which I *have* seen' (Kenyon, 2: 388). And in March 1861 Elizabeth had written to Sarianna Browning that Robert 'has material for a volume' (Orr, *Life*, p. 233). Furthermore, the book's pervasive theme of loss and gain – a recurrent phrase in the volume – is common to all Browning's poetry. What the poet seemed to intend was a working out of his long-held ideas in new ways.

The first of the love poems, 'James Lee's Wife' (originally 'James Lee'), is a monodrama similar to Tennyson's *Maud*, the poem the Brownings heard the Laureate read aloud in 1855. Different moods advance the poem through its various sections. The speaker is obsessed with change, fearful of it and full of foreboding for what it may bring. Idealizing her love and the perfection that she supposes to have found in it, she wishes to arrest time. Her husband however is made uneasy by such talk of perfect love and her anatomization of it. He, who does not wish to be her 'whole world' (109), feels suffocated. As he withdraws she looks to the natural world for some kind of consolation, only to find reflected there her own despair, and for distraction she takes up a book and reads a lyric poem. This turns out to be a lyric written by one Robert Browning at age twenty-three and published in Fox's *Monthly Repository* for May 1836. It is a song of the wind as the voice of human woes (152–81), which she recognizes as emanating from 'some young man's pride' (182) and which with experience he will sing in a different way. His future song of the wind will be in praise of change, and it will encourage her to accept the notion that all life is perhaps probation for advancement to a higher state. Love disappointed on earth must be sought on a higher, impersonal plane, and turning to art the wife finds there a confirmation of her intuition that, as Cleon had stated, 'imperfection means perfection hid' (185). Yet for all her disappointment with a husband who did not share a love as supreme as hers, she iterates her full belief in 'love that was life, life that was love' (359).

'James Lee's Wife', apparently composed in Brittany during the summer of 1862 (DeVane, p. 285), may perhaps have been inspired by – or be an answer to – George Meredith's *Modern Love*, published in the spring of 1862 and presented to Browning by the author a month or so later. Meredith's poem, consisting of a series of lyrics, had anatomized a failed marriage, as passion gave way to jealousy and discord. Browning, on the other hand, wanted to draw a portrait of a marriage in which jealousy or other outside influences had no part.[2] His aim, rather, was to show how love simply disappears, as a result of temperamental variation. He aimed to portray 'people newly-married, trying to realize a dream of being sufficient to each other, in a foreign land (where you can try such an experiment) and finding it break up,—the man being tired *first*,—and tired precisely of the love' (*Wedgwood*, p. 123).

Could it be that 'James Lee's Wife' had a biographical genesis? As we have seen, Robert threw himself into marriage wholeheartedly but became irritable and discontented when he was unable to work. Years before, in *Dramatic Romances & Lyrics*, he had written of one who at night impatiently sought the passionate moment of 'two hearts beating each to each' only next morning to acknowledge 'the need of a world of men' ('Meeting at Night' and 'Parting at Morning'). Here again he was suggesting something of the same feelings on the man's part. Had he not, at least from time to time, found Elizabeth's love suffocating?[3]

In the companion poem, 'The Worst of It', the speaker is a husband whose wife has been all to him. She was perfection, he thought, and in loving him she condescended to baseness. Now that she has proven false, he realizes that he loved not wisely but too well. His fear is that she, who was without stain, will suffer in the world's eyes as an unfaithful wife, although he himself will make no claim on her, even in Paradise, where 'if we meet, I will pass nor turn my face' (114).

'The Worst of It' may reflect the poet's determined efforts to sustain his wife's poetic reputation, which had begun to falter in comparison with his. To a person who admitted preferring his poems to Elizabeth's he said:

> You are wrong—quite wrong—she has genius; I am only a painstaking fellow. Can't you imagine a clever sort of angel who plots and plans, and tries to build up something—he wants to make you see it as he sees it—shows you one point of view, carries you off to another, hammering into your head the thing he wants you to understand; and whilst this bother is going on God Almighty turns you off a little star—that's the difference between us.

No, he insisted, 'The true creative power is hers, not mine' (Orr, *Life*, p. 235). Yet if one takes a close look at Browning's comparison, one cannot help feeling that Robert's poetry thus described is far more interesting than Elizabeth's and, moreover, that Robert could barely hide the fact from himself – and 'The Worst of It' may unconsciously mirror this.

Other love poems treat the situation narrated in 'The Statue and the Bust'. Lovers who defer to worldly considerations are destined to unfulfilled lives. In 'Dîs Aliter Visum; or, Le Byron de Nos Jours' a woman arraigns a man who loves, does not express it, and thus becomes the debased 'Byron de nos jours', for not making a 'wise beginning' of 'what cannot grow complete (earth's feat) / And heaven must finish' (121–3). In 'Too Late' a man realizes how much he loves a woman only when she is dead, while in 'Youth and Art' a woman regrets the choice that she and her young artist friend made, of money and fame over love and passion. These poems differ from 'The Statue and the Bust' in their contemporary settings and allusions to topical subjects and persons living or recently dead. In 'Youth and Art', for example, there are references to the sculptor John Gibson and the opera singer Giulietta Grisi, in 'Dîs Aliter Visum' to the composer Robert Schumann, the painter J. F. D. Ingres, the poet Heinrich Heine – all of which point up the actors as belonging to Robert Browning's modern theatre.

One of the chief performers is to be found in 'Mr Sludge, "The Medium"', the longest poem in *Dramatis Personae*. Based on the popular American medium Daniel Dunglas Home, whom Browning had met at the séance in 1855 and immediately detested, causing some pain to his wife, Sludge is a superlative actor ever aware of being on stage and engaged in 'acting, or improvising, make-believe' (428). Yet his is a different kind of performance in that his audience never wants to see him outside his role. When one goes to the theatre, he says, one sees an actor who plays first one part and then another. But in the case of the spiritualist theatre, 'Sludge acts Macbeth' and is 'obliged to be Macbeth' (651). He knows the difference but his audience does not, and he often is tempted to regard himself as the 'whole and sole reality / Inside a raree-show and a market-mob / Gathered about it' (909–11). This is why he, who lives in *commedia dell'arte*, is contemptuous of his audience's world: 'I slap it brisk / With harlequin's pasteboard sceptre' (1391–2). To the degree that his audience confuses the man with the performer, the medium is like the poet of 'One Word More', where 'never dares the man put off the prophet' (99).

Sludge makes the same claims as the poets who, in Browning's words, aim to put the infinite into the finite. But he knows as well as poets do that he cannot capture the Absolute, that he can only suggest its relation to the finite and the relative. And how does he do this? By lying, by cheating. All mediums – that is, all embodiments, like language for instance – are false representations. But it's a necessary lie: 'every cheat's inspired, and every lie / Quick with the germ of truth' (1324–5). For to focus his audience's attention on the miraculous and the supernatural, he must perform wonders that will essentially compel assent to belief in the spiritual world.

Furthermore, the medium presents the finite in a different way so as to make people in general, who lead a 'lethargic kind of death in life' (1417), see and appreciate the beauty of God's creation. Gifted like the poet with superlatively keen perception, the medium is ever sensitive to his environment: 'I'm eyes, ears, mouth of me, one gaze and gape, / Nothing eludes me, everything's a hint, / Handle and help' (1013–15). What he sees are signs of God immanent in creation. Signs are everywhere, and it is his business to make them wonders, to show how this world is 'pervaded by the influx from the next' (1397).

Near the end of his monologue addressed to Hiram H. Horsefall, the insensitive *homme moyen sensuel* who has accused the medium of cheating, Sludge makes plainer his sense of vocation similar to that of the poet's. He presents the ideal of a world of possibilities, of things about to be:

> No mere film
> Holding you chained in iron, as it seems,
> Against the outstretch of your very arms
> And legs i' the sunshine moralists forbid! . . .
> Thus it goes on, not quite like life perhaps,
> But so near, that the very difference piques,
> Shows that e'en better than this best will be—
> This passing entertainment in a hut
> Whose bare walls take your taste since, one stage more,
> And you arrive at the palace.
>
>   (1402–5, 1410–15)

What matter then if Sludge lies? 'Why, he's at worst your poet who sings how Greeks / That never were, in Troy which never was, / Did this or the other impossible great thing!' (1436–8).

In writing of the 'medium' Browning had obviously in mind other media, especially poetry. And in having Sludge talk, he was vicariously considering his own vocation: 'Really, I want to light up my own mind' (811). Poets have transcendental ideals but they are also mindful of their descendental natures; imaginatively they aspire on wings of song but physically they are of the earth, earthy. David Sludge, as his name implies, is endowed with lyric aspiration but restrained by a highly opaque medium. Browning and Sludge: 'You'd fain distinguish between gift and gift' (1179)? Maybe there's not such a great difference. 'Bless us, I'm turning poet!' Sludge says. Perhaps so, the poet allows: 'I can't help that. / It's truth! I somehow vomit truth today' (807–8).

There is, however, a good deal of slippage in the 'truth' of which Sludge speaks and which his name further implies.[4] It is one of the special characteristics of Browning's poetry after 1860 that truth in art and truth in religion are the chief topics that his monologists address, often in a casuistical fashion. Consequently the poems of his last three decades are generally more philosophical than the earlier ones. Whereas his poems of the 1840s and 1850s by and large dealt with these subjects separately, the later ones confront them simultaneously. If, for example, we compare 'Bishop Blougram's Apology' with 'Mr. Sludge', both highly casuistical monologues,[5] we see that 'Blougram' is almost exclusively concerned with religion while 'Sludge' deals with religion and art. Moreover, 'Sludge' deals with religion in a more complicated way.

With Browning's growing interest in German biblical criticism, especially as it became a topic of more general concern in England in the 1860s, the question of the historicity of the Bible and of textual authority becomes a matter for examination in his poetry. What is reliable evidence, the historical basis, for religious faith? In 'Sludge' Browning considers how doubt and uncertainty may in fact become the basis for belief.

Sludge begins – most curiously, it at first seems – by admitting that he is not a genuine medium. His strategy is to undermine his accuser's certainty that he is merely a trickster by demonstrating that truth cannot be attained on empirical grounds. For those for whom he performed, there was what appeared to be reasonable evidence for believing in him. They saw physical manifestations of spirit, they heard the voices: they were ocular and auricular witnesses to spiritual experience. But the truth was otherwise: the evidence was faked. What had seemed conclusively established was now shown empirically to be false. If reason can on the one hand prove something true and then on the other hand demonstrate it to be false, how can one then make reason the standard by which to judge truth?

Having placed credence as a matter beyond intellectual certainty, Sludge then asks how his audience can be sure that he is a deceiver. How, for that matter, can even he himself be certain that he is a cheat? 'Why, when I cheat, / *Mean to cheat, do cheat, and am caught in the act,* / *Are you, or, rather, am I sure o' the fact?*' (1282–4). It may well be that he was inspired and his feats served a divine purpose by educing others' faith in the supernatural. Paradoxically Sludge advances his case by denying his accuser the means of proving him false and claiming to be true by subverting the means by which truth can be ascertained.

In sum, there can be no certainty where truth is concerned. And this is as true of God as it is of Sludge. For faith – in God or Sludge – there is simply no reliable 'evidence'. What we are left with in the end is uncertainty, to believe as we will that there is an 'unseen agency, outside the world, / Prompt[ing] its puppets to do this and that' (898–9).

Sludge's argument proves persuasive to Hiram Horsefall. Browning does not, however, want his reader also to be convinced. In a coda, not unlike that to 'Bishop Blougram's Apology', Sludge is permitted a short soliloquy in which he admits his villainy and undercuts all that he had previously said. He first ponders, like the soliloquizer of 'Soliloquy of the Spanish Cloister', how he might seek retribution for all he has suffered, and then he remembers that all the world's a stage, that there are other theatrical sites, and that Horsefall is not 'the only fool in the world' (1525).

In 'A Death in the Desert' the question of evidence and biblical authenticity is the central concern. Here Browning replies to Ernest Renan's *Life of Jesus*, published in France in 1863 and in English translation in 1864.[6] Renan questioned the authorship of the Fourth Gospel and also accused St John, if he were indeed its author, of falsifying certain central

events in his reporting of the Christian story. In his poem Browning presents
John's testimony about his knowledge of Jesus' life. Admitting that he was
not present at the Crucifixion, as his gospel claims, and that he himself
did not perform a miracle, John stakes his apology on the paradoxical
grounds that certain falsehoods are necessary for communicating truth.

John is a very old man. He has outlived the other apostles and other
witnesses to Jesus' life and in effect has outlived his first vision of Christ.
Significantly, in his monologue Jesus does not figure at all. And it is precisely
the point of his account that the truth of Christianity is not dependent
upon historical fact. Whatever there was of 'plain historic fact' has for him
become 'reduced' and 'diminished', has served its purpose, 'proved a
point / And [is now] far away' (236–8). For, embracing the myth criticism
later to be expounded by the German Higher Critics, Browning's John
makes faith rest on internal rather than external evidence. 'To me, that
story . . . / Of which I wrote "it was"—to me, it is; / —Is, here and now'
(208–10).

Foreseeing future generations of persons like Renan and the Higher
Critics who will question not only the historical accuracy of his gospel but
also whether there was ever such a person as John at all, John argues that
the nature of evidence must develop along with the evolving nature of
mankind: 'to test man, the proofs shift' (295). In earlier times 'miracles'
and 'eye-witness testimony' were necessary to gain assent to the Christian
message of Love:

> minds at first must be spoon-fed with truth;
> When they can eat, babe's nurture is withdrawn.
> I fed the babe whether it would or no;
> I bid the boy or feed himself or starve.
>
> (455–8)

To a post-apostolic age relying exclusively on reason as a test of faith John
offers a prudential Christianity, 'the acknowledgement of God in Christ /
Accepted by thy reason' which will solve 'all questions in the earth and out
of it' (474–6). What he pleads for (from his yet-to-come nineteenth-
century readers) is an exercise of imaginative reason, entailing not a re-
jection of history but an imaginative grasp of the historical situation from
which 'history' sprang.

One of the most brilliant aspects of the monologue is the way in which
Browning equates the dying John with the experience of the Christian
community that has received his gospel throughout eighteen hundred
years. First, there is John's sense of loss of personal identity, the old man
not really sure that he is 'John' (71–9). He has almost outlived himself, as
it were; he has lost the feeling of exhilaration felt by the earliest Christian
community. Second, his monologue exemplifies the growing intellectu-
alization of the Christian community over the ages. He is deeply conscious
of loss but makes of it a gain whereby humankind can educe faith in more

or less the same way that David in 'Saul' could 'see the Christ stand'. As parrhesiastic truth-telling, John's apology boldly takes issue with the Enlightenment's glorification of reason as the sole path to truth.

In typical fashion Browning does not permit John's to be the last word. In fact, he does not allow it to be certainly and unequivocally John's word at all. Making the monologue something of a fictional edition, not unlike *Pauline*, 'A Death in the Desert', which purports to relate the apostle's deathbed remarks addressed to four auditors, is the manuscript 'supposed of Pamphylax' (1), who may or may not be the narrator who will 'tomorrow fight the beasts'. The other hearers of John's dying words are now dead or lost and so the 'I' will tell the story to one Phoebas (648–53). What is left unknown is who wrote the manuscript, which is in Greek, not the language of the apostle. As for the manuscript, it was at one time in the possession of someone identifying himself in the following manner: '*Mu* and *Epsilon* stand for my own name. / I may not write it' (9–10). At the end one Cerinthus is introduced but otherwise unidentified, and 'one' unidentified added the coda. Like the gospels themselves, the whole question of scribal authority and transmission of manuscripts is clouded in darkness. In the case of this poem, however, the effect of mystification is to call attention to the author, who is possibly 'ME', the mu and the epsilon that stand for Robert Browning.

In 'Caliban upon Setebos' Browning deals with the Higher Critics' thesis that God is created in the image of man and with the natural theologians' claim that the character of God can be derived from the evidences of nature. The poem was probably inspired by the brouhaha over biological evolution set off by Charles Darwin's *On the Origin of Species*, which had appeared in 1859, been immediately attacked as calling into question man's divine origin and become a matter of popular excitement when Samuel Wilberforce, the bishop of Oxford and the eminent biologist T. H. Huxley debated the matter before the British Association for the Advancement of Science in June 1860. This presumably set the poet to thinking of primitive man and the evolution of the race not only physically but also mentally and morally. The whole notion of change and development advanced in Darwin's book Browning would of course have found most congenial, although he was, as we shall later note, to take serious exception to the evolutionists' notion of *telos*. Further, the character of Caliban, the man–monster in Shakespeare's *The Tempest* who at the end of the play resolved to 'seek for grace', was a fitting subject for expression of such a view. In any case, the poet's chief purpose in the monologue is suggested by the subtitle, 'Natural Theology in the Island',[7] and the epigraph, 'Thou thoughtest that I was altogether such a one as thyself', which is what God said to the wicked in Psalm 50.

In a reversal of Genesis the poem makes God in man's own image. From what he has seen in nature and known of his own master, Prospero, Caliban conceives of a Higher Being who is capricious and cruel. Setebos is a god whose power can readily be discerned from all the evidences of the world around. But this god is not satisfying, does not fulfil the felt needs of the lowly Caliban, who almost unconsciously longs for a god of something more. He imagines the Quiet as one behind Setebos, indifferent to mankind but not actively antagonistic to human wishes. His conception of such a higher god results from a great stretch of the imagination, but Caliban can no farther go. It is beyond him to conceive of a god of love, as David in 'Saul' does. This, as we know from 'Cleon', requires a special revelation.

Strangely (but in characteristically Browningesque fashion), Caliban though low in the evolutionary chain does possess self-consciousness; that is, he sees himself as viewed by an other, as one more or less playing a role. This sense of theatricality seems to be indicated by the introductory and closing sections of the monologue, which are enclosed within brackets, suggestive of stage directions. Caliban sets the stage for his soliloquy as he comes out to sprawl in the sun and then 'talks to his own self, howe'er he please, / ... / Letting the rank tongue blossom into speech' (15, 23). As he speaks, he makes up his own little drama: a four-legged serpent he pretends is Miranda and his wife, a crane is Ariel, a sea-beast is Caliban. Thus he engages in role-playing: '"Plays thus at being Prosper in a way, / Taketh his mirth with make-believes"'. And he figures that what is true of himself is also true of the god Setebos, the great pretender: 'so He' (158–69). But Caliban recognizes that the fancy cannot cheat so well that it can make real what was theatrically imagined; thus in the final, bracketed lines, a cloud passes overhead and there drops 'a curtain o'er the world at once!' The play is ended with the actor–playwright's admission that 'it was fool's play, this prattling' (284, 287).

In not dissimilar fashion the soliloquizer of 'Abt Vogler' imagines a world that cannot be permanently realized. He regrets that he cannot arrest time. During his extemporization on the organ he believes he had reached a moment when the infinite and the finite met, when the past, present and future blended, when he was made perfect too, in brief a divine instant; but alas, it was only an instant. Had he painted or made verse it would exist in space to be preserved, permanently relished and analysed. But, he reflects, could such a moment have occurred in either visual art or poetry? They exist in obedience to laws, while music, stemming from 'the finger of God, a flash of the will that can' is 'existent behind all laws' (49–50). In other words, music is process, abstraction, existent purely in the realm of becoming and reflective of that realm. Vogler's is a bold claim, not only for music but also for himself as musician. Sounds are everywhere in the world, and each tone of the scale is naught. But

> Give it to me to use! I mix it with two in my thought:
> And, there! Ye have heard and seen: consider and
>   bow the head!
>   (55–6)

Moralizing on what he has played, he sees his unpreserved extemporization as a token of what is to come: good can never be lost, what was shall live as before, failure here is but promise of later accomplishment. Summing up his philosophy of the imperfect, he sees (and hears) 'on the earth the broken arcs' but intuits 'in the heaven, a perfect round' (72). In the end Abt Vogler returns to a more normal perspective, knowing that he must leave heaven for earth and finishing his playing where a 'resting-place is found, / The C Major of this life' (95–6).

The idea of earthly existence as provisional and probationary is expressed in personal terms in 'Prospice [Look Forward]'. Written soon after Elizabeth's death, it is 'Childe Roland to the Dark Tower Came' transformed lyrically. Here the end is death, not a tower, but reaching it is imaged in much the same way. The strong man endures the journey through all adverse circumstances, which he faces unflinchingly; he is 'ever a fighter' who can do no better than 'fare like [his] peers / The heroes of old'. This ordeal is his last and to arrive at an end will be success, for there, in what is the only (almost) open allusion to Elizabeth's death in the volume, 'thou soul of my soul! I shall clasp thee again'.

In slightly more dramatic terms the same story is told in 'Rabbi ben Ezra'. The setting is unclear, as is the audience; it may be that the rabbi is preaching to a congregation in a synagogue. What he preaches is the exact opposite both of the philosophy of *carpe diem* espoused in FitzGerald's *Rubáiyát of Omar Khayyám* (1859) and of the philosophy of stoic resignation expounded in Arnold's *Empedocles on Etna* (1852). Only 'fools propound', the rabbi says, '"Since life fleets, all is change; the Past gone, seize today!"' (154, 156). Of course all is change, he admits, setting forth like Browning's other heroes the doctrine of becoming, but this implies continuation and futurity, not termination and finality. The fool would arrest the present, not seeing that the present is dynamic, leading to an endless future of possibilities. All that was unachieved in past and present remains to be done in the future. Standing as surrogate for his poet–maker, Rabbi ben Ezra speaks of 'Thoughts hardly to be packed / Into a narrow act, / Fancies that broke through language and escaped' (145–7) – these will find true articulation in the hereafter.

Rabbi ben Ezra rejoices in the present, 'this dance / Of plastic circumstance' (163–4) that involves many missteps. His sermon embraces the 'paradox / Which comforts while it mocks' (38–9), namely that life succeeds while it seems to fail. Humankind is born into a world of flesh and spirit and is rightly sustained by the tension between the two. To attempt to live exclusively in either one or the other means either sinking in the evolutionary scale or committing hubris by aspiring beyond humanhood: 'All good things / Are ours, nor soul helps flesh more, now, than flesh helps soul!' (71–2). Imperfection is the perfect condition for advance in the endless process of becoming: 'What entered into thee, / *That* was, is, and shall be' (160–1).

'Gold Hair', a much misunderstood poem, approaches the question of perfection in a radically different way, although it too is professedly a sermon. It is a narrative told by the poet himself in a new manner, one characteristic of the poems of the 1870s. The story, which Browning heard on one of his summer visits to Brittany, is of a supposedly saintly young woman who secretly valued money more than heaven and whose love of pelf was discovered when her grave was disturbed and gold found in her gold hair. 'Why I deliver this horrible verse?' asks the poet, and answers: 'As the text of a sermon, which now I preach' (136–7). The sermon is generally understood to be about Original Sin and Browning's belief in man's natural depravity.[8] It is, however, about the Christian faith, which certain persons – many clerics among them, including the authors of *Essays and Reviews* (1860), which introduced German biblical criticism to England, and Bishop J. W. Colenso, whose *Critical Examination of the Pentateuch* (1862) questioned biblical historical facts – had recently seemed to suggest is false. With his inclination to look at all sides of a question, Browning examines the case of this girl who was thought perfect and finds, as he always does when it is a matter of supposed earthly perfection, 'a spider [in] the communion-cup' and 'a toad in the christening-font' (104, 105). And in this he sees a confirmation of the Christian faith, which denies human perfectibility. This is but one reason why, says the poet, 'I still, to suppose it true, for my part' (146).

'Apparent Failure' is a companion to 'Gold Hair', which might just as well have been titled 'Apparent Perfection'. Although from the beginning Browning had regarded phenomena of the world as semblances masking a higher reality, from the 1860s on he increasingly tended, almost perversely, to show that whatever is apparent cannot be what it seems. If most people regard a colour as black, then he will set out to demonstrate how it should properly be considered white. In the case of 'Apparent Failure' he deems the three bodies of suicides on display in the Paris Morgue to be not the failures most persons judge them. These men ended their lives, he fancies, because they did not attain the success they hoped for, abjuring, as we are told in the last stanza, the 'wiser', 'safer' and 'fitter' ways of keeping alive. This does not mean, however, that they were utter failures. It may be that they aimed higher than the contemporary political dignitaries named in the first stanza, that their reach exceeded their grasp. The speaker fancies that whatever of value was in them will remain, for in his opinion as in that of Rabbi ben Ezra, no good is ever lost: 'what began best, can't end worst, / Nor what God blessed once, prove accurst'.

The speaker in 'Apparent Failure' is identified as the poet himself, who did indeed witness 'seven years since' the baptism of Prince Louis Napoleon, the son of Napoleon III, in June 1856, spoken of in the opening stanza. In the 'Epilogue' to *Dramatis Personae* the poet likewise speaks out directly about religious matters touched on earlier in the volume. The poem is a little drama cast with three roles. The '*First Speaker*, as David' represents the period of triumph of the Church when theism held universal sway. The mysterious presence of the Lord was felt directly, and religious ceremony was one of the chief modes of worshipping and apprehending the divine. The '*Second Speaker*, as Renan', who has staked his faith on empirical evidence, expresses regret for the loss of special revelation. The Face that once enlightened has now receded, leaving only 'lesser lights' to be seen through the mist with great difficulty. It may be, this speaker fears, that the Face was never present at all but was created by humankind's longing for a higher reality that it could worship. The '*Third Speaker*' speaks only as himself, not 'as' someone else. 'Friends', he addresses the previous two speakers, in words similar to those of the presenter's in *Sordello*, 'I have seen through your eyes: now use mine' (68). The old Face cannot be recaptured, it is true, but a new Face, in reality an aspect of the old, can be discerned. The time of miracle and revelation is past, but this does not mean that the Face is lost. In a world of becoming no phenomenon, even a manifestation of the divine, can be expected to remain unaltered. The Absolute is ever embodying and accomplishing itself in new ways.[9] One island of cosmos slips into the sea of chaos only in time to be realized in a different form: waters 'hasten off, to play again elsewhere / The same part, choose another peak' and then 'feast and finish there' (84–6).

As in 'Christmas-Eve' Browning looks to faith beyond the forms of faith. In the creedless Christianity that he adopts there is no need of temple for worship; the world itself, ever evolving on its infinite upward spiral, is temple enough. For him that 'one Face' does not vanish but grows, 'Or decomposes but to recompose' (99–100). As his St John had said, the old forms of truth fade away when their purpose is served and new forms, more challenging because of their novelty, arise to take their place. But the Truth remains, always in advance of any formulation of it.

Dramatis Personae was such a critical and popular success that a second printing was soon called for. The young men of Oxford and Cambridge, like Rossetti and the Pre-Raphaelites earlier, had taken up the poet enthusiastically. Browning's reputation had changed dramatically within a year. The *Athenaeum* (4 June 1864), for example, hailed him as 'a great dramatic poet'. 'No one ever thought Mr Browning like unto any other poet', the *Athenaeum* reviewer said.

> He could not be if he would, and he would not be if he could. He pioneers his own way, and follows no one's track for the sake of ease and smoothness. His music is not as the music of other men. He frequently strikes out something nobly novel; but it is not to be quickly caught, for we have not heard the like before, and at first the mind of the reader finds it difficult to dance to the beat of the time. He has a horror of all that is hackneyed in poetry, and so he goes to the antipodes to avoid it, and finds things on the other side of the world with which we are not commonly acquainted.

Most other reviewers were equally encomiastic. At last Browning was recognized and appreciated as the distinctive, novel poet that he had always been.

10

The Ring and the Book

Although Browning became a celebrity soon after his return from Florence, known not only as a poet but also as a man of the world, dining at the great houses of London and meeting foreign and domestic dignitaries, he never neglected his son. He employed tutors for music, for drawing, for Latin and Greek, and for French, German and Italian. He was, in fact, so preoccupied with Pen's education that Isa Blagden accused him of being a 'monomaniac' about it. 'I shall always have plenty of anxiety, but none unduly, I think', he wrote to her. Pen was 'slow in development, but *sure* – retains all he has learnt & digests it'. In March 1863 Browning was sufficiently optimistic about his son's progress that he managed to get Pen entered on the books at Balliol College, Oxford, for residence in 1867 'if he will but resolve to rise to their high standard of scholarship' (*Dearest Isa*, pp. 104, 130, 156). Browning was drawn to Balliol primarily because Benjamin Jowett, Regius Professor of Greek, was a tutor (and soon to be master) there. Jowett, a liberal clergyman, was the author of one of the *Essays and Reviews*. With his love of Greek and his interest in liberal theology Browning was quick to find in Jowett a sympathetic friend, and the Oxonian was pleased to discover a perfectly sensible poet who could discuss the Greek *scholia* and world affairs. Jowett, who took a strong personal interest in his students and often remained a forceful influence on them for the rest of their lives, also seemed to like Pen and suggested how best he might prepare for admission to Balliol.

Yet it was increasingly evident that Pen's scholarship was not of a high standard. The father tried to console himself that his son was 'increasingly *considerate*'. Besides, Browning asked Isa, if Pen had interests that might take time away from his study of classical languages, 'how can I regret that he plays Bach & Beethoven understandingly?' (*Dearest Isa*, p. 202). Persevering, Robert read Virgil with him and corrected his Greek translations. In the spring of 1866 Jowett arranged for Pen to visit Oxford, where it was soon discovered that the boy's academic preparation was not all that it should be; the aspirant was sent home with suggestions for further reading and a strong indication that his entrance examination be post-poned. At Jowett's suggestion Pen went to stay at Oxford in 1867 so as to learn something of undergraduate life while studying for matriculation. But in 1868 Pen failed the matriculation examination and returned home to his disappointed father.

In the midst of Pen's scholarly preparations Robert was awarded an Oxford Master of Arts degree by diploma at Convocation in June 1867 – 'a very rare distinction said to have only happened in Dr Johnson's case!' (*Dearest Isa*, p. 268). This was followed by his election to an honorary fellowship at Balliol. He was happy about both honours especially because of Pen, whom he supposed would be enrolled 'at the College of which I am Fellow'. He was also 'not insensible to the strange liking for me that young & old Oxford' seemed to have (*Dearest Isa*, pp. 284, 269).

While overseeing Pen's studies Browning made regular visits to Paris to see his father and sister, never failing also to meet up with Milsand when-ever possible. In early spring 1866 he found his father unwell and for two weeks he sat constantly with the elderly man, making no social calls as he was accustomed to doing when in the French capital. Returning home when his father was somewhat better, he discovered that Jane Carlyle had died suddenly and that John Forster was in a paroxysm of grief and tending to necessary details while Carlyle was away in Scotland being installed as rector of Edinburgh University. Browning was much concerned at the effect the sad news would have on his old friend.

In June he received a telegram from Sarianna that their father was dying. Robert hurried over to Paris, arriving on the thirteenth to find his father in convulsions. Briefly the old man regained consciousness. Robert sent Sarianna, who had been watching for two sleepless nights, off to bed and assumed the nursing role at the bedside in the company of Milsand, who had been spending his days there. For the next twenty-four hours, as he slipped in and out of consciousness, Robert Browning senior kept up, according to his son, 'that divine gentleness and care for others that made him by far the *Finest Gentleman* I have ever known'. At night he asked to shake hands with Milsand and told Sarianna, who at Robert's insistence was going to bed, that if he did not see her again, he hoped to meet her in heaven. When Robert asked whether he would liked to be fanned, his father said, 'If you please, dear—I'm only afraid of tiring you' (Hood, p. 96). At approximately half-past eight in the morning of 14 June, just three weeks short of the completion of his eighty-fifth year, 'this good, unworldly, kind hearted, religious man' died. Possessing 'powers natural & acquired [that] would have so easily made him a notable man, had he known what vanity or ambition or the love of money or social influence meant', he was, said his son, 'worthy of being Ba's father—out of the whole world, only he, so far as my experience goes' (*Dearest Isa*, pp. 240-1).

After the burial Robert returned to England, leaving his sister to tend to closing down the Paris household. She was of course keenly aware of

her loss. 'All her life', Robert told Isa, 'has been spent in caring for my
mother, and, seventeen years after that, my father: you may be sure she
does not rave and rend her hair . . . but she loses very much' (Dearest Isa,
p. 241). Soon Sarianna, who never married, was to come live at 19 War-
wick Crescent, there and later in De Vere Gardens to be the companion,
confidante and housekeeper of her brother for the rest of his life. She was
apparently much of the same spirit as her brother; both he and Pen loved
her dearly. Callers found her intelligent and lively in conversation. Joseph
Arnould had earlier called her 'marvelously clever—such fine clear animal
spirits—talks much and well, and yet withal is so simply and deeply good-
hearted that it is a real pleasure to be with her' (Domett, p. 104). Robert
valued her opinion on all things and seems to have discussed his work in
detail with her.

Another confidante, whom he saw almost every day, was Elizabeth's
younger sister Arabel, who, like his own sister, had never married. It was
to her that Browning had first turned when he came to England after
Elizabeth's death. She had been 'perfect & it [was] a great relief to have
her at hand for Pen' (Hudson, p. 84). In June 1868 Browning learned that
she was seriously ill with a heart disease. Anxious about her, he insisted
that she see another doctor, who confirmed the first's prognosis that her
situation was not grave. On 10 June he went to hear the pianist Anton
Rubinstein play, returned home late, and was wakened early with a message
telling that Arabel was worse. He hurried over to her bedside, and in mid-
afternoon she died, as had Elizabeth, in his arms. It was almost seven years
exactly since Elizabeth's death.

As death narrowed his circle of loved ones, Browning turned more and
more to his work. His main business of the years 1864–8 was the writing
of a long poem. In June 1860, wandering as was his wont through the
markets of Florence, he had purchased at a bookstall an old book – the
Old Yellow Book, as he later named it – containing pamphlets, legal
documents and manuscript letters pertaining to a once-famous murder
trial in Rome of an impoverished nobleman from Arezzo who was found
guilty of multiple murders relating to his young bride, her rescue by a
possibly adulterous priest, her baby and her foster parents. Browning had
stopped for a while to leaf through its pages and continued looking at it
on his walk home to Casa Guidi. He was intrigued by the Roman murder
case, mainly because, as the Latin lettering on the volume related, the trial
'disputed whether and when a Husband may kill his Adulterous Wife
without incurring the ordinary penalty'. Here in this copious matter, written
in both Latin and Italian, was a mystery, perhaps even the stuff of a poem.
Always looking beneath and beyond the merely apparent, Browning began
to ask himself whether in fact the wife was adulterous and if so, what
prompted her to be so. By the time he reached home he had figured out
how he could make a poem out of such material. 'My plan was at once
settled', he said years later. 'I went for a walk, gathered twelve pebbles
from the road, and put them at equal distances on the parapet that

bordered it. Those represented the twelve chapters into which the poem is divided; and I adhered to that arrangement to the last'.[1] His mind was not, however, so made up on the matter as he later remembered. He offered the book as the basis for the narratives of novels and poems to various other writers, only in the end to take it on himself. But even before doing so, he made inquiries in Rome and Arezzo about the case, and in 1862 he obtained through Isa Blagden a supplementary manuscript account. He began writing and, fully at work on it in the autumn of 1864, he thought it would be finished by the summer of 1865. But despite daily hard work, writing energetically for three hours every morning, he was not to complete the approximately 21,000 lines of his poem till spring 1868.[2]

Browning had decided after the publication of *Dramatis Personae* that Chapman & Hall did not sufficiently promote the sale of the book and that he would do better with Smith, Elder and Co., whose senior partner, George Murray Smith, the poet had known since 1843 and who would prove extremely useful in the years to come.[3] Browning and Smith discussed the possibility of serial publication in magazines, a common mode of publication of novels, but in the end decided that the poem would appear in four volumes in monthly instalments. Browning was undecided about a title but finally chose *The Ring and the Book*, perhaps largely because it suggested his own initials. The poem duly appeared in the latter parts of the months of November, December, January and February 1868–9.

The poet always claimed that he invented nothing, that everything was in the Old Yellow Book. But in fact he rejected a great number of the details given in it, some of no little importance, such as the fact that the real Count Guido was mad. In addition, as the speaker notes in book one, only three-fifths of his material is in the primary source, the rest being 'written supplement' (1.119). Moreover, the speaker's several retellings of the story of this 'Roman murder-case' (1.121) serve further to call into question whether the 'truth' of the *The Ring and the Book* is fully congruent with the 'truth' of the Old Yellow Book.

The opening of the poem is not unlike that of *Sordello*. The setting and the atmosphere suggest a carnival or a fair,[4] and the speaker, like the presenter of the earlier poem, is a kind of Harlequin figure, the manager of the performance who is both in and out of the enactments of the entertainments and who both is and is not to be identified with the poet.[5] 'Do you see this Ring?' the showman asks his audience. It is an artefact, an imitation of old rings, the result of a 'trick' (1.1, 7) of an artificer who worked gold and an alloy together to make a manageable thing of the most ductile of metals: 'Prime nature with an added artistry' (1.28). This ring, he says, is 'a figure, a symbol' (1.30) of what he is now about to perform. For, 'Do you see this square old yellow Book . . . ?' (1.32). Before his audience's very eyes he will turn this book about an old, forgotten murder case into a living entity, in effect resurrecting the dead and

achieving the 'repristination' (1.23) attained by the artificer of the ring.
But first, a bit about the book and its contents.

The discovery of the book was an act of fate, since the producer like the
actors is a puppet controlled by a master playwright. For one day as the
resurrectionist and producer of the show that is to follow walked about
Florence, he felt himself pushed by 'a Hand, / Always above my shoulder'
– '(Mark the predestination!)' (1.40, 39) – to a certain square, which,
'crammed with booths' (1.42), was itself like a fair. And as he rummaged
in the market, among the odds and ends of the past, he came across and
purchased a certain book. Yet it was not what it seemed: 'A book in shape
but, really, pure crude fact / Secreted from man's life' for two centuries.
'Here it is,' the showman says. But no, 'Give it me back!' It's like a magic
charm, 'restorative / I' the touch and sight' (1.83–9), which must be
guarded.

Reading it as he walked along the streets of Florence, by the time he
reached home he 'had mastered the contents, knew the whole truth'
(1.115) about this case of the uxoricide, Guido Franceschini, wherein it
was disputed whether husbands might kill adulterous wives, in this case
one Pompilia. In the book, of Latin and Italian documents, lay the 'gold',
what the showman claims was 'absolutely truth, / Fanciless fact'. But al-
ready the 'gold' had been worked: the book not only consisted of 'print
three-fifths, written supplement the rest' but also was comprised of 'real
summed-up circumstance' that had been 'put forth and printed'. The
'trial' was only 'here in the book and nowise out of it', since the whole
'trial' consisted entirely of the documents presented to the proper au-
thorities. The prosecutor, like all the other participants in the case, 'only
spoke in print . . . (no noisy work at all,)' (1.139–72). As in a play, every-
thing is 'scripted', everything 'only on paper, pleadings all in print' (1.239).
Clearly the Old Yellow Book was not 'fanciless fact', a reproduction of the
thing itself.

But even as it is, what is the value of such 'gold, the fact untampered
with' (1.360)? In itself it is of no consequence – has no 'truth of force', is
not 'able to take its own part as truth should, / Sufficient, self-sustaining'
(1.367–9) – for the truth is not possessable from a summary of its con-
tents. As he considered revivifying the old story, the showman looked here
and there for confirmation of the facts put forth in the Old Yellow Book.
Persons he inquired of suggested that he should set the project aside.
Why, they asked, be limited to the so-called facts of the book? In addition,
they questioned whether the Old Yellow Book even existed: 'And don't
you deal in poetry, make-believe, / And the white lies it sounds like?' (1:
450–1).

In answering this question both affirmatively and negatively, the
showman, like Browning's St John and the last speaker of the epilogue to
Dramatis Personae, comes to realize that it is not the facts but the interpre-
tation of the facts that makes the ring, that 'fancy with fact is just one fact
the more'. By the power of sympathetic imagination he projects himself

into the facts – 'I fused my live soul and that inert stuff' – and then shuts the book and lays it aside as having no further value (1.458–66). His interpretation of the Roman murder story becomes then the basis for his re-presentation of it. He finds, however, that his interpretation is not stable, and he becomes increasingly sceptical that he can reach or present the truth of the matter.

In book one the narrator offers three distinct versions of the story, representing three possible ways of dramatizing it. The first (1.514–672) is his initial conception of it in Florence, when in a kind of vision 'then and there / Acted itself over again once more / The tragic piece'. 'I saw', the narrator keeps repeating, as if he were a visionary; and what he sees is the murder case in terms of black and white. Guido Franceschini, the murderous husband, is the 'main monster' of 'a dark brotherhood' and the devil incarnate, while Caponsacchi, who rescues the wife, Pompilia, and takes her to Rome, is the 'young good beauteous priest' and type of St George.

In this first version, conceived in Florence, the narrator believed that in his telling of it he 'disappeared; the book grew all in all' (1.681) and so the truth was reached in this 'tragic' re-enactment. But upon reflection he admits that this was not the case. Visionaries, or bards as they were called in *Sordello*, are but self-deluders and thus deceivers of others. For he recognizes that truth cannot be separated from content, text from interpretation, ends from means. 'Are means to the end, themselves in part the end?' he wonders. 'Is fiction which makes fact alive, fact too?' (1.697–8). Man can never create, present the thing itself; this is the prerogative of the master dramatist, God, alone. But by various tricks, 'by a special gift, an art of arts', the man who possesses 'more insight and more outsight and much more / Will to use both of these' than his fellows, can resuscitate, 'enter, spark-like, put old powers to play' and so, like Elisha and Faust, bring the dead to life (1.712–64).

In London the narrator turns to the Old Yellow Book once more, contemplates his 'historical' puppets, and ponders how he might 'have [his] will again with these' (1.778). In the second telling of the Franceschini case (1.772–815), he simply presents the characters in the story in a more objective and briefer fashion. And in considering how might 'this old woe step on the stage again! / Act itself anew' the showman–playwright ponders the role of language in the presentation of facts: 'For how else know we save by worth of word?' Language is a phenomenon, an embodiment subject to all the limitations of the phenomenal world. It can never present the absolute truth but rather 'truth with falsehood, milk that feeds [mankind] now, / Not strong meat he may get to bear some day' (1.816–29). Thus pure truth is ever deferred and cannot be reached by any 'tragic vision'.

In his third telling of the case (1.830–1370) the narrator adopts a more nearly Browningesque, ironic tone and point of view that allows, for example, some sympathy for Guido and some suspicion of Caponsacchi.

'Here are the voices presently shall sound / In due succession', he says,
as he then provides a longish (but not entirely accurate) précis of the play
to follow. The three divergent tellings of the story, as Adam Potkay re-
marks, do not necessarily converge in a kind of supertext. Instead, says
Potkay, book one 'offers a palimpsest of different interpretations, each
telling remaining "visible" beside its subsequent re-telling'.[6]

The narrator explicitly cautions the reader not to be guided by any
interpretation of the case that he the resuscitator might seem to make.
'See it for yourselves', the showman admonishes his audience, and then
further advises them to question 'your sentence absolute for shine or
shade'. Be open to other possibilities, he says in good Browningesque
fashion. The fact is that 'action now shrouds, now shows the informing
thought'. If one could see the good and the bad from all sides, one would
have a different opinion of them both. Viewed rightly, the ensuing drama
will issue forth in no pat moral of right and wrong, and it may be that the
audience will find itself able to arrive at no more than indeterinacy of
judgement (1.1356–70).

What the showman promises his audience is not a manichean melodrama,
in which the forces of darkness are pitted in warfare against the forces of
light, but rather a Bakhtinian carnival of contending figures and voices
resisting hegemony. Each actor in the drama at the fair claims that his or
her interpretation of the case is the right one, which means that the
commedia dell'arte is ultimately a commedia dell'interpretazione. Formally it is a
ring of monologues that his 'tricks' have made. But he asks, almost in the
persona of Robert Browning himself, 'A ring without a posy [an inscrip-
tion], and that ring mine?' (1.1382). Could Robert Browning consider
leaving one of his artefacts unsigned? Of course not. Whereupon he then
inscribes himself into his poem by personalizing the invocation to the
muse that the epic writer traditionally makes. In the final lines of book
one he invokes the spirit of Elizabeth, who melds into the figure of Christ
and the Madonna, to help him: 'Never may I commence my song', or,
some lines later, in a typically Browningesque evasion of an ending, 'Never
conclude' without looking up to where his eyes, 'that cannot reach, yet
yearn', and hope for benediction.

In 'ringing' his dramatization of the murder case in a form approximating
the epic in twelve books, Browning as the manager of the performance
provides his audience – the 'British Public, ye who like me not' (1: 405,
1371) – with a verbal labyrinth, the escape from which they will have to
find for themselves. The showman will be simply the resuscitator, not the
maker of meaning; in this sense he does 'disappear'. If everything seems
to be decentred, the poet can only remind his audience that a ring has at
its centre only an empty space until it is fitted to the finger. 'Meaning' is
but an abstraction until it is existentially appropriated. Having now
completed his introduction, the showman can make 'appear Rome' in
similar fashion to the necromancer's raising of the dead in Sordello to make
'appear Verona'.

Book two represents the segment of Roman opinion that sides with Guido. Meeting an acquaintance outside the church in which Pompilia's murdered parents, the Comparini, are exposed while awaiting burial, Half-Rome tells his version of the facts, which redounds to Guido's credit. A husband should have mastery over his wife and must act forcefully in protecting his honour. His seems to be a fairly impartial account, but in the end it turns out that Half-Rome's judgement is far from unbiased and that he, in fact, speaks for a purpose. For his situation is not unlike Guido's as he conceives it, and he uses the Franceschini story to convey a warning to his listener's cousin, who has been appearing at his wife's window as her suitor. Half-Rome is a perfect example of Browning's contention that all speech is conditioned.

The speaker in the following book, a sentimental bachelor, represents that part of Rome favourable to Pompilia. Having just left the dying young woman's house, he is totally preoccupied with thoughts of her and her suffering. Addressing an uncharacterized auditor, to whom he possibly is related,[7] he weighs the evidence and finds that Guido's forgeries of letters supposedly written by the illiterate Pompilia to Caponsacchi are spittings that spatter Guido himself and not the silly, sweet girl that he imagines Pompilia to be.

While both Half-Rome and Other Half-Rome are based on pamphlets in the Old Yellow Book, Tertium Quid of book four is without counterpart in the source. This speaker, who weighs and evaluates the evidence and opinions provided by the previous two speakers, is contemptuous of any mechanical method of interpretation. Yet he constructs aporias and antinomies in a mechanical fashion, as he tries to fit into his own logical scheme two alternatives that he fancies exclude all other possibilities. For example, Guido was reasonably jealous and punished his erring wife or he was not jealous for a reason (4: 914–15, 749–55); Caponsacchi acted rightly or he did not: in each case there is for Tertium Quid no other possibility. And on the basis of the information he is given, there is no way for him to know which alternative is true. So he will deny both, and suspend judgement, which means a levelling of good and evil. In the end he is morally evasive.

Like Tertium Quid, Guido is a relativist, admitting no absolute ground of truth. In book five, addressing his judges in court a few days after the crime, he adopts the sceptical position to argue that surface meanings deceive and that 'truth', 'love' and 'self' are but words that must be de-mystified and deconstructed.[8] All we can know about other people, he claims, are our interested and partial interpretations of them. There is no essential identity; self-definition is at best fluid; and judgement of any person's actions can only be made in the light of convention. The murders that he committed were an 'irregular deed' (5.99, 113) occasioned by 'irregular' acts on the part of his wife, her lover and her parents; and in his claim it had the sanction of custom. He performed the deed because of personal honour and protection of the family as an institution, and in so doing he martyred himself for the sake of the old established ways. Should he be punished for doing his duty? But Guido, who identifies himself before the court in terms of his social role,[9] does not admit that customs change, that the judgement of the late seventeenth (and nineteenth) century is not necessarily that of former times. Basing his defence on the personal nature of interpretation, he asks: 'Do your eyes here see with mine?' (5.1059). Yet in asking that question, he also allows for it to be asked in reverse and for himself to stand judged.

Where Guido is obsequious before his judges, Caponsacchi, whose testimony is presented in book six, is angry and hostile. He had appeared previously before them, and he recalls how they were slyly amused by the predicament that this young coxcomb priest had got himself into. At that time they could have acted in such a way as to save Pompilia, but instead they let Guido go free to murder her and her family. Caponsacchi's testimony is delivered in terms of an idealist discourse that portrays Pompilia as absolute good and Guido as absolute evil. His puzzlement is that the court could not have discerned this as well. For it was plain to him – him who previously had been unprepared for the recognition of the good and acting on it – from the moment he first saw Pompilia:

> Pompilia spoke, and I at once received,
> Accepted my own fact, my miracle
> Self-authorised and self explained. . . .
>   (6.903–5)

To assert his authority as a reliable *amicus curiae*, he must tell how this case has affected him: 'I need that you should know my truth' (6.338). And what he relates is a kind of *Bildungsroman* in which he traces his development from an indifferent priest committed only to an empty formalism to a Christian soldier in the service of the right and good, personified in Pompilia, whom he idealizes as a type of the Madonna. Dramatizing himself as a type of St George, he claims at last to have achieved true self-definition through Pompilia, the other who has tugged him into consciousness of what he should be: 'As I / Recognized her, at potency of truth / So she . . . knew me' (6.916–18).

If Caponsacchi finds self-definition by overstepping the bounds prescribed by the institutional Church, Pompilia's case offers an extraordinary example of the inability of established institutions to deal with what Guido called irregularities. In her monologue in book seven the dying Pompilia tells how she submitted to the institutions of the family and of marriage and was wronged by both. Then when she appealed for help to the institutions devised to offer redress for wrong – the law and the Church, in the persons of the governor and archbishop of Arezzo – they proved unable to do anything other than support an unethical status quo. It was Caponsacchi who came to her aid by doing exactly what priests should not do, namely, run off with married women. Dramatizing herself in idealist discourse as the Madonna and her child as the infant Jesus, she sees Caponsacchi as her angel, God's agent, the one who can read the signs of her saintliness, 'reads, as only such can read, the mark / God sets on woman, signifying so / She should—shall peradventure—be divine' (7.1483–5).

Convinced that she, like Caponsacchi, can read signs and penetrate to the signified, she is surprised that others do not share the ability to perceive what should be perfectly obvious. Where her saviour could hardly believe that her goodness was not self-evident to all who saw her, Pompilia laments the differences that varying perspectives yield:

> So we are made, such difference in minds,
> Such difference too in eyes that see the minds!
> (7.912–13)

She is amazed that others do not see the mark, the white light that radiates from Caponsacchi and all his acts with her. For her as for him there is no necessity of interpretation. Denying the deconstructive stances of Guido, they lay claim to idealistic vision, seeing not semblance but the thing, the white light of truth itself.

In the next two books, in which Browning has a great deal of fun satirizing the law and its practitioners, whom he had especially disliked ever since the breach-of-promise case against his father, lawyers for the defence and prosecution make no pretence of reaching the truth. The defence lawyer is more interested in his young son, home and its comforts than in anything having to do with Guido's case. But Hyacinthus de Archangelis, to give the records' Latin name for him, is a competent lawyer who loves the casuistical exercises that the law entails, and he argues, often ludicrously, that Guido's actions were justified by the laws of God, man and nature. Although his primary concern in the case is one of money and professional vanity, Archangeli as a family man is to some degree sympathetic with Guido's plea of *honoris causa* and the accused's desire for money that he would receive through his son.

The prosecuting attorney, on the other hand, is a bachelor for whom the law is a susbstitute for family. Bottini must try to prove that to whatever degree Pompilia was culpable was owing to fear, ignorance or weakness. Strangely, his prosecution is not so much of Guido as of Pompilia herself, against whom he considers not only the charges advanced by others but also those that he pruriently imagines. He treats the allegations as if true and then, adeptly if ludicrously, refutes them. But it is clear, almost from the beginning, that Bottini is less interested in the prosecution of this particular case than in displaying his splendid oratory based on classical rhetoric. To the lawyers for the defense and prosecution, words are never more than words. 'Anything, anything to let the wheels / Of argument run glibly to their goal!' (9.469–70). Where interpretation is required, it is merely a matter of employing mechanical modes.

In book ten the Pope ponders the law as a yardstick for measuring right and wrong and finds it defective on many grounds, the chief being that it is mechanical in operation. Employing the idealist discourse of Caponsacchi and Pompilia, the Pope addresses himself throughout his meditation to the question of interpretation. Disavowing history as a guide in the opening of his soliloquy, he turns from a survey of the judgements of his predecessors in the chair of St Peter, which he finds problematical, and concludes that he 'must give judgment on [his] own behoof' (10.160). Unlike Tertium Quid he is not immobilized by the uncertainties of history (or documents) resulting from the exposure of contradiction and deceit.[10] He therefore declares Guido guilty, finding a 'black mark impinge the man' (10.510); pronounces Pompilia 'perfect in whiteness' (10.1001); and exonerates Caponsacchi, the 'warrior- priest' who through his heroic rescue of Pompilia 'let light into the world' (10.1091, 1200). But how are such judgements made? The Pope says:

> Truth, nowhere, lies yet everywhere in these [documents]—
> Not absolutely in a portion, yet
> Evolvible from the whole: evolved at last
> Painfully, held tenaciously by me.
> Therefore there is not any doubt to clear
> When I shall write the brief word presently
> And chink the hand-bell, which I pause to do.
>   (10.228–34)

And in his 'pause' of almost 2,000 lines he explains that through an examination of motives he can issue an authoritative evaluation of the actions of the characters involved. And how does he get to knowledge of 'the seed of act' (10.271)? Through the exercise of dramatic sympathy.[11] Through negative capability he empathizes with the actors, becomes them so as to uncover their motives. In this sense the Pope is an actor as well as a spectator of a script entitled 'A Roman murder-case' (1.121). Initially he admits the possibility that his performative interpretation might be wrong (10.259–66), although he is forced by his office to interpret as best he can. Further, the Pope is unwilling to be immobilized by uncertainty and so resorts to questionable signs to support his verdict, such as the mark on Guido, and an insistence that such and such 'must not be' (10.2125). For all his willingness to let his interpretation of the facts evolve solely from the outcome of the little drama that he enacts, he nevertheless imposes on the drama his own beliefs and psychological needs. Never can the man who plays the imagined part escape his existential role: Antonio Pignatelli of Naples is also Innocent XII, bishop of Rome, who speaks 'in God's name' (10: 162). And so he cannot fail in his judgement? More tentatively he avows that it 'must not be'.

In his final appearance, the monologue in book eleven addressed to those who have come to confess him, Guido plays the deconstructionist more forcefully than in book five. His visitors have come to have his last words and to encourage penitence; they wish, he says, to know the essential Guido:

> Did not the Trial show things plain enough?
> 'Ah, but a word of the man's very self
> Would somehow put the keystone in its place
> And crown the arch!' Then take the word you want!
> (11.508–11)

He will speak because 'lucidity of soul unlocks the lips: / I never had the words at will before' (11.158–9). And thereafter the words fly. All Guido's monologue is self-consciously, lunatically verbal, as he takes the terms guilt and innocence, masculinity and femininity, faith and unbelief, institutional law and the Gospel, nature and society, master and slave and deconstructs them all in an effort to confound his listeners' Christian beliefs and thereby elude their demands. It becomes clear that his speech is not merely rhetorical but also evidential of a lack of a stable self. Guido is, in his own words, incomplete, made so by the devil,

> whose task it is
> To trip the all-but-at perfection . . .
> Inscribes all human effort with one word,
> Artistry's haunting curse, the Incomplete!
> (11.1550–6)

Thus it is written in the script by which one plays out one's life. Guido's most virulent charge against Pompilia is that she would not follow the script, believed in fact in what is an absurdity to a deconstructionist – an *hors texte*:

> Would not begin the lie that ends with truth,
> Nor feign the love that brings real love about:
> Wherefore I judged, sentenced and punished her.
> (11.1425–7)

In the end Guido repudiates all his words that have gone before as a bad script.

> Sirs, have I spoken one word all this while
> Out of the world of words I had to say?
> Not one word! All was folly . . . .

But now he will say his 'first true word, all truth and no lie' and that is 'save me' (11.2408–13). As he begs for his life, his last words seem to suggest penitence:

I am yours,
I am the Granduke's—no, I am the Pope's!
Abate,—Cardinal,—Christ,—Maria,—God,...
Pompilia, will you let them murder me?

Whether the words are sincere, as many critics have claimed,[12] or whether
they are not we will never know. Whether Guido fulfils the Pope's hope
for his salvation iterated at the end of book ten is a matter that is, like so
much in *The Ring and the Book*, indeterminate.

In the last book the ring is closed without bringing full closure, since
a ring after all has literally no beginning or end. 'Here were the end, had
anything an end', says the showman in the first line of book twelve. 'You
have seen [the] act, / By my power', he tells his audience, and 'may-be,
judged it by your own'. And now that the act is over, like a rocket it falls
and fades:

What was once seen, grows what is now described,
Then talked of, told about, a tinge the less
In every fresh transmission.
(12.10–16)

As Browning's St John said, faith in the thing changes to faith in the
report.

As in book one the manager of the performance offers several textual
versions of the story, this time of Guido's execution on the Feast of Fools
and the current happenings in Rome, each of them more or less stressing
the carnival aspect. From these and the other texts in the Old Yellow Book
the resuscitating showman has provided a living theatre; and in a gesture
of farewell to those who have watched the show – the 'British Public, who
may like me yet' (12.831) – he offers a 'lesson':

our human speech is naught,
Our human testimony false, our fame
And human estimation words and wind.
(12.834–6)

This lesson is very much like that proffered by Fra Celestino, Pompilia's
confessor, in his fragmentary sermon. Like the showman, Fra Celestino
adopts the position of disillusioned scepticism by assuming that every
interpretation is so false that no interpretation is true. Preaching on the
text 'God is true / And every man a liar',[13] he maintains that he

who trusts
To human testimony for a fact
Gets this sole fact – himself is proved a fool.
(12: 597–600)

Yet when we investigate it, we see that the claim of both the showman and
the Augustinian monk is a version of Zeno's paradox of the Cretan liar:
if every man is a liar, how can any statement he makes about truth be true?
Their condition of falsehood is thus incompatible with their claim that all
testimony is unreliable.

Clearly the narrator of book twelve is no more exempt from Browning's
irony than any of the other speakers in the poem. The poet knew very
well, as he had suggested in *Pippa Passes*, that no human can know what
God knows or in any way have knowledge of the ultimate order of things;
and even if he did know, he, like Paracelsus, would not have the means
to tell about it. The manager of the performance, however, seeks to find
a way around this paradox. Art, he asserts, is a different kind of speech
and thus 'the one way possible / Of speaking truth' (12.839–40). This is
because, as in *Sordello*, the audience for his art is a 'brother'. Speaking as
man or woman, the individual cannot tell the brother a truth, because,
given the speaker's and the hearer's self-interestedness, the truth looks
false when it reaches him. But art, which is not life but artifice that (in
Browning's hands, at least) foregrounds its representational inadequacy,
is addressed not to an individual but to mankind and as re-presentation
can tell a truth 'obliquely'. Calling on what Browning in the preface to
Paracelsus termed the brother/reader's 'co-operating fancy', art can 'breed
the thought' even though missing (while asking to be supplied) the 'me-
diate word' (12.841–57). *The Ring and the Book* stands thus in its author's
eyes as a type of the 'synthetist' art of 'brother's speech' outlined in the
fifth book of *Sordello*.

The audience for the resuscitation of this piece of Roman history is
presented not with the 'truth' but with the 'documental drama' from
which they must discover it for themselves: the only kind of truth that in
Browning's eyes is worth possessing. What the author–showman provides
is not *an* interpretation but a series of interpretations of an event from
which the reader may choose or, more importantly, may make his or her
own. This, as we have noted earlier, is what Browning, following Keats,
calls soul-making. The audience's proper experience of the drama that
the manager of the performance has presented is as a hermeneutic en-
terprise, an exercise in original thinking that will 'mean, beyond the facts,
/ Suffice the eye and save the soul beside' (12: 862–3).

The Ring and the Book is frequently and erroneously called a relativist
poem. It is surely not Browning's point that all truth is relative, that nothing
is true or false, good or bad except that our saying or feeling so makes it
so. Browning to some degree ranks the dramatized interpretations. The
sophistries of the lawyers and the mad nihilism of Guido are obviously not
the interpretations that the reader–viewer is to embrace. Nor are the ver-
sions rendered by the most winning characters such as Caponsacchi or
Pompilia, which vary fairly widely in their tellings of the facts of the case,
offered as central. Even the Pope, the most compelling of the judges of
the affair, arrives at his leap of faith in his judgement only after placing

the events of the case within a mythic framework of biblical rescue and salvation; his faith in a redeemed Pompilia is not based on verified fact admissible in a court of law. Far from saying that all truth is relative, Browning says that all truth is relational, that it depends upon a complex of things. He recognizes that in our moral economy good often conflicts with good and that any particular good we try to absolutize may be overridden by a subsequent good that the historical situation demands. Browning would have his brother/reader form his interpretation by surveying the possibilities, recognizing the limits of any particular one, and being open to new ones. A right interpretation of the Franceschini case, like that of the Bible, is thus in Browning's view always provisional: an approximation of truth for the time being.

That no part of The Ring and the Book renders the final 'truth' the manager of the performance makes almost explicit in the last seven lines. Speaking now, as at the end of book one, openly as Robert Browning, he tells that this 'ring' into which he has inscribed himself is a guard ring preserving the inner ring of facts – 'the rough ore' – of the murder case. Truth and its accessibility are thus refigured as rings within rings, circling round the truth but never getting there. In a final gesture of self-display Browning proffers the poem as a guard ring to the 'rare gold ring of verse' written by his dead wife, the 'Lyric Love' who has inspired its making. Textually shaped, it joins not only husband with wife but also Italy, where he found the Old Yellow Book and where the events took place, with England, where he has written it. In addition, it translates Elizabeth from Florence where she was buried – 'his Italy', the Tuscany of Nicolò Tommasei, who on the commemorative inscription at Casa Guidi speaks of her verse as linking Italy and England – to London, 'our England', where her spirit is 'resuscitated' by this ring that is a book. In one of his most daring acts of textual displacement Browning asserts the soul-saving value of art – 'to mouths like mine, at least' (12: 840).

11

Memory and Desire

I

The British public wooed by Browning in *The Ring and the Book* was won. The book sold well, and the reviewers who had been been warm in their praise of *Dramatis Personae* were now positively adulatory. The *Fortnightly Review* of 1 March 1869 declared that 'a striking human transaction has been seized by a vigorous and profound imagination, . . . its many diverse threads have been wrought into a single rich and many-coloured web of art'; and the *Athenaeum* of 20 March proclaimed it 'the *opus magnum* of our generation . . . beyond all parallel the supremest poetical achievement of our time, . . . the most precious and profound spiritual treasure that England has produced since the days of Shakspeare'.

'I find the British Public is beginning to like you well', wrote Julia Wedgwood, a young woman in her mid-thirties with whom Browning over the past four or five years had struck up a sentimental friendship that was soon to cease because she fell hopelessly in love with him (*Wedgwood*, p. 193). 'Yes', Browning replied, 'the British Public like, and more than like me, this week, they let their admiration ray out on me, and at sundry congregations of men wherein I have figured these three or four days, I have seen, felt and, thru' white gloves, handled a true affectionateness not unmingled with awe'. But, he said modestly, it was all because 'of the Queen's having desired to see me, and three other extraordinary persons' (*Wedgwood*, p. 195) – Carlyle, the historian George Grote and the geologist Sir Charles Lyell. The *Court Circular* of 13 March 1869 records that at this audience the Queen 'had the pleasure of becoming personally acquainted with two of the most distinguished writers of the age – . . . eminent men – who, so far as intellect is concerned, stand head and shoulders above their contemporaries'. Browning was much pleased with the audience and took it and the invitation to become Lord Rector of St Andrews University (which he declined) as signs that at long last he had captured popular esteem.

His pleasure in public acclaim was not sufficient, however, to counterbalance the misfortunes of the spring and summer of 1869. After some asking of special favours Browning had managed to have Pen, who had been unable to make his way at Balliol, admitted to Christ Church, Oxford, which, the father was certain, he would find more 'congenial' inasmuch as he would not be expected to prove himself 'an adept at grammatical niceties, which are the daily bread at Balliol' (*Wedgwood*, p. 148). But already, some few months after taking up residence there, Pen apparently was having trouble with his studies. In addition, the father seems to have learned of his son's sexual caprices in Brittany the previous summer. Moreover, Browning, normally so robust, was seriously unwell for several months, during which time he remained housebound. He was, he confessed, 'frightened a little by all this bad luck'.[1]

Forced by circumstances to forgo his summer holiday in Brittany, he and Sarianna and Pen therefore joined the Storys and their daughter Edith, who had come over from the Continent, on a trip to Scotland, where he had never been. The sightseeing tour did not, however, turn out as he had hoped. The weather was bad and the lodgings uncomfortable, and although he had earlier refused an invitation to visit Louisa, Lady Ashburton, at her splendid 'lodge' at Loch Luichart, he and his party were now entreated and eventually compelled by her insistence to accept her hospitality.

Lady Ashburton was the widow of the very wealthy William Baring, second Baron Ashburton, who had died five years earlier. In her early forties she was a Junoesque woman who struck many people as larger-than-life-size. She possessed both charm and taste and, being of a commanding personality, was accustomed to getting her way. Henry James described her as 'so striking and interesting a personage, a rich generous presence that, wherever encountered seemed always to fill the foreground with colour, with picture, with fine mellow sound'.[2] She sought out the great men of her day and showered them with gifts and invitations to visit at one of her grand homes. Among her closest acquaintances were the Carlyles, who adored her and her nine-year-old daughter, and Anna Jameson, the celebrated author who had accompanied the Brownings from Paris to Italy when they first married. Browning had originally met Louisa Mackenzie in Paris in 1851, eight years before she became Lady Ashburton, and since his return to London had seen her on various social occasions. Although initially reluctant to accept her repeated invitation to stay at Loch Luichart, Browning now welcomed the comfort of a well-run, luxurious household and the consequent buoyed spirits of Pen, Sarianna and the Storys. '[T]he worst is over', he wrote to Isa Blagden on 28 August, soon after his arrival, '& here, at an old friend's I am comfortable altogether... [and] all goes well now in this beautiful place' (*Dearest Isa*, p. 322).

Plate 9 'Robert and Pen Browning', c. 1869. Photograph. Courtesy of the Armstrong Browning Library.

Some days after the party had been installed in the house, Lady Ashburton apparently suggested to her famous guest, probably indirectly, that a marriage between these two widowed persons, each struggling with the upbringing of an only child, might be felicitous for them both. Browning, no doubt surprised, seems to have been not totally unsympathetic in his response, which was nevertheless politely evasive. When the visitors left some days later, everyone was still cheerful.[3] From Loch Luichart, where they had spent approximately three weeks, Browning and the Storys went to Naworth Castle, the Cumberland home of George and Rosalind

Plate 10 'Louisa Lady Ashburton (second wife of the second Baron Ashburton) with her daughter Maysie', 1862. Oil portrait by Sir Edwin Landseer. Reproduced by courtesy of the Marquess of Northampton.

Howard (later the Earl and Countess of Carlisle), who were special friends of the Storys, while Pen and Sarianna left for the south. There Edie, the twenty-five-year-old unmarried daughter of the Storys whom Browning had known since she was a little girl, confided to her hostess that Lady Ashburton had 'declared herself to be in love with Browning & shewed it to everyone'. Browning had asked Edie's advice and said that if she advised him to marry the lady he would do it, but Edie said that it was not right to marry a woman for her position and for his son's sake. When a letter came from Lady Ashburton expressing 'a wish to clinch the matter one way or another', Browning wrote to say no, 'taking advantage of an expression in her letter in which she said that perhaps it would be better for her child's sake that they should not marry. He appeared much more light hearted when he had disposed of that matter'.[4]

Edie further told Mrs Howard that the poet was in love with her, Edie, and was forcing his attentions on her. Rosalind Howard believed her and fancied that the poet 'was burningly in love & thinks he covers it all by being an old family friend, so that it is not apparent to people & he takes hold of her hand & once kissed her on the forehead (in the presence of her unsuspecting mother)'. Probably this was nothing more than the affectionate attention paid by an older man to a much younger woman whom he had known almost all her life. Browning was renowned for his gallantries to ladies – it was also frequently said that he was about to be married to some wealthy widow or other[5] – and whatever 'liberties' he took were generally accepted as the kindly, innocently flirtatious attentions of an elderly, respectable widower. In her diary recording Edie Story's confidences Rosalind Howard also noted that on an outing with her house guests and another young woman, Aggie Carnegie, 'Aggie let down her golden hair to please Browning as we sat by the waterfall – he said poets ought to be indulged by such sights'. In all likelihood Edie Story was the one who was in love with the man who was 'her best & greatest & oldest friend'. She was, Mrs Howard wrote, 'very unhappy for him & says she could at once sacrifice herself & marry him to make him happy but that it would not be right to do it'. In the last analysis, the 'passion' that Edie ascribed to Browning was probably her own.

Browning left Naworth Castle at the end of September. For the next seven or eight months he was often away from Warwick Crescent, visiting the country houses of the great and famous and spending a good deal of time with Pen at Oxford, where he enjoyed being lionized by the undergraduates. In June 1870 Pen failed his examinations and was forced to leave Christ Church. His father was disconsolate, in fact angry with his son not only for his academic failure but for being a spendthrift as well. What was to come of the boy who seemed to have only one talent, namely, for expensive living? Pen was weak and immune to any influence his father might exert. 'I am merely the manger at which he feeds', Browning wrote his brother-in-law George Barrett on 1 July, 'and nothing is more certain than that I could do him no greater good than by dying to-night and leaving him just enough to keep from starving' (*Letters to George*, p. 295).[6] A year later Robert wrote in somewhat the same vein to Isa Blagden: Pen 'has been assiduously labouring in that occupation to which Providence apparently hath pleased to call him, – that is, in shooting, idling and diverting himself' (*Dearest Isa*, p. 367).

The major diversion from his troubles with Pen was the Franco-Prussian War, which commenced with France's declaration of war on Prussia on 19 July. Browning recognized from the press reports that the French were little prepared for such an undertaking. In 'the interest of humanity', he

Plate 11 'Robert Browning, Naworth Castle, September 1869'. Drawings by William Wetmore Story. Reproduced by courtesy of The Pierpont Morgan Library, New York. Gift of Mrs Herbert N. Straus. 1954.5.

wrote, Napoleon III 'wants a sound beating this time & probably may get it' (*Dearest Isa*, p. 340). Almost immediately it was plain that the war was going in favour of the Prussians and that France was suffering serious defeats. But no war was going to stand in the way of a summer holiday in France, and so Robert and Sarianna met Milsand on the Normandy coast on 12 August. When the emperor capitulated on 1 September and things grew progressively worse as the Germans invaded the country, Milsand became alarmed for the safety of his English friends. They however were reluctant to give up their pleasant days on the beach, and only at Milsand's insistence did they make a hurried departure for home, where over the next seven months they followed the disasters and sufferings inflicted on the French by the Germans and by themselves.

By spring 1871 the Prussian King Wilhelm had been proclaimed emperor of the German empire in the Hall of Mirrors at Versailles, and it looked as though a good part of Europe and its past would be buried under Prussian militarism. Browning feared 'that we shall all be forced into the Prussian system' and that there would be 'nothing but soldiering to concern us for the next generation' (*Dearest Isa*, p. 344). Also in spring

1871 Elizabeth had been dead for nearly ten years. Probably with the recent war and the coming anniversary of Elizabeth's death in mind, Browning turned to the composition of a poem incorporating a translation of Euripides' *Alkestis*, 'imposed' on him, as the dedication relates, by the young Countess Cowper, 'a singularly pretty & kind person' (*Dearest Isa*, p. 364), and completed as 'the most delightful of May-month amusements'. The result was *Balaustion's Adventure: Including a Transcript from Euripides*, published in August 1871.

II

Balaustion is about salvation, through art and love. Its narrator is a young woman from Rhodes, in character very much like Pompilia in *The Ring and the Book*. Her native island is preparing to forswear its allegiance to Athens, which has been defeated by Sparta, so as to share in the spoil. Balaustion, however, refuses to turn her back on her beloved Athens, which is for her 'the life and light / Of the whole world worth calling world at all' (25–6), and embrace the militaristic, materialistic culture of Sparta.

In the first 357 lines of the poem, which serve as a prologue to the 'Transcript from Euripides', Balaustion sets forth her belief in the redemptive power of poetry, which is 'a power that makes' and which 'speaking to one sense, inspires the rest, / Pressing them all into its service', to the end that the audience sees, hears and feels simultaneously (318–28). Her 'transcript' of the *Alkestis* is her interpretation of the play in which she interweaves her own commentary on the characters with Euripides' dramatic colloquies. In her telling, Admetos learns the meaning of love and loss and Herakles is Christianized into a god-man dedicated to alleviation of the sufferings of others.

Admetos at first stands condemned because he opts for being rather than becoming. Unwilling to die, he has called on all possible powers to save him, with the result that his life can be rescued only if he can find someone to die in his place. His wife, Alkestis, alone is willing to pay the ransom; and only at her burial does Admetos, 'beginning to be like his wife' (2000), understand how wrong he has been in believing that 'of all evils in the world, the worst / Was – being forced to die, whate'er death gain' (1072–3). At this point Herakles, 'human and divine', appears, holding 'his life / Out on his hand, for any man to take', and reminding mankind that 'good days had been, / And good days, peradventure, still might be' (1049, 1076–7, 1253–4). Immediately setting about to help the grieving king, he harrows Hades and returns with the veiled Alkestis. Rejoined with his wife and now aware of his selfishness, Admetos is redeemed from his egoism and vows 'to begin a fresh / Existence, better than the life before' (2387–8).

Balaustion's interpretation is not a criticism but a 'higher criticism' of the text in which Euripides, stressing Admetos's self-control, was careless of or indifferent to certain moral implications of the story. Just as a modern hermeneuticist may look behind the literal accounts of the gospels to grasp the essence of the Christian message, Balaustion looks beyond the actual text to seize upon Euripides' essential meaning. Like the Pope in *The Ring and the Book*, she by imaginative sympathy will look beyond the facts.

Literalists will, of course, object to such an interpretation. After Balaustion recounted the play, a 'brisk little somebody, / Critic and whippersnapper' – surely intended for Alfred Austin, who had attacked Browning in the *Temple Bar* in June 1869 – objected to the liberties she had taken (306– 16). Balaustion replies that the person who can 'hear, see and feel, in faith's simplicity' is the one who really 'sees the play' for what it is (333– 5), whereas the literalists and 'friendly moralists' (2390), unwilling or unable to project themselves imaginatively and sympathetically into the text, fail to see that meaning is not fixed and final but ever open to fresh possibilities. Truth, she argues, has many facets and is approachable in many ways: different understandings or interpretions may 'glorify the Dionusiac shrine' without defiling it (2407). The validity of Balaustion's interpretive enterprise is proven by its effect, the saving of her and her companions from the harshness of their captors.

In *The Ring and the Book* the Pope envisioned Euripides as one who had intuited Christian virtues without a specifically Christian revelation. The Greek dramatist, the Pope implies, saw that the 'perfection fit for God' is 'love without a limit'; he knew that if there is 'strength' and 'intelligence' and love 'unlimited in its self-sacrifice, / Then is the tale true and God shows complete' (10.1362–7). To the Pope there can be 'first things made new' when there is 'repetition of the miracle, / The divine instance of self-sacrifice / That never ends and aye begins for man' (10: 1649–52). In his judgement every Christian must refashion the Christian story for himself, putting 'the same truth / In a new form' (10.1392–3).

Balaustion, who has 'drunk' Euripides' play and 'quenched' her thirst, nevertheless feels that 'yet more remains' (2431–2): the wish to dramatize the redemption that she personally has experienced from immersion in the text. In her version, which must reflect Browning's own feelings for his dead wife, Apollo's music tames all Admetos's selfish desires and induces in him the wish, shared by Alkestis, to perfect the people whom he rules. The king refuses his wife's sacrifice of herself, for to agree would violate the humanity for which he wishes to live. Yet it must be, she argues. He must live to carry out their ideals; and so entirely are they one being that the choice must be made regardless of each as an individual. As they embrace, her soul enters his; and when she dies and her spirit goes to Hades, it is refused entrance because the queen of the underworld re-cognizes that this is but a mock death. Before the embrace is relaxed, Alkestis is alive again and, with her husband, lives long and well.

In Balaustion's version there is no heroic redeemer to reclaim Alkestis as there was in Euripides' play. Indeed, it is precisely the point of the play that love redeems Alkestis from death and allows her to work with her husband for the good. In the 'Spartan' world in which all the traditional beliefs and loyalties have begun to decay, Balaustion, like the Pope of *The Ring and the Book*, foresees a time when the old mythology must be re-interpreted so that the essence of the myth will not be discarded along with its outer trappings. For her as for the Pope the 'true tale' is 'love without a limit'. For those grasping the essence of the 'tale' there is then no need for a mythical Herakles or an historical Jesus: 'Christ' is present in the individual's life when he or she assumes the Christian attributes and re-enacts the Christian story. If the instincts be right, if love be complete, the miracle of the Incarnation is repeated. Whatever the attacks made on the sacred text, the substance of faith is ever available to persons willing to immerse themselves in it and the commentaries on or rewritings of it.

Balaustion's version of the *Alkestis*, rendered in the most beautiful poetry of the work, is testimony to her belief that poetry can 'bring forth new good, new beauty, from the old' (2425). And her theory of the efficacy of poetry is further proven by the woman poet and the painter described at the end of her narrative who also produce art works in response to Euripides' play, which was originally scorned by the Athenians.

In the last 105 lines, serving as epilogue, Balaustion reveals herself most clearly as the mask of the poet. 'I know', she says, 'the poetess who graved in gold, / Among her glories that shall never fade', the title of Euripides as '*the Human with his droppings of warm tears*'. This is Elizabeth Barrett Browning, and the quotation is from a quatrain from her *Wine of Cyprus* (1844) that serves as epigraph to the poem. 'I know, too', she continues, 'a great Kaunian painter' who 'made a picture of it all'. This is Browning's friend Sir Frederic Leighton, who had recently exhibited his *Hercules Wrestling with Death for the Body of Alcestis* (1871). It is a piece 'worthy to set up in our Poikilé', which is surely to be identified with the National Gallery. And just think, Balaustion–Browning says, 'It all came of this play that gained no prize!' Still smarting from his earlier critical neglect, the poet nevertheless asserts his self-confidence by boldly asking in the final line, 'Why crown whom Zeus has crowned in soul before?'

Balaustion's Adventure is a much underrated poem. The 'transcript' of Euripides' *Alkestis* is a brilliant, ingenious means of dealing with commentary on an ancient text, and Balaustion's retelling of the Greek story is a perfect example of the revision or re-enactment that Browning always insists must be a part of the reader's participation in the text.[7] In addition, Balaustion herself, who resembles both Pippa and Pompilia but, in seeing beyond the facts, is more complex than either, is one of Browning's loveliest creations. She is, as her shipmates call her, the 'Wild-pomegranate-flower' that dethrones the rose (207–10).

III

Balaustion's Adventure was well received and the issue of 2,500 copies was sold out before Christmas. In late July, just before its publication, Browning and Pen set out for another holiday in Scotland. For two months they enjoyed themselves enormously. They called on Jowett, who was entertaining an Oxford reading party nearby, and there met Robert's old admirer, the poet Algernon Charles Swinburne, who had been one of Jowett's students before being sent down and who was now being entrusted to Jowett to keep him off drink. Knowing that the Brownings were fairly close by, Lady Ashburton invited them to Loch Luichart. Robert, however, was most reluctant to go, having already resisted her 'nine or ten months' teazing with her invitations' (Hudson, p. 170). Nevertheless, perhaps for the sake of Pen, who had visited Lady Ashburton and her daughter earlier in the year at their home in the south, he relented. On 2 October he went over to Loch Luichart, where he remained overnight. Apparently Lady Ashburton again raised the question of marriage, and this time, instead of temporizing, Browning told her forthrightly that his heart lay 'buried in Florence, and the attractiveness of a marriage with her lay in its advantage to Pen' (Hudson, pp. 170–1). Lady Ashburton's vanity was wounded. Browning left the next day. She however wrote to him, 'foamed out into the couple of letters she bespattered [him] with' (Hudson, p. 170). She also told others that the poet had ill-treated her, that she had broken with him, and that he was constantly 'making endeavours to renew a relationship of even ordinary acquaintance' (Hudson, p. 186). Six months later Browning wrote to Edie Story that he had met Lady Ashburton only once since he left Loch Luichart and 'felt excused from even looking at—much less, speaking to her' (Hudson, p. 170). Thereafter he was to see 'every now and then that contemptible Lady Ashburton, and mind her no more than any other black beetle—so long as it don't crawl up my sleeve' (Hudson, p. 175).

While in Scotland during August 1871 Browning commenced writing a poem that, so he noted at the end of the manuscript, was begun in rough draft in Rome in 1860. It was, he told Edie Story, conceived 'twelve years ago in the Via del Tritone—in a little handbreath of prose,—now yellow with age and Italian ink' (Hudson, p. 167). He brought his 'little sketch begun in *Rome in '60'* with him to Scotland, and by 1 October had 'written about 1800 absolutely new lines or more, . . . what *I* can't help thinking a sample of my very best work' (*Dearest Isa*, p. 367). The poem was based on Napoleon III, who had been released from captivity and taken refuge in England earlier in the year. Although Browning, as we have seen, had never shared his wife's admiration for Louis Napoleon, he had on occasion seen some good in the French emperor. As in the case of his own fictional characters, the poet believed there was at least a modicum of good in everyone. 'I thought badly of him at the beginning of his career', he wrote, but 'better afterward, on the strength of promises he made, and gave indications of intending to redeem,—I think him very weak in the last miserable year' (*Dearest Isa*, p. 371). Further, 'I don't think so much worse of the character as shown us in the last few years, because I suppose there to be a physical and intellectual decline of faculty, brought about by the man's own faults, no doubt —but I think he struggles against these . . .' (Hudson, p. 167). In short, Browning saw in Napoleon a man of complex character whose ideals and actions were frequently antithetical.

In the poem about him, entitled *Prince Hohenstiel-Schwangau, Saviour of Society*, Browning addresses the problem of why persons with good intentions fail to pursue them. And in getting to the answer he has his speaker undertake 'Revealment of myself' (22) to an imaginary auditor. The 'revelation', which is formally a dramatic monologue incorporating soliloquy and an interior dialogue, is of course apologetic. As Browning said of his speaker, he struggles against his own faults, 'and when that is the case, depend on it, in a soliloquy, a man makes the most of his good intentions and sees great excuse in them—far beyond what our optics discover!' (Hudson, p. 167).

In the first part the prince attempts to justify his conservative rule:

> To save society was well: the means
> Whereby to save it,—there begins the doubt
> Permitted you, imperative on me;
> Were mine the best means? Did I work aright
> With powers appointed me?—since power denied
> Concern me nothing.
>
> (701–6)

If he has not done all that social visionaries would have him do, it is because he had first to devote himself to the immediate needs of his people:

> No, my brave thinkers, whom I recognize,
> Gladly, myself the first, as, in a sense,
> All that our world's worth, flower and fruit of man!
> Such minds myself award supremacy
> Over the common insignificance,
> When only Mind's in question,—Body bows
> To quite another government, you know.
>
> (1101–7)

But the more he talks the more he comes to realize he has been speaking as a 'self-apologist' (1203) and that his career may not have been so altruistic or even so successful as he claims. If he has portrayed himself as 'a god whose fault was—trying to be man' (1208), he has nevertheless done the best he could. And so confessing himself a 'failure' and one of life's 'losers' (1212, 1217), he shifts perspective from 'autobiography' (1220) to biography, from first- to third-person narrative.

The second part of the monologue is devoted to 'what I never was, but might have been' (1224). Told from two points of view – those of the Head Servant, the idealized ruler, and Sagacity, the shrewd opportunist – this part is also another strategy in self-apology. The prince is, however, as unsuccessful in convincing himself that he has followed the highest ideals as he had been earlier in pretending that he acted practically but altruistically; and he is forced to admit that he has had no consistent philosophy but has acted as it suited him at the moment, his life an uneasy combination of good and ill, of democratic sympathies and imperial designs.

Yet for whatever he did or did not do, Hohenstiel-Schwangau refuses to be held accountable. He has acted only in accordance with the 'law' enjoined upon him by God. If he has done certain things, it is because he takes pleasure in doing God's will, ruling men and women 'for their good and my pleasure in the act' (282). Throughout the poem the monologist claims to have followed this 'law', a word that occurs more frequently in this poem than in any other by Browning. Like other Browning characters, the prince likes to fancy himself a puppet in the hands of a master playwright who has 'scripted' the 'law' that governs him.

At the end of the poem Browning engages in one of his playful surprises when the reader discovers that the speaker is not in a London café with a prostitute for his listener as he had pretended. He has been but daydreaming in the Residency: 'Alone,—no such congenial intercourse!' (2145). The pretence reveals the prince as the 'lazy and worn-out voluptuary' that Browning found Napoleon III 'when the mask fell' (*Dearest Isa*, p. 356). Far from the man of action that he claims to be, the speaker is an indecisive *homme sensuel* whose monologue properly closes without a conclusion, as in his capriciously casual way the speaker ends with a question to be answered by chance: 'Double or quits! The letter goes! Or stays?'

The prince also learns something about himself as the result of his imaginary theatrical.[8] He discovers that no matter how truthful one wishes to be – whether one speak from one's own point of view or whether one attempt to gain another perspective on oneself – one is ultimately forced to lie. All ratiocination is in the end but rationalization: 'yes, forced to speak, one stoops to say – one's aim / Was – what it peradventure should have been' (2113–4). In the 'ghostly dialogue' (2092) that takes place within the self without verbal language there is no need to justify or defend one's self and one's motives, because all claims are put 'to insignificance / Beside one intimatest fact—myself / Am first to be considered' (2101–3). But try to express one's aims in words, which implies the desire to communicate, the result is special pleading (2106–9). Ultimately, 'one lies oneself / Even in stating that one's end was truth, / Truth only, if one states as much in words' (2123–5). Yet words have to come because language is the only means humankind has for dealing with the world. No wonder then that the theatre of action is, as Browning constantly shows, a carnival world of contending voices, within as well as without.[9]

The few readers that *Prince Hohenstiel-Schwangau* has enjoyed have found the monologue to be filled with 'inconsistencies, . . . casuistries and tangled argument' resulting from the poet's lack of control over his material.[10] The verbal convolutions are not, however, owing to the poet's inability to manage his text but to the character of the speaker. The poem in fact presents a splendid (though perhaps overly long) verbal portrait of a complex man who, for the most part wanting to do right, failed to act in accord with his noblest aspirations. Browning's aim was to show that it is in the nature of things for one's best intentions frequently to be frustrated. Hopes are born in air but must be realized on earth. 'Once pedestalled on earth', the prince, like King Admetos, learns, 'I found earth was not air' (902–3). Whatever one's situation, one is always at the mercy of the world, the flesh and the devil – of all, in short, that constitutes phenomenal reality.

Prince Hohenstiel-Schwangau was published in early December 1871 and sold well. The reviewers however were baffled, some seeing it as a eulogy of the former French emperor and others as an attack on him. It was perhaps asking too much that the reader should be both sympathetic to and judgemental of the monologist and that the interest in him should be (as it always is in Browning) more psychological than political. To ask, as Hohenstiel-Schwangau did at the end, ' "Who's who?" . . . / Since certainly I am not I!' was to suggest that the supposed speaker was but a mask for the poet, an agency by which Browning could examine and come to terms with his own ambiguous feelings about Napoleon III.

IV

While writing *Prince Hohenstiel-Schwangau* Browning thought it among the best things he had done (*Dearest Isa*, p. 367), and when he had finished it he wrote to a correspondent that he had just sent 'a rather important poem to press' (Hood, p. 151). Yet when it appeared, his enthusiasm for it had waned. He told Edie Story: '. . . I expect you not to care three straws for what, in the nature of things, is uninteresting enough, even compared with other poems of mine which you have been only too good to. What poetry can be in a sort of political satire. . ?' (Hudson, p. 166). Perhaps it was owing to his dissatisfaction with *Prince Hohenstiel-Schwangau* that immediately after its publication he commenced another poem dealing with the same question: namely, why persons with good intentions fail to live up to their highest potentialities, why they are not true to themselves.

Browning worked on *Fifine at the Fair* at a furious pace, writing half of it in less than a month and finally finishing it – 2,355 rhymed alexandrines, with prologue and epilogue of 108 lines – in May 1872, about five months later. It seems to have engaged his energy and attention more intensely than any poem he had written in a long time; he speaks of it as '*growing* under me' (*Dearest Isa*, p. 376), almost as if it had a life of its own. Dealing with conjugal inconstancy, it touched on a matter very close to home.

Browning no doubt felt qualms of disloyalty to his dead wife for even momentarily considering Lady Ashburton's proposal of marriage. As Edie Story had told Rosalind Howard, he had thought of accepting for Pen's sake and she had advised against it. Furthermore, while he was writing *Fifine* his old friend Harriet Hosmer, the American sculptor whom he had met in Rome and come to know well over the past twenty years, was at Lady Ashburton's instigation going about telling anyone who would listen that it was *he* who had proposed marriage at Loch Luichart. The 'slanderous gossip' about which he wrote to Edie Story in early April 1872 (Hudson, pp. 170–1) rankled and probably focused his thoughts on his 'betrayal' of Elizabeth.

His own situation may also have reminded him of what he considered an affront to the memory of his mother committed by his father, who little more than a year after his wife died was looking to another woman for consolation and was, in fact, proposing to marry her. In addition, he probably also was reminded of his once-beloved Shelley, who, he had fairly recently learned, had deserted his wife and fled with another woman. Reading William Michael Rossetti's 1870 memoir of the Romantic poet, he could hardly 'avoid despising' himself for having so much misjudged the Sun-treader (*Dearest Isa*, p. 328). 'Talking of Shelley's history' in April 1872, noted his friend Alfred Domett, recently returned from New Zealand, 'Browning seemed to have adopted the most unfavourable view of his conduct with reference to his separation from his first wife. I don't much care to record what he said'.[11] Here in the two men whom he honoured most he found fickleness where he had expected fidelity. If such were the case among the best of men, what couldn't one expect of ordinary males? Is lifelong faithfulness only a dream and a mockery?[12]

Fifine at the Fair owes its setting to Browning's three visits to Brittany in the 1860s. In the prologue ('Amphibian') the speaker relates a 'fancy' he had that day. While floating in the bay and seeing a butterfly overhead, he pondered the impossibility of their exchanging their supporting elements, and this in turn caused him to wonder whether 'a certain soul' having left earth for heaven does look down on him who still lives on earth and has no desire, at the present time at least, to leave it. Yet, worldling though he be, there are times when he wishes to escape from earth to a finer sphere, and so he plunges into the sea: 'Unable to fly, one swims!' 'Emancipate through passion / And thought', the swimmer substitutes poetry for heaven and, like the 'spirit-sort' who live in air, imagines what they know and do but wonders whether one of them, the soul previously alluded to, looks at and pities him who mimics flight. Land however is always in sight, and after a long swim it is always pleasant to return to 'land the solid and safe'.

The body of the poem is an almost cinematic monologue of shifting perspectives in time and space. It is a narrative, but the story hardly matters.

The landscape and the people in it crowd the various scenes, yet they too are comparatively unimportant. What is significant is the internal action – what the preface to *Strafford* called 'Action in Character, rather than Character in Action' – the plunge into the depths of personality to discover what, if anything, is there *au fond*. The progression is not logical; everything seems to fade into something else by chance suggestion. It is an unreal world into which the reader is carried, and with great difficulty does one follow the kaleidoscopic movement in which nothing appears substantial. As Browning said of its composition, the poem *grows*.

The main monologue explores the nature of an 'amphibian', one placed on the isthmus of a middle state, seeing that his present home is earth but also perceiving that his true home is elsewhere, his real values different. Depicting the amphibian as held in tension by a polarity of opposing thrusts, the monologue is structured on the old Browningesque interplay between being, the wish for constancy and law, on the one hand, and becoming, the desire for change and lawlessness, on the other.

Browning appears to have borrowed his speaker from Molière's *Dom Juan*, a quotation from which serves as motto to *Fifine*. There Browning found a hero after his own heart, one who is described in this way: 'Vous tournez les choses d'une manière qu'il semble que vous avez raison, et cependant il est vrai que vous ne l'avez pas' (1.1). It was doubtless this aspect of Molière's Juan – the ability to turn things insidiously and make the false appear true and vice versa – that intrigued Browning and helped to mould his conception of the monologist. Moreover, by using the figure of Don Juan, the poet could show that just as the 'Byron de nos jours' is not the Romantic Byron ('Dîs Aliter Visum'), so the Victorian Don Juan is not the Don of legend: the great seducer would become a husband merely talking about seduction. Further, by naming his protagonist Don Juan, Browning, with his predilection for undercutting his speakers' arguments, could intimate that while in the beginning of the monologue the speaker has few, if any, similarities with the Don of popular tradition, in the end he would prove (like Prince Hohenstiel-Schwangau) to be a voluptuary after all. The ironic possibilities were practically unending.

Don Juan's monologue is addressed to his wife, Elvire, who nevers utters a word although her husband puts words into her mouth. It may be that Elvire is not even present. It may be that she is the 'certain soul / Which early slipped its sheath' of the prologue. In the closing sections the speaker seems to conceive of Elvire as a 'ghost' or 'phantom', 'a memory, a hope, / A fear, a conscience' (cxxx). 'Be but flesh and blood', he invokes more than once (cxxxi), only, in the last section, to admonish her to 'slip from flesh and blood, and play the ghost again'.

The action takes place at a fair in Brittany, where nothing is stable and nothing is as it seems.[13] It is a make-believe world inhabited by mountebanks and deceivers of all types. Aware of its unreality, Don Juan nevertheless wants to be a part of it, to be free like the losels there whose only law is lawlessness.

My heart makes just the same
Passionate stretch, fires up for lawlessness, lays claim
To share the life they lead: losels, who have and use
The hour what way they will,—applaud them or abuse
Society, whereof myself am at the beck,
Whose call obey, and stoop to burden stiffest neck!

(vi)

Just as the amphibian swam out to sea to escape worldly annoyance, so does the monologist trippingly and skippingly soar into metaphysical speculation to forget his earthly concerns.

Soon it becomes clear that the Don is drawn to the 'fizgig called Fifine' (xxxiii) and that this is the reason for his monologue. Fifine has only 'loveliness for law / And self-sustainment made morality' (xvi). What makes her so attractive, he claims, is that she is utterly true, never pretending to be other than what she is. Yet loveliness (described in highly erotic terms) is not law enough. Body's beauty cannot match soul's beauty, which Elvire exemplifies. Outlining their attractions and oscillating between them, Don Juan makes the two women into almost allegorical figures, ghosts and phantoms as he on occasion calls them. As soon as he reaches a pinnacle of loving praise for Elvire, he reverts almost immediately to the charms of Fifine.

Trying to justify his attraction to Fifine, the speaker argues that to get to the soul, the realm of the true, one must first deal with the body, the covering of the soul and hence the realm of semblances and the false. Take for example, he says, his morning swim in the bay. A swimmer breathes only by submitting to the water's limitations – that is, to law; if he attempts to rise too far out of the water, he drowns: 'Fruitless strife / To slip the sea and hold the heaven'. In like fashion the soul cannot live apart from the body; hence the spirit's life is betwixt 'false, whence it would break, and true, where it would bide' (lxv). The human being would reside 'in an element too gross / To live in' did not the soul inhale the air of truth above and thus capture just enough of truth to give the illusion that some day the obstructing medium will be transcended and the swimmer fly. But when the swimmer would rise into the air, just as the soul would leave the body, the body is no longer sustained by its supporting element and so sinks. Yet each soar upward and each resulting plunge beneath the water causes the soul more intensely to dislike the briny taste of falsehood. 'And yet our business with the sea / Is not with air, but just o' the water, watery': we must endure the false, hoping that 'our head reach truth, while hands explore / The false below' (lxv).

To howl at the sea, as Byron's Childe Harold did, is childish indeed (lxvii). In the magnificent passage in which Don Juan, like Carlyle's Teufelsdröckh, closes his Byron, Browning again takes issue, as he had years earlier in *Sordello*, with Romantic metaphysics that sought for the ideal untethered to the real. Although he yearns for the sky, man is of the earth, earthy – or 'of the water, watery' – and there is nothing he can, or should, do about it save accept it.

This morning, just after his noonday swim, the Don says that he sat down at the piano and played Schumann's *Carnaval*. As he played, he dreamed that the fair that they are now visiting expanded to the Carnival at Venice and the Carnival into the world: 'With music, most of all the arts, . . . change is there / The law' (xcii). In this reverie each musical theme caused him to realize that truth is always the same, change coming in the seasoning or the sauce, not truth but its expression being evanescent: 'Truth builds upon the sands, / Though stationed on a rock: and so her work decays, / And so she builds afresh, with like result' (cxiii).

From his reverie he also learned that mankind's apprehension of the truth is determined by the viewer's angle of vision. When he came down from the tower over St Mark's Square, he discovered that what had seemed defective in humankind from on high was, on a lower level, found to be purposeful. Thus the proper goal for wisdom is the ground and not the sky; further, 'one must abate / One's scorn of the soul's case, distinct from the soul's self' (cii). Finally Don Juan sums up the lessons of his dream in which Venice became the world, 'its Carnival – the state of mankind, masquerade in life-long permanence' (cviii). This is the 'lesson' that Browning had been dramatizing throughout his career: all the world's a stage. And with this understanding of the world we must, says Don Juan, 'bid a frank farewell to what – we think – should be, / And, with as good a grace, welcome what is' (cix). In other words, men and women must accept their status as participants in a giant carnival supervised by a supreme showman.

Eventually in his dream the diverse buildings of Venice blended into a common shape, the Druid monument where Juan and Elvire now stand. Tradition says that the edifice was built as a reminder that earth was made by Somebody and not by itself and that the Somebody remains permanent while everything else changes. But the great stone pillar now lying in the grass was and remains an object of phallic worship, and no matter how much the church over the years has tried to suppress such pagan practice, the pillar 'bides / Its time to rise again' (cxxiii). The point is that no matter how much humankind attempts to deny the claims of the flesh, it is always there to exert its demands. In addition to Elvire there is always also Fifine.

In the end the Don admits that his disquisition on 'abstruser themes' was ill begun. The subject should have been 'From the given point evolve the infinite'; not 'Spend thyself in space, endeavouring to . . . / Fix into one Elvire a Fair-ful of Fifines' (cxxix). Though man is an amphibian, he is better off as a landlubber keeping house than as a swimmer. Fifine is a mere foam-flake, while Elvire is a whole sea that could contain many such. Enough then of foam: 'Land-locked, we live and die henceforth' (cxxix).

Instead of swimming he will confine himself to the 'honest civic house' where there are 'no fancies to delude'; and so housed, he will wonder why he was ever tempted 'forth to swim'.

Forswearing the 'passionate stretch' and desire for 'lawlessness' expressed earlier (xi), the Don prepares to settle down into a life of bourgeois domesticity. Yet he does so without taking into account who he is. For in spite of all his noblest resolutions he is, after all, Don Juan, the man who always submits 'to the reign / Of other quite as real a nature, that saw fit / To have its way with man, not man his way with it' (cxxviii). And in the last section, having arrived home and said farewell to the fair and promised 'never to wander more' (cxxi), he apparently steals off to a tryst with Fifine.

In the epilogue ('The Householder') the former amphibian has indeed become a householder, and he is no happier housebound than we had reason to suspect. Now grown too old for swimming, he sits weary and bored in his house waiting for death. Quite unexpectedly his dead wife returns during a kind of waking dream. He tells her of all he has had to put up with since her departure: 'If you knew but how I dwelt down here!' he says to her. 'And was I so better off up there?' she replies. At last the speaker has his answer to the question posed in the prologue. Yes, the lady does still follow from another sphere his earthly pilgrimage, his 'swimming', and as she is mindful she is also forgiving. It does not matter that the swimmer-become-householder is Don Juan. What matters is love, which both transcends the flesh and even triumphs over death. In the epitaph that she helps compose, the wife ends with 'Love is all, and Death is nought!'

Early on Don Juan had allowed that it is 'not for every Gawain to gaze upon the Grail!' (iv). Nevertheless, 'through the fleeting' the Grail beckons, urging mankind on to 'reach at length "God, man, or both together mixed"' (cxxiv). This locution, which Don Juan borrows from Aeschylus' *Prometheus Bound*, is like the 'Fomalhaut', the bright star that the narrator believed Sordello to be in need of (3.430). It is the 'other than itself' (lix), a lodestar, the unchanging truth of the infinite-in-the-finite perceived by Aeschylus and Euripides and formulated by Christians as the Incarnation.

So closely is *Fifine at the Fair* tied to Browning's biography that many commentators regard the poet as the speaker of both prologue and epilogue. As is nearly always the case with Browning, the poet is and is not the protagonist. In the epilogue Browning fairly well gives himself away by literary quotation. The first quotation is from Poe's *The Raven*, in the opening lines where the speaker is 'sitting in my house, late, lone: / Dreary, weary'. In Poe's poem it is of course a raven that comes calling and allows that the speaker's lost love will never return. The second quotation is from Kingsley's *The Water-Babies*, in the antepenultimate line, '*Affliction sore long time he bore*'. In Kingsley's work, subtitled *A Fairy Tale for a Land-Baby*, little Tom runs away from harsh treatment, falls into a river and turns into a water baby. The quatrain relevant to the supposed amphibian-that-was is as follows:

> Instruction sore long time I bore,
> And cramming was in vain;
> Till heaven did please my woes to ease
> With water on the brain.

The third quotation is of Molière's *Dom Juan* in the last line. In the scene from the play that Browning uses as epigraph to his poem, Elvire says to Juan that he makes a poor defence and that he should adopt an attitude of noble impudence, swear that his love for her is unchanging, and vow that nothing will separate them save death.

Each of the allusions serves an ironic purpose – that is, to call into question the seriousness and finality of what appears to be the moral summation of this poem that Browning said was ' "the most metaphysical and boldest" he had written since *Sordello*'.[14] Placing his ending within a complex of literary allusions, the poet signals his audience that while Don Juan might have been the name of the monologist of *Fifine at the Fair*, it was really Robert Browning who was the carnival's producer and manager of this masterful performance, the most dazzlingly brilliant of his later career. The anonymous reviewer in the *Westminster Review* for 1 October 1872 percipiently observed of 'the meaning of his poem – it is an apology for himself and his poetry'.

12

Redefining Poetry

I

Browning completed *Fifine at the Fair* on 11 May 1872, four days after
celebrating his sixtieth birthday, and three days later he dedicated a new
volume of his *Selections* to Tennyson. He had been properly 'very doubtful
as to [*Fifine's*] reception by the public'.[1] Most of the reviewers were baffled
by it and, although it is one of Browning's most profound works, generally
condemned it on the old charges of obscurity. '[F]or the ordinary reader
it might just as well been written in Sanscrit', said the *Westminster Review*
of 1 October 1872. The poet was of course disappointed by the reviews:
the British public, whose esteem he had so recently won, had ceased to
love him. Yet he was contemptuous of those who would or could not
understand his work. Several months after *Fifine* appeared, he wrote on
the manuscript two passages in Greek, from Aeschylus and Aristophanes.
Translating them, DeVane renders the Aeschylean passage: 'And reading
this doubtful word he has dark night before his eyes, and he is nothing
clearer by day'. To this Browning added in English: '—if any of my critics
had Greek enough in him to make the application'. The quotation from
Aristophanes is dated 5 November 1872 and in translation reads: 'To what
words are you turned, for a barbarian nature would not receive them. For
bearing new words to the Scaeans you would spend them in vain' (DeVane,
p. 370).

One of the saddest events resulting from the publication of *Fifine* was
the rupture of his friendship with his long-time admirer Dante Gabriel
Rossetti. In 1847 Rossetti had written to Browning asking whether he was
the author of the anonymously published *Pauline,* and from this overture
a friendship developed when the Brownings visited London and Paris in
the 1850s. At a time when the reviewers were generally indifferent to
Browning's poetry, Rossetti was promoting Robert's work among other

younger men and women loosely grouped around the Pre-Raphaelites, poets and painters devoted to art and beauty who proclaimed realism as their aim. As we have seen, Rossetti had by 1855 become such an intimate that he was present when Tennyson visited Robert and Elizabeth and read *Maud*, and Robert read 'Fra Lippo Lippi' for the first time. When Robert returned to London in 1861, the poet and painter was among the first to call; and when Rossetti's wife died of an overdose of laudanum only seven months after Elizabeth's death, Robert was most sympathetic: '[M]y heart is sore for . . . poor Rossetti. . . . Poor, dear fellow!' (*Dearest Isa*, p. 98).

Although as the decade ended he became critical of his friend's bohemian ways and of his poetry as artificial, Browning continued to send the younger man copies of his poems. When he forwarded a presentation copy of *Fifine* slightly before it was published in early June 1872, Rossetti was enraged by what he took to be a satire of him and his poetry. His 'Jenny', published in 1870, presented a monologist attracted to a prostitute who inspired him to philosophize about the life of the senses. Was not Browning's Don Juan a direct allusion to and condemnation of his speaker? 'The Blessed Damozel', printed earlier and republished in 1870, expressed the longing of an earthly lover for a beloved whom he envisions as speaking to him from heaven. Was not the epilogue to *Fifine*, 'The Householder', a lampoon on that poem? To Rossetti, whose mind was addled by his addiction to opium, it was obvious that Browning was casting *him* as Don Juan, one riddled with guilt for a dead wife and all too eager to go chasing after loose women. Thereafter when their paths crossed Rossetti was insolent, and Browning, never understanding the cause, gave up on this relationship of twenty-five years' standing.

In August and half of September 1872 Robert and Sarianna were on the Norman coast with Milsand, who had been in London the previous March and who, said Browning, 'is increasingly precious to me': 'no words can express the love I have for him' (*Dearest Isa*, p. 376). As the poet was to say in his next poem, Milsand was the 'friend, who makest warm my wintry world, / And wise my heaven' (*Red Cotton Night-Cap Country*, 3.781–2).

On an earlier visit to Calvados, Milsand had told Browning an intriguing story about a man in the neighbourhood who had 'destroyed himself from remorse at having behaved unfilially to his mother'. And then subsequently he learned other particulars: 'they at once struck me as likely to have been occasioned by religious considerations as well as passionate woman-love,— and I concluded that there was no intention of committing suicide; and I said at once that I would myself treat the subject *just so*'. As in the case of his finding of the Old Yellow Book he threw himself imaginatively into the situation and believed that he had come up with the truth; and as in the case of the Roman murders he asked for 'legal documents' and 'collected the accounts current among the people of the neighbourhood, inspected the house and the grounds, and convinced [him]self that [he] had guessed rightly enough in every respect' (Hood, p. 309).[2] Involving

Plate 12 'Robert Browning with Joseph Milsand', c. 1882. The painting they are inspecting is probably by Pen Browning. Courtesy of the Armstrong Browning Library.

love, sex, religion and social roles, it was a tale after Browning's own heart.

Leaving Normandy the Brownings rented a house in Fontainebleau for a month, and from there Robert wrote to Isa Blagden that he had 'a capital brand-new subject for my next poem', which would be his 'winter-work in London' (*Dearest Isa*, p. 385). Back in London by the end of October, he told Domett in December: 'I have got *such* a subject for a poem, if I can only do justice to it'. According to notes he made on the manuscript, he began writing *Red Cotton Night-Cap Country or Turf and Towers* on 1 December and completed it on 23 January 1873, after having sworn not to ' "dine out for 2˙ months" '.[3] It was not published till May 1873 partly because the publisher, George Smith, feared a libel suit from some of the persons involved in the case. On the advice of legal counsel Browning changed the names of all the principal persons and places.

Red Cotton Night-Cap Country is a first-person narrative in four parts and 4,247 lines of blank verse that proceeds in a Conradian spiralling motion downward from the surface to the heart of the matter. Since early manhood Browning had been interested in the novel. His letters are full of references to nineteenth-century French novelists, especially Balzac, to whom his allegiance 'remained unshaken' and whose works he liked to read aloud in later years (Orr, *Life*, p. 363). Browning loved the realistic novel and felt a special affinity for it as a literary form because it respects the particularity of context and the uniqueness of personality. He was also probably aware of the naturalistic novel and doubtless intrigued by it in so far as it showed the 'normal' and the commonplace of modern times to be grotesque. It was not surprising then that he undertook to treat the material for *Night-Cap*, which is basically that of the naturalistic novel, in a novelistic manner.[4]

It cannot be determined whether Browning knew the work of Émile Zola, who had also recently visited St Aubin, the very locale from which the poet first heard the story of the man who had committed suicide. Milsand however knew Zola's writings and the novels of other French naturalists as well, and he detested them. 'When I hear them speak', Milsand said, 'of pathological studies and social anatomy, I shrug my shoulders. . . . A sensual obsession prevents them from taking a real interest in character, in the development of affection, or to see what is noble near what is ignoble'.[5] In all likelihood Browning shared Milsand's opinion of the naturalists; and it was characteristic that he should take the sordid material of the naturalistic novel, anatomize it in a similar fashion, and then transform it into analytical discourse pointing to a religious conclusion. This would really provide a paradigm of putting the infinite in the finite or, as Milsand said, showing 'what is noble near what is ignoble'.

The central act of the story, a man's falling to his death from a great height, was not in debate and in itself was of little interest. What was intriguing – and here lay the mystery to be unravelled – were the thoughts and motivations prompting the act.

> Along with every act—and speech is act—
> There go, a multitude impalpable
> To ordinary human faculty,
> The thoughts which give the act significance.
> Who is a poet needs must apprehend
> Alike both speech and thoughts which prompt to speak.
>   (4.24–9)

Like *Fifine* structured on a walk and having quest as its chief motif, the poem has as its objective the uncovering of the thoughts behind the act, the pressuring of the surface of the story, as in a detective novel, to make it yield its secret.

Part one begins with the poet speaking apparently *in propria persona* with his walking companion, Annie Thackeray, daughter of the novelist, who was staying five miles away from the Norman village where Browning spent the late summer of 1872. She calls the region 'White Cotton Night-Cap Country', referring to the head-covering appropriate for the inhabitants of this sleepy backwater cut off from the modern world. But the narrator, typically Browningesque, argumentative and perverse, will have none of it: the land should better be called '*Red* Cotton Night-Cap Country' in that behind the seeming innocence of the local people there surely lies some horror. No, he says, things are not what they appear; it is not enough to regard an object or an incident as merely 'normal, typical'. Everything has its own special truth, and a nightcap is not *just* a nightcap any more than a fiddle is just a fiddle. One must 'recognize / Distinctions', get to the bottom of things, even if it means that one has to 'rub to threads what rag / Shall flutter snowily in sight' (1.336, 256, 411–12). Then, almost immediately, the narrator glimpses the spire of the famous shrine La Ravissante, which looks something like a night-cap. Further, he remembers, it was associated with the recent death of the jeweller Léonce Miranda. Yes, there is the horror beneath the surface, there 'the Red is reached, / And yonder lies in luminosity!' (1.546–7).

Miranda's story is told in the following parts of the poem. It is a story, like Don Juan's, of a divided life, one torn between 'turf', the earthly realm of the flesh, and 'tower', the ethereal realm of spirit. Miranda, a son of the Roman Catholic Church, falls in love with Clara, a divorcee, whom he can never hope to marry; and to avoid social ostracism he takes her away from Paris to Clairvaux, in Normandy, where they lead a life of total absorption in each other, although he is never unaware that he stands condemned by the Church and the world. The Church and the world eventually forcefully intrude, and when he is recalled to Paris he becomes so charged with guilt that he attempts to drown himself and then later burns his hand in an attempt to purify himself. But whatever he does he finds himself unable to give up either the Church or Clara, and for two years thereafter he deludes himself that by presenting gifts to the Church he might stay in sin and yet stave off sin's punishment.

In the fourth part of the poem Miranda climbs to the top of his Norman home, which he has made into a palace and tower of art, and from there gazes at La Ravissante, which houses the splendid statue of the Virgin to which he has presented gorgeous jewels. In the magnificent meditation that ends with his death Miranda believes that he can be saved by miracles. Yet instead of being miraculously transported to the tower of La Ravissante when he steps off the roof of his home, he lands on the turf and dies.

The world considers Miranda insane for having put his faith in the Virgin to the test. The narrator, on the other hand, judges him sane, because, in light of his premises, Miranda at last acted in accordance with what he believed. 'Put faith to proof, be cured or killed at once', the speaker says, like the narrator in the coda to 'The Statue and the Bust'.

> In my estimate
> Better lie prostrate on his turf at peace,
> Than, wistful, eye, from out the tent, the tower,
> Racked with a doubt.
>
> (4.356–62)

In the narrator's eyes Miranda should mainly be condemned for having waited so long to choose. The spirit of compromise, urged on him in part two by the spirit of Molière's pusillanimous Sganarelle (of *Dom Juan*), infected his personality and ruined all his relationships. In addition Miranda is to be faulted because in accepting an inherited religious faith, its superstitions along with its doctrines and dogmas he did not use the intelligence granted him. La Ravissante and all it stands for belong to the past, and Miranda's attempt to 'bring the early ages back again' was both stupid and vain.[6] Finally, Miranda (and Clara too) never understood the meaning of love. For them it was a means by which 'self-entrenched / They kept the world off'. For them love was what James Lee's wife had wanted it to be: total absorption, autotelic, instead of the means by which the soul conquers the false in its journey towards the Absolute. In the end all the 'white' facts of life proved the 'red' of Miranda's undoing.

It is, Browning says, the poet's duty to do what the naturalists do not do: namely, to look beneath and beyond things as they appear. Thus a poet must perceive the red beneath the white, the 'spider [in] the communion cup' and the 'toad in the christening-font' ('Gold Hair'). After all, the poet is a seer. But more importantly he is a maker-see. And to make others see what he sees he must distort and rearrange, 'break through Art and rise to poetry'. If this results in the 'grotesque' style (of which Browning's critics have complained[7]) instead of a beautiful Tennysonian aesthetic surface, it is because it is totally functional and cannot be otherwise. 'Art' means 'work complete', which can only result from work 'inferiorly proposed'; art represents the order of being. 'Poetry', on the other hand, means 'incompletion', resulting from the attempt to put the infinite into the finite, 'to tremble nearer, touch enough / The verge of vastness to inform our soul / What orb makes transit through the dark above'; poetry bespeaks the chaos of becoming. If it succeeds in showing the relation of the Absolute and the relative, then

> there's the triumph!—there the incomplete,
> More than completion, matches the immense,—
> Then, Michelagnolo against the world!

Of course one can never capture the infinite, but this makes no difference. What counts is the attempt.

> Aspire, break bounds! I say,
> Endeavour to be good, and better still,
> And best! Success is naught, endeavour's all.
> (4.4015–33)

'Have I redeemed my promise?' Browning asks his companion at the end. Has he succeeded in showing that white is really red? Shifting from the dramatization of his story, he changes perspectives and in the coda situates himself in London writing the poem. The Miranda story and his imaginative resuscitation of it were all told months ago in France as they paced the Norman sands. But can 'gloomy London make a poem' of the insight 'flashed' to him in France? Such ought to be. 'How fail imbibe / Some foretaste of effulgence?' he confidently asks, as he dedicates his poem to Annie Thackeray and asks her to 'accept the moment's flashing, amplified, / Impalpability reduced to speech, / Conception proved by birth'. The poet–showman Robert Browning has worked his tricks, and here is *Red Cotton Night-Cap Country*, which disguises a profundity of ideas under the guise of conversational banter.

II

The poem was generally disliked, chiefly on the grounds that it was not 'art'. The review in the *Daily News* of 5 May 1873 was characteristic in wondering 'whether psychological puzzles are fit subjects for poetry, or whether explorations in the mournful phantom-haunted borderland between Illusion and Guilt are the best exercises of the poet's genius'. Browning however bore up manfully, and told Annie Thackeray that he didn't feel the criticisms as most people might: 'Remember that everybody this thirty years has given me his kick and gone his way'.[8]

   Probably as a diversion he made another 'transcript' of Euripides, this time of *Herakles*, the manuscript of which is dated 17 June 1873. He then laid this aside and turned his attention to another Greek dramatist, Aristophanes, who had mocked and denigrated Euripides. His interest may have been stimulated by the general hostility to Euripides rampant in the 1870s and to be found, for example, in A. W. von Schlegel's *Lectures upon Dramatic Art and Literature*, a new edition of which had appeared in 1871. Schlegel claimed, as did Nietzsche in *The Birth of Tragedy* (1872), that Euripides had wrecked classical Greek poetry, and Browning wanted to prove that this was not so. From France, where he was spending his annual summer holiday, he wrote to a correspondent in August 1873 that he was deeply involved in a study of Greek books, especially Aristophanes (Hood, p. 158). Apparently over the next year he read everything about the Greek dramatists that he could lay his hands on, including a great deal of arcane scholarship. And, as he indicated on the manuscript, he began the material surrounding *Herakles* in mid-August 1874 and completed it the following November. 'I felt in a manner bound to write it', the poet told Carlyle, 'with so many blunders about Aristophanes afloat, even among the so-called learned'.[9]

Aristophanes' Apology: Including a Transcript from Euripides, Being the Last Adventure of Balaustion was published on 15 April 1875. Composed of 5,705 lines, it is the third longest of Browning's works (after *The Ring and the Book* and *Sordello*). Formally it is extremely complex. It progresses by statement and counterstatement and is divided into three main parts in three different modes – the apology of Aristophanes, Balaustion's admonishment of him and a translation of Euripides' *Herakles* – with a prologue and a conclusion. Aristophanes and Balaustion offer subjective evaluations and the *Herakles* stands as an objective resolution of the two conflicting points of view. The subsuming formal locus, however, is Balaustion's monologue, which will 're-enact' (168) the tragedy of the fall of Athens.

Balaustion speaks as the representative of 'soul' and upholds Euripides as the dramatist who affirmed her (and incidentally Athens's) highest ideals. In defending Euripides against Aristophanes, therefore, she is in fact defending herself; which is to say that hers is as much an apology as her antagonist's is. Aristophanes speaks for 'body' and like Balaustion believes that there is but one way to understand life. His quarrel with Euripides is that he (like Robert Browning) questioned everything, looked beneath the surface of all he saw and heard to the point where he left 'no longer one plain positive / Enunciation incontestable / Of what is good, right, decent here on earth' (2221–3). Where Aristophanes has urged the populace to 'accept the old, / Contest the strange' (2649–50), Euripides, the advocate of the philosophy of becoming, has introduced the notion of 'restless change' (2024). In short, Aristophanes' argument is for being at the expense of becoming, and his debate with Balaustion centres on the conflict between the conservative values that his comedy upholds and the radical notions that Euripidean tragedy instils. The dialogue between Balaustion and Aristophanes ends as it began, as two monologues, an expostulation and a reply.

It is plain from the dialogue, however, that Euripides is not the antagonist

Redefining Poetry

that Aristophanes thinks him to be nor the disembodied spirit that
Balaustion fancies him. Recognizing that Athens was in a period of tran-
sition, from a mythifying past to a more secular future, Euripides con-
ceived of his task as helping to ease the pangs of change. He did not
shrink from teaching that if the gods are strong and wicked, mankind
could nevertheless 'prove their match by willing to be good' (428–30). He
showed how man must forgo dependence upon the gods and rely upon
himself, accept 'fact in figment's place, / Throned on no mountain, na-
tive to the mind' (2148–9).

Euripides saw that in this trying period of history art too must change.
Realizing that the old categories of tragedy and comedy were no longer
adequate modes and vehicles, he envisioned a new type of drama in which
comedy and tragedy would meet. Bringing the tragic grandeur of Aeschylus
and Sophocles 'down to the level of our common life' (conclusion, 482),
he attempted a dramatic mode that 'fain would paint, manlike, actual
human life, / Make veritable men think, say and do' (1312–13). It was to
be the art of the maker-see; and while he had attempted such a new mode,
he had not perfected it, that task awaiting 'the novel man / Born to that
next success myself foresee' (1321–2). Believing that the death of art means
working in traditional, inherited modes, Euripides steadfastly embraced
the idea that 'never needs the Art stand still' (1304).

His last play presented to Athens, the *Herakles*, embodies all these ideas.
In the *Alkestis*, which played such a major role in Balaustion's first adven-
ture, Herakles was the heroic redeemer. In this play, which forms part of
Balaustion's last adventure, Herakles is no longer a god–man but a fully
human being who realizes that human love is adequate compensation for
a lost heroic, godlike strength. 'Who rather would have wealth and strength
/ Than good friends', he says in the final lines, 'reasons foolishly therein'.
In that it shows the human condition to be a dialectic between strength
and weakness, good and evil, hope and despair, the play points up the
deficiency of the views expounded by both Balaustion and Aristophanes
when considered singly. Balaustion comes to recognize and accept the
tension of these oppositions when at the very close of her monologue she
joyfully expresses the paradox in song: 'There are no gods, no gods! /
Glory to God—who saves Euripides!'

Aristophanes' Apology is Browning's boldest experiment with the dramatic
monologue. The poet was attempting exactly what Balaustion (3435–45),
Euripides (1302–5) and Aristophanes (1468–94) speculate on in their
discussions of a new type of drama and what he himself had posited in his
Essay on Shelley, where he considered how the subjective and objective modes
of poetry might be combined. And in the defence of Euripides he was in
fact defending himself against such critics as Alfred Austin, the 'Dogface
Eruxis' (1671–6), who could not comprehend what he was doing.[10] He was
aiming at a poetry that would take in both body and soul, right and wrong,
high and low, 'every side at once, / And not successively' (conclusion, 57–
9). Seeking, as he had in *Sordello*, the depiction and expression of life not

sequentially but simultaneously, Browning presented two long monologues and a complete play through the medium of one speaker, one consciousness. It was a marvellous trick for the showman to perform, but in doing so he was, he realized, stretching the dramatic monologue to or beyond its limit. That he could go no further is indicated by the fact that after *Aristophanes' Apology* he never returned to the dramatic monologue again as the mode for a long poem.

Domett remarked to the poet upon the great demands that the poem makes of its readers and said that he believed 'no one, even classical scholars, unless they were in the daily habit of reading Aristophanes, as tutors or schoolmasters, would be able to understand all the numerous allusions in it without referring over and over again to his Comedies; and that Browning thus wilfully restricted the number of his readers to comparatively few'. Carlyle told Browning that he liked the poem but asked 'why he could not tell it all in a plain straightforward statement'. Browning acknowledged the difficulty and said 'he was not likely to try anything of the sort again'. Domett commented: 'And here is this wonderfully fertile genius, after . . . years of varied productiveness, still working away— writing as vigorously if not always as fascinatingly as ever—and still making resolutions as to what is to be avoided in his *future* creations!'[11]

When *Aristophanes' Aplology* was published in mid-April 1875 the reviewers were even more bewildered. Practically all of them found it too abstruse for the general reader, and some of them reported it, said Browning furiously, as ' "the transcript of the talk of the Master of Balliol" ', the Greek scholar Benjamin Jowett, 'with whom I never had a conversation about Aristophanes in my life' (Hood, p. 171). Only John Addington Symonds, upon whose studies of the Greek poets Browning may have drawn, hinted in his review in the *Academy* for 17 April 1875 at what the poet was up to with his 'special pleading': 'The point of view is modern' and expresses 'the views of the most searching and most sympathetic modern analyst', who compares Euripides' 'work with that of all the poets who have ever lived'. Browning was, in other words, using Balaustion as his own mouthpiece.

III

In his next work, *The Inn Album,* according to the manuscript begun on 1 June and finished on 1 August 1875, Browning did not entirely abandon the dramatic monologue but embedded a series of monologues within a narrative. It may best be characterized as a dramatic poem not unlike *Sordello,* in that the narrator is a typically Browningesque manager of the performance who sets the scene to introduce the action and at the end says, 'Let the curtain fall'. As in 'A Death in the Desert' and *The Ring and the Book* the point of departure is a text. Yet here the text is not one that the narrator or any of the actors is to interpret but, almost in Pirandellan fashion, is in fact a text written by the characters themselves. As the action proceeds, almost the entire story is inscribed into the album: the noble-man's calculation of his gambling debts, his blackmail note to the lady and her exoneration of the young man. In the end it becomes the 'queer reading' that the youth had found it at the beginning (1.130), and its 'defacement' becomes paradoxically its 'enrichment' (1.122).

'Hail, calm acclivity, salubrious spot!' is the first line in the album and, as it turns out, the prooftext for demonstrating what Browning's poems so frequently display: that things are not what they seem, that white is in fact red. Set on 'neutral ground' at an inn called only the 'Something-Arms', the poem brings four nameless characters together to discover, 'by strange chance', 'who is who and what / Is what' (5.99, 17–18). The older woman and the older man have led unhappy, ruinous lives because, like the pair in 'The Statue and the Bust', they acted in cowardice, failing to seize the moment and follow their love for each other. They have lost what each of them figures as Paradise, the Garden of Eden, and each holds the other responsible. She, assuming the role of Eve (5.156–60), assigns him the role of Satan – the 'tempter' (4.225), the 'Adversary' (4.669), the 'reptile' (5.153) – who is her 'hell' and 'Death' (4.30, 34). He, a poor Adam, makes her his evil genius (4.41–63), his 'woman-fiend' (4.70), a lamia haunting and enchanting him (4.72–83, 111–19).

Where the elder pair claim experience and knowledge, the younger represent innocence and ignorance. Seeking guidance from the older man and woman, who both assert their status as teachers, the young man and the young woman eventually learn that life cannot be learned or lived vicariously. No person can ever instruct another how in the Garden of Eden one should 'strip the tree / Of fruit desirable to make one wise' (6.196–7). These are lessons that can only be learned experientially. In the end, forswearing such teachers, the young persons gain the Tree of Knowledge that is the Tree of Life, while the older pair are left with the Tree of Knowledge that is the Tree of Death.

The Inn Album is one of Browning's most topical poems.[12] With allusions to Trollope, Carlyle, Ruskin, Landseer and Tennyson, among others, it touches on nearly every aspect of English artistic life of the 1870s.[13] Yet none of the actors in this melodramatic piece has any real concern or apprecia-tion for art. Pictorial art is regarded as mere decoration, and literature is mined for the stereotypical roles that each of the *dramatis personae* might play. The art that figures in the poem is much like the inn itself, which once may have been 'a veritable house' but which now houses view-hunters who have 'fingered blunt the individual mark / And vulgarized things comfortably smooth' (1.32–3). No wonder that they prefer the dog-gerel inscribed in the inn album to 'Browning' who, his critics say, 'neglects the form' (1.17).[14]

It is the formal experimentation that makes *The Inn Album* significant among Browning's works. Quite unlike anything he had attempted earlier, it combines melodrama with the narrative technique of the novel. Observing the unities of time and place, it turns the popular sensation novel into a play that our old friend the manager of the performance gives us by glimpses. As the action ends, he writes, 'And so ends the Inn Album'. But *The Inn Album* does not conclude till the showman appears as Robert Browning, writing in the mid-1870s, who in the last lines reports on a voice 'outside' that alludes to productions in 1875 of *The Merchant of Venice* and *Lohengrin* before letting 'the curtain fall'.[15] It is 'a voice that sounds like song, / And is indeed half song though meant for speech', and what it says is 'the oft-quoted, long-laughed-over line— / *"Hail, calm acclivity, salubrious spot"'*. It is the ironic voice of the author, who having introduced himself can now 'let the curtain fall'.

13

Fame is the Spur

I

The *Athenaeum* for 27 November 1875 proclaimed *The Inn Album* a greater poem than *The Ring and the Book*, and John Forster wrote to the author that he had been much moved and affected by it and believed that Browning had 'done nothing finer' (*NL*, pp. 231–2). Forster's words were especially cheering, for the poet's relationship with him had been fairly stormy over the past ten years. They had had a number of fallings out. One of these, especially memorable, occurred in the early 1870s when they clashed in company over a lady's truthfulness, about which Forster was sceptical. Browning seized a bottle of claret and had to be forcibly restrained from throwing it at Forster's head. Relations between the two were thereafter entirely interrupted and Forster's letter about *The Inn Album* was the first resumption of contact. Browning replied gratefully, terming Forster his first and best critic and, referring to their most recent quarrel, saying that their 'friendship was too vital to succumb at the interruption of *that*' (*NL*, pp. 229–30). Two months later Forster was dead.

In general, however, *The Inn Album* was not well received. Browning 'laughed at some abuse',[1] but he was nevertheless irritated that the reviewers were bringing up the old charges of obscurity and prosiness that had checked his reputation in the 1840s and 1850s. Not far beneath the surface was his displeasure with Alfred Austin, whose hostile article in the *Temple Bar* for June 1869 he could not put out of his mind. Austin had not only attacked his poetry as unmusical, unintelligible, pretentious and pseudo-philosophical, but had also made mention of his personal life. 'Small London literary coteries, and large fashionable London salons, cannot crown a man with the bays of Apollo', Austin wrote. To Browning, the least 'official' of poets, the thought of gaining a reputation through his acquaintance with the great and influential was both ridiculous and hurtful. He was glad, he said to Isa Blagden, to consider how 'it "riles" such a filthy little snob as Mr. Alfred Austin to read in the Morning Post how many dinners I eat in good company'; and he was stimulated by the reflection that Austin was stung 'to the quick that I "haunt gilded saloons"' (*Dearest Isa*, pp. 332, 359). When he learned that Austin, who had met Miss Blagden in 1865 and become friendly with her, was to edit a volume of verse by his cherished Isa, who died suddenly in Florence in January 1873, he was beside himself to think of 'the association of a dearly-loved name with that of Mr. Alfred Austin' (*Dearest Isa*, p. xxvi). Though he had already made, as we have noted, veiled allusions to Austin in several poems, he now felt compelled to confront him more directly, to give him 'one fillip in return for fifty or more flea-bites' (*Learned Lady*, p. 36).

Though Browning almost never wrote a poem that was not a vehicle for self-display, he was paradoxically a very private person who loathed the idea of any public intrusion into his private life. One of his ways of keeping the world at large was to adopt the mask of the man of the world who delighted in being mistaken for a financier. People meeting him at dinner parties for the first time were amazed that *this* could be Robert Browning the poet. Mary Gladstone, daughter of the prime minister, said of the man who was represented to her as the poet: 'I tried to think of Abt Vogler but it was no use—he couldn't ever have written it'. Lady Knightley of Fawsley was disillusioned when she was introduced to 'a loud-voiced, sturdy little man, who says nothing in the least obscure or difficult to understand'. Sidney Colvin found that 'Browning's talk had not much intellectual resemblance to his poetry. That is to say, it was not apt to be specially profound or subtle; still less was it ever tangled or obscure'.[2] The American journalist W. J. Stillman saw him as a person who seemed to have something to hide, 'a strong man armed in the completest defensive armour'.[3] An anonymous writer in the *New Review* claimed 'that no one meeting Mr Browning for the first time . . . would guess his vocation. He might be a diplomatist, a statesman, a discoverer, or a man of science'.[4] Henry James, who was disappointed to find Tennyson unTennysonian, was distressed to discover that Browning was not 'Browning'. He believed that the public and private aspects of the poet's personality were

> dissociated in him as they can rarely elsewhere have been; . . . the wall that built out the idyll . . . of which memory and imagination were virtually composed for him stood there behind him solidly enough, but subject to his privilege of living almost equally on both sides of it. It contained an invisible door through which, working the lock at will, he could swiftly pass and of which he kept the golden key—carrying the same about with him even in the pocket of his dinner-waistcoat, yet even in his most splendid expansions showing it, happy man, to none.[5]

James was so intrigued by the man who led a double life that in time he wrote a story, 'The Private Life', about him.

Yet no matter how thick a wall the public man tried to raise, with his formal manners and his almost aggressive *bonhomie*, he was subject to constant questions of a personal nature. Concerning an unauthorized publication of some of his wife's letters, he wrote to Isa Blagden: 'But what I suffer in feeling the hands of these blackguards . . .—what I undergo with their paws in my very bowels, you can guess & God knows!' (*Dearest Isa*, p. 149). He was determined that the world would never know the man who wrote the poems that they now seemed to despise; and to assure his posthumous privacy he burned every letter he could get his hand on except those between himself and Elizabeth. As he had said to Julia Wedgwood, 'I live more and more—what am I to write?—for God not man—I don't care what men think now, knowing they will never think my thoughts' (*Wedgwood*, p. 53).

Ill treatment by some of the reviewers and his determination to keep closed the door of his private life were uppermost in his mind when he composed the poems in *Pacchiarotto and How He Worked in Distemper*, which was published in July 1876. In the prologue the speaker lives in a 'house, no eye can probe'. In 'Of Pacchiarotto' the critics come to it under the pretence of helping with the housekeeping but in fact bring in filth, and the speaker warns them to keep away from his door. Whether they like his house or not is a matter of indifference. For he is concerned only to please the 'Landlord' to whom he pays rent for the 'freehold' ('Pacchiarotto'); he is deaf to human praise or blame, his interest being only in the approval of the 'Mightiness yonder' ('Pisgah-Sights.II'). In 'House' the 'I' will not allow anyone to enter and see him at home. While his work doubtless reflects the man, it still is not his whole life. Browning is not 'Browning'; he is more than the sum of his poems. Yet it is only 'Browning' who matters, his identity as a poet transcending questions of who he was and what he did. Hence his poetry, like Shakespeare's, is 'blank of such a record' ('At the "Mermaid"').

Housekeeping, which entails strict attention to and upkeep of a provisional home, is, as the epilogue to *Fifine at the Fair* suggested, mankind's proper business. To attempt to deny or rise above this responsibility is to lapse into lethargy or hubris. In the title poem the artist Pacchiarotto, who dealt with 'fancy' rather than 'fact' (55), wished to refashion his earthly home according to his conception of what it should be, because in his view men should be angels, not mere housekeepers. But when forced to spend two days in a tomb with a rotting corpse, he begins to change his mind; and when he seeks refuge in a monastery, he learns from the abbot what Don Juan in *Fifine* affirms: that '*Earth is earth and not heaven, and n'er will be*'. This does not mean, however, mere acceptance of things as they are: 'Man's work is to labour and leaven— / As best he may—earth here with heaven' (367–9). One must adopt an 'as if' philosophy, working to move earth to heaven but 'not dream of succeeding' (371–2). One cannot redeem the world; one can only save oneself by tending to one's earthly home in preparation for a later one.

In poem after poem Browning maintains that the present takes on meaning only when being is viewed within the context of becoming. Some persons, he says, are weighted down by material considerations, forgetting soul and seeing life solely in terms of body; they live in a shop and not in a home. Of course one must tend to everyday concerns, yet

> Because a man has shop to mind
> In time and place, since flesh must live,
> Needs spirit lack all life behind,
> All stray thought, fancies fugitive,
> All loves except what trade can give?
> ('Shop')

Among the good housekeepers in this volume are Shakespeare, who finds this provisional existence 'not grey but rosy' ('At the "Mermaid"'); the speaker in 'Pisgah-Sights.I', who accepts that life is 'rough-smooth' and 'mixed—man's existence'; and Hervé Riel, who, combining love and duty, can 'save the squadron, honour France, love his wife'. The bad housekeepers, on the other hand, are those who tend towards absolutism and see life in terms of either/or. Among these are the lovers in 'Bifurcation', who are torn between love and duty; the wife in 'A Forgiveness', who demands that duty yield completely to love; and the pair in 'St. Martin's Summer', who cannot decide whether to erect a 'mansion' or a 'bower' and end by building nothing.

The philosophy that Browning adumbrates in the *Pacchiarotto* volume is closely akin to Kierkegaard's. Absurdist in nature, it is essentially based on hope. 'Hold on, hope hard in the subtle thing / That's spirit', the prologue advises. But to sustain this hope is one of the most difficult aspects of housekeeping. Nowhere is this made more evident than in 'Numpholeptos', the most beautiful poem in the collection. Here the Absolute is figured as a nymph who imposes impossible tasks on the lover who seeks to grasp her. From her dwelling in the white, cold light of purity she demands that he gather all the experience of the seven colours into which her white light resolves and then come back to her unstained by it. But even though he 'break through bounds' (98) as she demands, every time he is rewarded not with love but with her 'old statuesque regard, / The sad petrific smile' (132–3). Tired of trying he rebels, acting out 'the true slave's querulous outbreak' (148), but soon he returns to his task in hope that his 'crimson-quest' may one day 'deepen to a sunrise, not decay / To that cold sad sweet smile' (150–2).

In 'Numpholeptos' as in the other poems of the volume Browning sets forth his aesthetic theory in terms of the philosophy of becoming. In his concern with art as with all matters of householding his focus is more on questing than on the object of the quest, and here the stated aim of art is primarily *Bildung*, the 'Author's evolvement' ('Of Pacchiarotto', 438). As the poet told Julia Wedgwood, '. . . I need increasingly to tell *the truth*—

for whom? Is it that *I* shall be the better, the larger for it, have the fairer start in next life, the firmer stand? Is it pure selfishness, or the obedience to a natural law?' (*Wedgwood*, p. 53). Whatever his purpose, it is definitely neither magisterial nor reformatory. Pacchiarotto is shown to betray his art when he takes 'reform' for his motto. Shakespeare is praised for encouraging no 'revolt', 'song-sedition' or 'scism in verse' ('At the "Mermaid"'). The artist works, as the speaker of the last book of *The Ring and the Book* implied, to save his soul. And throughout this volume Browning, though constantly repudiating self-delineation, delights in enunciating his own artistic principles while denouncing his detractors. Changing metaphors in the epilogue, from householding to drinking, he bids farewell to his critics by offering them new wine, admittedly a 'stiff drink', that in time will be savoured; but since they are not true oenophiles, perhaps they would be better served with nettle broth.

Most critics, now as well as then, have found in the *Pacchiarotto* volume evidence of the poet's bad humour, of 'a growing perversity not wholly attributable to age, a new failure in self-control and more deeply in self-assurance'.[6] This is, however, to misread the poems and the showman presenting them. Believing that the poet mistakenly 'thought he sung while he whistled', his critics have not seen that his purpose here is to 'whistle, not sing at all'. He begins his book 'with a chuckle' and ends his introduction with a 'laugh on this mirth-day', 1 May, one week before 'dawns [his] birth-day' ('Of Pacchiarotto', 495–6, 538, 572–3). Moreover, Browning's revisions of the poems in the volume give not an iota of evidence of a loss of self-control but instead 'point to a composed mind that had control over its emotions in answering the charges of the critics'.[7]

II

It is not surprising that the reception of the nineteen poems of *Pacchiarotto . . . With Other Poems* was less than cordial. Browning had probably expected no more. 'It was not worth my while, perhaps', he wrote to George Barrett, 'to amuse myself for once (first time and last time) with my critics—I really had a fit of good humour—and nothing worse' (*Letters to George*, p. 303). The volume was largely a *jeu d'esprit*, among other things a way of keeping occupied. Over the past five years his output had been enormous, six long poems totalling about 20,000 lines. They were highly experimental poems, formal essays with the dramatic monologue and other kinds of first-person narratives; and they had proven taxing. They were monumental accomplishments that the world had by and large not appreciated (as it does not to this day).

It was probably also with a sense of keeping busy that Browning undertook to translate the *Agamemnon* of Aeschylus. Carlyle had suggested to him that he 'ought to translate the whole of the Greek tragedians' (Griffin and Minchin, p. 256), and he himself was eager to prove his mastery of the Greek language after critics had hinted that *Aristophanes' Apology* owed more than a little to the poet's acquaintance with Benjamin Jowett. Moreover, during the nineteenth century Aeschylus was by and large regarded as an obscure writer and, it has been suggested, Browning initially aligned himself with Aeschylus so as 'to dramatize a vexed relationship with his reading public'; and his decision 'to translate Aeschylus may therefore be understood as an implicit response to his critics'.[8] Browning worked on the translation during the late winter and early spring of 1877, and it was published in October as *The Agamemnon of Aeschylus Transcribed by Robert Browning*.

The piece is indeed more of a literal transcription than a translation, Browning's aim being, as he says in the preface, to offer 'a mere strict version of thing by thing' and 'to furnish the very turn of each phrase in as Greek a fashion as English will bear'. The result, Greek English, is almost unreadable.[9] Browning however was very pleased with it, not least because it proved the inadequacy of Greek writers as models. Matthew Arnold had argued in the preface to his *Poems* of 1853 that Greek literature is the best model for contemporary poets. To Browning this was foolishness: 'Learning Greek', he wrote in the preface, 'teaches Greek, and nothing else: certainly not common sense, if that have failed to precede the teaching'. He had long agreed with his wife that it was mindless to 'go back to the antique moulds..classical moulds' when what was needed was 'new *forms*..as well as thoughts' (Kintner, 1: 43). For a man who so passionately expounded the philosophy of becoming and based his whole aesthetic theory and practice on it, the very notion of using antique models, Greek or otherwise, was to be deplored.

III

From 1874 Browning and his sister had spent their summer holidays with Anne Egerton Smith, an old acquaintance from Camberwell days with whom the poet in recent years frequently attended musical events. Miss Smith and the Browning brother and sister were close; she was almost a member of the family. In August 1877 the three had settled in a chalet, 'La Saisiaz', in the Jura mountains, near Geneva. On 14 September Robert and Miss Smith had planned to climb Mt Salève. The night before she had been in the best of spirits, but when Sarianna went to wake her the next morning, she was found dead on the floor.

In 1877 Browning was sixty-five years old, and doubtless when he considered an elegy for Miss Smith he also reflected on his own death, immortality and posthumous fame. 'Does the soul survive the body? Is there God's self, no or yes' (144): this was the question that he wished to face up to, and it was the one which his commemorative poem 'La Saisiaz' would attempt to answer.

The elegy is, like *Red Cotton Night-Cap Country*, a re-enactment in the poet's study in London of a previous experience and, further, is structured on a walk, this time up and down Mt Salève. The quest is, however, internalized, in that the answer to what he seeks must come from within: 'I will ask and have an answer,—with no favour, with no fear,— / From myself' (208-9). This would provide a moment of stock-taking, the first since 'Easter-Day', to examine 'how much, how little, do I inwardly believe / True that controverted doctrine' (209-10).

Browning and Miss Smith had been following a series of articles in the new journal *The Nineteenth Century* during the summer and early autumn 1877 on 'The Soul and the Future Life' under the general heading 'A Modern Symposium'. The whole question of the Christian revelation was deliberately set aside, as the contributors were both believers and non-believers. 'La Saisiaz' was conceived as Browning's contribution to the 'fence-play' that 'sundry minds of mark engaged in "On the Soul and Future Life"' (163-4). As he works his way through the arguments for and against an afterlife, through 'facts' and 'fancies', he finds that he is certain of only two things: his own being, 'soul', and a power outside and independent of himself, 'God'. That these 'facts' overpass his power of proving them, in fact 'proves them such: / Fact it is I know I know not something which is fact as much' (223-4). Whether this power outside ourselves is good is impossible to prove. Experience has taught that wisdom, good and power cannot be reconciled with the ignorance, evil and failure to be discerned daily. The only way that the miseries of life can be regarded as meaningful – that is, permitted by a wise, benevolent and omnipotent deity – is to see them as prelude to something better: 'Only grant a second life, I acquiesce / In this present life as failure' (358-9).

This reformulated belief in the doctrine of becoming is but surmise, and to test it as fact the speaker resorts to interior dialogue, as in *Prince Hohenstiel-Schwangau*, in which competing voices, here called Fancy and Reason, argue the case. The contenders conclude that an afterlife is not provable, and the speaker is in the end left to hope and act as if 'surmise' were 'fact'.[10] This is, alas, the 'sad summing-up of all to say' (545), as he can only affirm in conclusion that which he had declared at the beginning: 'God, . . . soul, . . . the only facts for me' (222).

Somewhat dejected, the speaker all of a sudden throws off his religio-philosophical mask to reveal himself as none other than Robert Browning, who to the great questions could truthfully only say, 'I don't know'. Other writers, on the other hand, have been ready and willing to speak out and proclaim their easily attained beliefs, and they have been listened to. Pope had preached that this is the best of all possible worlds, Rousseau had taught man's natural goodness, and Byron had boldly preached a gospel of despair; and for this they had gained fame. '*Athanasius contra mundum*' indeed (546)! Why should Pope or Rousseau or Byron be heeded? Why should people be swayed by the unnamed Tennyson, whose elegy *In Memoriam* had had such far-flung influence and whose eight-stressed rhymed couplets in 'Locksley Hall' are borrowed for this memorial to Miss Smith? Why, the underlying question implicitly asks, does Tennyson have the fame denied to Browning? Simply because men are so made that 'such magnetic virtue darts / From each head their fancy haloes to their unresisting hearts!' (547–8). People believe simply because 'the famous bard believed' (572).

Since men will listen only to the famous, then let him, Robert Browning, so long unheeded, for a moment have the requisite fame to lift the black torch of influence so that he too will be paid attention to and 'by help of mine, they may / Confidently lay to heart and lock in head their life long —this:'

> 'He there with the brand flamboyant, broad o'er night's forlorn abyss,
> Crowned by prose and verse; and wielding, with Wit's bauble, Learning's
> rod...
> Well? Why, he at least believed in Soul, was very sure of God.'
>
> (600–4)

Even so bedecked, Robert Browning cannot really be a 'bard'; he cannot provide the key to unlock the mysteries of life. He remains here what he has always been – the showman in life's carnival where contending voices in 'fence-play', like those of Fancy and Reason, hold sway. This frame or fragment of the play – 'Life is stocked with germs of torpid life' (615) – is what he offers as his elegy in his unconcluding conclusion: 'Least part this: then what the whole?'

IV

Published in the same volume with 'La Saisiaz' in May 1878 was a sequel, 'The Two Poets of Croisic', which begins (leaving aside the brief prologue): ' "Fame!" Yes, I said it and you read it'. Seated with another person before a fire, the speaker lets his mind drift to the Breton village of Croisic, just north of the mouth of the Loire, which Browning had visited in the summers of 1866 and 1867. It is a poor place that has little to recommend it. Yet even here there is something to be gained: 'For point me out the place / Wherever man has made himself a home, / And there I find the story of our race / In little, just at Croisic as at Rome' (XVIII). In Croisic lived two poets famous in their own day but now largely forgotten.

The first was René Gentilhomme, who, feeling himself inspired by a bolt of lightning, wrote a poem prophesying the birth of a new king. When the dauphin was indeed born the next year, Gentilhomme was made royal poet and proclaimed 'bard and seer' (XLVI). His fame however was short-lived and he soon sank into oblivion. What interests Browning about him is the French poet's feeling that he was divinely inspired. It was right that he wrote no more after his prophetic poem and retired to a secluded life. Divine illumination, as Karshish discovered in the case of Lazarus, means death to ordinary life, so it is better that we live without it, discovering only in the end what we should know. To be a true seer and bard one must cease to be a poet entirely: 'after prophecy, the rhyming-trick / Is poor employment' (LXVI).

The second poet of Croisic was Paul Desforges Maillard, who wrote worthless verses that no one would publish. When his sister, who perceived that fame depends more on wile than merit, copied and signed them with her own name, she immediately became famous, courted by all the leading literary persons of the day. Eventually her brother revealed the ruse. Those who praised his work when they believed it his sister's turned their backs on him and without their sponsorship he was unable to gain fame.

From the stories of these two poets the speaker concludes that fame is dependent upon externals and cannot be a criterion for valuation. To determine the worth of poets he proposes a simple test: 'Which one led a happy life?' (CLV); that is, which best observed life with all its sorrows and was not undone by it? It is easy to wail about the world as do the so-called bards, who supposedly feel and see more deeply than others (CLV-VI). Yet the true poet looks at life, accepts it for what it is, and remains a 'strong since joyful man who stood distinct / Above slave-sorrows to his chariot linked' (CLVI). Furthermore, unlike 'bards' the true poet is reluctant to proclaim a universal truth: 'Who knows most, doubts most; entertaining hope, / Means recognizing fear' (CLVII). Of course he has intimations of and insights into the supersensible world, but he keeps his eye on men and women, not forgetting the ground while looking at the stars.

The poet who finally wins the prize is the one of the Browning world, the one who will 'yoke Hatred, Crime, Remorse, / Despair' but through the 'whirling fear' and 'tumult' will let 'break the poet's face / Radiant' (CLIX). 'Therefore I say...', the speaker says in an unfinished sentence, 'no, shall not say, but think' (CLX). But those who have attended the many Browning productions will know that it is the showman Robert Browning who lets his Harlequin face break radiantly from the theatre of men and women, and they will complete the sentence by saying that it is Robert Browning who wins the prize.

14

An Idyllic Interlude

I

Browning's sadness over the death of Anne Egerton Smith was not relieved by the writing of the elegy in her memory. For almost a year after the loss of this favourite companion he felt restless and despondent. 'In my own experience, this has been a trying year for me', he wrote in August 1878 to the wealthy, slightly bookish widow Mrs Thomas FitzGerald, whose acquaintance he had cultivated over the past six years (*Learned Lady*, p. 54).

Adding to his distress was his concern for Pen. During the years following his removal from Oxford, Pen lived a dilettantish life, trying his hand at verse at one time and then turning to drawing at another, all the while making the rounds of fashionable clubs and salons or visiting one of the great country houses so as to enjoy the riding and shooting. 'He wants the power of working', his father wrote to Isa Blagden, '& I give it up in despair: but his natural abilities are considerable,—and he may turn out a success, after all, though not in the way which lay most naturally before him' (*Dearest Isa*, p. 362). In 1874 Pen impressed the former Pre-Raphaelite painter (and now Royal Academician) John Everett Millais with one of his watercolours, and Millais recommended formal training. After making enquiries Browning sent his son off to Antwerp to study in the atelier of the Dutch painter Jean-Arnould Heyermans. Pen, delighted with both his *maître* and Belgium, sent some of his giant canvases home to his father and aunt, who extolled his talents to all who would listen. At last, Browning believed, his son had found himself.

The fact was however that Pen's paintings were quite ordinary. Artists and literary people said kind things about them to please a doting father. Mrs FitzGerald purchased one his pictures and became Pen's 'Original Patroness' (*Learned Lady*, p. 55). But soon the young artist became involved with a young Belgian woman, offered to marry her and refused to return to Heyermans' studio. Robert was furious and for a while all communication between father and son ceased. Only through various intermediary efforts, apparently on the part of the ever-helpful Milsand, was the marriage prevented from taking place.

Robert's life was upset and he could not bring himself to sit down to work. 'I am increasingly lazy. . . . I confess to having been quite idle of late', he wrote Mrs FitzGerald. Perhaps a visit to Italy, not seen since Elizabeth's death, 'might stimulate me a little' and help 'to emerge from the effects of the earlier months' (*Learned Lady*, pp. 54–5).

Robert and Sarianna set off in August, spending a little over a month in Switzerland before going on to Italy. The trip proved even more restorative than he had expected. Stopping at Splügen the sexagenarian pair were 'renewed like eagles' after walking 'daily for some four or five hours at a stretch – generally managing seventeen miles about, in that time' (*NL*, p. 248). Here Robert composed two poems and apparently one or two more soon thereafter. 'And to think', he wrote, 'that none of this was in my mind when I set out—very unwillingly—from London! All that reconciled my laziness to the step was the notion of seeing once again *Venice* – and perhaps Asolo' (*Learned Lady*, p. 61).

In the event Asolo was reached before Venice. Sarianna, who was seeing Italy for the first time, was as enthralled by the charms of Asolo as was Robert, who was returning after an interval of forty years. Indeed, she was, said Robert, 'the perfect fellow-traveller . . . : so that I have no subject of concern,—if things suit me they suit her—and *vice versa*'. Robert visited the ruined tower on the hilltop to see if, as on his earlier visit, he could still cause an echo, 'and thereupon it answered me plainly as ever, after all the silence' (*Learned Lady*, pp. 69, 68).

Next came Venice, where Robert delighted in introducing his sister to the city – to canals and gondolas, to the giant square of San Marco where one could take tea to musical accompaniment, to the large English and American community. Both Brownings liked it so much that they returned there in seven autumns over the next eleven years, although Robert would never visit any of the parts of Italy intimately associated with Elizabeth.

Browning seems to have feared that his poetry was becoming over-intellectualized, and even the prospect of a visit to Asolo and Venice revived in him some of the old feelings experienced during his visit in 1838 when he was worried that the poem on which he was then working, *Sordello*, was too far removed from real life. Perhaps as a way of getting his poetry again in touch with common life he could employ the idyllic mode that Tennyson had of late made so popular. Obviously he could have no thought of writing in the Tennysonian manner. As he told Isa Blagden almost a decade earlier, 'We look at the object of art in poetry so differently! . . . I should judge the conflict in the . . . soul the proper subject to describe: Tennyson thinks he should describe the [scenery] . . . , anything *but* the soul' (*Dearest Isa*, p. 328). Although he never articulated, probably even to himself, the rivalry that he felt with the Laureate, it seems indisputably to have existed; and he may have felt, more or less unconsciously, that by using the idyll he could beat Tennyson at his own game and gain the popularity that should rightfully be his.

In Greek literature the idyll is a short, descriptive poem dealing with pastoral or rural life. As employed by Tennyson in his so-called English Idyls, it was a little verse picture that rendered the emotional and moral signficance of an event through elaboration. Reflecting upon this form of the narrative mode, Browning saw how he could transform it. Where Tennyson's idylls were descriptive and usually morally unambiguous, Browning's would explore a brief scene or situation psychologically, in effect replacing signification by characterization.[1] Thus his idylls would be dramatic. 'An idyl', he explained to a correspondent,

> is a succinct little story complete in itself; not necessarily concerning pastoral matters, by any means, though from the prevalency of such topics in the idyls of Theocritus, such is the general notion. These of mine are called 'Dramatic' because the story is told by some actor in it, not by the poet himself. (DeVane, p. 430)

Dramatic Idyls, containing six poems, was published in late April 1879. They are webs of narrative spun round a central puzzle, which is enclosed within a narrative of a narrative, embodied in long swinging, rhyming lines. Browning resorts to such narrative complexity and to a verse form that constantly calls attention to itself in order to suggest that it is difficult or impossible ever fully to understand the truth of a situation, that in any case the arguments are about as good on one side as the other and, further, that the complexities of existence are merely highlighted and not resolved in art, which, neither magisterial nor reformatory, pretends to be nothing other than itself.

Most of the 1879 idylls, however, deal with moral problems. The main character in each is motivated at a critical moment by his emotional sensitivity to a power, often supernatural, greater than himself. But is this power God or the devil? Browning's point is that it is impossible to know. 'Martin Relph' is a monologue set within a narrative frame that tells how Martin failed to act to prevent two deaths and how each year he retells the story. Is his guilt simply the hallucinations of old age? Or if his story is true, might it not as well be the guilt of cowardice as of murderous revenge? 'Pheidippides' is a personal account of a runner's effort to seek help for the Athenians at Marathon, concluded by a detached narrator. The runner is led by the demigod Pan to believe that he will receive a worthy reward, which he thinks will be retirement from running and settling down to domesticity; and he ends his part of the poem with 'I too have a guerdon rare!' The narrator of the second part tells what the guerdon was: Pan allows Pheidippides to 'never decline, but, gloriously as he began, / So to end gloriously—... Pheidippides dies in the shout for his meed'. Some meed! 'Halbert and Hob', related entirely by an omniscient narrator, intimates in its last line that it takes the supernatural to awe men into decent behaviour. But is Hob moved, after his father's death, to cursing and swearing as the children say, or to prayer as the elders believe?

The question of a divine voice figures even more importantly in 'Ivàn Ivànovitch'. Introduced as a tale told to the narrator by a Russian friend and probably reflecting Browning's memories of the Russian landscape from his visit in 1834, it is comprised largely of a woman's monologue. If Ivàn's action results from 'God's voice', as he claims, then there is a sharp division between divine severity and human weakness. What the reader is left with in the end is what the narrator refers to in the beginning as an 'unprobed undreamed abyss' – nothingness filled by the woman with her monologue of self-justification, by Ivàn with his axe and by the priest with his judgement. Whether Ivàn acted according to divine law or whether his murder of the woman was a perversion of the sacred is left indeterminate. The mawkish 'Tray', inspired by the antivivisectionist controversy of the 1870s, presents three tales, only one of which (where a dog is the hero) the narrator judges satisfactory to quench the soul's thirst. The bystanders in this last believe that it is the dog's 'divine' instinct to help people in distress, although in fact the dog is just as ready to rescue a child's doll from the water as the child himself; and a scientist among the crowd hopes to discover the dog's soul by dissecting its brain.[2] Whether in fact the dog has a soul and whether it is divinely informed is left in question. In 'Ned Bratts', basically a tale told in the third person, the eponymous hero and his wife, through a misunderstanding of Bunyan, confess to many crimes in court, which confession the judge curiously ascribes not to Bunyan's influence but to the restoration of Charles II.

In one way or another, all the idylls have one central subject – judgement; and all have characters facing death in some manner or other. It may be that they reflect the sixty-seven-year-old Browning's concern with his own mortality and enduring fame.

II

Dramatic Idyls was well received by both critics and public, and Browning was so pleased that he wrote another series of six in less than six months, publishing them as *Dramatic Idyls, Second Series* in June 1880. The prologue tells explicitly that those who claim to have a hold on the highest truth cannot in fact comprehend the more accessible truths of everyday life. In 'Echetlos', a companion to 'Pheidippides', and like it also about fame, the narrator tells the story of how the gods give fame to a hero at Marathon whose name is to remain for ever unknown. Again, some fame! 'Clive', the most psychologically penetrating of all the idylls and thought by Browning to be his best (Hood, p. 235), is a narrative within a narrative, in effect two dramatic monologues of two fully realized characters. The speaker of the outer narrative frame reveals his need for a hero who can serve as a model for his own unheroic life. If Clive had not killed himself, then the speaker could have maintained the illusion that he shared in Clive's heroic life throughout. The narrator justifies himself by showing that in the end he has survived, morally, while Clive is dead, immorally. He is, however, just as wrong and just as right in his attitude towards life as Clive had been. The speaker of 'Mulèykeh' shares with Clive a belief in the worth of abstractions like honour and fame and so is willing to endure the loss of his most prized possession, a horse, rather than have her fame for speed be diminished.

'Pietro of Abano' deals with the irony of a mage, despised and unfairly dealt with during his lifetime, who believes that the genuine lover of knowledge and mankind can expect only spiritual rewards but who centuries later is widely commemorated. 'Doctor ———' recalls Faustian narratives, but here the bargain is imposed by Satan and the fruits of it are for the devil himself. 'Pan and Luna', the most beautiful of the idylls, is a gloss on Virgil, a commentary on three lines of a *Georgic*. The speaker begins his gloss with scholarly detachment but then starts to respond to the sensuality of the story until he finally says, 'enough!' It is as though he were conscious of the goat half of Pan within himself. He then returns to a reportorial style and a moral evaluation: Luna fell not through a fault in herself but from virtue – 'unmatched modesty' – while Pan is recognized as the villainous demigod who in this instance is full brute. The speaker then tidies up the myth by pronouncing, 'Never say, kiss her! that were to pollute / Love's language', as 'who finds thorns / Where she sought flowers'. Yet in the last stanza he turns once more to Virgil and learns that Luna followed her seducer, 'by no means spurning him'. Virgil's text, in other words, will not allow the exegete to moralize: he is left with a 'ruin' – the ruin of his moral expectation – but also with the memory of how he first thrilled to the sensual aspects of the story. He tried to shape the myth to his conscious liking but failed. Nevertheless, his reward is something without shape: a list of five words of enormous suggestive potential, words that may be related to each other in a variety of ways – 'Arcadia, night, a cloud, Pan, and the moon'.[3]

The best of the *Dramatic Idyls* are expressive of the double vision of the ironic showman, who presents contradictory views without resolving them. As ironist the poet reminds us constantly, with his long, heavily stressed lines and insistent rhymes, of his presence in as well as his transcendence of the enacted drama. In the epilogue to the second series Browning himself comes forward (though not by name) to bid farewell by announcing his poetic purpose. He is not, he says, the kind of poet the public generally expect their poets to be. First, they want songsters: 'Touch him ne'er so lightly, into song he broke', as 'song would song succeed / Sudden as spontaneous'. Second, they want moralists whose chief interest is 'Vitalizing virtue'. He however is different. He produces neither flowers of song nor moral exhortations. Instead he offers a pine that springs from rocky soil and aspires upwards towards heaven: unappreciated during its growth, it becomes in an after-age valued as 'a nation's heritage'.

III

The second series of Browning's dramatic idylls was received far less enthusiastically than the first had been. But no reviewer could now possibly make the vituperative comments that had characterized earlier critical remarks about the poet. By 1880 Browning had become something of a national institution and was generally recognized, along with Tennyson, as one of the greatest poets of the period, in testimony to which Cambridge had awarded him an LL D degree in 1879. The most public attestation to his fame came in the summer of 1881, when a group of his admirers, headed by F. J. Furnivall, proposed the founding of a Browning Society.[4]

In 1879 Furnivall – a lawyer, philologist, agnostic, socialist, vegetarian, pioneer in adult education, founder of the Early English Text Society and the Chaucer Society – had persuaded Browning to accept the presidency of the New Shakespeare Society. Browning was most taken with this man who, no fawning sycophant, could nevertheless speak to the poet as though it could be taken for granted that he belonged in the company of Chaucer, Shakespeare and the other great names of English literature. Unfortunately, Furnivall was given to scholarly feuds, and no sooner had Browning become the nominal head of the New Shakespeare Society than Furnivall began squabbling with the poet Algernon Charles Swinburne. As an Oxford undergraduate and later as part of the group associated with the second generation of the Pre-Raphaelites, Swinburne had done much to promote Browning's poetry among the young; even in 1881 he sent Browning a copy of his volume of poems that contained his 'Song for the Centenary of Walter Savage Landor', which had as its motto the opening lines of Landor's poem 'To Robert Browning'. In the slugging match between Furnivall and Swinburne, in which epithets such as 'Pigsbrook' and 'Flunkivall Brothelsbank' were exchanged, Browning tried to remain impartial. But Swinburne saw him as the figurehead of a ship the captain of which was an impudent liar and he could, so he wrote to Browning, no longer in conscience be associated with the president of the New Shakespeare Society.

When Furnivall proposed on 3 July 1881 a Browning Society for the study and appreciation of the works of an intellectual poet often thought to be obscure, Browning was taken aback. There was a Wordsworth Society and a Shelley Society in addition to the other societies already originated by Furnivall, but a society in honour of a living poet might provoke all sorts of humour and raisings of eyebrows, especially from someone so given to satirical mischief as Swinburne. After all, there was no society

Plate 13 'Mr Robert Browning, taking tea with the Browning Society'. Cartoon by Max Beerbohm. F. J. Furnivall, a founder of the Society, is the bearded figure to the poet's right. Courtesy of the Ashmolean Museum, Oxford. © Sir Rupert Hart-Davis.

named for the Laureate, whose sales from verse were many, many times greater than Browning's. But Furnivall urged and Browning relented, even while fearing that such an enterprise might subject him to ridicule.

After a good deal of preparation Furnivall was successful in gathering over three hundred admirers to attend the inaugural meeting of the Browning Society on 28 October 1881 in a hall at the University of London. Furnivall was elected president and soon after he enlisted Leighton, Domett and Milsand as vice presidents. Browning himself, who refused to attend any of the society's meetings, was amazed and delighted by this outpouring of support from persons largely unknown to him. And he was even more surprised and elated as Browning Societies began to spread around the world, so that within three years there were twenty-two of them. Reflecting on the society's first publication, a bibliography of his works, he said: 'It makes me feel ... as if I were dead and *begun* with, after half a century' (*Learned Lady*, p. 124).

Other honours soon followed. Oxford gave him an honorary DCL at the Sheldonian Theatre in 1882, during which prankish undergraduates in the gallery managed to drop a red cotton nightcap upon his head. A Browning craze began in America, as clubs dedicated to the study of his works sprang up throughout the United States. Browning had for years

been far more popular in America than in England. Elizabeth had re-
ported to Sarianna in 1861 that the American minister in Florence had
said 'there is not so poor a village in the United States' where Robert was
not known. In America, she said, 'he is a power, a writer, a poet—he is
read – he lives in the hearts of the people' (Orr, *Life*, p. 234). More re-
cently his works were printed on railway timetables in Chicago, where
bookstores were unable to keep up with the demand for copies of his
poems. In St. Louis a Sordello Club was initiated. The Browning craze
even manifested itself in clothing and interior decor, as brown dresses,
brown curtains and brown bread became *de rigueur*. No less—and more
unlikely – a personage than Mark Twain held Browning classes and gave
readings from Browning throughout the country, vowing, 'I can read
Browning so Browning himself can understand it'.[5] Foreign sightseers in
London were delighted with a glimpse of the poet and besieged him for
autographs. Browning loved it all, although feigning a certain diffidence.
He was, he said in reference to his many admirers, somewhat embarrassed
and was himself 'quite other than a Browningite':

> The exaggerations probably come of the fifty-years'–long charge of un-
> intelligibility against my books; such reactions are possible, though I never
> looked for the beginning of one so soon. That there is a grotesque side to
> the thing is certain. (Hood, p. 212)

At the height of his fame he could for the time being rest on his laurels,
as he and Sarianna continued to spend their summers abroad. 'I feel a
poor sinner indeed when such praises are given me', he said; 'the bracing
effect always came of the blame . . .' (*Learned Lady*, p. 132). For almost three
years he published nothing. According to his manservant for his last seven
years, William Grove, who gave an account of his employer's habits in the
Pall Mall Budget for 19 December 1889, a week after the poet's death,
Browning's routine involved rising at seven and remaining in his room till
eight, at which time he bathed. He then came down to breakfast at nine,
having earlier eaten some fruit left in his bedroom the night before. Then
after reading the *Times* and the *Daily News* and perhaps playing the piano
he wrote in his study from ten till one. After a light luncheon he went out
to pay calls on friends or to visit art galleries.

Certain days were generally set aside for specific visits. On Saturday he
went to the Athenaeum, where he read the weekly papers. On Sunday he
visited Mrs FitzGerald and other friends. On Tuesday and Friday he went
to Kensington to call upon Alexandra (Mrs Sutherland) Orr, the widowed
sister of Frederic Leighton, who after Isa Blagden was his closest woman
friend and who after his death was to write the *Life and Letters*. On Monday
he dined with A. P. Stanley, dean of Westminster, and afterwards would
help show tradesmen around the Abbey. When he dined out, he returned
home so as to be in bed by half past midnight.

He became a more strenuous diner-out than ever. 'I have dined out—
and been to a "Ball"—on each of the two days since I saw you', he wrote
to Mrs FitzGerald in the first of his extant letters to her (*Learned Lady*, p.

31). He was to be encountered at all sorts of social events, where he made his presence known. The press took him up as a public figure. The weekly *World* of 7 December 1881 referred to his frequent appearance on the social scene and described his 'compact little figure, the urbane and genial bearing, the well-made clothes'. He was, said the writer, 'as far a dandy as a sensible man can be'. The young Browning who affected yellow gloves remained a dandy till his dying day.

It is evident that for Browning the world was a stage on which he himself wished (and was expected) to figure. His dandyism was part of his act, as was his theatrical heartiness. In a sense, Browning stylized himself as a means of making himself and his attributes more visible. He was as intent on fashioning himself as on fashioning his poetry. Both were a way of 'making' in that both fashion and poetry originate in the verb 'to make' or 'to do' (*facere* in Latin, *poein* in Greek). It was evidently part of his scheme to complicate and problematize the drawing of boundaries between persona and personality, self and theatrical mask. Which, Browning implicitly asks, is primary: the literary fact or the fact of life? Or to use his own terminology, which Robert Browning was the 'fact' and which the 'fancy'? He made sure there would be no easy answer, as he trotted himself out on to various stages to deliver his lengthy monologues. W. H. Mallock was but one to find him given to theatrical gestures and almost ceaseless talk. Edmund Gosse noted 'the loud trumpet-note' of welcome that the carefully groomed man with the white hair and the white beard boomed to his guests, 'the talk already in full flood at a distance of twenty feet'. Charles Hallé remembered a dinner party where Browning talked the whole time during dinner and ate nothing.[6]

For a while the energetic man of the world subdued the energetic poet. For three years Browning the poet was silent, until *Jocoseria* appeared in March 1883. Containing ten poems, the volume was 'a collection of things grav*ish* and gay*ish*' (Hood, p. 213) in the mode of the dramatic idylls. The theme they treat is desire, as announced in the slightly ridiculous first line of the prologue ('Wanting is—what?'). The only poem worthy of mention in this undistinguished volume – 'this Olla Podrida', as Browning referred to it (Hood, p. 213) – is 'Ixion', which deals with the kind of complex, ironic situation found in Browning's earlier, shorter poems.

Shunned by all mankind, Ixion was taken up to heaven by Zeus, who bade him enjoy all the pleasures of the gods. Yet when Ixion tried them, Zeus angrily sent him to the underworld to be bound on a wheel of fire. Where is the justice in it all? Why did not the gods take pity on him and show him how he had gone wrong? Why must his punishment be eternal? As he reflects on these questions, Ixion comes to the Shelleyan perception that from suffering can spring hope: 'Strive, my kind, though strife endure thro' endless obstruction, / Stage after stage, each rise marred by as certain a fall!' (97–8). Further, he discerns that beyond the 'gods' there is a greater power. For Ixion, somewhat like Shelley's Prometheus, perceives that the gods are but phantoms of man's own making and that man can reconceptualize his old formulations and so rise 'past Zeus to the Potency o'er him' (21). 'Zeus' is but a stage in the evolutionary spiral of human thought towards the Absolute. As Balaustion said at the end of *Aristophanes' Apology*, 'There are no gods, no gods! / Glory to God'.

Surprisingly, even to its author, *Jocoseria* was well received. 'This little "Jocoseria" (joking even in the title)', Browning wrote not long after its publication, 'has had the usual luck of the little-deserving,—got itself sold ... at the rate of 2000 very early, and is now reprinting' (Hood, p. 218). The volume is the least important and (with the possible exception of *A Blot in the 'Scutcheon*) least worthwhile that the poet ever published. Clearly the idyllic mode was not for him, since he had little interest in narrative exposition. He had tried it mainly because 'it is undeniable that the common reader is suceptible to plot, story, and the simplest form of putting a matter "Said I", "Said He" & so on'.[7] If his idylls had offered, as he said they would, 'a succinct little story complete in itself ... told by some actor in it', the focus would have been on character revelation, Browning's speciality, as in the splendid example of 'Clive'. Too often, however, the idylls such as those in *Jocoseria* are narratives told by a third-person narrator that serve as vehicles for the poet's own moralizing, as in the case of 'Donald', a mawkish little poem dealing with the wretchedness and guilt visited upon a man who killed a stag that presented itself defenceless before him. The narrator in such cases is fairly explicitly the poet himself. As we have constantly seen, Browning somehow inserts himself into practically all his work. But here self-display is different: it is not playful or ironic; the master of the performance presents a drama that is little more than a morality play.

'Donald' is exemplary. Like 'Tray' in the first *Dramatic Idyls*, it reflects Browning's strong antivivisectionist beliefs, in furtherance of which he had become vice-president of the Victoria Street Society for the Protection of Animals. Donald, who killed the stag that trusted him, fell while committing the perfidious deed and was crippled for life. He thereafter wandered from place to place, braggingly telling his story and showing the stag's head and hide so as to earn a beggar's livelihood. To this the narrator has the last word: 'Rightly recorded,—Ingrate'. Such poems, so uncharacteristic of Browning, do not permit the reader of the three volumes of 'dramatic idyls' to escape the feeling that the poet wrote them to keep himself occupied and published them to satisfy public demand for new poems from the great poet so recently canonized by his admirers. As he said of the popularity of *Jocoseria*, 'It all comes of the Browning Societies' (Hood, p. 218).

IV

Browning himself was not overly pleased with his idylls, recognizing them as the bagatelles that they are. The day after *Jocoseria* appeared in March

1883, he said that they were 'probably the last of the kind I shall care to write' (Hood, p. 214). What was expected of him, now proclaimed a sage by the Browning Societies that seemed to be springing up everywhere, was poetry addressed to philosophical and religious issues. Yet he was, as he well knew from the experience of writing 'La Saisiaz', not the kind of poet who could speak as a bard. 'Crowned by prose and verse; and wielding, with Wit's bauble, Learning's rod', what he could he say? 'Well? Why, he at least believed in Soul, was very sure of God' ('La Saisiaz', 603–4). No, he could do only what he had done in the past: assume a mask.

About this time Browning was trying to improve his knowledge of German (Orr, *Life*, pp. 362–3), and it may be that in seeking a suitable setting and persona for a religio-philosophical poem, he turned to Goethe's *Westöstlicher Divan*, a collection of poems with a Persian backdrop divided into twelve books of unequal length. In any event, after versifying a fable from Bidpai that he had read as a boy, it 'then occurred to him to make the poem the beginning of a series, in which a Dervish, who is first introduced as a learner, shall reappear in the character of a teacher' (Orr, *Handbook*, p. 331).

Ferishtah's Fancies, published in November 1884, contained twelve of 'Ferishtah's Fancies' plus a prologue and an epilogue. The fancies – analogies and parables of the great theological problems – are followed by lyrics grounded in everyday life, thereby joining 'things visible and invisible, / Fact, fancy' ('A Pillar at Sebzevah', 124–5). The prologue presents us with a speaker with whom we have been long familiar, the self-mocking showman-poet. He is like the Shakespeare described by Jeremy Collier, a quotation from whom serves as one of the two epigraphs to the volume: 'His genius was jocular, but, when disposed, he could be serious'. What he announces, employing a risible analogy, is the form his poems will take: like ortalans skewered and cooked in the Italian fashion, they will be hard on the outside, piquant next and meaty finally, thus blending sense (the story), sight (the moral) and song (the lyrical expression of the idea) into a succulent mixture.

The parts, loosely joined, trace Ferishtah's development as a sage. Called to be a dervish, he nevertheless follows God's admonition to forgo an ascetic and speculative existence for life among men and women ('The Eagle'). As he wanders in fulfilment of his vocation, he learns that it is better to thank God for life's joys than to curse him for its sorrows ('The Melon-Seller'). Become a full dervish, he instructs his followers in matters of faith, stressing not the forms or doctrines but the basic problems of belief.

Ferishtah discourses on the historical grounds of faith, on prayer, on the Incarnation, on the problem of pain, on punishment, on asceticism, on thanksgiving to God, on justification of sensual gratification, on the limitations of knowledge and on the predominance of good over evil. These are all topics on which Browning has touched at one time or another, and they are treated as he has treated them in the past: by the use

of the image, addressing 'the symbol, not the symbolized' ('The Sun', 21).
And although his protagonist is a Moslem, Browning has him, like Cleon
and Karshish, induce from his own personal needs and observations a
Christian God of love who made the earth for man's enjoyment.

Ferishtah is always careful to represent his thoughts not as dicta but as
expressions of a point of view:

> I know my own appointed patch i' the world,
> What pleasures me or pains there: all outside—
> How he, she, it, and even thou, Son, live,
> Are pleased or pained, is past conjecture, once
> I pry beneath the semblance,—all that's fit,
> To practise with,—reach where the fact may lie
> Fathom-deep lower. There's the first and last
> Of my philosophy.
>
> ('A Bean-Stripe', 165–72)

From his own angle of vision there is in the world a compensatory light
for every instance of darkness, but he is willing to allow that his basically
cheerful view of life might well not be shared by someone else, who sees
in the row of mixed beans more black than white ones.

Browning himself, thoroughgoing realist as he was, was never willing to
base belief in anything on abstraction. Unless it is felt in the blood and
proven upon the pulses, faith is void and formless. The existence of God,
the Incarnation, the afterlife – any religious question could find verifica-
tion only in his own experience. And the experience that was most real to
him was the experience of love. As he showed in *Fifine at the Fair*, all is
shadow except the heart's affections. This is why each of Ferishtah's
theological speculations is followed by a love lyric, expressing in emotional
terms the thought or idea of the discourse. The 'fancies' of the intellect
are authenticated by the 'facts' of love.

Following his last fancy Ferishtah asks why the world should praise his
work. He has not worked for the world's sake and is therefore indifferent
to its praise or blame. 'I looked beyond the world for truth and beauty:
/ Sought, found and did my duty'. In the epilogue the speaker, sounding
even more like the poet than the Ferishtah of the closing lyric, declares
that he has kept his eye on the world's moanings and groanings, weariness
and woe – 'none of Life I lose!' But he also hears the voices of the great
of old who battled for the just and true asking why their names and deeds
are so soon erased from the tablet 'where Life's glory lies enrolled'. Is it
in fact worth dealing with the world, the speaker wonders, only then to
assure himself that the world and its ways have their worth, 'man's strife
and strife's success'. But what if – what if it were only a dream? 'What if
all be error – / If the halo irised round my head were, Love, thine arms?'

The assumption in all the lyrics is that human love is a reflection of
divine love: 'God is soul, souls I and thou' (lyric following 'The Eagle').
And part of the 'terror' in the last stanza of the epilogue derives from the

fear that the 'I' has created the fiction that love and Love are the same. What if love were only love and his own circumstance and opinion insignificant of the principle of Love at work in the universe? The question is unanswered because it is the point of the poem that nothing worth knowing can be proven or disproven. It can only be provisionally answered by the questioner, Robert Browning the maker of the poem.

Although smacking too much of the orientalism sweeping Western Europe at the time, *Ferishtah's Fancies* is the most impressive work Browning had completed since the long poems of the first half of the 1870s. In its sometimes brilliant analogies of religious questions, posed at the beginning of each of Ferishtah's discourses, it recalls the proem to Kierkegaard's *Fear and Trembling*. In its structure – 'fancy' manifested in 'fact' – it perfectly reflects Browning's incarnational view of poetry iterated in his letter of 1855 to Ruskin quoted earlier: 'all poetry [is] a putting the infinite within the finite'.

15

Looking Backwards and Forwards:
The *Parleyings*

'I can't at all guess how people will like it', Browning wrote to Furnivall of *Ferishtah's Fancies* shortly before its publication, 'but I have managed to say a thing or two that I "fancied" I should like to say' (Peterson, p. 100). The book was in the event well liked by both the public and the reviewers. Domett wrote to the author that he liked it but found it 'so full of subtle and profound thought on abstruse and difficult subjects' that he was inclined to say, '"Out with your *nut-crackers*, you Browning Societies!"'[1] The author was probably not overly pleased with the observation. There was, in any case, still more that he would like to say, on a grander scale and without the Persian disguise. As one of the two mottos to *Ferishtah*, Browning had chosen a passage from *King Lear*, which reads in part: 'I do not like the fashion of your garments: you will say they are Persian: but let them be changed'. Now he would indeed change costumes and present himself in the dress of his own time.

Browning was seventy-three years old when he apparently began composition of *Parleyings with Certain People of Importance in Their Day*. 'I am writing another poem', he confided to Furnivall from his autumn holiday in Italy in 1885 (Peterson, p. 116); and he wrote to Mrs FitzGerald two months later that, though enjoying Venice, he looked forward to coming home 'because I have work to finish' (*Learned Lady*, p. 187). A year later he was still excitedly working on it, convinced that the poem was 'to be my best' (Hood, p. 254). When he had finished a first draft, he started to revise and found doing so unusually difficult (Orr, *Life*, p. 347).

Writing the poem was hard because it was to be the summation of his career, 'full of reminiscences' and dealing with 'men whose works connect themselves with the intellectual sympathies and the imaginative pleasures of his very earliest youth' (Orr, *Handbook*, p. 339). While it was to be something of an intellectual autobiography told in a familiar, conversational style, it was also to be of epic, encyclopedic scope – a kind of *Divina Commedia* rooted in *commedia dell'arte*.

'Parleying' was a carefully chosen word, one of Browning's own manu-facture (which is still unlisted in the *Oxford English Dictionary*). For it signifies not only a conversation but also a discussion of terms with an opponent; in addition, the phrase 'to beat or sound a parley' means to call for a parley by sounding a drum or trumpet. Almost certainly in Browning's mind it had all three meanings. For as he uses the term a parleying is a monologue in which a figure from the past is summoned up by a nec-romancer, in a way not dissimilar from that in which the speaker in *Sordello* conjures up Verona or the narrator in *The Ring and the Book* resuscitates Rome. Each ghost so evoked is presumably harmless, but as each ectoplasm is encountered, strange thoughts arise in the speaker's mind: old feelings come to life in new strength to be embraced or cast aside. 'Could I . . . / Boast, with the sights I see, your vision too?' asks the necromancer in the parleying 'With Gerard de Lairesse'. 'Advantage would it prove or detriment / If I saw double?' (116–19).

The parleying trick, however, permits more than dual vision. For with the appearance of each ghost from the past there also arises a current thought or attitude to be argued with, so that each section presents three points of view: those of the speaker, the figure summoned from the dis-tant past, and a contemporary.[2] With its multiple perspectives the parley-ing was of great advantage for the person who believed that 'one thing has many sides' (*Balaustion's Adventure*, 2402).

The *Parleyings with Certain People of Importance in Their Day* is not, how-ever, simply a series of complicated monologues. It is a unified poem of epic proportions modelled on *Faust* and the *Divine Comedy*. It begins with a prologue analogous to the prologue in Heaven in Goethe's poem or the descent into Hell in Dante's, and ends with the salvation of one John Fust, made the inventor of the printing press. Structurally the *Parleyings* form a symphony of four movements, with an introduction and a coda. The action in the beginning is downward, Apollo proceeding 'down to the depths— dread hollow' to encounter the Fates (3), and works upward to the epi-logue, where Fust's friends climb 'up, up, up' (1) to the abode of the apostle of enlightenment. The light imagery, basic to the entire work, operates in the same way. In short, the structure of the *Parleyings* is re-flective of Browning's evolutionary view of history.

The work is chiefly concerned with two basic questions: is life good or bad? and what makes it tolerable? The prologue presents a debate be-tween Apollo, who sees life as good and happy, and the Fates, who view it as evil, he arguing that darkness is an unreality that can be cleared away by light, they insisting that light is an illusion that soon fades. While acknowledging that 'debarred / Of illusion . . . / Man desponds and de-spairs' (105–7), Apollo also claims that man has a 'power in himself' that makes life meaningful and bearable (109–10). This is wine, the product and symbol of man's art; and to prove its power he induces the Fates to drink, whereupon they perceive that life is 'no defeat but a triumph' (221).

Like Nietzsche, Browning presents art as an 'Apollonian', illusionist activity that casts a veil of the cosmos of being over the chaos of becoming; but unlike Nietzsche, he offers it as a performance, a showman's trick. And to suggest its temporarily illusory efficacy, he characteristically undercuts much of that which has gone before by concluding the action in the prologue with a theatrical explosion from the centre of earth, which recalls the Fates from ecstasy to sobriety and leaves them with the knowledge that the true significance of life cannot be gained by the living.

In the parleying 'With Bernard Mandeville' the speaker's chief argument is with Thomas Carlyle, Browning's old, admired friend who had died in 1881. Although it has not here been possible to trace directly Carlyle's influence on the poet – that would take a separate, book-length study – it is none the less safe to say that with the possible exception of Shelley, Carlyle had a greater influence on Browning's thought than any other nineteenth-century writer. Browning acknowledged this. Writing a month after the older man's death, he said that if it had not been for his acquaintance with Carlyle, 'very likely I might have figured in some corner of a page as a poor scribbling-man with proclivities for the turf and scamphood. . . . No, I am his devotedly' (*NL*, p. 263). And while he was writing the *Parleyings* he said, in December 1885, in answer to a request for a personal account of the Sage of Chelsea: 'I cannot undertake to write any account of our beloved friend at present: I feel . . . hardly able to say my whole mind aright just now, from abundance rather than lack of matter'.[3]

'With Bernard Mandeville' invokes the eighteenth-century philosopher to come to the speaker's aid in his argument with Carlyle about life's harmonious combination of good and evil for a beneficent purpose. In the fancied debate Carlyle argues the impossibility of learning God's purpose and the foolishness of trying to understand the infinite in terms of the finite; agnosticism, he urges, is the only stance possible. The speaker responds that mankind's understanding can come only through signs, symbols and myths. In a drawing one does not complain that the letter 'A', which designates the house, is not the house itself; no, one 'look[s] through the sign to the thing signified' (192). It is precisely the purpose of myth and of fables such as Mandeville wrote to help us with our limited vision: 'A myth may teach' (204). But of course myths, like all living things, change and fade, and in helping create new myths poets assume a religious function. Euripides, for example, humanized the old myths instead of dealing with them in the earlier forms; he taught Balaustion to say the 'master-word' at the close of *Aristophanes' Apology*: 'There are no gods, no gods! / Glory to God'. That is why in dealing with myth 'who better would expound it thus / Must be Euripides not Aeschylus' (205–6).

Carlyle himself had addressed the question of myth in *Sartor Resartus*, a book that Browning confessed had had an immense influence on him (*NL*, p. 263). The 'Mythus of the Christian Religion looks not in the eighteenth century as it did in the eighth', Teufelsdröckh in that book said, and what was now needed was someone to 'help us to embody the divine

Spirit of that Religion in a new Mythus, in a new vehicle and vesture, that our Souls, otherwise too like perishing, may live'.[4] This was precisely what Browning had considered and attempted for most of his career, certainly since *Christmas-Eve and Easter-Day*. Here, following in the footsteps of Euripides, the speaker offers a variation on the Prometheus myth that suggests the importance of artists – among whom must be included Mandeville, the 'Fabulist' of the 'Grumbling Hive', and Carlyle, who 'himself wrote fables short and sweet' (93–4) – in the formulation of the new mythus that is to be. Moving from midnight to an image of the sun, the parleying-myth indicates that life is a mixture of good and evil, whose harmonious combination may be discerned through the imagination and its embodiment in art.

'With Daniel Bartoli' mitigates 'Mandeville's' high claim for art and myth, the poet reiterating his often repeated insistence on the superiority of life to art. Words, he shows, even when ordered into art, pale into insignificance before the Word as manifested in human love. The seventeenth-century moralist Bartoli is invoked only to be dismissed as a hagiographer, while the speaker confronts a contemporary antagonist who is none other than Robert Browning. The story told is of a duke's choice of material gain over a woman's self-sacrificing love and his subsequent sorrow for that error. The speaker insists that the lady has a far greater claim to devotion than does a St Scholastica, who miraculously tamed a ferocious lion; nothing marvellous in this narrated story, simply a tale of human love that would yield all for love's sake. In the end the speaker even grants sainthood to the man, who escapes from the enchantments of a 'bold she-shape' that attempts to cut him off from his past love.

As Browning resurrects the Lady Ashburton episode of some fifteen years earlier, the poetry springs to life with the same tension marking the close of *Fifine at the Fair*, which had also covertly figured his supposed disloyalty to his dead wife for even briefly considering Lady Ashburton's proposal.

> Fancy's flight
> Makes me a listener when, some sleepless night,
> The duke reviewed his memories, and aghast
> Found that the Present intercepts the Past
> With such effect as when a cloud enwraps
> The moon and, moon-suffused, plays moon perhaps
> To who walks under, till comes, late or soon,
> A stumble: up he looks, and lo, the moon
> Calm, clear, convincingly herself once more!
> How could he 'scape the cloud that thrust between
> Him and effulgence?
> (276–86)

Admitting his guilt, the speaker ends with an affirmation of 'the main fact that love, when love indeed, / Is wholly solely love from first to last— /

Truth—all the rest a lie' (267–9). God is revealed not in the miracles of
'legend but [in] a chronicle' of an ordinary life (260).

The second movement of the *Parleyings* takes its point of departure from
'Bartoli', which located the infinite in human love. 'With Christopher
Smart' begins with a consideration of the possibility of divine revelation,
a subject treated in the first of 'The Two Poets of Croisic'. The eighteenth-
century poet wrote one poem, 'The Song of David', that seemed to bear
the stamp of divine authority, while everything else of his was nothing
more than unexceptional verse. 'What if, in one point only, then and
there / The otherwise all-unapproachable / Allowed impingement?' (104–
6). Whatever the reason, in this one instance Smart perceived nature and
truth undisguised and expressed his vision in matching language.

In his description of the power of poetry (113–20, 157–61), Browning
leaves no doubt that that power resides in the poet's ability to act as a
moral force, although without moralizing. 'First give us knowledge, then
appoint its use!' the speaker apostrophizes Smart as the representative of
all poets. And with his eye on Rossetti, Morris, Swinburne and the whole
art-for-art school, Browning denounces any conception of the poet as the
idle singer of an empty day.

Though, as we have noted, he had liked Rossetti as a young man and
had appreciated Rossetti's promotion of his work among his friends and
disciples, he grew increasingly weary of Rossetti as a poet. The Pre-
Raphaelite's poems were, he told Isa Blagden,

> *scented* with poetry, as it were—like trifles of various sorts you take out of a
> cedar or sandal-wood box: you know I hate the effeminacy of his school,—
> the men that dress up like women,—that use obsolete forms, too, and
> archaic accentuations . . . : Swinburne started this with other like Belialisms . . . ;
> then, how I hate 'Love,' as a lubberly naked young man putting his arms
> here & his wings there, about a pair of lovers. . . . (*Dearest Isa*, pp. 336–7)

When Rossetti fell out with him over *Fifine*, Browning tried to overlook the
younger man's continuing hostility; but eventually he found his 'inso-
lence' intolerable.[5] As for Swinburne, prior to the break over the New
Shakespeare Society, Browning had liked him and thought 'he had gen-
ius' but 'wrote verse in which to my mind there was no good at all'; in fact,
Browning thought his poems of the 1860s 'moral mistakes' (*NL*, p. 150).

In Browning's mind beauty is the means and not the end of art. Nature
is of course to be enjoyed, but it also can tell us something about God's
goodness. Smart was, the parleyer says, the only poet between Milton and
Keats to pierce the screen separating thing and word, to look into nature
and 'tell / Us others of her majesty and might / In large, her lovelinesses
infinite / In little' (142–5). Possessed of extraordinary power of sight, Smart
scrutinized the rose before studying the heavens; and from him a poet
should learn to begin with the little before ascending to the large. Hu-
mankind's business is with earth, and there or nowhere will we discover
'Will, Power, and Love' (258).

Where the parleying with Smart unfolds in images of blazing light, 'With George Bubb Dodington' is carried on in darkness. In summoning up the eighteenth-century political opportunist, the speaker adopts the role of the cynical manipulator in order to parley with his recently deceased contemporary, Benjamin Disraeli, whom he regards as a political charlatan. Without mentioning Disraeli's name he instructs Dodington in the methods of demagoguery so successfully employed by the Tory politician who became prime minister and the first earl of Beaconsfield.

Browning was first a political radical and afterwards a liberal. As Mrs Orr, who knew the poet well, said, 'His politics were, so far as they went, the practical aspect of his religion. Their cardinal doctrine was the liberty of individual growth; removal of every barrier of prejudice or convention by which it might still be checked' (Orr, *Life*, p. 354). In no sense was he a party man or doctrinal in any respect. This is brought out in his sonnet 'Why I Am a Liberal', published in 1885 in a collection of statements entitled *Why I am a Liberal, Being Definitions by the Best Minds of the Liberal Party*. The poet declares himself a liberal because he believes in liberty:

> Who, then, dares hold—emancipated thus—
> His fellow shall continue bound? Not I,
> Who live, love, labour freely, nor discuss
> A brother's right to freedom. That is "Why".

Yet he fell out with Gladstone, the leader of the Liberal Party, and 'many valued friends' over Irish Home Rule, 'and no pain of Lost Leadership was ever more angry or more intense, than that which came to him through the defection of a great statesman whom he had honoured and loved, from what he believed to be the right cause' (Orr, *Life*, p. 355). It was not, then, because of partisan politics that he was at odds with Disraeli, the leader of the Tories. In fact, Browning condemns Disraeli in this parleying not because he lied, was a hypocrite or achieved ill-gotten gains, but because he perverted the truth to the extent that he made lies look like truth and, worse, truth look like lies.

The beginning of the third movement of the *Parleyings* presents the seventeenth-century Italian naturalistic painter Francis Furini, whose aim was to reveal God's work in all its freshness and glory. Like Browning's Lippo Lippi, Furini painted men and women not as if they were saints or devils but just as God made them. Pointing out earth's common beauties that are so frequently overlooked, he believed that 'art hangs out for sign / There's finer entertainment underneath' (530–1). In parleying with him the speaker takes on two contemporary groups of adversaries, those who embrace an exclusively moral aesthetic and those who base their philosophy on biological evolution.

Furini was charged with indelicacy and immorality in painting female nudes, and the speaker is quick to jump to his defence. The reason for this was that Pen Browning, after his dalliance in Belgium, had returned to the study of art, including a brief residence in Paris to learn sculpture under the direction of Rodin, and had become a fairly successful painter and sculptor. With the exhibition of his big painting *A Worker in Brass, Antwerp* at the Royal Academy in 1878 Pen had won modest acclaim, and his proud father made every effort possible to promote his work. Robert hung Pen's enormous pictures in a rented empty house in Queen's Gate Gardens, whither he invited Tennyson, Carlyle and other friends to view them and wealthy socialites and businessmen to buy them. In 1882, Robert told Domett, Pen made £1,200 by his pictures and had sold one for £300 to 'a Philadelphian Museum of Art, or some such Institution there'.[6] All who had unflattering remarks to make about Pen's works were immediately anathematized. One influential critic, who himself was a painter and patron of painters, had refused to allow the younger Browning's statue of a nude to be shown at Burlington House in 1884, had objected to the exhibition of Pen's paintings of nudes at London galleries in 1885 and 1886, and had attacked the nude in art in the *Times*, 20–5 May 1885. Browning was furious. 'I am amused', he wrote to Furnivall in May 1886,

> at the objection taken by some of the critics to the Eve-like simplicity of Pen's peasant-girl [Joan of Arc about to bathe], who before going on to saintliness ... was satisfied with the proverbially next step to it—cleanliness. If they knew anything of Joan's habits even when advanced in her saintly career, they would remember she was no prude by any means: her favoured young cavalier ... mentions that he had frequently seen her undress ... (Peterson, p. 132)

Browning had written seven lines of verse to accompany Pen's picture, *Joan of Arc and the Kingfisher*, and included it in the parleying (601–7) as a description of a painting by Furini.

In taking aim at Pen's critics the poet was also objecting to those who evaluate art solely in terms of its moral content. As much as he was opposed to Rossetti's and Swinburne's conception of art as autotelic, he took issue with those who viewed art as an exclusively moral vehicle. The artist's business is with God, as he was fond of saying, and not with those who 'dare advance / This doctrine that the Artist-mind must needs / Own to affinity with yours' (215–17).[7]

In addition to being a painter Furini was also a priest, and the speaker invites him to preach to a London congregation of 'Evolutionists', who focus their interest downwards to the animal origin of life instead of looking upwards towards humankind's quest for the Absolute. The burden of Furini's imaginary homily is that mankind gains knowledge by proceeding from the tangible to the abstract, from sense to soul. Like the speaker of 'La Saisiaz' he professes to know only two things, soul and God: 'my self-consciousness,— / 'Twixt ignorance and ignorance enisled,— / Knowledge: before me was my Cause—that's styled / God: after, in due course succeeds the rest' (351–4). His art is a record of his growth of consciousness and of his understanding of soul that lies beneath sense. Yet whatever veil he or any other artist manages to pluck from nature, the cause is never discovered, and this leads him to know for certain that cause is external to manifestation. In opposition to the new evolutionary science and speaking from what he admits is only his point of vantage (259–60, 518–19), Furini affirms that nature is not one with rapine, that good predominates over evil and that both exist to enable human growth. In testimony to such belief he had exercised his imagination.

'With Gerard de Lairesse' takes up the theme of time adumbrated in Furini's sermon to the evolutionists. Where the Italian painter looked to the future and to progress, the Dutch seventeenth-century painter and writer on art looked to the past as the height of man's achievement. The brilliant light of the close of the preceding parleying is lost in the blindness, both physical and spiritual, of the subject of 'With de Lairesse'. The speaker had once respected and been influenced by the Hollander, but he cannot admit the validity of Lairesse's contention that the best one can do is to imitate the Ancients. Nor can he cede to contemporaries like Matthew Arnold that the Greeks are the best models for modern poets: 'Plain retrogression, this!' (165).

De Lairesse was the author of a book on art that contained a section entitled 'The Walk', and to prove that he, Robert Browning, can see as his predecessors saw, he himself begins a 'walk', going, in a series of symbolic vignettes described in the classical grand manner, from the dawn of Hellenic culture to its death. This 'walk' through history includes glances at Arnold, Tennyson, Swinburne, Morris and possibly Shelley, in each vignette mimicking their style in the treatment of Greek subjects. His point is that Greek civilization is a record of progressive dehumanization and that, moreover, it is dead and done with. Fit model indeed! Surely there is 'some fitter way express / Heart's satisfaction that the Past indeed / Is past, gives way before Life's best and last, / The all-including Future!' (364–7). The past has marked a beginning on which men and women have built and will continue to build; nothing that truly lived can ever die: 'What here attains / To a beginning, has no end, still gains / And never loses aught: when, where, and how / Lies in Law's lap' (413–16).

The last movement consists of one section containing the dialectical components of the preceding ones. On a dreary March morning the speaker is reminded of another 'March', by the eighteenth-century English organist Charles Avison whom he had loved as boy, and he wonders whether Avison's music is as dead as the winter landscape before him. Once it had captivated audiences, seemed perfect. Yet now when one is accustomed to the complex harmonies of Wagner, Brahms and Lizst, it seems so simple; it no longer has the power to stir as it once had. Since no truer truth is obtainable than that which music offers, does this mean that truth itself loses its power?

Just as a river flows under a bridge, soul, emanating from the depths of feeling that cannot be understood or described, underlies mind, which is knowledge. All the arts attempt to '"shoot / Liquidity into a mould"' (209–10), arrest the soul's movement and make what we feel as hard and fast as what we know. Music more nearly succeeds in doing this, yet paradoxically it gives less permanence to its truth than do its sister arts. A Handel's grasp on feeling soon loses its power, and then a Haydn or a Mozart comes along to recapture the hold the earlier musician once had: 'So perfections tire,— / Whiten to wanness, till...let others note / The ever-new invasion!' (274–6). The expression of truth that energized the past seems to be utterly lost. Momentarily this is for the speaker a cause for sorrow. But then as he plays the bold C major of Avison's march, his sorrow lightens. First, he considers how it is possible for our present life to rekindle the life of the past: by putting ourselves in sympathy with the age that produced Avison's music, we can make it live again. Secondly, he reflects on how truth was in humankind from the beginning: though the forms may fade, the art that captured the truth for its age is of infinite value in preserving the truth of that time. Art history therefore is the history of the changing vestures of truth. Winter comes but spring is not far behind, bringing fruits as 'not new vesture merely but, to boot, / Novel creation' (377–8). What is true of music is true of all manifestations of truth: 'Soon shall fade and fall / Myth after myth—the husk-like lies I call / New truth's corolla-safeguard: Autumn comes, / So much the better' (378–81).

Forty years earlier Robert had written to Elizabeth: 'The cant is, that "an age of transition" is the melancholy thing to contemplate and delineate— whereas the worst things of all to look back on are times of comparative standing still, rounded in their impotent completeness' (Kintner, 2: 710). And here in 1887 he was as vigorous an adherent of the doctrine of becoming as he had been in 1846, ending 'Charles Avison' with a mighty symphony of sound in which the past is recaptured and Avison with Bach, Strafford with Pym march while the dim antique grows clarion clear. March, the month in which the parleying begins, leads on to May and June, as Avison's 'March' provides the harmonic seeds for progress towards new musical moulds. At the end Browning prints four bars of the 'March', of which his father had once owned a manuscript copy.

The epilogue, 'Fust and His Friends', brings the *Parleyings* to a close with a comedy, in which the inventor of printing is mistaken for a Faust-like mage and miracle-worker. The final scene of this epic is no beatific vision, as in the *Divine Comedy*, but the everyday world of men and women. Humans haven't reached heaven yet; history remains open. The epilogue, in the same verse form as 'Apollo and the Fates', simply marks the end of *this* history of human consciousness that moves from superstition, belief in gods and fates removed from the human world, to a faith in existential reality, the divine manifested in the actual.

John Fust has invented a marvellous machine that, like art, will fix facts, '"shoot / Liquidity into a mould"' – for a time at least. Like all advances it will undermine the old established formulations of truth and, in that it can be used for the dispersion of lies, will serve both the good and the bad. Yet the heretic Martin Luther, who will benefit from the press, will be the agent of more good than bad; and in the end Fust fancies that he hears his Creator's benediction:

> 'Be thou saved, Fust! Continue my plan . . .
> Far and wide, North and South, East and West, have dominion
> O'er thought, winged wonder O Word!'
>
> (284, 291–2)

When he was twenty, Browning conceived a plan of producing a series of works in various media that the unsuspecting world would never guess were by the same individual. In the *Parleyings*, with its many comparisons of music, painting and literature, Browning seems to have cast a retrospective glance at what possibly might have been had he not elected to devote himself to the theatrical world of his poetry. The epilogue indicates that, to his own satisfaction at least, he had made the right choice. As Maisie Ward says, the epilogue brings 'the message that Browning felt his own choice in life had been the right one . . . The written word will outlast all else'.[8]

Parleyings with Certain People of Importance in Their Day is the boldest work of Browning's later career, more philosophically complex than *Fifine at the Fair* and more daring in design than *The Ring and the Book*. Ranging from classical Greece through the Middle Ages and the Enlightenment to the later nineteenth century, it takes into account the evolution of man's thought, morals, art and religion. Characteristically, it does not end. Bespeaking the poet's view of human history, it drops off with the half-line 'I foresee such a man'.

16

Death in Venice and Burial in London

I

Parleyings with Certain People of Importance in Their Day was dedicated to Milsand, who had died in September 1886 and whose loss the poet felt deeply. The reviewers, who had heard that the poem was to be retrospective, looked in vain for autobiographical details. 'The supposition that Mr. Browning's new work was to be of an autobiographical character', said the *Times* (28 January 1887), 'is entirely erroneous'. Most critics were bewildered and shared the opinion of the reviewer in the *Spectator* for 5 February 1887 that 'Mr. Browning does not condescend more generously to the minds of his readers in age than he did in youth'.

Soon after publication of the *Parleyings* Robert and Sarianna set their minds to the problem of moving house, owing to the faulty construction of 19 Warwick Crescent that with time had become evident. Instead of renting, Robert bought a new house in early April and moved into the larger and somewhat grander 29 De Vere Gardens, Kensington, in June. 'Everybody competent to give an opinion thinks the bargain an excellent one', he wrote; 'and Pen will have, in due course of time, a property pretty sure to increase in value' (*Learned Lady*, p. 195).

Pen, however, was not to stand in need of as much money as his father had previously been giving him. In the summer of 1887, soon after exhibiting a bust of his father at the Grosvenor Gallery, he became engaged to marry the heiress Fannie Coddington, who was American by parentage but English in upbringing. She was a great admirer of Robert's, and he was delighted with her: 'there is no young person I know at all comparable'. As for Pen himself, his father told him, 'you are just at the time of life when you may "take a fresh departure" with the greatest advantage' and settle down. 'Miss C. has spoken to me with the greatest frankness and generosity of the means she will have of contributing to your support—for

Plate 14 'The wedding of Pen Browning and Fannie Coddington, Pembury, near London, 4 October 1887'. Photograph. (Sarianna Browning is seated slightly in front of the bride and the poet is standing behind his sister.) From *The Tragi-Comedy of Pen Browning* by Maisie Ward, p. 98 (photograph: Elaine Baly).

my part, I can engage to give you £300 a year' (Hood, pp. 265, 266). On 4 October 1887 the couple were wed, and after honeymooning first in Venice and then in America, Pen and Fannie settled in Venice the following year.

The poet's main business during 1887 and 1888 was the preparation of his collected works in sixteen volumes. He made a number of revisions, especially in the text of *Pauline*, and carefully corrected the proofs of each volume, which were issued by Smith, Elder at monthly intervals between April 1888 and July 1889.[1] As Mrs Sutherland Orr points out, 'the power of detail correction either was, or had become by experience, very strong in him' (*Life*, p. 381). At first he had thought of adding notes to the poems, but then changed his mind. He wrote to George Smith on 12 November 1887: 'I am so out of sympathy with all this "biographical matter" connected with works which ought to stand or fall by their own merits quite independently of the writer's life and habits, that I prefer leaving my poems to speak for themselves as they best can—and to end as I began long ago' (Peterson, p. 198n). Like Goethe, Browning seems to have

Plate 15 'Robert and Pen Browning outside the Palazzo Rezzonico, Venice, 1889'.
Photograph. Reproduced courtesy of Michael Meredith, Browning Collection,
Windsor.

thought of all his works as 'nur Burchstücke einer grossen Konfession' ('only fragments of a great confession').[2] He was consciously preparing his work to preserve it in the form in which he wished posterity to receive 'Browning'. As Alexander Pope had said, 'I *must* make a perfect edition of my works, and then I shall have nothing to do but to die'.[3]

Browning, however, was by no means ready to die. In late summer 1888 he and Sarianna set off for Venice, where they were to stay for three months and where he corrected proofs of his collected edition. Pen, who discovered that he really had more talent for interior decorating than for painting and sculpting, had set his heart on the once grand but now sadly deteriorated baroque Palazzo Rezzonico with its Tiepolo ceilings, and Fannie was willing to give him the money to buy and restore this great palace on the Grand Canal. The elder Brownings excitedly followed the negotiations for its purchase and refurbishment before returning to London in December. 'You will be amused, and I think greatly interested', Browning wrote to Fannie's sister Marie, 'when you see the famous palazzo their property, which Pen is doing his best to make as comfortable as it is magnificent' (Hood, p. 300).

Back at De Vere Gardens the poet was besieged by his admirers, both domestic and foreign, while he continued to dine out among the great and famous several nights a week. Although his health seemed to be good, he found that he had not the energy he previously had had, and numerous acquaintances noted that he often appeared weary. In July 1889 he opened a recently published collection of letters by the poet and translator Edward FitzGerald, who had died in 1883, and therein read a letter of 1861 referring to Elizabeth:

Mrs Browning's Death is rather a relief to me, I must say: no more Aurora Leighs, thank God! A woman of real Genius, I know: but what is the upshot of it all? She and her Sex had better mind the Kitchen and the Children; and perhaps the Poor: except in such things as little Novels, they only devote themselves to what Men do much better, leaving that which Men do worse or not at all.[4]

Browning was seized with anger and immediately wrote and sent off a vituperative sonnet to the *Athenaeum*, where, although he tried to retract it, it was published on 13 July. The poem caused an uproar and its writer felt that he had humiliated both himself and his dead wife.

The incident took its toll on Browning's health, and he fell ill. But in late spring he was nevertheless at his usual rounds of dinners and celebrations. He went up to Oxford to be with Jowett, who also had been unwell, at the Balliol Commemoration in June and stayed on for the Gaudy dinner given by the college to the provost and fellows of Eton. In July he attended a dinner at Lord Rosebery's held in honour of the Shah of Persia. He was invited by Millais to meet Princess Louise and her husband, the Marquess of Lorne. He was expected, as usual, at the annual soirée at the Royal

Academy, of which his friend Frederic Leighton was president. Although he had earlier felt, as he told Mrs FitzGerald, 'tired and "washed out"', doing the duties expected of him as a public man had quite 'restored' him (*Learned Lady*, p. 199). In addition, the thought of visiting Italy, which had been planned earlier, was rejuvenating, as it always was, and by the first of September he and Sarianna were on their way, first of all to Asolo, his 'old attraction' (Hood, p. 316).

When they arrived, Robert found that Asolo remained 'what I first conceived it to be—the most beautiful spot I ever was privileged to see. It is seldom that one's impressions of half-a-century ago, are confirmed by the present experience but so it is . . .' (*NL*, p. 383). To all his correspondents he spoke of his extreme pleasure 'in this lovely Asolo,—my spot of predilection in the whole world'.[5] He thought of buying a small property there, which he proposed calling Pippa's Tower, where he might come hereafter for a few months; but owing to inefficiency and stubbornness on the part of the town council was unable to conclude the purchase. Asolo stimulated a new burst of creative energy, and he began to prepare a new volume of poems – 'some few written, all of them supervised, in the comfort of your presence', he said in the dedication to his hostess in Asolo, Katherine Bronson, the wealthy American expatriate whom he had earlier met and been lionized by in Venice.

Before leaving Asolo Robert and Sarianna were able to greet the Storys, who arrived for a few days just to see them. At the end of his friends' visit, Robert, reluctant to say goodbye, held on to Story's hand and said: 'We have been friends for forty years—aye—more than forty years—and with never a break' (Hudson, p. 197). And just before bidding Mrs Bronson farewell in mid-October, Robert sent off his collection of poems to his publisher and then went on with Sarianna to stay with Pen and Fannie at the splendidly restored Palazzo Rezzonico, which now contained central heating and a chapel dedicated to the memory of Elizabeth. It 'excites the wonder of everybody—so great is Pen's cleverness, and extemporized architectual knowledge', said the proud father (*Letters to George*, p. 329).

Hordes of admirers called on Browning in Venice, and he assented with pleasure and alacrity to requests to read his poetry at various homes. Although friends had noted some wheezing in Asolo and although he admitted to a few bouts of asthma, he busied himself in Venice by visits and sightseeing, pushing himself to the limit of his physical endurance. He also read proofs of his new volume, *Asolando*.

Robert and Sarianna planned to return to London before the end of November in order to oversee the printing of a collected edition of Elizabeth's works. However, in late November he confessed to a cold, whereupon a physican was called. The diagnosis was bronchitis and a weakened heart. Pen and Fannie stayed up to apply poultices and then hired a Venetian nurse. As the poet grew steadily worse, friends were notified of his critical condition. Mrs Orr took an express train from France to be at his bedside. News of his illness reached the press, and to satisfy the world's curiosity about the great man bulletins about his condition were posted

Plate 16 'The Last Life-Picture of Robert Browning, Venice, 24 November 1889'. Drawing by G. D. Giles. Courtesy of the Armstrong Browning Library.

outside the porter's lodge of the Rezzonico. Telegrams from all parts of the world began to arrive.

Conscious until almost the end, Browning opened copies of *Asolando* that had come from London. He read to Fannie and Sarianna from the epilogue and remarked on these lines:

> One who never turned his back but marched
>   breast forward,
> Never doubted clouds would break,

> Never dreamed, though right were worsted,
>   wrong would triumph,
> Held we fall to rise, are baffled to fight
>   better,
> Sleep to wake.

'It almost sounds like bragging to say this, and as if I ought to cancel it', he admitted; 'but it's the simple truth; and as it's true, it shall stand'. On 12 December his publisher sent a telegram saying that the book, published that day, had received most favourable reviews and that the edition was almost sold out. Pen read it to his father late that afternoon. 'More than satisfied', he murmured to Pen, and then whispered, 'I am dying. My dear boy. My dear boy'.[6] Several hours passed, during which he slipped in and out of consciousness; then, around ten o'clock, the poet of *Asolando* breathed his last.

II

Asolando: Fancies and Facts, which within a short time went through nine reprintings, is a collection of what the dedication calls 'disconnected poems' united by the title, derived from '*Asolare*—"to disport in the open air, amuse oneself at random"'. This makes them seem trifling, like most of the verse in *Jocoseria*, but in fact they are important not only for themselves but also for the information they provide about the poet and his development.

Asolo was for Browning literally a city of dreams. He had had recurrent dreams 'of seeing Asolo in the distance and making vain attempts to reach it' until at last he 'saw it again, and the dreams stopped'.[7] Even the drive there 'seemed to be a dream' (Orr, *Life*, p. 388). And his return to Asolo in 1889 symbolized the changes his 'dreams' – his 'facts' and 'fancies' – had undergone during his lifetime.

The prologue tells how, though Asolo has remained the same, the poet himself has changed. Once, as he cast a haze of fancy over them, natural objects seemed clothed in fire. Now the burning bush is bare, and God is no longer where the poet had thought to find him. Like Wordsworth of the ode on the 'Intimations of Immortality', he has lost what the Romantic poet called the 'visionary gleam', 'the glory and the dream'.[8] This is, however, no reason to be 'sad', for in giving up one habit of seeing he has gained a new, truer one, 'which straight unlinked / Fancy from fact'. As in the epilogue to *Dramatis Personae*, the poet, while maturing, has witnessed 'dwindling into the distance' the star of God's presence on earth; and as he relates in another poem in this volume, God has become like an 'unseen friend' who 'keeps absent' ('Fear and Scruples').

That the real world is preferable to any fancifying of it is expressed in most of the poems of *Asolando*. 'Poetics' illustrates how figurative language itself can falsify. 'Speculative' evinces the poet's preference even in heaven for the love he knew on earth to a dreamed-of new life for man, nature and art. 'Inapprehensiveness' portrays a lady absorbed in a fancy about the landscape while her lover is left to weigh 'fancies that might be' with 'facts that are'.

But, the question remains, what is fact? This is probably best answered in the disarmingly biographical poem 'Development', which pretty well sums up a good deal of what Browning had to say not only in *Asolando* but also in much of his earlier work as well. Nowhere else does the poet set forth so succinctly his well-known philosophy of the imperfect, which can be better understood as a philosophy of inadequacy.

In this deceptively charming poem the poet describes the progress of his knowledge from early childhood to ripe maturity. Early on he learned about the *Iliad* as the siege of Troy was presented to him in an impromptu game by his father, 'who knew better than turn straight / Learning's full flare on weak-eyed ignorance' (20–1). Then a few years later his father gave him Pope's translation to read and finally, after helping him learn Greek, 'the very thing itself, the actual words' that Homer wrote (42). Here, so the boy thought, was 'an end of learning'(50). At the age of twelve he was, he believed, fully acquainted with Homer: who the historian and poet was, with what he wrote, indeed with all the known facts about him. But soon after this 'comfortable time' he was introduced to the historical criticism of Friedrich August Wolf and other German scholars and was given to understand that his 'facts' were questionable: he learned that 'there was never any Troy at all, / Neither Besiegers nor Besieged,— nay, worse,— / No actual Homer, no authentic text, / No warrant for the fiction I, as fact, / Had treasured in my heart and soul so long' (62, 69–73). Yet for all the efforts of the big bad Wolf he retains 'fact's essence freed and fixed / From accidental fancy's guardian sheath' (76–7), still holds in his heart and soul the 'fiction' of the Trojan War, just as Browning had declared in the epilogue to *Dramatis Personae* and elsewhere that he would continue to hold dear the 'fiction' of the Christian story in spite of the Higher Critics who are bent on 'unsettling one's belief' (65).

Why, some enlightened modern educationist might ask, did his father, who was familiar with German scholarship, ever introduce him to this falsehood, 'ever let me dream at all' (92)? He could have given the boy Aristotle's *Ethics* and so have avoided the 'pretty lying that improves' (107). Yet how could the boy have dealt with material that the now gray-haired man, who knows there is no end of knowledge, can hardly manage?

The whole force of 'Development' turns on the question of adequacy: what will suffice? Or to put the question another way: when will that sufficiency prove inadequate? Growth, development, metamorphosis, moving on, *Bildung*, a metaphor drawn from biology, is opposed to the mechanical metaphors of the Enlightenment, with the thought of which Browning, as we have seen, constantly takes issue. Behind it lies the idea of the universe as a living process, growing according to its inner rules and potentials. For Browning there is especially attached to the notion of *Bildung* the Heraclitean idea of energy, motion and change whereby an entity becomes something so as to become something else, is created so as to be de-created, is formed so as to become transformed. The principle of becoming, the poet makes explicit in 'Development', is at the very heart of his thought and practice as a poet. As he sees it, for the individual and for humanity as a whole, becoming is the perennial process of development whereby, first, contradictions are felt to be momentarily resolved and the limitations of an outmoded form of consciousness temporarily overcome and then, secondly, this stage is perceived as deficient so that, thirdly, a new stage of consciousness is attained.[9] Never amenable to formalization and precision, development may none the less be characterized as a series of provisional resting places – 'approximations' Browning has called them – which are the best attainable at a given time but which eventually prove inadequate.

It will be recalled that speaking through a fairly thin fictional disguise in *Pauline*, the young Browning portrayed his as an intensest life that would 'be all, have, see, know, taste, feel, all' (278). He would call on all things to minister to his sense of self and so participate in his growth of consciousness. His aim was the total comprehension of the world of his experience. But already by the time of *Pauline* the poet had learned that this is impossible: he 'cannot be immortal, nor taste all' (810). And even were it not impossible, it would be deadly, for were his soul to have 'its utmost pleasure filled, . . . complete / Commanding for commanding sickens it' (816–17). In the world of becoming to have all and know all would mean having arrived at a fixed point and so being no longer alive. The idea of the necessity of striving for conditional accommodations for what the poet characteristically calls 'soul' is foremost in Browning's work from first to last.

From this point of view the sixteen-volume *Poetical Works of Robert Browning* of 1888–9 plus *Asolando* (later added as the seventeenth volume) record a progression of stages that the Browning carnival follows on the road to the Absolute in full knowledge that it will never be attained. As John Fust says in the *Parleyings*, 'As still to its asymptote speedeth the curve, / So approximates Man—Thee, . . . reachable not' ('Fust and His Friends', 425–6). Indeed, it is the business of a poet, Browning insisted in the *Essay on Shelley*, to behold the universe and all therein 'in their actual state of perfection in imperfection' and then, in addition, to look to 'the forthcoming stage of man's being' and so suggest 'this ideal of a future man', thereby striving 'to elevate and extend' both himself and mankind. Of course, Browning hastened to add, 'an absolute vision is not for this world, but we are permitted a continual approximation to it'. His poems are these approximations – exhibits at the fair offering representations of life whose progress towards the Absolute is determined by their own inadequacies. One representation or form of consciousness fails and another is chosen to take its place. Yet the new representation is not in any way a deductive necessity, nor are the connections entailments: Browning recognizes that there could always be different starting-points and different routes taken to arrive at provisional ends, to reach the 'facts'. As his Ferishtah said, new occasions 'may wreck / My life and ruin my philosophy / Tomorrow, doubtless' ('A Bean-Stripe', 203–5). Today's truth is tomorrow's falsehood. The music that once moved us to tears can lose its hold on us, the picture that once we adored can cease to exert its charm: art, like everything else, can wear out, as the speaker in the *Parleyings* discovered to his great dismay: 'So will it be with truth that, for the nonce, / Styles itself truth perennial: 'ware its wile! / Knowledge turns nescience,— foremost on the file, / Simply proves first of our delusions' ('With Charles Avison', 357–60).

Early in his career Browning had learned that what is regarded as fact is the end of a process, a period of doubtful experimentation eventually leading to something asserted as certain. And he knew that in a world of becoming nothing can be accepted as final: the fact is dead unless it is enlivened, by 'fancy' or imagination. As his putatively Persian speaker said in *Ferishtah's Fancies*, 'To cope with fact—wants fiction everywhere!' ('A Bean-Stripe', 288); it is a way of joining 'things visible and things invisible' ('A Pillar at Sebzevah', 124). Thus in *The Ring and the Book* the poet revivified inert fact, given in the Old Yellow Book, by the exercise of his imagination, creating 'fiction which makes fact alive' and merging 'fancy with fact [which] is just one fact the more' (1.699, 458). In Browning's world the process never stops. That is why in 'Development' each stage in the child's or adult's life suffices only for the time being.

On the one hand, then, Browning's philosophy is negative. For the poet continually dramatizes his belief that no philosophical point of view, no conceptual framework, no demonstrative proof – however persuasive it might be – can ever be adequate by itself. As the perspectivist art of his monologues suggests, for every premiss there is a context and a set of presuppositions taken for granted. For every argument there is a perspective unchallenged. For every moral or religious principle there are a social milieu, a set of cultural needs and a history that make such exercises intelligible and plausible. Like Michel Foucault later, Browning recognized the reality of imprisonment, the incarceration of human beings within systems of thought and practice that have become so much a part of them that they do not experience these systems as a series of confinements but instead embrace them as the very structure of being human. Seeking to escape these restrictions and thereby liberate himself and others from conventional modes of thinking and seeing, Browning attempted in effect to denature Kant's great questions about epistemology, ethics and metaphysics. He does not ask 'what can I know?' but rather 'how has my way of knowing been conditioned?' He does not ask 'what ought I to do?' but 'how may I experience the real and meaningful?' He does not not ask 'what end can I hope for?' but 'in what ways can I engage with an endless universe?' Browning's heroes, especially his lovers and artists, are always

determined to break bounds, ethical as well as aesthetic, to escape enclo-
sures that the world has imposed upon them. His failures, on the other
hand, are those who submit to the limitations of what has been permitted
them.

Over the years Browning had been particularly concerned to locate his
actors within an historical setting so as to investigate the role history plays
in the determination of consciousness. He wanted to show how even those
who could lay claim to all the advantages their civilization had to offer
could nevertheless be victims of that which their culture granted them.
This was the case with, to take one example, Cleon, who summed up
within himself the whole Greek cultural accomplishment. Though pos-
sessing all the material rewards that his society could provide, he neverthe-
less longed for something more, for an afterlife. Yet he could not embrace
the Christian answer that lay so readily at hand because, conditioned by
his culture, he could not believe that a mere barbarian could possess
knowledge not vouchsafed to a Greek. It was Browning's point (among
others) not to condemn Cleon but to suggest that such a refusal is entirely
understandable in terms of Greek society in the first century AD. Here as
in other cases of his historicism, Browning attempted to rethink history
and then to dramatize it so as to bring into relief that which was buried
in the silence of the repressed and forgotten. Indeed, it was the poet's
effort throughout – from 'Porphyria's Lover', one of his two first-published
monologues, to '"Imperante Augusto Natus Est—"' of *Asolando* – to
demonstrate that, considered in terms of his own milieu, every man, no
matter how villainous he may seem to a modern-day audience, has his own
logic for being what he is and acting the way he does. Contrary to what
many of his critics believe, it was not simply a love of casuistry, making the
worse appear the better and vice versa, that motivated Browning to drama-
tize such figures; instead it was part of his philosophy that when all the
circumstances are considered, a plausible case can be made for all human
activity. Browning would have nothing to do with ethnocentrism or chau-
vinism in any of its guises. Unlike Kant he did not believe that a single
universal theory of the Good and the Proper could ever be provided,
which is probably one of the chief reasons why he is, without doubt, along
with Shakespeare and Keats, among the most sympathetic of all poets.

Yet, granting the intelligible motives, Browning was also concerned to
show how the positions arrived at are, emotionally and intellectually, only
temporarily valid. The narrator and his protagonist in *Sordello* thus viewed
the history of poetry as a never-ending process of setting up and dismantling
of various machines. Rabbi ben Ezra thus saw the present, 'plastic cir-
cumstance', as mere 'machinery' meant to be discarded (164–6). The
narrator of *The Ring and the Book* thus iterated that just when we think we
have formulated the truth in a given situation, it turns out that 'our human
speech is naught, / Our human testimony false, our fame / And human
estimation words and wind' (12.838–40). Browning constantly shows how
it is always the case that when a person, like the Duke of Ferrara in 'My

Last Duchess', fancies he possesses the world, the world in fact possesses him. In Browning's universe of endless becoming those who think that they are firmly established in their positions are in imminent danger of being undone, not, as in Greek tragedy, because they will be punished by the gods for their hubris but because, thinking to have arrested time and circumstance, they have become spiritually dead. There is a logic for it all and it is the logic of inadequacy.

On the one hand, then, Browning's philosophy is negative. But on the other hand it can be considered optimistic. For to the poet everything counts: the phenomenal world, the sensible world of everyday reality, is endowed with traces of the ideal, the supersensible, of which it is a manifestation. Behind every object there is meaning: every phenomenon is a sign, a sign pointing to the infinite and the Absolute, which cannot exist in the finite, conditional world. As Cleon said, 'imperfection means perfection hid' (185). Phenomena, myriad and diverse as they are, are thus all parts of a whole. Fragmentation, discontinuity, ugliness, evil – these are readily discernible even to the most unpractised eye. It is the artist's business however to show how they fit into the whole. For the artist is what is called in *Sordello* the 'Maker-see', one who sees and makes what he sees and then makes others see what and how he has seen. He is what is named in the *Essay on Shelley* the 'whole poet', whose function is to behold and present 'with an understanding keenness the universe, nature and man, in their actual state of perfection in imperfection'. As Fra Lippo Lippi said, 'This world's no blot for us, / Nor blank; it *means* intensely, and *means* good: / To find its *meaning* is my meat and drink' (313–15; italics added). By uncovering what has been hidden, by defamiliarizing what has been dulled by the blindness of custom, by lifting the phenomenon out of the field of ordinary perception and placing it within a network of relationships that consititute the work of art – by so doing the artist makes us experience the becoming of an object in the boundless universe of change. From one point of view Browning's poems can be regarded as a series of questions – what was it like to paint in a realistic style in the mid-fifteenth century ('Fra Lippo Lippi')? how was it possible to accommodate oneself to the new science and the old religious formulations in the early Renaissance (*Paracelsus*)? – questions that interpenetrate, transform and fructify each other. Which is to say that Browning's poems establish a discourse among themselves, a discourse of exposure to the infinitude of language.

Critics have frequently remarked, often in derogation, on the wealth of details in Browning's works. George Santayana, for example, was distressed by the 'barbarism' of the poet's multitudinousness, his seeming inclusion of everything.[10] Yet it is precisely this dwelling on detail that exemplifies the poet's philosophy. For he wanted to show that nothing can be omitted, that everything is meaningful, is part of a holistic unity. In poem after poem Browning dramatizes a power continually able to appropriate the most trivial details. It is a power in which he himself exults, often inducing the heartiness and rollicking jauntiness that have disturbed his detractors and admirers alike. In 'How It Strikes a Contemporary' (1855) the poet, like a detective or a spy, roams widely and closely inspects everything; he is 'a recording chief-inquisitor, / The town's true master if the town but knew!' But it is a power that is to be feared: because if all were known, nearly everyone would be incriminated; even the saints have something to hide.

In *Pauline* the subject would subjugate and violate all things so as to penetrate, possess and know them fully. In *Paracelsus* the protagonist, who began with a desire for Godlike power, learns finally that love should precede power, desiring power to set it free, and that under such circumstance new power would always mean a growing access of love (5.856–9). Nevertheless the fact remained that for Browning the dialectic of love and power was never reconciled: power remained primary and dominant, in the world and within himself. In 'Reverie', the penultimate poem in *Asolando*, the speaker admits, 'Even as the world its life, / So have I lived my own— / Power seen with Love at strife'. Yet 'Life has made clear to me / That, strive but for closer view, / Love were as plain to see'. But 'When see?' Not on earth but 'yonder, worlds away'. Till the end of his career Browning shows good to be passive: his virtuous characters, because they are largely passive, are uncontaminated by the power plays going on around them.

None the less the fact remains that in Browning's eyes, although mankind tends mainly to see evil, there is good hidden. What we see depends on our points of view. Illustrating with a row of black and white beans, his Ferishtah demonstrates that if the eye is allowed to range over the entire row the general effect is to him grey, while for others it might appear dun ('A Bean-Stripe'). In the *Parleyings* Francis Furini views history as progress in man's knowledge of good, although he is careful to state that he speaks only from his point of vantage: 'All—for myself—seems ordered wise and well / Inside it,—what reigns outside, who can tell?' ('With Furini', 519–20). As Browning looked at the whole of human history, with its conflicts, brutalities and stupidities, he was ever concerned to locate what good underlies the human's every thought and action, to display it for others to see, and to suggest development in human affairs, not towards some attainable absolute but to more comfortable and congenial accommodation.

The delusion of finality, of the end of *Bildung*, was to Browning perhaps the greatest of all evils, and although touched on in 'Development', is more specifically addressed in 'Rephan' and the last poem in *Asolando*. In the former the speaker could not tolerate life on another planet where all was perfect, everything merging in a neutral best, but longed for the imperfection, pain, growth, doubt and change that would startle him up towards the infinite. 'Not rest content with a wealth that's dearth?' he was asked. Well, 'thy place be Earth!' The epilogue conceives of life as energy and motion and of death as the beginning of a new phase of activity.

Regarding as slothful, aimless, helpless and hopeless the individual who settles fully into a resting place, the speaker looks forward to an afterlife and asks those who mourn him to cease their tears and instead bid him, '"Strive and thrive! . . . fight on, fare ever / There as here!"' The next life may or may not be the one in a finer tone that Keats envisioned, but in Browning's eyes it will be one of continuing energetic movement. In all the poems of 1889 the poet remained concerned to remind us that 'philosophy' as a means of development entails engaging in the thought of the other, the different and the alien. To the end development was for him the process of endeavouring to experience alterity and to examine to what extent it is possible to think differently, instead of legitimating that which is already known. To this extent Browning was a subversive, indeed a revolutionary dedicated to undermining the status quo.

And yet for all the seriousness with which he iterates his belief, Browning would not allow his reader to close with metaphysics – or politics, for that matter. After all, what he has to say is no revelation from Horeb or Sinai; it is but a 'fancy', a 'dream': and as the speaker in 'Development' allows, '"No dream's worth waking"—Browning says' (l. 84). The poem ends not with statement or meaning but irony, with facts that are also fancies. Yes, here in 'Development' as elsewhere, there's always 'Browning' – Browning the showman practising his art of the maker-see.

In the dedication to *Asolando* the poet said, as we have noted, that he derived his title from '*Asolare*', meaning 'to disport in the open air, amuse oneself at random'. 'Development' exemplifies this ludic exercise, the free play of the mind over possibilities, paths taken and roads unexplored. Like his other poems, 'Development' is, in the last analysis, an approximation, a form of consciousness, another of those representations (of representations) of the various forms that make up the poet's view(s) of human life. Although it is ultimately inadequate there has however been some improvement over the past: 'At least I soil no page with bread and milk, / Nor crumple, dogsear and deface—boy's way' (104–5). The playfulness of the final lines signals that 'Development' is another 'fact' turned 'fancy', an additional display at the carnival where 'Browning' hangs out his wares.

III

At Sarianna's suggestion Pen Browning sought permission to bury his father next to his mother in the Protestant cemetery in Florence but learned that the burial ground was closed and could not be opened even by the municipality. A message then arrived from the dean of Westminster with an offer of burial in the Abbey, which was accepted. But first there was a preliminary funeral service in Venice, held in the great hall of the Palazzo Rezzonico, followed by a cortège of funeral gondolas down the Grand Canal and out to the temporary resting place on the island of San Michele. 'As we passed under the Rialto Bridge', said one of the mourners, 'the setting sun burst out of the clouds which had covered the sky all that day and shone with fantastic lights upon the funeral barge and the gilded ornaments'.[11] Soon afterwards the body was returned to London by train.

The splendid funeral in Westminster Abbey, attended by a crowd of distinguished mourners, was held on the last day of 1889. Long queues of ticket-holders waited in the foggy morning for their admission to the service while a bell tolled. At half-past noon the service began; it ended with the burial of the body in Poet's Corner. 'The consignment of his ashes to the great temple of fame of the English race', said Henry James, 'was exactly one of those occasions in which his own analytic spirit would have rejoiced'.[12] In a word, it was great theatre.

Epilogue

'Is there no more to say?' the manager of the performance asked at the close of *Sordello.* Where Browning is concerned, of course there is. After the funeral Fannie and Pen stayed on in London till the spring of 1890 to settle the poet's affairs. Browning's will, executed on 12 February 1864 in the presence of Tennyson and the poet and critic Francis Palgrave, was proved on 19 February 1890, and admistration of his effects was granted to Pen, the residuary legatee. The estate was valued at £16,744.

Sarianna, who became seriously ill for six months, stayed on at De Vere Gardens for another year and then went to live with Pen and Fannie in Venice. In April 1891 seventy-six cases of household effects, many of which had been shipped from Florence in 1861, were forwarded to Venice. Also offered sanctuary there were Pen's old nurse Wilson and her husband, Ferdinando. Pen installed a memorial plaque for his father on the Palazzo Rezzonico and subscribed to a window commemorating him in the English Church in Venice. He purchased the property in Asolo that his father had wished to buy, there constructed 'Pippa's Tower' in his father's honour and, hoping to resuscitate the silk works, bought the disintegrating factory where Pippa was supposed to have worked.

Pen continued to spend large sums of money on the Palazzo Rezzonico, and Fannie drifted into invalidism. Various quarrels – about money, their childlessness, Pen's flirtations with his model, Fannie's penchant for building Christian missions in odd foreign places – were reported as fact by various visitors of 1892 and 1893, but these may have been nothing more than rumours. Whatever the case, Fannie left Venice on several occasions in search of medical help and eventually did not come back.

In 1895, at the urging of her elder sister, Fannie demanded the furniture in the palazzo for herself, and Pen thereafter visited the Rezzonico infrequently. He did not however abandon his painting, although he no longer exhibited; nor did he give up his hobby of renovating old buildings. He bought houses in Asolo and Florence (including the Casa Guidi), but it was in Asolo where he more or less settled. Sarianna lived with him until her death in 1903.

Robert had told his son to turn to his publisher George Smith whenever he needed advice. Smith himself did as much as he could to look after Pen, and it was Smith who persuaded Pen to allow his firm – Smith, Elder & Co. – to publish Robert and Elizabeth's love letters in 1899. Pen's Barrett relatives were enraged and charged their nephew with making public for either financial gain or notoriety what they felt should have remained private.

Pen grew obese, sickly and almost blind. He died of a heart attack at age sixty-three on 8 July 1912, soon after the centenary of his father's birth, which he had helped celebrate in the town square of Asolo. The little town of Asolo gave him a splendid funeral: the shops were closed, the flags flew at half-mast, and the mayor praised the 'Cavaliere Browning'. A decade later Fannie, who did not attend the funeral, had her husband's body (they were never divorced) removed from Asolo to Florence. Fannie lived till 1935.

Two of Pen's wills were discovered and it was believed that still a third existed. Eventually it was agreed that Pen had died under circumstances amounting to an intestacy, and attorneys in Florence acting on behalf of Fannie and a Barrett cousin (representing himself and other Barrett cousins) began to make legal arrangements for disposition of his property. On six days in 1913, between 1 and 8 May, his effects – which included his parents' manuscripts, pictures, books and furniture – were auctioned in London at Sotheby's. There were 1,417 lots, described in a 170-page catalogue.[1] After Pen's enormous debts were paid, the residue of the sale of his property under Italian law went one-third to Fannie and two-thirds to sixteen Barrett cousins.

During the last years of his life Browning had been chiefly admired as a philosopher and thinker. Although he was honoured by a society founded for the study of his works, he was never a popular poet in the sense that Tennyson was: the sales of his poems were only a fraction of those of the Laureate's. He was admired more than read. True appreciation of his poetry was the province of a comparative few, mainly poets such as Rossetti and Swinburne and prose writers such as George Eliot, George Meredith and Oscar Wilde. His fame – and by the time he died he was one of the most famous persons in the English-speaking world – was spread by persons such as Furnivall, who looked to his work for moral instruction that could be inculcated in adult education classes, church socials and the like. To this end the London Browning Society served Browning well, acting as a stimulus to the horde of publications devoted to the poet as a thinker during the decade following his death.

At the same time, however, moral instruction as the end of art (which Browning had constantly denied) came to be considered as something 'Victorian', and even though Victoria was to reign till 1901 it was widely proclaimed in the 1890s that the *fin de siècle* meant also the *fin de*

Victorianisme. The last public meetings of the London Browning Society were held during the 1891–2 session, although private meetings continued to be held in members' homes over the next several years and other Browning Societies continued to operate in America.

Sir Henry Jones's *Browning as a Philosophical and Religious Teacher* (1891) maintained that while an examination of Browning's work showed the poet as the exponent of a system of ideas on religious and moral subjects, there was no consistent philosophical framework to be found. George Santayana's treatment of Browning in the chapter 'The Poetry of Barbarism' in his *Interpretations of Poetry and Religion* (1900) pronounced the poet's imagination truncated, his thought and art inchoate and his moral teaching faulty. John M. Robertson's *Browning and Tennyson as Religious Teachers* (1903) likewise attacked Browning's approach to serious thought. All three works took their toll on Browning's reputation, which was chiefly as a thinker.[2]

They were, nevertheless, offset by the centennial celebrations in 1912, which produced a large number of books as well as two editions (the Centenary and the pocket version of the Florentine) of the poet's work that remained more or less standard for more than half a century; and for the rest of the decade Browning enjoyed something of the adulation afforded him earlier. With the 1920s, on the other hand, the revolt against almost everything of the preceding century meant derogation of Browning, who was attacked for his optimism and his wilful refusal to face the evils of Victorian society. Browning's general reputation (along with Tennyson's and that of most other Victorian writers) almost totally collapsed, kept alive by a few poets and lovers of Victorian verse; and this situation continued until the mid-1950s, when scholarly interest in his verse began to revive.

Among poets Browning's verse lived on continuously. Both Hardy and Yeats admitted their indebtedness to Browning. Indeed, the night before he died Hardy insisted that his wife read to him all thirty-two stanzas of 'Rabbi Ben Ezra'. Yeats, in the final poem ('Are You Content?') of the last volume of his verse he oversaw (*New Poems*, 1938), alluded to Browning by name and suggested his own descent from Blake and Shelley through Browning. The main preserver of Browning's poetry as a potent influence on modern poetry was, however, Ezra Pound, who acknowledged Browning as his poetic father. 'Und überhaupt ich stamm aus Browning', he wrote in 1928 in his usual polyglot fashion. 'Pourquoi nier son père?' ['In general I am descended from Browning. Why deny one's father?'].[3] Before and after that date he made similar acknowledgements of his poetic lineage and praised Browning as a poet without parallel in the nineteenth century for his musicality and imagery. On occasion, T. S. Eliot, although his relation to Browning was more problematical in that he had both good and bad things to say about him, felt the influence of Browning on himself and others and certainly in his use of the dramatic monologue owed more than a little to his Victorian predecessor. In 1915 Robert Frost, just beginning to be recognized, said that 'his favorite poets were Chaucer, Shakespeare, Wordsworth, and Browning'.[4] John Crowe Ransom admitted it as 'a fact that Browning started me on my own, and no other poet did'.[5]

Ransom's student Robert Lowell consistently employed the Browningesque monologue, even eventually turning it into a mode for confessional poetry. Lowell praised Browning for opening up the subject matter allowable for poetry, explaining that 'there is almost nothing Browning couldn't use'. Further, he acknowledged his specific indebtedness to 'My Last Duchess' and *Sordello*, their couplets 'run-on with . . . rhymes buried. . . . I wanted something as fluid as prose you wouldn't notice the form, yet looking back you'd find that great obstacles had been climbed'.[6] Auden also aimed for verse as fluid as prose, and his prose monologues 'Herod' and 'Caliban to the Audience' surely stem from Browning. Richard Howard's monologues in *Untitled Subjects* are written directly in imitation of the Browning manner.

The centrality of Browning in the history of English poetry is today pretty much taken for granted. There are many signs of this. There are Browning Societies in both Britain and America; there is a Browning Institute in New York; there is the Browning apartment preserved at the Casa Guidi in Florence; there is even a Browning shrine, the Armstrong Browning Library at Baylor University. There are *Browning Society Notes, Browning Institute Studies* (soon to be renamed *Victorian Literature and Culture*) and *Studies in Browning and His Circle*. Books on Browning, biographies and scholarly studies, have appeared in increasing numbers over the past twenty-five years. Perhaps the best testimony to the importance of Robert Browning is the fact that, in addition to the Yale–Penguin edition of 1981, there are three scholarly editions of his works now under way. The manager of the performance is still putting on his show.

Notes

Notes to Chapter 1

1   For the notebooks and sketchbooks by the poet's father, see Joseph C. Carson, 'A Collection of Books from the Brownings' Personal Library' (MA thesis, Baylor University, 1970); Jack W. Herring, *Browning's Old Schoolfellow: The Artistic Relationship of Two Robert Brownings* (Pittsburgh: Beta Phi Mu, 1972); and Maynard, appendix B, 'Checklist of Sketchbooks, Notebooks, and Manuscripts of Robert Browning Sr.', pp. 376–8.

2   Sir Charles Gavan Duffy, *Conversations with Carlyle* (London, Paris, Melbourne: Cassell, 1896), p. 58.

3   *The Diary of Alfred Domett, 1872–1885*, ed. E. A. Horsman (London, New York: Oxford University Press, 1953), pp. 74, 73.

4   Moncure D. Conway, *Autobiography, Memories and Experiences* (Boston: Houghton Mifflin, 1904), 2: 24.

5   For a summary account of Fox's influence, see O. P. Govil, 'Browning's "Literary Father"', *Indian Journal of English Studies*, 9 (1968): 1–7.

6   The most authoritative study of Browning's discovery of Shelley's poetry is Frederick A. Pottle, *Shelley and Browning: A Myth and Some Facts* (Chicago: Pembroke Press, 1923). An outstanding study of the dynamics of Browning's psychological response to Shelley is Herbert F. Tucker, Jr, *Browning's Beginnings: The Art of Disclosure* (Minneapolis: University of Minnesota Press, 1980). Loy D. Martin, *Browning's Dramatic Monologues and the Post-Romantic Subject* (Baltimore: Johns Hopkins University Press, 1985), ch. 2, studies Shelley's influence on Browning mainly by comparing syntax and structures of metaphor. Negative views of Browning's revision of Shelley are expressed in Roland A. Duerksen, *Shelleyan Ideas in Victorian Literature* (The Hague: Mouton, 1966), ch. 2, and in Harold Bloom, *The Anxiety of Influence: A Theory of Poetry* (New Haven: Yale University Press, 1973), p. 69. Richard C. Keenan, 'Browning and Shelley', *BIS*, 1 (1973): 119–45, surveys Browning's later views of Shelley.

7   *Table Talk* (27 April 1823) in *The Complete Works of Samuel Taylor Coleridge*, ed. W. G. T. Shedd (New York: Harper, 1884), 6: 265.

8   Vivienne Browning, 'The Real Identity of Pauline', *BSN*, 13 (1983): 2–10.

9 Mill's copy of *Pauline* with his penciled notes is in the Forster and Dyce Collection of the Victoria and Albert Museum. Mill's comments on the poem are treated fully in William S. Peterson and Fred L. Standley, 'The J. S. Mill Marginalia in Robert Browning's *Pauline*: A History and Transcription', *Publications of the Bibliographical Society of America*, 66 (1972): 135–70.

10 On 1 February 1833, less than a month after *Pauline* was completed, Browning received from his father a copy of Mandeville's *Fable of the Bees*, which apparently had been in the household for some time. Mandeville's book is an 'edition' of the poem 'The Grumbling Hive', which is surrounded by editorial apparatus. Browning later speaks at some length of the *Fable* in his *Parleyings*.

11 Compare Keats: 'The Genius of Poetry must work out its own salvation in a man: It cannot be matured by law & precept, but by sensation & watchfulness in itself— That which is creative must create itself'. The poet must, in other words, submit to something greater. Keats speaks a few weeks later of how the true poet is not the man himself: 'But even now I am perhaps not speaking from myself; but from some character in whose soul I now live' (*The Letters of John Keats*, ed. Hyder E. Rollins (Cambridge, Mass.: Harvard University Press, 1958), 1: 374, 378). The beginnings of modern literary careers are treated in Edward Said, *Beginnings* (New York: Basic Books, 1975), pp. 226–8. For the shape of poets' entire careers, see Lawrence Lipking, *The Life of the Poet: Beginning and Ending Poetic Careers* (Chicago, London: University of Chicago Press, 1981).

Notes to Chapter 2

1 W. David Shaw, *The Lucid Veil: Poetic Truth in the Victorian Age* (Madison: University of Wisconsin Press, 1987), p. 49.

2 DeVane's remarks are typical: 'This critique changed the course of Browning's poetical career. He had exposed his callow soul.... But his main resolve was that never again would he reveal his own soul so crudely – henceforth his poetry would be "dramatic in principle, and so many utterances of so many imaginary persons, not mine." From this incident dates Browning's "extreme repugnance" to *Pauline*' (p. 47). The misunderstanding of the effect of Mill's remarks stems in large part from a misunderstanding of the genre of the poem. Traditionally it has been deemed a confessional lyric, 'thoroughly autobiographical' to the extent 'Browning is the speaker, hardly disguised at all' (DeVane, p. 42). In reaction to this view of the poem as a confessional lyric, still held by critics writing years after DeVane – Eleanor Cook, *Browning's Lyrics: An Exploration* (Toronto: University of Toronto Press, 1974), pp. 12–13, for example – others have held that the poem is totally impersonal; see Roma A. King, Jr, *The Focusing Artifice: The Poetry of Robert Browning* (Athens: Ohio University Press, 1968), p. 3, and Michael Hancher, 'The Dramatic Situation in Browning's *Pauline*', *Yearbook of English Studies*, 1 (1971): 149–59. As I hope to have made clear, I believe that *Pauline*, like nearly everything that Browning ever published, is both personal and impersonal. The complicated story of how Mill's copy got back to Browning and then to Forster is told by Michael A. Burr, 'Browning's Note to Forster', *VP*, 12 (1974): 343–49.

3   This has been suggested by Alice Chandler, '"The Eve of St. Agnes" and "Porphyria's Lover"', *VP*, 3 (1965): 273–4, who also notes similarities in plot, phrasing and theme. U. C. Knoepflmacher, 'Projection and the Female Other: Romanticism, Browning, and the Victorian Dramatic Monologue', *VP*, 22 (1984): 149–56, says that the poem carefully inverts Keats and simultaneously parodies Browning's own desire to flatten women into immovable objects. The dramatic monologue, he argues, allowed the poet to ironize the Romantic process of projection and yet restore to prominence the Female Other on which he and the Romantics had projected their desire.

4   For Monclar's influence on *Paracelsus*, see Richard Purdy (with revisions by Philip Kelley), 'Robert Browning and André Victor Amédée de Ripert-Monclar: An Early Friendship', *Yale University Library Gazette*, 61 (1987): 143–53.

5   Donald S. Hair, *Browning's Experiments with Genre* (Toronto: University of Toronto Press, 1972), rightly insists that generic considerations were always in the forefront of the poet's mind.

6   As W. David Shaw, *The Dialectical Temper* (Ithaca: Cornell University Press, 1968), p. 14, remarks, the auditors are essentially what Henry James called *ficelles*, mere conveniences. The reviewer of *Paracelsus* in the *Spectator* of 15 August 1835 in similar fashion observed that 'the fundamental plan renders the whole a virtual soliloquy, each person of the drama *speaking up* to Paracelsus, in order to elicit his feelings, thoughts, or opinions'.

7   Quoted from David E. Latané, Jr, *Browning's* Sordello *and the Aesthetics of Difficulty* (Victoria, BC: University of Victoria, 1987), p. 17.

8   Mrs F. L. Fridell-Fox, 'Browning', *The Argosy*, 49 (1890): 112.

9   *The Diaries of William Charles Macready 1833–1851*, ed. William Toynbee (London: Chapman & Hall, 1912), 1: 277. Mary Russell Mitford, the novelist and dramatist, saw Browning for the first time at the affair and later, in 1847, recalled her impressions of him: 'he resembled a girl drest in boy's clothes— ... he seemed to me about the height and size of a boy of twelve years old— Femmelette—is a word made for him' (*Elizabeth Barrett to Miss Mitford*, ed. Betty Miller (London: John Murray, 1954), p. xiii).

10 In 1840 Browning declared his 'republicanism' to his friend Fanny Haworth (*NL*, p. 18).

11 *Diaries of Macready*, 1: 382.

12 Ibid., 1: 387, 389.

13 Ibid., 1: 394.

14 Ibid., 1: 362, 355.

15 *Autobiographical Notes of the Life of William Bell Scott*, ed. W. Minto (London: James R. Osgood, McIlvaine, 1892), 1: 124–5.

16 Terry Otten, *The Deserted Stage: The Search for Dramatic Form in Nineteenth-Century England* (Athens, Ohio: Ohio University Press, 1971), p. 109. Denis Donoghue, *The Third Voice: Modern British and American Verse Drama* (Princeton: Princeton University Press, 1959), p. 21, says that Browning was 'an experimental dramatist, trying to clarify and exploit ideas of drama which Macready would have found bewildering'. James P. McCormick, 'Robert Browning and the Experimental Drama', *PMLA*, 68 (1953): 991, sees Browning as an experimental dramatist who 'appeared in the theater at a time when there was no one capable of interpreting his plays or encouraging what was really original, and vital, and realistic'.

Notes to Chapter 3

1　See Browning's letters to Monclar of 5 December 1834 and 9 August 1837 in which he outlines the history of the composition of his works up to this time (*Correspondence*, 3: 109–10, 264–5). Curiously he refers in the latter (p. 265) to *Sordello* as 'my first *poem*'.

2　*Harriet Martineau's Autobiography, with Memorials by Maria Weston Chapman*, 2nd edn (London: Smith, Elder), 3: 207.

3　The best account of the composition of *Sordello* and the stages of change through which it probably passed is DeVane, pp. 72–85.

4　For discrepancies between the historical characters and Browning's characters based on them, see *The Poetical Works of Robert Browning*, ed. Ian Jack and Margaret Smith (Oxford: Clarendon Press, 1984), 2: 175–6.

5　Lionel Stevenson, 'The Key Poem of the Victorian Age', in *Essays in American and English Literature Presented to Bruce R. McElderry, Jr.*, ed. Max F. Schulz, with William T. Templeman and Charles R. Metzger (Athens, Ohio: Ohio University Press, 1967), pp. 260–8, sees the technique of *Sordello* as a response to the popularity of prose fiction. Characterizing it as 'a poem about a poet writing a poem about a poet writing poems', he compares *Sordello* with *Sartor Resartus*, a treatise 'about a philosopher writing a treatise about a philosopher writing a treatise' (p. 278). Latané, *Browning's* Sordello *and the Aesthetics of Difficulty* looks at the poem in relation to the poetics of the 1830s.

6　See Lionel Stevenson and Daniel Stempel, 'Browning's *Sordello*: The Art of the Makers-See', *PMLA*, 80 (1965): 554–61.

7　The question is considered in Robert R. Columbus and Claudette Kemper, '*Sordello* and the Speaker: A Problem in Identify', *VP* 2 (1964): 251–67, and Michael G. Yetman, 'Exorcising Shelley Out of Browning: *Sordello* and the Problem of Poetic Identity', *VP*, 13 (1975): 79–98.

8　Cf. Alan J. Chaffee, 'Dialogue and Dialectic in Browning's *Sordello*', *Texas Studies in Literature and Language*, 23 (1981): 52–77, who treats the poem as psychoanalytic discourse in which the narrator is the analyst and Sordello the analysand.

9　Browning was later to say that Sordello's fault of 'thrusting in time eternity's concern' was a major theme of the poem (Hood, p. 92). The last two passages quoted are from the revised *Sordello*.

10　Cf. Tucker, *Browning's Beginnings*, p. 38, speaking of *Pauline*:'It is impossible to tell whether Browning's strategic humility arises from a need to come to terms as a young poet with so proud a path-breaker as Shelley or whether Browning's early fascination with the power of secondariness simply meets in Shelley a worthy and convenient antagonist'.

11　Browning seems to have borrowed the term 'synthetist' as well as many of his notions about synthetist art from Friedrich Schlegel. See Clyde de L. Ryals, *Becoming Browning: The Poems and Plays of Robert Browning, 1833–1846* (Columbus: Ohio State University Press, 1983), p. 114.

12　The last half of the second line is from the 1863 edition. In 1840 the words after the ellipsis were 'but enough!'

13　This passage on power and love has had many interpretations. For example: Stewart Walker Holmes, 'Browning's *Sordello* and Jung: Browning's *Sordello* in the Light of Jung's Theory of Types', *PMLA*, 56 (1941): 758–96; Earl Hilton, 'Browning's *Sordello* as a Study of the Will', *PMLA*, 69 (1954): 1127–34; Thomas

J. Collins, *Robert Browning's Moral–Aesthetic Theory, 1833–1855* (Lincoln, Neb.: University of Nebraska Press, 1967), p. 60; Lawrence Poston, III, 'Browning's Career to 1841: The Theme of Time and the Problem of Form', *BIS*, 3 (1975): 79–100; Tucker, *Browning's Beginnings*, p. 90.

14 Isobel Armstrong, 'Browning and the "Grotesque Style"', in *The Major Victorian Poets: Reconsiderations*, ed. I. Armstrong (London: Routledge and Kegan Paul, 1969), pp. 97, 102, notes Browning's ability to render in *Sordello* 'the structure of experience as a fluid, unfinished *process* on which we continually try to impose a shape, an order' and observes how the 'grammar, assisted by the breaks in the lines, constantly creates and dispels illusions of meaning and relationship and required a continuous reorientation and adjustment to its direction'.

15 *Poetry*, 10 (1917): 113.

Notes to Chapter 4

1 When he completed *Paracelsus*, Browning wrote to W. J. Fox in 1835 about *Sordello*: 'I have another affair on hand, rather of a more popular nature, I conceive, but not so decisive and explicit on a point or two . . .' (*Correspondence* 3: 134). And in the preface to *Paracelsus* he spoke of 'other productions which may follow in a more popular . . . form'.

2 *Browning: The Critical Heritage*, ed. Boyd Litzinger and Donald Smalley (London: Routledge and Kegan Paul, 1970), p. 6. The introduction provides a convenient and brief survey of the poet's reputation.

3 *Diaries of Macready*, 2: 64.

4 Speaking of *Sordello*, Michael Mason, 'The Importance of *Sordello*', in *The Major Victorian Poets*, ed. Armstrong, p. 148, says: 'The most important constituent of this new, unideal figure of the poet is reliance on his audience; poetry is not the effusion of genius, but a dynamic co-operation of audience and poet; gone is the old notion of poetry as the overheard solitary audience, still expressed by Mill in 1833'.

5 For example, E. D. H. Johnson, *The Alien Vision of Victorian Poetry: Sources of the Poetic Imagination in Tennyson, Browning, and Arnold* (Princeton: Princeton University Press, 1952), p. 88.

6 Dale Kramer, 'Character and Theme in *Pippa Passes*', *VP*, 2 (1964): 247, observes that 'Luigi's bravado and his disregard for life are based more on egoism and youthful glory than on a reasonable, if not reasoned, basis that Browning could respect, however much he might sympathize with the cause of Italian freedom'. For a study of Browning's political views as reflected in his works of the early 1840s, see Lawrence Poston, III, 'Browning's Political Skepticism: *Sordello* and the Plays', *PMLA*, 88 (1973): 260–70. Poston offers a healthy correction to H. B. Charlton, 'Browning as Dramatist', *Bulletin of the John Rylands Library*, 23 (1939): 33–67, who sees the plays as political dramas.

7 Fortunately critical understanding of Browning has advanced beyond the point where Pippa's views can be considered as expressive of the poet's. Once Pippa's 'God's in his heaven— / All's right with the world!' was considered Browning's own optimistic belief. But there remain those who hold that Pippa's final lines reflect the poet's religious belief and that the poem portrays 'the irony of God's ways when regarded from man's point of view' (Margaret

Eleanor Glen [Cook], 'The Meaning and Structure of *Pippa Passes*', *UTQ*, 24 (1955): 412, 426). E. Warwick Slinn, '"God a Tame Confederate": The Reader's Dual Vision in *Pippa Passes*', *UTQ*, 45 (1976): 158–73, offers a corrective.

8   Cf. David G. Riede, 'Genre and Poetic Authority in *Pippa Passes*', *VP*, 27 (1989): 61: 'Pippa is the ultimate puppet . . . She thinks she is God's puppet, but her mere instrumentality in the extreme artifice of the play makes it clear that she is in fact the author's puppet. She is repeatedly trotted out as a sort of regina ex machina to bring scenes to a climax; she is the string that moves the other puppets. Her lack of more than superficial characterization further signifies her mere instrumentality. She can hardly be said to have her own voice at all – the songs she sings, of course, are not of her devising, and even when she speaks in her "own" voice in the "Introduction" and "Epilogue" she sounds far more like the author of *Sordello* than an adolescent silk-weaver. To the extent, then, that Pippa's lyric voice exercises power in this work, it is a power delegated by the author, the poet who fills the void of meaning if God's presence does not fill the world'.

9   *The Collected Letters of Thomas and Jane Welsh Carlyle*, ed. Clyde de L. Ryals, K. J. Fielding, et al. (Durham, NC: Duke University Press, 1987), 13: 155–6.

10   *Diaries of Macready*, 2: 23.

11   Ibid., 2: 73, 80.

12   Ibid., 2: 76.

13   Ibid., 1: 362, 355, 389.

14   Mary Ellis Gibson, *History and the Prism of Art: Browning's Poetic Experiments* (Columbus: Ohio State University Press, 1987), p. 164, says that in Browning's plays 'heroic tragedy became ironic stalemate'.

15   John Woolford, *Browning the Revisionary* (New York: St Martin's Press, 1988), p. 21, observes: 'The conflict between love and power forms one aspect of the larger conflict between individuality, answerable only to God, and the collectivity which society imposes on its individuals. Political power, whoever yields it, necessarily entails an instrumentalist strategy and a social/collectivist view of men; Browning sees this as inherently tyrannical, whatever the political colour of the régime. The pattern of abdication/apostacy enacts the resulting belief that political power corrupts even . . . the liberal'.

16   Mary Rose Sullivan, 'Browning's Plays: Prologue to *Men and Women*', *BIS*, 3 (1975): 17, similarly notes: 'The primary pattern in the plays seems to be historical or political rather than moral, but Browning uses the conflict between dispossessed liberal and entrenched reactionary not out of interest in statecraft, but as a vehicle for exhibiting in action two character types, the divided idealist and the single-minded realist'. Gibson, *History and the Prism of Art*, p. 164, says that in *A Soul's Tragedy* 'politics is presented as a form of theater, and all action is ironized'. Paul E. Coggins, *Egoism versus Altruism in Browning's Drama* (Troy, Michigan: International Book Publishers, 1985), finds a pattern of conflict between the characters' self-interest and a concern for the welfare of others, egoism and altruism being the 'controlling ideas in Browning's dramas' (p. 123).

17   Vladimir Jankélévitch, *L'ironie, ou la bonne conscience*, 2nd edn (Paris: Presses Universitaires de France, 1950), p. 23.

18   The most influential study of the dramatic monologue has been Robert Langbaum, *The Poetry of Experience: The Dramatic Monologue in Modern Literary Tradition* (New York: Random House, 1957), to which I and all others who

write on Browning must acknowledge indebtedness. Stressing the tension between sympathy and judgement in the auditor's or reader's understanding of the monologist, Langbaum tends to regard the speaker as having a self – a life or character – of his own, more or less independent of the poet, his creator. Ralph W. Rader, 'The Dramatic Monologue and Related Lyric Form', *Critical Inquiry*, 3 (1976): 131–51, takes issue with Langbaum by looking at the lyric nature of the genre and insisting upon the relationship between the poet and the poem, which, he argues, does not stand apart in linguistic indeterminacy. Herbert F. Tucker, 'Dramatic Monologue and the Overhearing of Lyric', in *Lyric Poetry: Beyond New Criticism*, ed. Chavra Hosek and Patricia Parker (Ithaca: Cornell University Press, 1985), pp. 226–43, also considers the lyric aspects. Dorothy Mermin, *The Audience in the Poem: Five Victorian Poets* (New Brunswick, NJ: Rutgers University Press, 1983), looks at the auditor's role. Investigating the reader's role are Lee Erickson, *Robert Browning: His Poetry and His Audiences* (Ithaca: Cornell University Press, 1984), and John Maynard, 'Speaker, Listener, and Overhearer: The Reader in the Dramatic Monologue', *BIS*, 15 (1987): 105–12. Loy D. Martin, *Browning's Dramatic Monologues and the Post-Romantic Subject* (Baltimore: Johns Hopkins University Press, 1985), looks at the genre from a semiotic and Marxist perspective and attemps to show how it allows both acceptance and rejection of the autonomy of the individual as constitutor of meaning.

19   Although nearly every critic considering the dramatic monologue as a genre tends to regard 'My Last Duchess' as paradigmatic, interpretations of it vary widely. Some (Langbaum, for example) hold that the duke commits his outrageous indiscretion – telling the envoy from a prospective duchess that he has murdered his last wife – because he becomes too absorbed in the lyric element of his utterance, allowing himself to be carried away by song and thus oblivious of his audience or, aristocratic autocrat that he is, careless of what he says. Others (like Rader) maintain that the duke's speech is not gratuitous but calculating, designed to indicate that the envoy should warn the prospective duchess to act in a way befitting the wife of the duke of Ferrara. Many of the critical opinions on the poem are fanciful in the extreme.

20   For a survey of various critical views of 'Count Gismond', see Sidney Coulling, 'The Duchess of Ferrara and the Countess Gismond: Two Sides of Andromeda Myth', *SBHC*, 14 (1986): 66–84. Coulling himself believes that 'My Last Duchess' and 'Count Gismond' are true companion poems and can best be understood when read together. William E. Harrold, *The Variance and the Unity: A Study of Browning's Complementary Poems* (Athens: Ohio University Press, 1973) studies these (pp. 37–51) and other poems that Browning placed as companions.

21   Addressing the question of canon formation Patricia Parker, in her introduction to *Lyric Poetry: Beyond the New Criticism*, p. 18, asks: 'Can we really be certain . . . that of the two poems Browning himself thought of as a pair, "My Last Duchess" . . . is a "better" poem and thus more worthy of inclusion in the curriculum than "Count Gismond", whose inconsistencies more immediately frustrate the translation of its written characters into the characters of psychologically coherent utterance?'

22   Gibson, *History and the Prism of Art*, p. 165, notes: 'A close reading of Browning's historical monologues suggests that although the theatrical metaphor

itself appears infrequently, pretense, role-playing and imposture – the theat-rical side of human relationships – are central'. E. Warwick Slinn, *Browning and the Fictions of Identity* (London: Macmillan, 1982), is concerned 'with the nature of the histrionic in his poetry, with the way characters are engaged in verbal acts which dramatise themselves' (p. ix).

23   See, for example, Irvine and Honan, pp. 119–20, and George Santayana, 'The Poetry of Barbarism', in his *Interpretations of Poetry and Religion* (New York: Scribner's, 1900), p. 194.

24   For example, William Lyon Phelps, *Robert Browning: How to Know Him* (Indianapolis: Bobbs-Merrill, 1919), pp. 116–24, and W. O. Raymond, *The Infinite Moment and Other Essays*, 2nd edn (Toronto: University of Toronto Press, 1965), pp. 218–19.

25   Questioning the speaker's clear-mindedness are Clyde S. Kilby, 'Browning's *Cristina*', *Explicator*, 2 (Nov. 1943): item 16, and Marylyn J. Parins, 'Browning's "Cristina": The Woman, the Look, and the Speaker', *SBHC*, 7 (1979): 33.

26   Examining the Victorian concern with the gender of poetic sensibility, Carol Christ, 'The Feminine Subject in Victorian Poetry', *ELH*, 54 (1987): 396, says that while Tennyson repeatedly 'represents the danger of absorption in the female', Browning's 'absorption of the lyric within the dramatic effectively contains the feminine'.

27   For the religious overtones see Bernadine Brown, 'Robert Browning's "The Italian in England"', *VP*, 6 (1968): 179–83.

28   Robert Viscusi, '"The Englishman in Italy": Free Trade as a Principle of Aesthetics', *BIS*, 12 (1984): 25, sees more of an economic than a political motive in the poem: 'Abolishing the Corn Laws, those final bastions between the great landlords and the flood of inexpensive European produce and grain, would make this vast catalogue of the delicious . . . part of the everyday English bill of fare. . . . Browning's political motive cannot have been more unexceptionable. Still, the poem is, to put it bluntly, an advertisement. Its dialect is precisely the mouth-watering diction of advertisement'.

29   J. Hillis Miller, *The Linguistic Moment: From Wordsworth to Stevens* (Princeton: Princeton University Press, 1985), p. 228, claims that the poem repeats the triumph of Shelley's 'The Triumph of Life', which is 'to enact so brilliantly in words both the urge to symbolic appropriation and the inhibition of this by the medium itself, its memorial inscription in words'.

30   A. Dwight Culler, *The Victorian Mirror of History* (New Haven and London: Yale University Press, 1985), p. 247. Fred Kaplan, *Miracles of Rare Device: The Poet's Sense of Self in Nineteenth-Century Poetry* (Detroit: Wayne State University Press, 1972), pp. 109–15, sees Browning revealing in 'Pictor Ignotus' his concern with himself and his art.

31   Gerald L. Bruns, 'The Formal Nature of Victorian Thinking', *PMLA*, 90 (1975): 904–18, maintains that it is specifically the appeal to time that sets off Victor-ian meaning-making from that of the Romantics.

Notes to Chapter 5

1   For the rescue myths as they figure in Browning's life and works, see William Clyde DeVane, 'The Virgin and the Dragon', *Yale Review*, n.s. 37 (1947): 33–46,

and Daniel Karlin, *The Courtship of Robert Browning and Elizabeth Barrett* (Oxford: Clarendon Press, 1985).

2   Constance W. Hassett, *The Elusive Self in the Poetry of Robert Browning* (Athens: Ohio University Press, 1982), p. 45.

3   Karlin, *Courtship*, p. 79, says that Browning saw Elizabeth Barrett as 'other', stably and genuinely so, opaque and elusive but compared with himself 'integral' and 'self-sustaining'.

4   In her letters Elizabeth Barrett remarks frequently on Browning's poems published in *Dramatic Romances & Lyrics*, and in addition she wrote fifty-six manuscript pages about them and the two plays that were to follow in 1846. See Kintner, 1: 134, n. 1.

5   Cf. Betty Miller, *Robert Browning: A Portrait* (London: John Murray, 1952), pp. 154–7, who holds that dependence is an essential part of Browning's character.

6   Most of the commentators addressing the subject of Browning's religious beliefs take this poem as a central document in the poet's religious history. See, for example, Raymond, *The Infinite Moment*, pp. 29–31, and E. LeRoy Lawson, *Very Sure of God: Religious Language in the Poetry of Robert Browning* (Nashville: Vanderbilt University Press, 1974), pp. 59–72.

7   Linda H. Peterson, 'Rereading *Christmas-Eve*, Rereading Browning', *VP*, 26 (1988): 364, says that the poem is primarily 'about the problem of determining meaning, about hermeneutics broadly conceived'.

8   Benjamin Jowett, whom Browning was later to know well, considered *Christmas-Eve and Easter-Day* 'Browning's noblest work, written in his highest, though a fluctuating mind. . . . He deepens many things, unveils and unfolds human nature, but he deepens them into greater scepticism; there is no rest in him' (Evelyn Abbott and Lewis Campbell, *The Life and Letters of Benjamin Jowett* (London: John Murray, 1897), 2: 355). On the similarity of Browning's and Jowett's religious beliefs, see Brahma Chaudhuri, 'Browning, Benjamin Jowett and English Higher Criticism', *SBHC*, 4 (1976): 119–32; this is a good corrective to Raymond, *The Infinite Moment*, ch. 2, which argues that Browning's attitude towards the Higher Criticism was one of marked antagonism.

Notes to Chapter 6

1   C. R. Sanders, 'The Carlyle–Browning Correspondence and Relationship. II', *Bulletin of the John Rylands University Library of Manchester*, 57 (1975): 437. Sanders provides, in his two-part study (57: 213–46, 430–62), the fullest factual account of Browning's relationship with Carlyle.

2   *New Letters and Memorials of Jane Welsh Carlyle*, ed. Alexander Carlyle (London and New York: John Lane, The Bodley Head, 1903), 2: 39.

Notes to Chapter 7

1   W. M. Rossetti, *Some Reminiscences* (New York: Scribner's, 1906), 1: 235–36.

2   For the biographical circumstances surrounding the poem and for 'Mesmerism' as a 'discourse of power', see Daniel Karlin, 'Browning, Elizabeth Barrett, and "Mesmerism"', *VP*, 27 (1989): 65–77.

3   Letter of 6 April 1886, *SBHC,* 2 (1974): 2: 62.
4   Jacob Korg, 'Browning's Art and "By the Fire-Side"', *VP,* 15 (1977): 147–58,
    studies the complex interplay between autobiographical and impersonal ele-
    ments in the poem. Korg holds that Browning's use of personal experiences
    as elements of an imagined situation illustrates his usual method of intruding
    himself into the poem without (because of his distrust of Romantic egoism)
    revealing himself. In other words, Browning adapts subjective feelings to ex-
    pression of general truth. Leslie Brisman, 'Back to the First of All: "By the Fire-
    side" and Browning's Romantic Origins', in *Robert Browning: A Collection of
    Critical Essays,* ed. Harold Bloom and Adrienne Munich (Englewood Cliffs,
    NJ: Prentice-Hall, 1979), pp. 39–58, also sees the poem as calling into ques-
    tion the boundary between objective, dramatic monologue and subjective,
    autobiographical narrative.
5   William Cadbury, 'Lyric and Anti-Lyric Forms: A Method for Judging Brown-
    ing', in *Browning's Mind and Art,* ed. Clarence Tracy (Edinburgh and London:
    Oliver and Boyd, 1968), p. 42, finds that 'we cannot tell whether Browning
    intends us to take the narrator as right or wrong, as a spokesman for the poet
    with whose thought we are to agree, or as a deluded character . . . who does
    not know what we know'. Cadbury is made uneasy in general by the ambiguity
    of several of Browning's monologues and insists on an either/or interpretation
    of them, faulting them when they offer only both/and possibilities. Ann Farkas,
    'Digging Among the Ruins', *VP,* 29 (1991): 33–45, surveys the vast critical
    literature on the poem, most of it devoted to identifying the ruined city. She
    maintains that Browning placed it first in *Men and Women* because it is em-
    blematic, forming a 'complex hieroglyphic summary of the contents of the
    volumes' (p. 42). Thus the city and the poem 'must be at once real and not
    real' (p. 33).
6   See Russell M. Goldfarb, 'Sexual Meaning in *The Last Ride Together',VP,* 3
    (1965): 255–61.
7   Lippo's aesthetic is very much like that proposed a few years later by John
    Ruskin in *The Elements of Drawing*: 'The whole technical power of painting
    depends on our recovery of what may be called the *innocence of the eye*; that
    is to say, of a sort of childish perception of these flat stains of colour, merely
    as such, without consciousness of what they signify,—as a blind man would
    see them if suddenly gifted with sight' (*The Complete Works of John Ruskin,* ed.
    E. T. Cook and Alexander Wedderburn (London: George Allen, 1903–12),
    15: 27n). Cf. also the Victorian philosopher John Grote: 'we do not, in know-
    ing or perceiving, *make* things, but *find* them' (*Exploratio Philosophica* (Cam-
    bridge, 1865), pt 1, p. 58, quoted by W. David Shaw, 'Browning and
    Pre-Raphaelite Medievalism: Educated versus, Innocent Seeing', *BIS,* 8 (1980):
    82). See David J. DeLaura, 'The Context of Browning's Painter Poems: Aes-
    thetics, Polemics, Historics', *PMLA,* 95 (1980): 367–88.
8   Tucker, *Browning's Beginnings,* p. 195. In later, collected editions Browning
    put 'Pictor', 'Lippo' and 'Andrea' together.
9   Richard D. Altick, '"Andrea del Sarto": The Kingdom of Hell is Within', in
    Browning's Mind and Art, ed. Tracy, pp. 18–31, sees Andrea as one who has
    too much self-knowledge and lacks the saving grace of rationalizations that he
    can accept.
10 Betty Miller, however, sees 'Andrea' as a reflection of Browning's feeling that
    his wife was stifling his genius (*Robert Browning,* pp. 175–6) and, further, of
    the poet's psychosexual weakness (p. 187).

11 W. David Shaw, *The Dialectical Temper* (Ithaca: Cornell University Press, 1968), p. 136, says that the 'sermonizing speech . . . fixes the speaker as a man of his generation, of the age that produced Thomas Arnold and his resolution to "abolish levity"'. W. Craig Turner, 'Art, Artist, and Audience in "A Toccata of Galuppi's"', *BIS*, 15 (1987): 124, says: 'Galuppi's unsettling music . . . speaks – always through the attribution of meaning by the nineteenth-century English speaker – not only of the light-hearted character of the soulless Venetians, but also of their earned immortality in contrast with his own equally merited immortality'.

12 Julia Markus, '"Old Pictures in Florence" Through *Casa Guidi Windows*', *BIS* 6 (1978): 43–61, sees the poem in relation to Elizabeth's poem published in 1851.

13 Joe McClatchey, 'Interpreting "Karshish"', *BSN*, 13 (1983): 3–16, finds the poem a hermeneutic paradigm. It mimics the New Testament: an encyclopedic form including epistle, report, confession, gospel and apocalypse. See also Michael J. Berens, 'Browning's "Karshish": An Unwitting Gospeller', *SBHC*, 12 (1984): 41–53.

14 See the epilogue to Tucker, *Browning's Beginnings*.

15 Langbaum, *The Poetry of Experience*, examines in detail how Browning's monologists arrive at conclusions without any appeal to outside moral codes or religious dogma.

16 See J. S. McClatchey, 'Browning's "Saul" as a Davidic Psalm of the Praise of God: The Poetics of Prophecy', *SBHC*, 4 (1976): 62–83.

17 F. E. L. Priestley, 'Blougram's Apologetics', *UTQ*, 15 (1946): 139–47, holds that Blougram argues on Gigadibs' own grounds and finally exposes the poverty and inconsistency of Gigadibs' view while affirming the value of his own faith. R. G. Collins, 'Browning's Practical Prelate: The Lesson of *Bishop Blougram's Apology*', *VP*, 13 (1975): 1–20, questions Priestley's view and maintains that Gigadibs learns nothing from Blougram but has gone to Australia to make his fortune and forget philosophical nonsense. Sarah Gilead, '"Read the Text Right": Textual Strategies in *Bishop Blougram's Apology*', *VP*, 24 (1986): 47–67, sees the poem as an elaborate game of reading whose paradoxical strategies deny or defer meanings even as they formulate them: 'Blougram reads Gigadibs and Gigadibs' reading of Blougram, Gigadibs vehemently reads Blougram and rereads himself, the narrator reads Blougram and Gigadibs, the readers read [them all] . . . The game that all the players within and without the poem play is the game of "logos", the game that hides and seeks the signifier and its elusive capacity to point to what Browning's version of Saint John calls "The Way, the Truth, the Life"' (pp. 66–7).

18 Cf. Slinn, *Browning and the Fictions of Identity*, pp. 161–2: 'In seeking in the tower an external object as the goal of experience, Roland discovers instead the self as a subject which is the centre of experience, and this is an irony which makes the poem, like so much of Browning's work, at once a fulfilment and a betrayal of the Romantic mythos of salvation through experience. In attempting to actualise the paradox of meaningful action in a meaningless wasteland, Roland may discover the nub of self . . . , but that is a pyrrhic victory, for meaning is only what he provides himself. All he can do is proclaim his existence, since anything more is but a fiction of consciousness. Thus the poem is essentially the vision of a man who finally realises that he is imprisoned within consciousness'. See also Harold Bloom, *The Ringers in the Tower* (Chicago: University of Chicago Press, 1971), pp. 157–67.

19 On Browning's belatedness as figured in the poem see Harold Bloom, 'How To Read a Poem: Browning's *Childe Roland*', *Georgia Review*, 28 (1974): 404–18.
20 Richard D. Altick, '*A Grammarian's Funeral*: Browning's Praise of Folly', *Studies in English Literature*, 3 (1963): 449–60, says condemned. Martin J. Svaglic, 'Browning's Grammarian: Apparent Failure or Real?' *VP*, 5 (1967): 93–104, says praised.
21 *The Brownings to the Tennysons: Letters from Robert Browning and Elizabeth Barrett Browning to Alfred, Emily, and Hallam Tennyson 1852–1889*, ed. Thomas J. Collins (Waco, Texas: Armstrong Browning Library, 1971), p. 30. Collins provides the best factual account of the Browning–Tennyson relationship.
22 K. W. Grandsen, 'The Uses of Persona', in *Browning's Mind and Art*, ed. Tracy, p. 55.

Notes to Chapter 8

1 Quoted in W. G. Collingwood, *The Life and Work of John Ruskin* (London: Methuen, 1893), 1: 199–202.
2 Sanders, 'The Carlyle–Browning Correspondence and Relationship', 431.
3 Browning told Edward Chapman: 'I am the church-organ-bellows' blower that talked about *our* playing, but you know what I do in the looking after commas and dots to the i's' (*NL*, p. 97). Cf. Laura E. Haigwood, 'Gender-to-Gender Anxiety and Influence in Robert Browning's *Men and Women*', *BIS*, 14 (1986): 115: 'After his book's apparent failure he threw himself into what must be called a feminine role – as long as the assumption remains that the supporting role is necessarily the woman's part – overseeing the printing of his wife's very successful *Aurora Leigh* . . . These years, spent mainly in looking after the interests of his more prolific and successful wife or in dilettantish pursuits, suggest that Browning was not fully able to maintain the self-confidence and autonomy necessary to continue to write prolifically and for the public in the face of widespread misunderstanding and in the shadow of a spouse whose own success was inevitably a species of silent reproach, though her encouragement and loyalty toward him remained unswerving'.
4 Gardner B. Taplin, *The Life of Elizabeth Barrett Browning* (New Haven: Yale University Press, 1957), p. 311.
5 Letter of W. W. Story, 15 August 1861, in Henry James, *William Wetmore Story and His Friends, from Letters, Diaries, and Recollections* (Boston: Houghton, Mifflin, 1903), 2: 65–6.
6 James, *Story*, 2: 66.
7 Jacob Korg, *Browning and Italy* (Athens, Ohio, and London: Ohio University Press, 1983), p. 154.

Notes to Chapter 9

1 Lawrence Poston, III, *Loss and Gain: An Essay on Browning's* Dramatis Personae (Lincoln: University of Nebraska Press, 1974), p. vii.
2 Patricia M. Ball, *The Heart's Events: The Victorian Poetry of Relationships* (London:

Athlone Press, 1976), ch. 4, compares Browning's poem with *Modern Love* and *Maud.*

3 Reading the Brownings' marriage through their poems, Nina Auerbach, 'Robert Browning's Last Word', *VP*, 22 (1984): 161–73, discerns many hidden tensions. She maintains that Elizabeth's celebration of her authority as a woman and as a poet were to become in *The Ring and the Book* the apotheosis of an illiterate girl whom the poet loves because she dies unheard. 'The spiritual authority of Elizabeth Barrett Browning's women [in *Aurora Leigh*] is [in the instance of Pompilia] thrust to the margins of the social and political life Barrett Browning's poetry of the 1850s celebrated ... It may be Robert Browning's victory over his celebrated wife that he robs Pompilia of a public voice' (pp. 170–1). On the other hand, Dorothy Mermin, 'The Domestic Economy of Art: Elizabeth Barrett Browning and Robert Browning', in *Mothering the Mind: Twelve Studies of Writers and Their Silent Partners*, ed. Ruth Perry and Martine W. Brownley (New York: Holmes and Meier, 1984), pp. 82–101, sees their life together as one of mutual solicitude that nurtured both their lives and art. They gave each other 'psychic space in which they could work freely, and the confidence to explore previously repressed or inaccessible desires and fields of experience' (p. 99).

4 See Isobel Armstrong, 'Browning's *Mr. Sludge, "The Medium"*', *VP*, 2 (1964): 1–9, for an analysis of the poem, its structure and imagery.

5 For Sludge and some of Browning's other casuists, see Raymond, 'Browning's Casuists', *The Infinite Moment*, pp. 129–55.

6 Elinor S. Shaffer, 'Browning's St. John: The Casuistry of the Higher Criticism', *VS*, 16 (1972): 205–21, offers a brilliant analysis of the poem in terms of its relation to biblical criticism, especially to that of Ernest Renan. Demonstrating that St John is 'Browning's archetypal casuist' (p. 221), the essay calls into question the notion of 'Browning the Simple-Hearted Casuist', which is the title of an essay by Hoxie N. Fairchild, *UTQ*, 48 (1949): 234–40. Shaffer's essay is reprinted in her *'Kubla Khan' and the Fall of Jerusalem: The Mythological School in Biblical Criticism and Secular Literature, 1770–1880* (Cambridge: Cambridge University Press, 1975), pp. 191–224.

7 See Michael Timko, 'Browning upon Butler; or, Natural Theology in the English Isle', *Criticism*, 7 (1965): 141–50.

8 See, for example, Watson Kirkconnell, 'The *Epilogue* to *Dramatis Personae*', *Modern Language Notes*, 41 (1926): 215.

9 Shaw, *The Lucid Veil*, p. 217, says that Browning's God is 'neither a supreme fiction nor a grammatical subject, but a verb implying a process of development'. Cf. Samuel L. Chell, 'Robert Browning's Evolving God', *Christianity and Literature*, 28 (1979): 51–62, who finds that Browning conceived of the Incarnation in dynamic and evolutionary terms. Shaw examines Browning's use and challenge of Strauss's methods of scientific historiography, Schleiermacher's theology of dependence, Jowett's liberal hermeneutics and Hegel's concept of the double Trinity.

Notes to Chapter 10

1 Rudolf Lehmann, *An Artist's Reminiscences* (London: Smith, Elder, 1894), p. 224.

2 See DeVane, pp. 319–46, for an account of the composition of the poem, the contents of the Old Yellow Book and translations of the source material.

3 For Browning's relations with Smith and the part that Smith played in establishing the poet's reputation, see Michael Meredith, 'Browning and the Prince of Publishers', *BIS*, 7 (1979): 1–20.

4 The carnival aspects have been noted by Susan Blalock, 'Browning's *The Ring and the Book:* "A Novel Country"', *BIS*, 11 (1983): 39–50. The importance of comic elements in the poem has been noted by Richard D. Altick and James F. Loucks II, *Browning's Murder Story: A Reading of* The Ring and the Book (Chicago and London: University of Chicago Press, 1968), pp. 281–326. While I do not agree with its insistence that the poem basically moves from partial truths to 'a transcendent Truth' (p. 37), Altick and Loucks's book is a fine study of many elements – rhetoric and metaphor, for example – of this very long, complex poem.

5 Gibson, *History and the Prism of Art*, p. 99, calls him the 'dramatic presenter'. William E. Buckler, *Poetry and Truth in Robert Browning's* The Ring and the Book (New York: New York University Press, 1985), holds that the poem is really the poet's story; that is, the truth it created for its author is re-enacted for the reader.

6 Adam Potkay, 'The Problem of Identity and the Grounds for Judgment in *The Ring and the Book*', *VP*, 25 (1987): 154–5.

7 For a consideration of the auditor and the speaker's possibly impartial judgement of the Franceschini case, see C. Stephen Finley, 'Browning's "The Other Half-Rome": A "Fancy-fit" or Not?', *BIS*, 11 (1983): 127–48.

8 For an identification of the attitudes and judgements on the part of the various speakers in the poem with modern critical positions, see W. David Shaw, 'Browning and Mystery: *The Ring and the Book* and Modern Theory', *VP*, 27 (1989): 79–98. The essay is reprinted in Shaw's *Victorians and Mystery: Crises of Representation* (Ithaca and London: Cornell University Press, 1990), pp. 300–21.

9 On the nature of self and discourse in *The Ring and the Book*, see E. Warwick Slinn, 'Language and Truth in *The Ring and the Book*', *VP*, 27 (1989): 115–33. The essay is reprinted in Slinn's *The Discourse of Self in Victorian Poetry* (Charlottesville: University of Virginia Press, 1991), pp. 149–84; Slinn also treats the textualization of truth, pp. 119–48. To both Slinn and Shaw I am deeply indebted for many observations in this chapter.

10 For studies of the ways in which Browning treats history and the recoverability of the meaning of historical documents, see Morse Peckham, 'Historiography and *The Ring and the Book*', *VP*, 6 (1968): 242–57, and *Victorian Revolutionaries: Speculations on some Heroes of a Culture Crisis* (New York: George Braziller, 1970), pp. 84–129. Peckham was the first to consider Browning's use of history in terms of contemporary developments in historiography, particularly as practised by the German historian Leopold von Ranke. Myron Tuman, 'Browning's Historical Intention in *The Ring and the Book*', *SBHC*, 3 (1975): 76–95, finds parallels with Ranke and other German historians and philosophers such as Herder and Humboldt. More recently Lee C. R. Baker, 'The Diamond Necklace and the Golden Ring: Historical Imagination in Carlyle and Browning', *VP*, 24 (1986): 31–46, finds parallels with the French historian Jules Michelet. The kinship to Michelet is developed in Hilary Fraser, 'Browning and Nineteenth-Century Historiography', *AUMLA*, 71 (1989): 13–29, who sees

Michelet's theatricality reflected in Browning; that is, both see history as a stage on which actors play out their parts. Gibson, *History and the Prism of Art*, maintains that Browning had a contextualist conceptualization of history, which means, as Hayden White, *Metahistory: The Historical Imagination in Nineteenth-Century Europe* (Baltimore: Johns Hopkins University Press, 1973), p. 18, says, apprehending (like Michelet) history as spectacle. Gibson says, 'History itself, in Browning's texts, can be understood as ironic drama' (p. 163).

11 Langbaum, *The Poetry of Experience*, pp. 109–36, finds that the Pope's are precisely the right judgements because they are judgements of character.

12 For example, Robert Langbaum, 'Is Guido Saved? The Meaning of Browning's Conclusion to *The Ring and the Book*', *VP*, 10 (1972): 289–305. Vivienne J. Rundle, '"Will you let them murder me?": Guido and the Reader in *The Ring and the Book*', *VP*, 27 (1989): 99–114, says that the reader must understand Browning's concern for his reader's involvement and Guido's plea for his listeners' sympathy before he or she can consider the question of Guido's salvation. The truth, in other words, lies in the reader's response.

13 In the preface to *The Poetry of Experience*, Langbaum claims this as the 'moral' of the poem.

Notes to Chapter 11

1 Letter of 27 June 1869, in Rudolf Chambers Lehmann, *Memories of Half a Century: A Record of Friendships* (London: Smith, Elder, 1908), p. 119.

2 James, *Story*, 2: 196.

3 For years it was assumed that Browning himself had made the proposal. Through newly discovered letters Virginia Surtees proved, almost conclusively, that it was Lady Ashburton who made the overture concerning marriage. For the story of the relationship and its ensuing bitterness, see V. Surtees, *The Ludovisi Goddess: The Life of Louisa Lady Ashburton* (Wilton: Michael Russell, 1984), pp. 137–49.

4 The story of the events at Naworth Castle is told in Rosalind Howard's diary. See Virginia Surtees, 'Browning's Last Duchesss', *London Review of Books*, 9 October 1986, pp. 17–18.

5 See Gordon Haight, 'Browning's Widows', *TLS*, 2 July 1971, for a list of some of the nominees. For an informative summary of Browning's relations with women generally, see Ashby Bland Crowder, 'Browning and Women', *SBHC*, 14 (1986): 91–134.

6 See Maisie Ward, *The Tragi-Comedy of Pen Browning (1849–1912)* (New York: Sheed and Ward, 1972), for an account of Pen's peccadillos and ineptitudes from this time forward.

7 Speaking of this 'most hermeneutical Greek poem in Browning's canon', Shaw, *Victorians and Mystery*, pp. 307–8, discusses the influence of Benjamin Jowett's essay 'On the Interpretation of Scripture' (1860) on the poem, showing that any text requires that 'readers must always project their own values, applying the warrants of their own beliefs as well as the warrants of history, logic, and the law courts'. Robert Langbaum, 'Browning and the Question of Myth', *PMLA*, 81 (1966): 575–84, regards the poem as employing the mythical method and sees it as 'actually more successful than *The Ring and the Book*

in achieving what it sets out to do. If I hesitate to rank it above or even with *The Ring and the Book*, it is only because the poem is after all mainly Euripides. Yet I am not sure this matters. We probably ought to understand the poem as we understand Ezra Pound's translations – as a creative appropriation of ancient material, a way of giving an ancient poet a historical consciousness he himself could not have had' (p. 583).

8   Thomas E. Fish, 'Questing for the "Base of Being": The Role of Epiphany in *Prince Hohenstiel-Schwangau*', *VP*, 25 (1987): 27–43, says that in his epiphanic moments the prince exemplifies one of Browning's favourite themes – the discrepancy between what one is and what one could or should be. Ashton Nicols, *The Poetics of Epiphany: Nineteenth-Century Origins of the Modern Literary Moment* (Tuscaloosa: University of Alabama Press, 1987), pp. 107–43, argues that the 'epiphanic imagination' underlies moments of crisis and character revelation in all of Browning's work.

9   When Browning seeks a metaphor for human activity, he almost instinctively turns to the theatrical or carnival world. He says of Napoleon III's decision to declare war against Prussia: it was because '"*something*" must be done to brighten matters at the end of his life,—just as when, at the Fair in my young days, Richardson the show man, at any crisis of his tragedy found the action halt, he set the blue fire burning, and ended the scene with éclat' (*Dearest Isa*, p. 356).

10 J. M. Cohen, *Robert Browning* (London: Longmans, Green, 1952), p. 129.

11 *Diary of Alfred Domett*, p. 53.

12 Samuel B. Southwell, *Quest for Eros: Browning and 'Fifine'* (Lexington: University of Kentucky Press, 1980), provides a biographical reading of the poem and sees it as evidence of Browning's theory of culture as an elaboration of libido.

13 Slinn, *Browning and the Fictions of Identity*, pp. 134–50, discusses the carnival or 'pageant' aspects of the poem.

14 *Diary of Alfred Domett*, p. 52.

Notes to Chapter 12

1   *Diary of Alfred Domett*, pp. 52–3.

2   Mark Siegchrist, *Rough in Brutal Print: The Legal Sources of Browning's* Red Cotton Night-Cap Country (Columbus: Ohio State University Press, 1981), gives source documents that provide insight into the process whereby Browning altered the unadorned facts of the case.

3   *Diary of Alfred Domett*, p. 67.

4   For considerations of Browning's narrative techniques see Hugh Sykes Davies, *Browning and the Modern Novel* (Hull: University of Hull Publications, 1962), and Philip Drew, *The Poetry of Browning: A Critical Introduction* (London: Methuen, 1970), pp. 321–31. Roy E. Gridley, *The Brownings and France: A Chronicle with Commentary* (London: Athlone Press, 1982), makes interesting comparisons between Browning and French nineteenth-century novelists.

5   Th. Bentzon, 'A French Friend of Browning – Joseph Milsand', *Scribner's Magazine*, 20 (1896): 118.

6   Brendan Kenny, 'Browning as a Cultural Critic: *Red Cotton Night-Cap Country*',

BIS, 6 (1978): 137–62, regards the poem as a radical and ironic critique not only of French Catholicism but also of the entire French socio-economic system.

7   The first critic to characterize Browning's poetry as 'grotesque' was Walter Bagehot, 'Wordsworth, Tennyson, and Browning; or Pure, Ornate, and Grotesque Art in English Poetry', *National Review*, 19, ns. 1 (1864): 27–67. Isobel Armstrong has interesting remarks to make on the subject in her essay 'Browning and the "Grotesque" Style', in *The Major Victorian Poets*, ed. Armstrong, pp. 93–123. See also the chapter on Browning in her *Language as Living Form in Nineteenth-Century Poetry* (London, Harvester, 1982).

8   Annie Thackeray Ritchie, *Records of Tennyson, Ruskin, and Browning* (New York: Harper's, 1892), p. 181.

9   William Allingham, *A Diary* (London: Macmillan, 1907), p. 240.

10 For an account of Browning's quarrel with his critics carried on in the poem, see Donald Smalley, 'A Parleying with Aristophanes', *PMLA*, 55 (1940): 823–38. Jane A. McCusker, 'Browning's *Aristophanes' Apology* and Matthew Arnold', *Modern Language Review*, 79 (1984): 783–96, thinks the poem is particularly concerned with the current poetic situation. Specifically it is in her view a debate with Arnold over what constitutes the best poetry of the age.

11 *Diary of Alfred Domett*, pp. 149–50, 161, 150.

12 See Ashby Bland Crowder, '*The Inn Album*: A Record of 1875', *BIS*, 2 (1974): 43–64.

13 Charlotte C. Watkins, 'Form and Sense in Browning's *The Inn Album*', *BIS*, 2 (1974): 65, says that the many references 'to contemporary styles in the arts call attention to the poem *as a poem*'.

14 Walter Kendrick, '*The Inn Album*: Browning's Marginal Poem', *BIS*, 11 (1983): 124, finds the poem 'a sarcastic attack on the very people who were expected to buy it, . . . a calculated affront to anyone who might fancy himself cultured enough to read Browning'.

15 See A. B. Crowder, 'A Note on Section VIII of Browning's *The Inn Album*', *SBHC*, 1 (1973): 21–3.

Notes to Chapter 13

1   *Diary of Alfred Domett*, p. 162.

2   Mary Gladstone Drew, *Diaries and Letters*, ed. Lucy Masterman (London: Methuen, 1930), pp. 116–17; *The Journals of Lady Knightley of Fawsley, 1856–1884*, ed. Julia Cartwright (New York: Dutton, 1916), p. 251; Sir Sidney Colvin, *Memories and Notes of Persons and Places, 1852–1912* (New York: Scribner's, 1921), p. 80.

3   W. J. Stillman, *Autobiography of a Journalist* (London: Grant Richards, 1901), 2: 115.

4   Quoted in Edward Dowden, *Robert Browning* (London: J. M. Dent, 1904), p. 330.

5   James, *Story*, 2: 89. See also Richard D. Altick, 'The Private Life of Robert Browning', *Yale Review*, 41 (1951): 247–62. The subtitle of the second volume of Maisie Ward's biography, *Robert Browning and His World* (London: Cassell, 1969), is subtitled *Two Robert Brownings?*.

6   Irvine and Honan, p. 483. Walter Kendrick, '*The Inn Album*: Browning's Marginal Poem', *BIS*, 11 (1983): 114, says that the decade 1869–79 is 'Browning's most disagreeable phase . . . It seems as if in those years Browning himself did distempered work, thrusting upon the public – the very readers he had wooed and won with *The Ring and the Book* – a series of crabbed, opaque, uncongenial poems designed to test and challenge the popularity that at last was his'.

7   Ashby Bland Crowder, 'Browning and How He Worked in Good Temper: A Study of the Revisions of *Pacchiarotto*', *BIS*, 17 (1989): 94.

8   Yopie Prins, '"Violence bridling speech": Browning's Translation of Aeschylus' *Agamemnon*', *VP*, 27 (1989): 152.

9   George Steiner, *After Babel: Aspects of Language and Translation* (Oxford: Oxford University Press, 1975), p. 315, considers Browning's 'Greek English' within the context of Walter Benjamin's essay *Die Aufgabe des Übersetzers*, which reflects on the difficulty and impossibility of translation and fixes the translator's task not as a matter of making a foreign language one's own but of making one's own language foreign. The reviewer of Browning's translation in the *London Quarterly Review* for April 1878 reported that a young Oxford BA said that 'at almost every page I had to turn to the Greek to see what the English meant'.

10 See Roma A. King, Jr, 'The Necessary Surmise: The Shaping Spirit of Robert Browning's Poetry', in *Romantic and Victorian: Studies in Memory of William H. Marshall*, ed. W. Paul Elledge and Richard L. Hoffman (Rutherford, Madison, and Teaneck, NJ: Fairleigh Dickinson University Press, 1971), pp. 346–61.

Notes to Chapter 14

1   See John R. Reed, 'Tennyson, Browning, and the Victorian Idyll', *SBHC*, 9 (1981): 27–31.

2   C. R. Tracy, 'The Source and Meaning of Browning's Tray', *PMLA*, 55 (1940): 615–16, relates the poem to the 'Symposium' in the *Nineteenth-Century* that was the point of departure of 'La Saisiaz'.

3   Susan E. Lorsch, 'Browning's "Pan and Luna": A Victorian Approach to Nature', *SBHC*, 9 (1981): 32–8, sees the poem as Browning's dramatization of a failed attempt to infuse nature with meaning.

4   See William S. Peterson, *Interrogating the Oracle: A History of the Browning Society* (Athens: Ohio University Press, 1969).

5   *When Huck Finn Went Highbrow*, ed. Benjamin de Casseres (New York: Thomas F. Madigan, 1934), p. 7. For Twain on Browning, see Alan Gribben, '"A Splendor of Stars & Suns": Twain as a Reader of Browning's Poems', *BIS*, 6 (1978): 87–103.

6   W. H. Mallock, *Memoirs of Life and Literature* (London, Chapman & Hall, 1920), p. 53; Edmund Gosse, *Personalia* (Boston and New York: Houghton Mifflin, 1890), pp. 81–2; *Life and Letters of Sir Charles Hallé*, ed. C. E. Hallé (London, Smith, Elder, 1896), p. 9.

7   Letter to John Kenyon, 1 October 1855, in the Houghton Library, Harvard University, quoted by Eleanor Cook, *Browning's Lyrics*, p. xv.

Notes to Chapter 15

1   *Diary of Alfred Domett*, p. 298.
2   William Clyde DeVane, Jr, *Browning's Parleyings: The Autobiography of a Mind* (New Haven: Yale University Press, 1927) provides the most extended treatment of the biographical background of the *Parleyings*.
3   *New Letters of Thomas Carlyle*, ed. Alexander Carlyle (London: John Lane, 1904), 1: 235n.
4   Thomas Carlyle, *Sartor Resartus*, ed. C. F. Harrold (New York: Odyssey Press, 1937), p. 194.
5   Quoted in Oswald Doughty, *A Victorian Romantic: Rossetti* (Oxford: Oxford University Press, 1960), p. 517.
6   *Diary of Alfred Domett*, p. 248.
7   Rowena Fowler, 'Browning's Nudes', *VP*, (1989): 29–47, surveys Browning's attitudes towards the female body and concludes: 'In his poetry Browning gives expression to the facet of himself that enjoys contemplating the female body as spectacle; he also shared, by sympathetic acts of the imagination, its predicament and its paradoxical power. Through identifying with female nakedness he extends but ultimately recognizes the bounds of the male perspective' (p. 45).
8   Ward, *Robert Browning and His World*, 2: 282.

Notes to Chapter 16

1   For Browning's preparation of the text and his revisions of the 1888–9 edition, see Philip Kelley and William S. Peterson, 'Browning's Final Revisions', *BIS*, 1 (1973): 87–99.
2   *Dichtung und Wahrheit*, book 7, *Goethes Werke*, ed. Erich Trunz (Hamburg: Christian Wegner, 1949), 9: 283.
3   Joseph Spence, *Observations, Anecdotes, and Characters of Books and Men*, ed. J. M. Osborn (Oxford: Clarendon Press, 1966), 1: 258.
4   *Letters and Literary Remains of Edward FitzGerald*, ed. W. A. Wright (London: Macmillan, 1889), 1: 280.
5   'Letters from Robert Browning to the Rev. J. D. Williams, 1874–1889', ed. Thomas J. Collins, *BIS*, 4 (1976): 56.
6   Bernard Jerman, 'The Death of Robert Browning', *UTQ*, 35 (1965): 50, 59–60. 'Without death, which is our crapelike churchyardy word for change, for growth, there could be no prolongation of that which we call life', Browning is reported to have said. 'Pshaw! it is foolish to argue upon such a thing even. For myself, I deny death as an end of everything. Never say of me that I am dead!' (William Sharp, *Life of Robert Browning* (London: Walter Scott, 1890), pp. 195–6).
7   Lilian Whiting, *The Brownings: Their Life and Art* (Boston: Little, Brown, 1917), pp. 282–3.
8   Phillip D. Sharp, '"The Poet's Age is Sad": Browning's Late Reference to Wordsworth', *SBHC*, 9 (1981): 86–91, finds that the imagery of the opening lines is taken from Wordsworth's 'Peter Bell' and is used against him to argue

that visionary poetry cannot be sustained. Sharp sees the poem as primarily a defense of realism, as in 'Transcendentalism'. Lawrence Kramer, 'The "Intimations" Ode and Victorian Romanticism', *VP*, 18: 332–5, sees the prologue as the most direct response by a major Victorian poet to Wordsworth's 'Intimations Ode'.

9 I use consciousness in the sense that R. C. Solomon says Hegel uses it: 'Most generally, it means having experience; more specifically..., knowing something.... Following Kant, Hegel sees consciousness primarily as an *activity*. Furthermore, consciousness does *not* refer to a particular person's awareness or knowing, but only knowing in general: e.g. "It is known that life on earth originated at least 3.5 billion years ago". The question that follows is not "By whom?" but "Known how? – On what ground?"' (Robert C. Solomon, *In the Spirit of Hegel: A Study of G. W. F. Hegel's* Phenomenology of Spirit (New York and Oxford: Oxford University Press, 1983), pp. 276–7).

10 Santayana, 'The Poetry of Barbarism', pp. 188–216.

11 Quoted in Donald Thomas, *Robert Browning: A Life within Life* (New York: Viking, 1982), p. 296.

12 'Browning in Westminster Abbey', *Speaker*, 1 (4 January 1890): 12.

Notes to the Epilogue

1 A magnificent reconstruction of the contents of the sale and their disposition is to be found in *The Browning Collections: A Reconstruction with Other Memorabilia*, compiled by Philip Kelley and Betty A. Coley (Winfield, Kansas: Wedgestone Press, et al., 1984). For a succinct account of Pen's disposition of his parents' effects and preservation of his father's fame, see Michael Millgate, 'Robert and Pen Browning', in his *Testamentary Acts: Browning, Tennyson, James, Hardy* (Oxford: Clarendon, 1992), pp. 6–37.

2 For the fate of Browning's fame as a philosopher, see Boyd Litzinger, *Time's Revenges: Browning's Reputation as a Thinker, 1889–1962* (Knoxville: University of Tennessee Press, 1964).

3 *The Letters of Ezra Pound 1907–1941*, ed. D. D. Paige (New York: Harcourt Brace, 1950), p. 218.

4 Joseph Warren Beach, 'Robert Frost', *Yale Review*, 43 (1953): 210.

5 Quoted by G. Robert Stange, 'Browning and Modern Poetry', in *Browning's Mind and Art*, ed. Tracy, p. 197. The essay originally appeared in *The Pacific Spectator*, 8 (1954): 218–28. Stange was the first to trace in some detail Browning's influence on modern poetry. For a book-length study of the subject, see Betty Flowers, *Browning and the Modern Tradition* (London and Basingstoke: Macmillan, 1976).

6 'The Art of Poetry. III', *Paris Review*, 7 (1961): 92, 66.

Selected Bibliography

WORKS BY BROWNING
(ARRANGED CHRONOLOGICALLY WITHIN EACH SECTION)

Collected Editions

Editions overseen by Browning
Poems. 2 vols. London: Chapman & Hall, 1849.
The Poetical Works of Robert Browning. 3 vols. London: Chapman & Hall, 1863.
The Poetical Works of Robert Browning, M.A., Honorary Fellow of Balliol College, Oxford.
    6 vols. London: Smith, Elder, 1868.
The Poetical Works of Robert Browning. 16 vols. London: Smith, Elder, 1888–9. Vol.
    17, ed. Edward Berdoe, added 1894.

Later Editions
Complete Works of Robert Browning. Ed. Charlotte Porter and Helen A. Clarke.
    Florentine (in full levant) or Camberwell Edition (in flexible leather or
    buckram). 12 vols. New York: Thomas Y. Crowell, 1898.
The Works of Robert Browning. Ed. Frederick G. Kenyon. Centenary Edition. 10 vols.
    London: Smith, Elder, 1912.
The Complete Poems of Robert Browning with Variant Readings and Annotations. Ed. Roma
    A. King, Jr, et al. 9 vols to date. Athens: Ohio University Press, 1969–.
Robert Browning: The Poems (excluding The Ring and the Book). Ed. John Pettigrew
    and Thomas J. Collins. 2 vols. New Haven and London: Yale University Press;
    Harmondsworth and New York: Penguin, 1981. Complemented by *The Ring
    and the Book.* Ed. Richard D. Altick. New Haven and London: Yale University
    Press; Harmondsworth: Penguin, 1981 (first printing 1971).
The Poetical Works of Robert Browning. Ed. Ian Jack et al. 4 vols to date. Oxford:
    Clarendon Press, 1984 –.
The Poems of Browning, ed. John Woolford and Daniel Karlin. 2 vols. to date. Harlow:
    Longman, 1991–.

Individual Volumes (with dates of first publication)

Pauline; A Fragment of a Confession. London: Saunders & Otley, 1833.
Paracelsus. London: Effingham Wilson, 1835.
Strafford: An Historical Tragedy. London: Longman, Rees, Orme, Brown, Green, & Longman, 1837.
Sordello. London: Edward Moxon, 1840.
Bells and Pomegranates. No. I.—Pippa Passes. London: Edward Moxon, 1841.
Bells and Pomegranates. No. II.—King Victor and King Charles. London: Edward Moxon, 1842.
Bells and Pomegranates. No. III.—Dramatic Lyrics. London: Edward Moxon, 1842.
Bells and Pomegranates. No. IV.—The Return of the Druses. London: Edward Moxon, 1843.
Bells and Pomegranates. No. V.—A Blot in the 'Scutcheon. London: Edward Moxon, 1843.
Bells and Pomegranates. No. VI.—Colombe's Birthday. London: Edward Moxon, 1844.
Bells and Pomegranates. No. VII.—Dramatic Romances & Lyrics. London: Edward Moxon, 1845.
Bells and Pomegranates. No. VIII And Last. Luria; and A Soul's Tragedy. London: Edward Moxon, 1846.
Christmas-Eve and Easter-Day. A Poem. London: Chapman & Hall, 1850.
Men and Women. 2 vols. London: Chapman & Hall, 1855.
Dramatis Personae. London: Chapman & Hall, 1864.
The Ring and the Book. 4 vols. London: Smith, Elder, 1868–9.
Balaustion's Adventure: Including a Transcript from Euripides. London: Smith, Elder, 1871.
Prince Hohenstiel-Schwangau, Saviour of Society. London: Smith, Elder, 1871.
Fifine at the Fair. London: Smith, Elder, 1872.
Red Cotton Night-Cap Country or Turf and Towers. London: Smith, Elder, 1873.
Aristophanes' Apology: Including a Transcript from Euripides, Being the Last Adventure of Balaustion. London: Smith, Elder, 1875.
The Inn Album. London: Smith, Elder, 1875.
Pacchiarotto and How He Worked in Distemper: With Other Poems. London: Smith, Elder, 1876.
The Agamemnon of Aeschylus Transcribed by Robert Browning. London: Smith, Elder, 1877.
La Saisiaz; The Two Poets of Croisic. London: Smith, Elder, 1878.
Dramatic Idyls. London: Smith, Elder, 1879.
Dramatic Idyls, Second Series. London: Smith, Elder, 1880.
Jocoseria. London: Smith, Elder, 1883.
Ferishtah's Fancies. London: Smith, Elder, 1884.
Parleyings with Certain People of Importance in Their Day. London: Smith, Elder, 1887.
Asolando: Fancies and Facts. London: Smith, Elder, 1890.

Letters

Robert Browning and Alfred Domett. Ed. Frederick G. Kenyon. London: Smith, Elder, 1906.

Letters of Robert Browning Collected by Thomas J. Wise. Ed. Thurman L. Hood. London: John Murray, 1933.

Robert Browning and Julia Wedgwood: A Broken Friendship as Revealed in Their Letters. Ed. Richard Curle. London: John Murray and Jonathan Cape, 1937.

Dearest Isa: Robert Browning's Letters to Isabella Blagden. Ed. Edward C. McAleer. Austin: University of Texas Press, 1951.

New Letters of Robert Browning. Ed. William Clyde DeVane and Kenneth Leslie Knickerbocker. London: John Murray, 1951.

Letters of the Brownings to George Barrett. Ed. Paul Landis with the assistance of Ronald E. Freeman. Urbana: University of Illinois Press, 1958.

Browning to his American Friends: Letters between the Brownings, the Storys, and James Russell Lowell. Ed. Gertrude Reese Hudson. London: Bowes and Bowes, 1965.

Learned Lady: Letters from Robert Browning to Mrs. Thomas FitzGerald. Ed. Edward C. McAleer. Cambridge, Mass.: Harvard University Press, 1966.

The Letters of Robert Browning and Elizabeth Barrett Barrett, 1845–1846. Ed. Elvan Kintner. 2 vols. Cambridge, Mass.: Belknap Press of Harvard University Press, 1969.

The Brownings to the Tennysons: Letters from Robert Browning and Elizabeth Barrett Browning to Alfred, Emily, and Hallam Tennyson 1852–1889. Ed. Thomas J. Collins. Waco, Texas: Armstrong Browning Library, 1871.

'Letters from Robert Browning to the Rev. J. D. Williams, 1874–1889', ed. Thomas J. Collins, *BIS*, 4 (1976): 1–56.

Browning's Trumpeter: The Correspondence of Robert Browning and Frederick J. Furnivall, 1872–1889. Ed. William S. Peterson. Washington: Decatur, 1979.

More than Friend: The Letters of Robert Browning to Katharine de Kay Bronson. Ed. Michael Meredith. Waco, Texas: Armstrong Browning Library, 1985.

The Brownings' Correspondence. Ed. Philip Kelley and Ronald Hudson. 10 vols to date. Winfield, Kan.: Wedgestone Press, 1984–.

BIBLIOGRAPHIES, CONCORDANCE AND CATALOGUE

Anderson, Vincent P. *Robert Browning as a Religious Poet: An Annotated Bibliography of Criticism.* Troy, NY: Whitston, 1983.

Broughton, Leslie N., and Stelter, B. F. *A Concordance to the Poems of Robert Browning.* 2 vols. New York: G. E. Stechert, 1924–5; repr. 4 vols, New York: Haskell House, 1982.

Broughton, Leslie N., Northrup Clarke Sutherland, and Pearsall, Robert, comps. *Robert Browning: A Bibliography, 1830–1950.* Ithaca: Cornell University Press, 1953.

Drew, Philip. *An Annotated Critical Bibliography of Robert Browning.* London: Harvester Wheatsheaf, 1990.

Kelley, Philip, and Coley, Betty A., comps. *The Browning Collections: A Reconstruction with Other Memorabilia.* Waco, Texas: Armstrong Browning Library, Browning Institute, Mansell Publishing, Wedgestone Press, 1984.

Peterson, William S. *Robert and Elizabeth Barrett Browning: An Annotated Bibliography, 1951–1970.* New York: Browning Institute, 1974.

BIOGRAPHIES, STUDIES AND CRITICISM

Armstrong, Isobel, ed. *Robert Browning*. London: G. Bell, 1974.

Bloom, Harold, and Munich, Adrienne, eds. *Robert Browning: A Collection of Critical Essays*. Englewood Cliffs, NJ: Prentice-Hall, 1979.

Chesterton, G. K. *Robert Browning*. London: Macmillan, 1903.

Collins, Thomas J. *Robert Browning's Moral-Aesthetic Theory, 1833–1855*. Lincoln: University of Nebraska Press, 1967.

Cook, Eleanor. *Browning's Lyrics: An Exploration*. Toronto: University of Toronto Press, 1974.

DeVane, William Clyde. *A Browning Handbook*, 2nd edn. New York: Appleton-Century-Crofts, 1955.

DeVane, William Clyde. *Browning's Parleyings: The Autobiography of a Mind*. New Haven: Yale University Press, 1927.

Domett, Alfred. *The Diary of Alfred Domett, 1872–1885*. Ed. E. A. Horsman. London, New York, and Toronto: Oxford University Press, 1953.

Drew, Philip. *The Poetry of Browning: A Critical Introduction*. London: Methuen, 1970.

Drew, Philip, ed. *Robert Browning: A Collection of Critical Essays*. London: Methuen, 1966.

Erickson, Lee. *Robert Browning: His Poetry and His Audiences*. Ithaca: Cornell University Press, 1984.

Gibson, Mary Ellis. *History and the Prism of Art: Browning's Poetic Experiments*. Columbus: Ohio State University Press, 1987.

Gridley, Roy. *Browning*. London: Routledge and Kegan Paul, 1972.

Gridley, Roy. *The Brownings and France: A Chronicle with Commentary*. London: Athlone Press, 1982.

Griffin, W. Hall, and Minchin, Harry Christopher. *The Life of Robert Browning*, 3rd rev. edn. London: Methuen, 1938.

Hair, Donald S. *Browning's Experiments with Genre*. Toronto: University of Toronto Press, 1972.

Hassett, Constance W. *The Elusive Self in the Poetry of Robert Browning*. Athens: Ohio University Press, 1982.

Honan, Park. *Browning's Characters: A Study in Poetic Technique*. New Haven: Yale University Press, 1961.

Irvine, William, and Honan, Park. *The Book, the Ring, and the Poet*. New York: McGraw-Hill, 1974.

Jack, Ian. *Browning's Major Poetry*. Oxford: Clarendon Press, 1973.

Karlin, Daniel. *The Courtship of Robert Browning and Elizabeth Barrett*. Oxford: Oxford University Press, 1985.

King, Roma A., Jr. *The Focusing Artifice: The Poetry of Robert Browning*. Athens: Ohio University Press, 1968.

Korg, Jacob. *Browning and Italy*. Athens: Ohio University Press, 1983.

Langbaum, Robert. *The Poetry of Experience: The Dramatic Monologue in Modern Literary Tradition*. New York: Random House, 1957.

Latané, David E., Jr. *Browning's* Sordello *and the Aesthetics of Difficulty*. Victoria, BC: English Literary Studies, University of Victoria, 1987.

Litzinger, Boyd. *Time's Revenges: Browning's Reputation as a Thinker, 1889–1962*. Knoxville: University of Tennessee Press, 1964.

Litzinger, Boyd, and Knickerbocker, Kenneth L., eds. *The Browning Critics*. Lexington: University of Kentucky Press, 1965.

Litzinger, Boyd, and Smalley, Donald, eds. *Browning: The Critical Heritage*. London: Routledge and Kegan Paul, 1970.

Martin, Loy D. *Browning's Dramatic Monologues and the Post-Romantic Subject*. Baltimore: Johns Hopkins University Press, 1985.

Maynard, John. *Browning's Youth*. Cambridge, Mass.: Harvard University Press, 1977.

Miller, Betty. *Robert Browning: A Portrait*. London: John Murray, 1952.

Miller, J. Hillis. *The Disappearance of God: Five Nineteenth-Century Writers*. Cambridge, Mass.: Harvard University Press, 1963; repr. New York: Schocken, 1965.

Orr, Mrs Sutherland. *A Handbook to the Works of Robert Browning*, 6th edn. London: G. Bell, 1927.

Orr, Mrs Sutherland. *Life and Letters of Robert Browning*, new edn. rev. Frederick G. Kenyon. London: Smith, Elder, 1908.

Peckham, Morse. *Victorian Revolutionaries: Speculations on some Heroes of a Culture Crisis*. New York: George Braziller, 1970.

Peterson, William S. *Interrogating the Oracle: A History of the Browning Society*. Athens: Ohio University Press, 1969.

Poston, Lawrence, III. *Loss and Gain: An Essay on Browning's* Dramatis Personae. Lincoln: University of Nebraska Press, 1974.

Raymond, William O. *The Infinite Moment and Other Essays in Robert Browning*, 2nd edn. Toronto: University of Toronto Press, 1965.

Ryals, Clyde de L. *Becoming Browning: The Poems and Plays of Robert Browning, 1833–1846*. Columbus: Ohio State University Press, 1983.

Ryals, Clyde de L. *Browning's Later Poetry, 1871–1889*. Ithaca: Cornell University Press, 1975.

Shaw, W. David. *The Dialectical Temper: The Rhetorical Art of Robert Browning*. Ithaca: Cornell University Press, 1968.

Shaw, W. David. *Victorians and Mystery: Crises of Representation*. Ithaca: Cornell University Press, 1990.

Slinn, E. Warwick. *Browning and the Fictions of Identity*. London: Macmillan, 1982.

Slinn, E. Warwick. *The Discourse of Self in Victorian Poetry*. Charlottesville: University of Virginia Press, 1991.

Thomas, Donald. *Robert Browning: A Life Within Life*. New York: Viking, 1982.

Tracy, Clarence, ed. *Browning's Mind and Art*. Edinburgh and London: Oliver and Boyd, 1968.

Tucker, Herbert F., Jr. *Browning's Beginnings: The Art of Disclosure*. Minneapolis: University of Minnesota Press, 1980.

Ward, Maisie. *Robert Browning and His World*, 2 vols. London: Cassell, 1968–9.

Whitla, William. *The Central Truth: The Incarnation in Robert Browning*. Toronto: University of Toronto Press, 1963.

Woolford, John. *Browning the Revisionary*. New York: St Martin's Press, 1988.

Index